Managerial
Cost
Accounting

Harold Bierman, Jr.

*The Nicholas H. Noyes Professor
of Business Administration, Graduate School of Business
and Public Administration,
Cornell University*

Thomas R. Dyckman

*Professor of Accounting and Quantitative Analysis,
Graduate School of Business
and Public Administration,
Cornell University*

The Macmillan Company, New York

Managerial Cost Accounting

Collier-Macmillan Limited, London

The Macmillan Company
866 Third Avenue, New York, New York 10022

Collier-Macmillan Canada, Ltd., Toronto, Ontario

Library of Congress catalog card number: 73-123454

Second Printing, 1971

Preface

This book is designed to be used in a second course in managerial accounting. The general orientation is toward decision-making situations which involve the use of accounting data and which practicing accountants (or other business managers) are frequently called on to resolve or assist in resolving. It will therefore be helpful to the person whose job requires an understanding of the analysis and use of accounting data.

It is assumed that the reader already has a knowledge of accounting entries for both general financial accounting and basic cost accounting. Although some repetition of introductory topics could not be avoided (readers of this book may have widely different backgrounds), no attempt has been made to include introductory material which describes debit-credit procedures, or to include in a complete or extensive manner the material of cost accounting concerned with determining the unit cost of product and the flow of costs through the accounts. The authors have assumed that readers will have had at least one semester of managerial accounting or two semesters of financial accounting with some cost accounting or equivalent training. No attempt has been made to develop systematically the reader's ability to record financial transactions, close accounts, and prepare financial reports.

Some knowledge of elementary economic theory, introductory statistical decision theory, and organizational theory and behavior is required to complete the material successfully. However, a student need not know the calculus to profit from this volume. The reader will also find that occasionally a knowledge of linear programming and basic regression analysis will prove to be useful.

Several topics (such as capital budgeting) have received particularly detailed treatment, since these topics are especially relevant to practicing accountants and managers. The report of the Committee on Education and Experience Requirements for CPA's (*AICPA*, March 1969) that describes the cost-accounting requirement states "... it is believed important that he know how cost accounting can contribute to decision making and planning. Typical problems might involve make or buy decisions, product mix, capital budgeting, and inventory planning. The methodologies might include present value analysis, models, and incremental analysis."

The report of the American Accounting Association's Committee to Compile a Revised Statement of Educational Policy (*Committee Reports,*

American Accounting Association, 1968) reaches a similar conclusion. "In recent years management has come to recognize that accountants are in a strategic position to make significant contributions in the area of resource planning." The committee then presents a long list of relevant topics and includes such items as lease or buy decisions, capital budgeting, investment decisions, and return on investment.

There is no question that any of the items cited and found in this book might be covered elsewhere in a curriculum. We have included only items for which no other functional area in business or basic skill courses has obvious first claim, and which we think are highly relevant to the job of the management accountant.

The questions and problems are an integral part of each chapter. In answering them it will often be necessary to refer to the text. Indeed, problem solving is a necessary step toward understanding the main ideas in each chapter. In other words, the reader should not expect to have full command of the material after a first reading. Problem solving followed by additional readings is recommended.

In many ways the present volume serves only as an introduction to the topics covered. In order that the reader may pursue an interest in one or more of the subject areas, a selected bibliography is provided for each chapter.

We owe debts to many individuals for the ideas contained in this volume; occasionally their names appear in the footnotes. Perhaps foremost among our debts, however, is that owed to our teachers at the University of Michigan who started us on our present path, our colleagues at Cornell who refined many of our ideas, our students who challenged us, and our families who sustained our efforts and tolerated our venture. We also wish to thank Professor Myron Uretsky of Columbia University for his particularly helpful comments on an early draft of the manuscript. Many of his suggestions were incorporated in the final version. Finally, we owe our gratitude to the administration of the Graduate School of Business and Public Administration at Cornell which provided the constructive and supportive environment necessary to complete the task, and to Mesdames Snedden, Tubbs, Lovell, Towner, and Burns for their long hours of difficult typing.

Comments from users would be most welcome.

H. B.
T. R. D.

Contents

Chapter 1

Cost-Accounting Systems

This is a book about the role of cost accounting in decision making. It would be easy to conclude that only future and not historical costs are relevant to managerial decisions. This position is common since it is generally agreed that the manager must use the relevant future costs to make decisions. However, historical cost data are relevant to the estimation of relevant future costs as well as the control of present costs.

Figure 1.1 shows how historical costs feed into the model which generates relevant costs for decision making.[1]

The environment influences both internal and external data as well as the need for decisions. The decision requirements then are used to define a model for the decision. The choice of the decision model then influences the data selection, and the model, together with the data, leads to a decision. The decision in turn affects the environment and hence the data for future decisions. The environment and the data may, for a given decision, be internal, external or both. The arrow from the decision to the decision model represents the feedback mechanism by which the results of a decision are retained for evaluation purposes and possible revision of the model itself. There is also a path from the decision model to the relevant data that permits the model and the data to respond iteratively to the decision requirements.

---

[1] This figure is based on a report presented by the American Accounting Association Committee on Managerial Decision Models, *Supplement to the Accounting Review*, 1969, p. 48.

After a decision model is selected, five elements must be specified.

1. The set of variables under the manager's control.
2. The set of variables not under the manager's control.
3. The goal or objective function.
4. The constraints under which the manager must operate.
5. The estimates of the parameter values for the objective function and constraint requirements.

The information requirements of the decision model are dictated by the need to determine the relevant variables, the constraint formulations, the objective function, and the proper parameter values in order to predict the optimal values of the controllable variables. Similarly, information is required to detect significant variations in these factors and to implement the resultant solution.

There are many ill-structured problems requiring solution in a subjective setting. When this is the case, many aspects of the decision process are

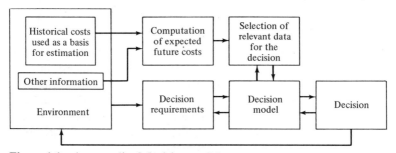

Figure 1.1   A generalized decision model

heuristic. The result is that in these situations the task of determining the precise information needs of an organization is impossible. The alternative is to make available an extensive data bank from which data can be obtained easily by the manager for application to the problem at hand.

The generalized decision model presented in Figure 1.1 is applicable to a wide range of managerial decisions. These decisions include: capital budgeting, cost control, performance evaluation, pricing, cost estimation, inventory levels, and many others. Cost data are also relevant to the production of useful financial reports on which outsiders may place substantial reliance in their own decision making. Although this book is oriented primarily to internal decisions, some attention is given to the relevance of cost data to external reporting.

It is frequently suggested that decision models should attempt to maximize the profits of the firm. Each decision, then, should take into consideration its effect on the other sections of the firm so that the firm's profits are maximized in a global sense. There are, however, two major difficulties with global profit maximization from an operational point of view.

First, rather than maximize profits, the firm may reasonably prefer to maximize something else (which will be called utility). The use of profit maximization (even when profits are correctly defined) has several disadvantages as a goal for the firm. For example, it generally does not adequately take into account nonmonetary factors (such as growth, market size and prestige), indirect contributions to society (such as the creation of jobs), or costs to society (such as pollution). In addition, expressing the consequences of decisions in monetary terms may not adequately reflect the impact of these events on the firm.

For example, suppose it is believed that with event A, a loss of one million dollars will lead to certain bankruptcy while with event B, a loss of one-half million will not lead to bankruptcy. Under these conditions, the first loss may in some very real sense be more than twice as serious as the second. The fact that businessmen take out insurance to protect themselves against large losses even when the premium is greater than the mathematical expectation of the loss provides evidence of the incompleteness of monetary values as the sole guide to decisions. Thus, in the previous example the manager may be unwilling to pay more than $500 for insurance against the event B (with a loss of $500,000 and a probability of occurrence of 0.001), and yet be willing to pay more than $1,000, say $1,200, for insurance against the event A (with a loss of $1 million and the same probability of occurrence, 0.001). Furthermore, another equally likely event C (with a loss of $2 million and a probability of occurrence of 0.001) may not lead to a willingness on the part of management to pay a much higher insurance premium than $1,200 since any loss greater than $1 million also leads to bankruptcy and nothing more serious can occur.

A similar situation often exists for positive monetary values as well. Thus a one million dollar increase in profits may not be considered twice as desirable as a one-half million dollar increase. Utility theory can be used to take into consideration the psychological reactions to gains and losses that the profit measure alone ignores.

The second difficulty with global profit maximization is that the decision maker's ability to cope with global optimization may be limited. In a dynamic economy many things are changing continuously. These changes may prevent the decision maker from reacting optimally on several fronts at once. Furthermore, he may be unable to digest all the information available to him resulting from the ripple effects of a decision, and even the simplest decision may become impossible to make if the decision maker insists on analyzing all its implications. Despite this difficulty, global maximization should be the goal. Frequently however, only sub-optimization decision-making procedures may be feasible.

An alternative approach is to view the manager as maximizing profits or some alternative factor subject to a set of constraints.[2] For example, the

[2] See A. Charnes and W. W. Cooper, "Some Network Characteristics for Mathematical Programming and Accounting Approaches to Planning and Control," *The Accounting Review*, January 1967, pp. 24–52.

manager of a division may wish to maximize net cash flows, market values, or something else subject to restrictions on liquidity and total capital expenditures. The manager of a cost center may desire to minimize costs subject to output requirements and the likelihood of a cost investigation analysis of his activity. To make the approaches feasible only the most critical variables would be considered. This alternative is not used in this book.

Both of the major difficulties (choosing what to maximize and the limited ability to cope) may combine in specific situations. Consider the optimization problem of the cost-center manager again but this time from a utility viewpoint. Suppose this manager is concerned about a cost that seems to be excessively high although the firm's operating procedures do not require a report or an investigation. If he investigates and finds a correctable cause, he may save the firm several thousand dollars. On the other hand, perhaps he should spend his time and resources on other activities that, although likely to benefit the company less, are more visible to his superiors. There is the further problem associated with the reporting techniques used in the firm. How will the discovery and report of an out-of-control cost look on his record? Finally, the utilization of the firm's resources to investigate the suspected activity should theoretically be considered as only one among several uses to which these resources might be put. Opportunities available throughout the firm should be considered as alternatives to undertaking the proposed cost investigation. This could be an extremely difficult procedure in practice, however.

For the above reasons, this book deals with decisions on a suboptimization basis. Suboptimization should, however, include the more relevant effects each decision may have on the overall well-being of the firm. For example, an optimal advertising policy may lead to disaster if productive capacity is not simultaneously taken into consideration. In addition decisions will be linked together by a rate of interest in order to take into account, in a common manner, time discounting.

Decisions are often approached in this book as if they might be solved using a quantitative approach exclusively. There is no question that qualitative considerations should also enter into decisions. For example, a decision to close a plant may be indicated from a quantitative analysis, but the parent firm may still accept the responsibility to keep the plant open for a period of time while its employees find employment elsewhere.

Despite the limitations of a quantitative approach to many decisions, this approach is frequently of great assistance in at least narrowing the area of debate concerning the relevant qualitative aspects. Indeed, it may then be possible to see how much the firm would pay for the qualitative advantage of a given action. Any decision maker then should have at his disposal the best quantitative tools which are available so that he may establish a frame of reference for the decision.

This book deals with cost control as if accounting could make a significant contribution toward effective decisions in the control of costs. It might be argued that a nonaccounting method (such as making all workers part owners of the plant) would be more effective. But even in this situation some workers would tend to avoid work and others would excel; thus, some means of measuring efficiency is still desirable. Therefore the implicit assumption is made that quantitative measures of efficiency are useful, and the task remaining is to seek the best available measures.

This chapter briefly reviews different cost classifications and investigates the objectives of cost accounting.

1.1   The Classification of Costs

A cost is defined and classified in many different ways. Some examples are:

How it reacts to changes in activity (fixed or variable).
Responsibility (plant, department, process, or cost center where it was incurred).
The product which the cost helped produce.
Degree of ability to trace the cost of the end product (direct, indirect).
Natural characteristics (labor, material, supplies, etc.).
Function (manufacturing, administrative, selling).
Reference to a particular decision; and by miscellaneous economic characteristics (joint, common, out-of-pocket, opportunity, unavoidable, etc.).

The accountant does not set up accounts in the bookkeeping records for every one of the above classifications; in fact, it would not be desirable to do this. A good accounting system is a ready source of cost information, but generally analysis and rearrangement of the costs is necessary for specific decisions. In some cases it is evident that certain types of useful data for decision purposes are not now being gathered and processed by the firm's information system. When this is the case, steps should be taken to remedy the apparent deficiencies after a study of the costs and benefits of obtaining and processing the desired data.

1.1.1 Changes in Activity

The terms *fixed* and *variable* are generally used to describe how a cost reacts to changes in activity. A variable cost is a cost which is proportional to the level of activity (total cost increases as activity increases), and a fixed cost is constant in total over the relevant range of expected activity under consideration. Sometimes the terms *avoidable* and *nonavoidable* are used in place of the words *fixed* and *variable*. These terms are better used, however, to describe costs associated with particular decisions. For example, the salary of a particular foreman would be avoidable if he has not yet been hired, but once hired, his salary is fixed regardless of the level of activity (assuming he cannot, or will not, be fired because of a decrease in activity).

If there is a decrease in activity, there is the option of not replacing the next foreman that leaves the company. While this type of long-run change cannot be relied on in the short run to adjust the firm's costs, supervisory costs may still be graphed as a step function if it is recognized that the adjustment of cost to volume changes may lag. It is best not to use the terminology *variable cost* interchangeably with *avoidable costs*, since a fixed cost may also be avoidable (although perhaps with a lag).

The terms *variable* and *fixed* may be made more useful by the addition of prefixes. The modified terms are: *semivariable, semifixed,* and *avoidable-fixed* (See Figure 1.2). *Semivariable* can be used to refer to a cost that is basically variable but whose slope may change abruptly when a certain activity level is reached. For example, hours of work in excess of the normal forty-hour week give rise to overtime or shift premiums and result in direct labor increasing

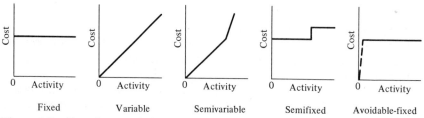

| Fixed | Variable | Semivariable | Semifixed | Avoidable-fixed |

Figure 1.2   Cost characteristics

more rapidly as activity increases than if additional overtime premiums were not incurred at that point.

Semifixed refers to a cost which is essentially fixed over the relevant activity range but which may have to be increased substantially at several activity levels if production is increased. Thus quality-control costs may be fixed over wide ranges, but an additional man may be required if production is above a given activity level. The result of adding identical machines at discrete intervals, as output requirements increase, provides another example of a *semifixed* cost.

Avoidable-fixed refers to costs that may not be incurred under certain circumstances. For example, if the firm is shut down (or its activities scaled down) many of the costs associated with running staff functions, such as accounting, are avoidable. Accounting supplies and the salaries of personnel who could be laid off provide specific illustration of *fixed* costs that can be avoided.

Figure 1.2 shows some cost-characteristic possibilities but does not include all the possibilities. For example, a cost such as maintenance may have an avoidable-fixed component at very low levels of activity but may vary directly with increases in activity at higher levels. This type of cost is sometimes said to be *semivariable*. (Compare Figures 1.2 and 1.3.)

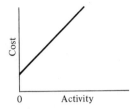

Figure 1.3   Variable cost with a fixed-cost component

1.1.2 Responsibility

Classification of costs by responsibility is important because it provides the basis of cost control. The first step in the control of costs is knowledge of where the cost was incurred and who was responsible.

The allocation of service department costs (building, power, heat, cafeteria, accounting, etc.) to operating departments for purposes of computing unit costs or profits by product line often thwarts the cost-control function. These allocations are thought to be essential to the control of costs, but costs must be controlled where they are incurred, and allocations to operating departments are generally not useful for cost-control purposes. An exception to this rule is illustrated by some repair department costs which are controllable both by the repair department (to ensure that repairs are implemented efficiently) and by the operating department (to ensure that preventive maintenance and proper operation reduces the need for repairs).

Cost-control reports should be prepared so that only costs for which the manager has responsibility are reported as being controllable. While some- one can be held responsible for the ultimate decision for any cost even the leasing or buying of equipment that took place many years ago, the inclusion of costs that a manager cannot control merely acts as a detraction. This does not prevent other allocated costs, about which the firm's officers believe the manager should be aware, from being reported to him. It does imply that these latter costs should be separately listed and appropriately described as not (currently) controllable by the manager in question. Deci- sions made in one cost center can affect costs incurred in another center.

1.1.3 Product Line: Direct and Indirect Costs

The classification of costs by product line is essential in determining the profitability of various activities of the firm. The total contribution margin earned (as well as the profitability per dollar of sales) in the various activities is often relevant to decisions involving expanding or contracting the activity, product promotion, product research, improving the productive process, and developing better cost-control techniques. If a cost is not changed by a decision it is not relevant to that decision.

The main problem in classifying costs by product line is that many costs cannot be directly identified with any one product because they are associated with several products. A cost of this nature is called an indirect cost. The term *indirect* is used with a cost which cannot be directly identified with a product line, job, process, department, etc. It is necessary then, to know for what purpose a cost is being identified and, thus, whether it is being associated with a product line, sales area, department, or some other activity before a classification of direct or indirect can be made. For example, if one salesman simultaneously handles several product lines, his salary is an indirect cost for each product line but a direct cost to his sales area.

If there are indirect costs, then reports by product line must be carefully prepared. Instead of showing one income figure it is desirable to show a series of subtotals. The report in Exhibit 1–1 highlights those costs directly associated with the product line and subordinates those costs indirectly associated with the product line. Additionally, it distinguishes between variable and fixed costs.

Exhibit 1–1   Income Statement for Product A

Sales	$5,000
Less: Direct-variable costs	2,000
	$3,000
Direct-fixed costs	800
Excess of revenues over direct costs	$2,200
Less: Indirect-variable costs	1,000
	$1,200
Indirect-fixed costs	400
Net Income—product A	$ 800

Instead of first subtracting the costs directly identified with the product line, the variable costs can be subtracted first and the fixed costs second, as in Exhibit 1–2. This report highlights the contribution of the product to the total fixed costs of the firm.

The choice as to which report is better depends upon the purpose for which the data are required. If a decision is being made to expand or contract this product line, a decision maker would want to know the change in the total contribution margin that would result from such a decision. If some indirect- or direct-fixed costs are avoidable, then neither statement is ideal for a decision to contract operations. It is worth adding that other considerations including future market expectations, complementarity to other product lines, other opportunities, the time value of money, and so on, would also be relevant to and perhaps controlling in a given decision situation. The analysis of accounting information is only a single step, albeit a desirable one. Furthermore, a decision maker is well advised to question closely the origin, nature,

Exhibit 1-2   Income Statement for Product A

Sales		$5,000
Less: Direct-variable costs	$2,000	
Indirect-variable costs	1,000	3,000
Excess of sales over variable costs		$2,000
Less: Direct-fixed costs	$ 800	
Indirect-fixed costs	400	1,200
Net income—product A		$ 800

relevance, and validity of the data supplied to him by the accounting information system. For example, one of the direct costs associated with product A is probably depreciation, based on the original cost using the straight-line or an accelerated depreciation method. If a decision is to be made on whether to retain product A or cease production, the conventionally determined depreciation cost is not the relevant cost measure.

1.1.4 Natural and Functional Classifications

The term *natural classification* refers to the basic physical aspects of the cost (labor, material, supplies, etc.). *Functional* refers to how the cost was used (manufacturing, administrative, or selling). A need for both natural and functional classifications exists. The prime conflict between the two classifications is in the preparation of income statements; that is, for product-costing purposes rather than for decision purposes. Should the expenses be classified according to natural or functional classifications? The answer must depend on the use of the report, but no matter which classification is used additional information should be supplied. For example, if the functional classification is used, the depreciation expense and labor expense of the period should also be shown, perhaps in a footnote.

1.1.5 Economic Characteristics of Costs

The accountant can classify costs in many ways, but he cannot record a cost as relevant or irrelevant to decisions, this will depend on the particular decision being made. In like manner the principle of opportunity costs is of great importance to decision making, but the accountant does not record opportunity costs because these generally depend on the alternative uses of the resources at the time of the decision. Opportunities foregone at the time a decision is made should be noted, however, and the *ex post* payoffs recorded if possible for feedback and decision-control purposes. Yet, even if an alternative decision would have been best in an *ex post* sense, the decision actually made may still have been the best given the information available at the time the decision had to be made. *Ex ante* estimates of the payoffs for different alternatives and under different future states may be made, but if an alternative is not selected, the *ex post* payoff, and therefore the *ex post* opportunity cost, is likely to be unknown. *Ex post* estimates may, however, still be possible.

Suppose, for example, that two alternate new products are under consideration, call them A and B, and three future market conditions exist, call them S_1, S_2, and S_3. The estimated profits (each the expectation of a frequency distribution) are given in Exhibit 1–3.[3] If the actual state is S_1 then product A is best because the profit expected, 20, is highest for product A given the state S_1. The opportunity cost for alternative B given state S_1 is five

Exhibit 1–3   Hypothetical Marketing Problem Estimated Payoffs (thousands of dollars)

Alternatives	States S_1	S_2	S_3
A	20	16	10
B	15	17	12

thousand dollars (for alternative A given state S_1 it is zero). Similarly, the opportunity cost for alternative A given state S_2 is one thousand (for B given state S_2 it is zero).

Suppose the decision maker believes the probability of the future state being S_1 exceeds the probability for S_2 and S_3 combined. Then he would probably select product A. But assume the actual state turns out to be S_2 and the profit actually realized is $16,236. Because alternative B was not selected, there is no way to know whether $17,000 the *ex ante* estimate or some other value would actually have been earned. Thus it is impossible to do more than estimate this figure and thereby estimate the *ex post* opportunity cost. It is still true however that the initial decision was best given the data available at the time.

Because of the inability to observe actual *ex post* opportunity costs and the accountant's preoccupation with reporting objectively determined profit figures to outsiders, he does not typically record opportunity costs. Nevertheless the present example suggests the usefulness of recording both the data used in making decisions and the *ex post* opportunity cost estimates as one

---

[3] It is assumed here that the relevant utilities are adequately represented by the dollar amounts (estimated profits).

element necessary in the continual evaluation of the decision-making procedures in use.

1.1.6 Sunk Costs

The term *sunk cost* is frequently used to refer to a cost such as the historic cost of a machine. The historic cost, once incurred, is not relevant for decisions (taxes aside). The accountant must be careful to recognize that the relevant measure of both the machine's worth and the periodic decline therein depend on the potential usefulness of the machine through time.

The accountant does allocate indirect costs to different products, but for decision making these allocations should be examined to determine their relevance. This is not to say that the accountant is wrong to make the allocations for purposes of income and inventory determination, but it would be incorrect to use these allocations for purposes for which they were not intended and for which they are not correct.

A transaction may have important economic characteristics that do not enter the accounting records. When there is occasion to make decisions, the relevant costs must be extracted from the accounting records and properly arrayed. It is not possible for the accounting system automatically to record and report costs in all relevant ways, for all possible decisions. However, the availability of high-speed computers has increased the amount of information which can be stored and obtained quickly.

1.2   The Objectives of Cost-Accounting Systems

To justify the dollars spent on accounting for costs, the cost-accounting system must be useful to management. Among the most important functions of a cost-accounting system is the provision of the necessary information for:

1. Determination of income and financial position.
2. Control and reduction of costs.
3. Motivation of employees toward organization goals.
4. Decision making and planning.

The above items are listed neither in order of importance, nor are they all inclusive and they do overlap.

1.2.1 Determination of Income and Financial Position

While this objective is frequently cited as a prime justification for elaborate cost-accounting systems, it is a relatively unimportant justification compared to the other three objectives. Determination of income and financial position is important, but any determination is going to be inexact and subject to numerous assumptions. For example, are fixed costs period costs, or are they costs which should be attached to product? While a certain amount of cost accounting is necessary to accomplish the objectives of income determination, the necessary system could be much simpler than the cost-accounting systems commonly used in manufacturing companies. Much of the detail could be eliminated with little loss of accuracy. For example, if a department manufactures automobile generators, the total cost incurred in the department must be known before the unit cost can be determined, but it is not necessary to know the cost of each step in manufacture of each part and the exact nature of each cost.

There would still exist the problem of common costs (costs of a single resource used in more than one cost center or incurred in the production of more than one product), but the importance of common-cost problems would be reduced because more interest would center in the broad measures needed for financial accounting purposes than in the exact measures needed for cost control and decision making. Problems of accounting for costs common to more than one time period would still exist.

It is interesting to note that no matter how elaborate the cost-accounting system, there would still exist problems of income and financial position determination. One problem, for example, is whether fixed costs should be considered costs of product (see Chapter 7). If the fixed costs are absorbed to product, there is, in turn, a problem of determining the basis for fixed-overhead absorption and the proper treatment of cost variances resulting from idle capacity and other factors. Should all the fixed costs be considered as costs of the product, or should some of the fixed costs be considered as costs of idleness when less than normal activity is attained? The problems of joint and common costs also prevent exact financial measures of financial activity, especially where there are inventory changes involving one or more of the joint products.

These examples do not provide a complete list of the complications arising in the use of cost-accounting information for purposes of determining income and financial position. If income measurement and determination of financial position were the only objectives of a cost-accounting system, the system could be much simpler. Added accuracy in this area is frequently an illusion. Few managerial decisions can be made using the value of accounting income which is the product of the conventional cost-accounting system. Mere general impressions are formed, which can lead to decisions only after further information is gathered. The user of information coming from a cost-accounting system must realize that this is a relatively rough tool. A manager who receives a measure of income that is inexact, and who knows that the measure is inexact, has better information than a manager who receives a somewhat more elaborate measure of income but is misled into thinking that the measure can be used for specific decisions such as expanding or contracting a product line. It is very important to distinguish between product costing and the other purposes of cost data. Many of the problems in cost accounting arise because data derived for one purpose are inappropriately used for another.

1.2.2 Control and Reduction of Costs

Control or reduction of costs requires a detailed cost-accounting system. It is necessary to know when and where the costs were incurred (the accounting period and the department or cost center where they were incurred), as well as the nature of the costs. Equally important, the actual amount of the cost and the amount that the cost should have been (the budgeted or standard amount) must be known. Unless all this information is available, the cost-accounting system cannot be effective in the control of costs.

The setting of cost standards is an important part of the cost-control system. These standards can be used by management to pick out those areas where there are difficulties (costs significantly in excess of standard) and to take action where action is required. This is an application of managing by exception (see Chapter 2 for a further discussion).

What should be the policy in regard to the difficulty of attaining the cost standards? Should the standards be very difficult to attain or relatively easy to attain? Actually, there is an entire range of possibilities. The problem of setting standards is to a degree analogous to the problem of setting par for a golfer.

The theoretical standard is analogous to shooting an eighteen-hole golf course in eighteen strokes. While this is theoretically possible, it is extremely unlikely to occur. Setting standards which are almost certain not to be attained is discouraging to workers and should be avoided.

The practical standard is analogous to shooting an eighteen-hole golf course in seventy-two (assuming that seventy-two is par). This seventy-two is difficult to attain, but a very good golfer can shoot seventy-two and sometimes do even better. There is more to be said in favor of this type of standard, difficult to attain but attainable, than for theoretical standards.

The normal standard is analogous to setting a par consistent with the golfer's ability (often by means of a handicap). Par for the course may be seventy-two, but if the golfer is just a "duffer" his par may be ninety-eight, where the term par is used in the sense of a goal or standard of performance based on the individual's ability. The standard becomes the mean or expected value of the golfer's score. The use of standards that take into consideration not only the present state of experience and skill of the worker but the variability in his performance as well are needed. Ideally, the skill of the worker should increase until the standard finally approaches the high level of performance called par (the seventy-two of the golf-course analogy), however, not everyone can shoot seventy-two no matter how hard he practices or how much pressure is applied from above (the learning concept discussed in Chapter 4 is relevant here). Loose standards are in a sense not standards, but they are reference points. Thus, if a golfer averages ninety, he may set a *standard* for himself of ninety-five just to make sure that his variance is generally favorable. In like manner the standards of a factory may be set so that the worker's performance is generally favorable, even though he could and should do better.

The use of standards leads to the necessity of interpreting the differences between actual costs and standard costs. (The term *standard* as used here means budgeted costs adjusted to the actual level of operation.) The analysis of cost variances could be accomplished by comparing the actual costs and standard costs and merely noting the difference. While this would be a step in the right direction, differences between actual and standard costs have traditionally been identified with a greater degree of accuracy by the use of a technique called variance analysis.

1.2.3 Cost Variances[4]

A cost variance results from the comparison of an actual cost with a preset standard (or budgeted) amount. The sign of the variance indicates whether the variance is favorable or unfavorable (the convention of specifying a positive variance as being unfavorable is arbitrary). It is generally (but incorrectly) assumed that an unfavorable variance reflects inefficiency and a favorable variance indicates efficiency. They may instead, for example, merely reflect changed conditions since the standards were established or, alternatively, the effects of random factors over which the firm has no control.

Cost variances are frequently classified into material, labor, and overhead variances. Each of these three variances can be further subdivided into price variances (caused by paying unit prices different than the standard or budgeted prices) or efficiency variances (caused by using a different amount of real resources, such as labor, hours, or material than the amount budgeted to accomplish the task).

Overhead variances are still further divided into variable and fixed overhead variances. In addition to a price variance (sometimes called a fixed overhead budget variance) and efficiency variances there are also several fixed overhead activity variances that can be used to examine the economic significance of under utilization of capacity (see Appendix 1A). A manager must be very careful in interpreting the significance of a cost variance. For example, the significance of the material and the direct-labor variances depends on the choice of the policy concerning the type of standard used. If the standard reflects

---

[4] The details and mechanics of the calculation of the cost variances are contained in two appendices in this chapter. This was done so that the text might concentrate, without distraction, on their uses and limitations.

an attainable level of performance (say, a normal cost standard), then an unfavorable variance of substantial size should be considered a candidate for investigation (this is discussed more precisely in Chapter 2).

The variances described above are measured in dollar terms. Physical measures could also be used for the material-usage and labor efficiency variances (although not for the spending variances). Since the standard wage rates and the standard unit prices are reasonably easy to establish however, the dollar measures of the efficiency variances are likely to be useful.

Frequently cost variances, even of large sizes, are not controllable by the manager whose performance is being measured. For example, the cost of steel may increase throughout the country after standards are set creating an unfavorable price variance for the user of the steel. But the purchasing agent of a using company does not have control over this event. For another example, an unfavorable labor efficiency variance may reflect a power failure rather than a situation that is correctable by the company or the cost center. It is important for the manager to realize that the report of cost variances indicates places where something is causing excessive costs, not that inefficiency necessarily exists. In fact, if the standard has been set incorrectly, there might not even be excessive costs, but rather an incorrect measure.

The variable overhead variances exhibit a similarity to the material and labor variances and their interpretation is similar. For example, an unfavorable variable-overhead efficiency variance tends to show the amount of variable overhead that was incurred because of an excessive amount of direct labor. The variable-overhead budget variance indicates the difference between the variable-overhead incurred and the variable overhead budget (the variable overhead-budget is first adjusted, however, to the actual level of activity attained, thus the term "flexible budget"). Direct-labor hours (or labor dollars) is frequently used to accomplish this adjustment. This is generally not a bad approximation, but it must be recognized that the procedure implicitly assumes either a linear relationship between variable-overhead costs and the activity measure used or a very close correlation. Particular variable-overhead costs may vary with other measures of activity. For example, the number of accounts receivable clerks varies with the number of billings. Also, the overhead cost may lead or lag behind the direct-labor cost. Thus a variable-overhead budget variance may be the result of excessive expenditures or merely of the method of computation. Relationships here are often multiple and complex. The goal is an activity measure (or set of measures) that provides useful data; an exact measure is not likely to be found.

In the case of overhead costs, physical measures may be even more relevant. In the first place, most overhead costs are of a fixed nature and cannot be changed in the short run. Furthermore, the historical fixed overhead costs (sunk costs) are of limited value in control, pricing, and other decision situations.

The analysis of *fixed overhead-capacity variances* is somewhat more complex, and different variance breakdowns have been suggested by different authors. Unfortunately the variances computed as by-products of product costing techniques are often inappropriately used for control purposes as well.[5]

The fixed overhead-capacity variances (or activity variances) are not usable for control purposes. Decisions such as pricing and output are marginal decisions and the fixed costs of the firm should not affect those decisions if profits are to be maximized. While fixed costs do affect nonmarginal decisions such as adding and abandoning a product, the relevant costs are not the historical fixed costs but rather the opportunity costs of the factors of production. It is true that the capacity variances can bring to management's attention the presence of slack resources. It is not clear that monetizing this calculation of slack by computing a cost variance adds to management's useful information. Hence these variances are, perhaps, most appropriately calculated in physical terms.

1.2.4 Product Costing

When overhead rates are determined for product-costing purposes and applied to these physical variances, the rates are usually based on either practical or normal capacity.

Practical capacity is difficult to define. It is sometimes defined (Appendix 1A) as the most efficient point of operations (where average variable costs are a minimum for a given set of fixed factors of production). However, many firms have relatively flat average variable-cost and average total-cost curves over a wide range of activity, and thus can produce past that point with little loss of efficiency. Practical capacity is also defined as the minimum of the average total-cost curve or the point at which the firm would operate if there were no shortage of orders. The latter would make practical capacity equivalent to the point where marginal cost equals marginal revenue. A common practice is to resort to industry usage. Thus, if the industry works six days a week, twenty hours a day, this becomes practical capacity. Another industry may commonly work only eight hours a day, five days a week, and this becomes practical capacity.[6]

---

[5] See C. T. Horngren, "A Contribution Margin Approach to the Analysis of Capacity Utilization," *The Accounting Review*, April 1967, pp. 254–264 and K. Schwayder, "A Note on a Contribution Margin Approach to the Analysis of Capacity Utilization," *The Accounting Review*, January 1968, pp. 101–104. The essential ideas in these articles are contained in Appendix 1A.

[6] Stigler defines capacity (in the terms of this book, practical capacity) as the output at which long- and short-run costs are equal. If the firm wants to produce more than the amount where this equality exists it should obtain more fixed factors of production. See G. J. Stigler, *The Theory of Price*, New York: Macmilian, 1966, pp. 157–158.

If a firm usually operates below practical capacity, the use of practical capacity for product costing would tend to understate unit costs with a similar effect on inventory values. Pricing decisions that are cost oriented may be improperly made if the decision maker is not careful.[7]

Because practical capacity is so difficult to define, normal activity is frequently used. Normal activity has as its objective the absorption of all overhead to product in a normal year; thus it is the mean or expected activity not of one year but of several years. Some accountants maintain that each year should carry its own weight and thus an expected capacity concept should be used for product costing. The result is to reduce unit costs in periods of high activity and raise unit costs in periods of low activity. This can again lead to unwise decisions if these decisions are made using historical costs.

The use of a normal activity base implies that year-end variances are expected to average out over time. In practice the variances left at the end of each accounting period are written off or allocated between inventory and expense.

1.2.5 Cost Accounting and Cost Control

The use of cost accounting for cost-control purposes implies that more costs would be incurred if the cost system were not being used. There are basically two reasons why costs may be higher if they are not controlled. For one thing, there would be ignorance of physical waste. Thus a leak in a water pipe may go unnoticed unless the water bill is compared to the budgeted amount. Cost savings of this nature probably would rarely justify the installation of a cost-control system because the water in the basement would probably indicate the leak before the accounting system did. Nevertheless it is one reason for a cost-accounting system.

The second reason is that workers do not tend to work at the highest rate of efficiency unless their performance is being controlled or unless they are very highly motivated. This statement implies that human beings have certain personality characteristics and that costs may be controlled either by authoritative methods or by incentives, or both. It is desirable to integrate the control and incentive devices. The implementation of the system of rewards and penalties requires great skill and judgment; that is, it requires managerial skill.

Despite the difficulties described, control of costs is the prime justification of a cost-accounting system. The fact that cost control requires not only a cost-accounting system but also managerial judgment is not surprising. If management jumps to conclusions and takes hasty action, or at the opposite extreme ignores indications of inefficiency, accounting will be criticized as a cost-control mechanism. In such cases the wrong person may be blamed. A

---

[7] The lack of relevance of fixed costs to pricing should also be noted.

cost-accounting system can assist management; it is not a substitute for managerial skill.

1.2.6 Motivation of Employees Toward Organizational Goals

Budgets and performance reports have an impact on motivation. Furthermore, a firm will find that the reporting procedures in use have motivational effects not only in relation to cost control but toward risk-taking behavior and creativity. The cost-variance reports used by most firms have motivational influences. In some of these firms an unfavorable variance requires the responsible manager to write a detailed explanation including a description of the remedial actions to be undertaken. Favorable variances may be overlooked or ignored. Such behavior is bound to have a motivational impact on the manager reporting.

The use by many firms of participatory budgeting techniques is in part a recognition of the importance of motivational factors. This subject is important enough to justify a separate chapter. (See Chapter 6.)

1.2.7 Decision Making and Planning

Often the criticism is made that cost information supplied by management information systems cannot be used for decision making but must be adjusted. The function of the cost-accounting system is not to supply cost information on a regular basis for decision making and planning but rather to act as a storage space where the information is kept until it is needed. It would be too costly if not impossible for any one accounting report to supply management with all the data necessary to assist in every possible decision. First the decision under consideration should be determined and then the costs should be supplied on the basis of the data requirements of the decision model selected by the manager. (Data availability may affect model choice.) The regular reports produced by the cost-accounting system should be useful both for purposes of measuring performance, and cost control.

Isolation of the cost variance, however, is only the first step in its eventual correction. Variations between actual and expected results may result from employee performance, equipment condition, nature of input materials, decision errors, measurement error, or some combination of these factors. The interaction effects in particular make the detection, assessment of significance, and correction tasks difficult. Nevertheless, the job of tracing back the results of operations to the assumptions underlying the original decisions and the implementation of those decisions is critical.

General cost reports cannot be useful for specific decision-making purposes because accountants cannot know what decisions are to be made. The following list gives some indication of the variety of decisions which may be made, each requiring different information.

1. Pricing a product line.
2. Expanding productive facilities for a product line.
3. Abandoning a product line.
4. Making or buying a product or part.

The first decision (pricing a product line) is a marginal decision; marginal costs and revenues are relevant to the making of this decision. The other three decisions are nonmarginal in nature. To expand a product line the expenditures required to purchase the new facilities and the total costs connected with the expansion must be known. To make a decision on whether or not to abandon a product line, the differential revenues that will be lost and the differential costs that will be saved should be known or estimated. The same is true of the decision to make or buy. All these decisions are also functions of factors not typically part of the accounting records, such as the opportunity costs connected with the building space required and the additional time that will be spent on the project or freed if the product is dropped.

A good cost-accounting system does not necessarily report costs in a form that is usable for all these decisions. However, a good system has stored the information required to make these decisions so that it is readily accessible when needed. A qualification to be noted is that all decisions are based on future costs and revenues; the past is merely an aid in making a judgment of the future. Recorded costs, to be useful, must be projected into the future.

1.3   The Reliability of Accounting Data

One of several problems faced by the users of accounting information is the validity of the data. Indeed, it is easy to impart to figures, somewhat mystically obtained, a degree of validity that they do not possess. A high, degree of self-control is required not to use these figures for purposes for which they are not intended. The wise decision maker investigates the relevance and the reliability of any data he intends to use in a given decision situation. The timeliness of the data may be thought of as one aspect of relevance.

The concept of reliability can be treated as being composed of two elements, bias and objectivity.[8] If the measurement process is stochastic, then the individual measures will differ. The variability of the measures around their average, as measured by the variance, indicates the objectivity in the measurement process. In other words the greater the propensity of a measuring

[8] The development of this section draws on Y. Ijiri and R. K. Jaedicke, "Reliability and Objectivity of Accounting Measurements," *The Accounting Review*, July 1966, pp. 474–483.

process to reproduce the same values for the same set of events, the greater the objectivity of the measure. In symbols

$$\text{Objectivity} = 1/n\Big[\sum_{i} (x_i - \bar{x})^2\Big]$$

where the x_i represents the individual observations and $\bar{x}$ represents the average of the observations.

Unfortunately, the average, $\bar{x}$, of the measurement process may not be equal to the value that the investigator wishes to estimate. In other words, the measurement process may be biased. However, if the bias in the measurement process is known it could be allowed for by adding the bias to the measure obtained. In symbols:

$$\text{Bias} = (\bar{x} - \mu)$$

where μ is the value to be estimated.

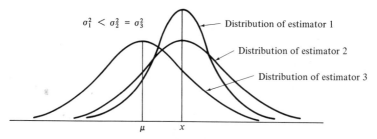

Figure 1.4   Reliability and its components

Reliability refers to the variability of the measure around the value to be estimated, μ in the equation for bias. Reliability may also be measured by a variance, but in this case the variance of the measure around the value to be estimated. In symbols:

$$\text{Reliability} = 1/n\Big[\sum_{i} (x_i - \mu)^2\Big].$$

After using some algebra this expression can be rewritten as

$$\text{Reliability} = 1/n\Big[\sum_{i} (x_i - \bar{x})^2\Big] + (\bar{x} - \mu)^2$$
$$= \text{Objectivity} + (\text{Bias})^2.$$

Reliability is equal to objectivity plus the square of the bias. In statistical terminology it is the efficiency of the measurement process.

The concepts involved here are illustrated graphically in Figure 1.4.

Suppose there are three measurement processes, (or estimators as they are called in statistics) whose measures are distributed according to the three distributions illustrated in Figure 1.4, available to estimate some cost level μ.

Estimator 1 is the most objective but it is biased. Estimator 3 is unbiased but it is not as objective as 1. Estimator 3 is more reliable than 2 but it is not clearly more reliable than 1. There is a tradeoff between bias and objectivity here. If the bias in estimator 1 were known then it would be preferred because knowledge concerning the bias permits the bias to be eliminated from the measure.

All other things equal, the larger the measure of reliability the poorer the measurement process. Small values are desired. But a reliable measure is not necessarily a relevant one. The relevance of a measure depends on the use for which it is required. The use must be specified before the relevance or irrelevance of a measure can be established.

1.4 Summary

The role of costs is extensive in decision making. This is the case even though management can often be viewed most appropriately as maximizing utility and not profits. It seems also to be the case that organizations tend to suboptimize or adopt satisficing strategies in the face of "real world" complexities.

Costs may be defined and categorized in a number of different ways. The proper classification will depend on the particular use or decision under consideration. It would not be desirable for cost records to be kept for each category. Rather, a good accounting system will act as a ready source of cost information that can be assembled to suit specific needs. If some data of the type needed for decisions is not now being recorded, then this situation requires correction. The cost-accounting system should provide information that can be used in control and reduction of costs, in performance measurement, in the determination of income and financial position, and for decision making and planning. Care needs to be taken, however, so that the motivational effects of cost systems are taken into account. The calculation of cost variances is discussed in an appendix.

The chapter concludes with a brief discussion of some desirable properties of cost measures. The notion of reliability is introduced as a combination of variability and objectivity (lack of bias). The characteristics of timeliness and relevance are also of critical importance to cost-measurement data.

APPENDIX IA
DEFINITION AND CALCULATION OF COST VARIANCES

This appendix discusses some of the commonly used cost variances. It also examines in some detail the information that can be obtained from the fixed-overhead variance calculations.

Material Variances

The material-usage variance is the difference between the standard and actual quantities of material priced at the standard price per unit. $(Q_A - Q_S)P_S$.

The material-price variance (spending variance) is the actual quantity of material used times the difference between the standard and actual price per unit of material. $(P_A - P_S)Q_A$. When both the price and quantity used exceed the standard, the additional expense due to the higher price for the extra quantity may arbitrarily be assigned to the price variance.

Direct-Labor Variances

The Efficiency variance is the difference between the actual and standard direct-labor hours, priced at the standard wage rate per hour. $(H_A - H_S)W_S$.

The wage-rate variance (spending variance) is the actual number of hours times the difference between the actual and standard wage rates per hour. $(W_A - W_S)H_A$.

When both the wage rate and hours used exceed the standard, the expenditure attributable to the higher rate for the extra hours may be arbitrarily assigned to the wage-rate variance.

Variable Overhead Variances

The variable-overhead efficiency variance is the difference between the actual and the standard direct-labor hours at the variable overhead rate. $(H_A - H_S)V_S$.

The variable-overhead budget variance (spending variance) is the difference between the actual and standard rates multiplied by the actual number of direct-labor hours. $(V_A - V_S)H_A$.

Fixed-Overhead Variances

The fixed-overhead budget variance is the difference between the budgeted and actual fixed costs for the period.

Fixed-overhead activity variances require a definition of capacity. The following several different capacity concepts are commonly found in the literature.

THEORETICAL CAPACITY: The output level that could be obtained operating continuously at peak maintainable output. (For example, the plant is assumed to operate 24 hours a day, 365 days a year, without breakdowns.)

PRACTICAL OR ATTAINABLE CAPACITY: The level of output at which the activity operates most efficiently (where variable cost is at a minimum). Unavoidable delays, maintenance, and normal waiting time are considered.

NORMAL CAPACITY: The level of output necessary to satisfy average consumer demand. Typically, this concept represents a long-run notion covering cyclical as well as trend and seasonal influences. The result is a more nearly constant overhead rate over time.

EXPECTED CAPACITY: The output level anticipated for the period in question.

A useful way to describe the relevant variances is through an examination of the schematic presented in Figure 1.5. It should be noted that there is no implied permanent pattern to the ordering of the various measures. In any actual situation their numerical ordering could be quite different: the present one is useful only for discussion purposes. Units of output are used for concreteness of the discussion. The units could be converted into the related direct-labor hours if desired. (In line with the previous discussion, all positive variances are considered undesirable.)

The theoretical-capacity variance is the difference between the activity level at theoretical capacity and at practical capacity.

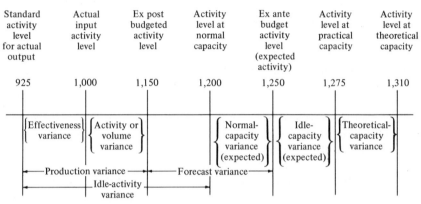

Figure 1.5   Activity levels relevant to cost control

This variance provides a measure of the excess capacity of the plant that might be utilized on a short-run basis if resources could be obtained. (1,310 − 1,275 = 35 units.)

The idle-capacity variance is the difference between the activity level at practical capacity and the activity level budgeted at the beginning of the period. (1,275 − 1,250 = 25 units.)

This variance represents the difference between the expected activity level for the budget period and the practical capacity of the activity. Since the firm's practical-capacity level is its most efficient operating level, there should be a close relationship between the expected activity level and practical capacity. Large and persistent variances here reflect on long-range planning decisions. Period differences are expected. This is an *ex ante* concept.

The normal-capacity variance is the difference between the budgeted (expected) activity level and a normal level of activity. (1,250 − 1,200 = 50 units.)

Variances between the normal activity level and the budgeted activity are expected due to trend, cyclical and seasonal influences. Sometimes the normal-capacity variance and the idle-capacity variance are combined and called the expected-capacity variance.

The normal activity to be encountered over a period of several years should be one important input to the design of the plant and thus there should be a close relationship between normal and practical capacity. Indeed the relationship would probably be closer than that suggested by the figures in the present example, although (due to the nonsymmetric nature of cost behavior) practical capacity would be planned to exceed the normal demand for capacity. Wide differences (between normal activity and practical capacity) might reflect poor long-run activity forecasts in the past. If, on the other hand, the utilization of an asset is expected to increase through time the normal activity level as well as the budgeted (expected) activity level in the early years could easily be substantially less than the activity level at practical capacity.

The forecast variance is the difference between the *ex ante* and *ex post* (or revised) budgeted activity levels. (1,250 − 1,150 = 100 units.)

This variance is typically a result of disruptions in marketing plans but it may be due to inaccurate economic projections, or calamities such as strikes. This variance has an expected value of zero when the *ex ante* budget is prepared.

The production-variance is the difference between the *ex post* budgeted activity level and the standard activity level needed to produce the actual output. (1,150 − 925 = 225 units.)

This variance is a function of the productive apparatus of the firm. For some reason the actual activity of the firm did not equal the revised (*ex post*) sales budget. There may be many reasons for this variance, including some reasons that are not attributable to the production department. For example, changes in raw material quality or labor skills might be involved. This variance can in turn be broken into two parts.

The activity or volume variance is the difference between the *ex post* budgeted activity and actual input activity level. (1,150−1,000 = 150 units.)

The variance represents the failure of actual activity to correspond to the *ex post* budgeted level. An unfavorable variance might be due to poor scheduling or equipment breakdowns that prevented the firm from reaching the revised budgetary sales levels. The reader is warned that the terminology "volume variance" is used differently here than in its usual definition.[9] It is useful to have a name for the difference between activity at normal capacity and actual output. This variance will be known as the idle-activity variance. (1,200 − 925 = 275 units.)

---

[9] The terms activity or volume variance are often used to represent the difference between the level of activity at normal capacity and either actual activity (1,200 − 1,000 = 200 units here) or standard activity for the actual output (1,200 − 925 = 275 units here). Neither interpretation given in this note lends itself as readily to interpretation and analysis as the breakdown given in the text.

The effectiveness variance is the difference between the actual activity level and the standard activity level for the actual output. (1,000 − 925 = 75 units.)

This variance provides a measure of how effectively the actual activity was conducted. For example, an unfavorable effectiveness variance may indicate poorly motivated or poorly skilled workers.

The analysis and use of variances in a given situation requires that interrelationships be considered as well as the causes for individual variances. For example, a favorable effectiveness variance combined with a large unfavorable labor wage-rate and a favorable labor-efficiency variance may indicate that a higher labor skill level than necessary is being employed.

Similarly, an (expected) idle-capacity variance for the next period can be reduced to at least zero if necessary to allow for some, if not all, of an expected unfavorable effectiveness variance. Thus in the present example, if a repetition of the production variances were anticipated, the *ex ante* budget could be increased (at least) to 1,275 units. The idle-capacity variance for the second period would be zero. If both parts of the production variance were also zero in the second period, an idle-capacity variance of 25 units would be budgeted and expected, *ceteris paribus*, in the third period.[10,11]

To the extent an unfavorable effectiveness variance exceeds the idle-capacity variance and contributes to an unfavorable production variance, it helps explain why the *ex post* budgeted level was not reached. This part of the variance might reasonably be considered as part of the activity variance if it were due to ineffective labor. Alternatively, if it does not exceed the idle-capacity variance, it may suggest inadequate planning.

The Calendar Variance

The normal-capacity variance may be split into two components, the calendar variance and a residual variance which should be treated as the normal-capacity variance. This practice helps to extract out from the normal-activity variance that part of the variance which is caused by changes in the number of working days in the month. Supposedly, the variance which is left is controllable by management. In the example illustrated in Figure 1.5, it is assumed that the budget figures are for the actual time period and not for an average period. Thus there is no calendar variance. An analogous separation could be made for the idle-capacity variance.

APPENDIX IB
MIX VARIANCE

In some manufacturing situations factors of production may be substituted for each other. Thus, in an emergency or during slack activity a highly paid

---

[10] The implicit assumption is made that absolute and not relative measures are relevant.

[11] To the extent operations are more efficient at the increased activity level, the cost of expanding activity may be offset somewhat.

worker may be used in a task which ordinarily requires a worker of a lower grade. In like manner one grade of steel may be substituted for another grade. This type of transaction gives rise to mix variances. A mix variance is defined as a variance which is caused by the substitution of one factor of production for another factor of production. The variance caused by differences in wage rates (or prices) can be determined relatively easily but the change in efficiency that results from the substitution is more difficult to establish since the necessary information to compute it is usually not available. Hence it is often difficult to measure the total effect of a shift in mix.

The mix variance can be illustrated by the use of a shift in direct labor. The mix variance is computed by multiplying the number of direct-labor hours which are shifted, by the difference between the standard wage rate for the workers who were transferred and the standard wage rate for the task. Several other possible definitions of mix variance would be equally reasonable; thus there is no implication that this is the only correct method of computation. There is too much jointness connected with the incurring of these variances to allow precision in the method of computation.

Example

Assume there are two types of workers, "skilled" and "unskilled," working on two processes, grinding and assembly. The standard cost information and the facts for March are given in Exhibit 1–4

Exhibit 1–4   Standard Costs for One Unit of Product

Process	Type of worker	Standard hours	Standard wage rate	Totals
Assembly	Unskilled	4	$2.00	$ 8.00
Grinding	Skilled	6	3.00	18.00
				$26.00

Actual Costs for Month

Type of worker	Actual hours	Actual wages	Actual wage rate
Unskilled	380	$ 836	$2.20
Skilled	610	2,074	3.40
		$2,910	

Assume skilled workers work on the assembly line for 10 hours (the total hours worked on assembly operations are 390 and on grinding 600). There are 100 units of product manufactured. The standard cost is $2,600 and actual cost is $2,910; thus there is an unfavorable variance of $310.

The computation of variance is as follows:

Efficiency variance: The standard wage rate times the difference between standard and actual hours worked.

Assembly	$2(400 − 390) = $20 favorable
Grinding	$3(600 − 600) = 0
	$20 favorable

Wage-rate variance: The actual hours times the difference between the actual and standard wage rates (for both types of workers, the actual hours worked by that type of worker is used)

Skilled	610(3.40 − 3.00) = $244 unfavorable
Unskilled	380(2.20 − 2.00) = 76 unfavorable
	$320 unfavorable

Mix variance: The number of hours shifted, multiplied by the difference between the standard wage rate for the men shifted and the standard wage rate for the task performed

$$10(3.00 − 2.00) = \$10 \text{ unfavorable}$$

Total variance:
The algebraic sum of the three variances

Efficiency	$ 20 favorable
Wage rate	320 unfavorable
Mix	10 unfavorable
	$310 unfavorable

(Note that nothing is said of whether the 100 units were produced quicker or whether some other advantage was obtained; nor is the value of the advantage, if any, given.)

QUESTIONS AND PROBLEMS

1–1 The New York Oil Company owns one tanker that has a value of $10 million. A careful study indicates there is a 0.005 probability of the ship being a total loss in the coming year as a result of a nautical disaster.

The company has contracted to pay $60,000 insurance for the year against this event.

The company has an opportunity to acquire a small oil wildcating firm at a cost of $10 million. The present value of the expected benefits from owning the firm are $11 million gross and $1 million net. The probability distribution of outcomes has a large variance. The opportunity is rejected despite its favorable expectation.

The New York Oil Company has an annual income of $1 million and assets of $100 million.

Required: Explain the thinking that may have lead to the two decisions. Are the decisions consistent?

1–2 A credit manager of Chase Manhattan Bank has to decide whether or not to offer credit to a small manufacturer. There is a significant risk of the firm failing, but the expected value of the loan is positive.

Required: Discuss the considerations that might affect the credit manager's decision.

1–3 The manager of the grinding department of a manufacturing plant has recommended the acqusition of a new machine that is fully automatic and that is fed information from a central computer station. The computer is currently being used for a variety of purposes within the company.

The analysis used to justify the acquisition compared the direct economic savings (essentially savings in labor) with the explicit cost of the equipment (assume the basic investment analysis was done in a reasonable manner).

Required: If the analysis were to be made on a global basis what other factors might be considered?

1–4 Assume a situation where you can hire workers when you need them but you cannot fire them when they are not needed except at a very large cost.

How would this information affect decision making?

1–5 It is difficult for a firm to separate its costs into fixed and variable costs but it can be done. As an illustration, take the costs of owning and operating an automobile and divide the costs into fixed and variable classifications.

1–6 Consider education as a product. What are the direct costs and what are the indirect costs to a university of facilitating the education of a student?

1–7 The concept of *opportunity cost* is extremely important to decision making. Discuss the following:

  a. Deciding how space in a department store is to be used.

b. Deciding how much salary to offer to a college graduate who is being considered for employment.

c. The importance of the reserve clause to professional baseball (a ball-player plays for the one team he has signed with or does not play).

d. The decision of a student to obtain a MBA degree.

1-8 The demand for a product can be 0, 1, or 2 each with equal probability. The payoffs for three alternative order decisions are:

	States: (Demand is)		
Alternatives: (Order)	0	1	2
0	0	0	0
1	-5	8	8
2	-10	3	16

Required:

a. Assuming that one unit is ordered, what is the opportunity cost for the three possible states that might occur?

b. What is the expected opportunity cost of ordering one unit?

c. If one unit is ordered and the event "demand is two" occurs, what is the opportunity cost?

d. What additional information might be desired to make an order decision?

1-9 The New York Oil Company has just bought 1 million barrels of oil. A consultant has argued that now the cost of the oil is a sunk cost and thus the cost is not relevant to any decision the company faces. The president of the firm realized that the cost of his pipelines was a sunk cost but found it difficult to consider his inventory to be sunk.

Required: Discuss whether or not the cost of the inventory is a sunk cost.

1-10 Do you think cost standards should be easy or difficult to attain? Discuss.

1-11 The following information applies to a day's production:

Units of good product started and finished	5,000
Standard material per unit	2 lb
Actual material used	11,000 lb
Standard price per pound of material	$2.25 per lb
Actual price per pound of material	$2.35 per lb

Required: (Appendix IA may be useful)

a. Compute the material-usage variance.

b. Compute the material-price variance.

c. Compute the total variance from standard cost.

d. Part of the variance was caused by a higher price paid for units that should not have been used. Compute this amount. Compute a price and usage variance to accompany it so that the total variance is equal to the answer of part c. Explain the difference in results in relation to parts a and b and discuss the value, if any, of the refinement in calculation.

1–12 Using average total cost, average variable cost, marginal cost curves, and any other curves that you think useful, indicate on a diagram the practical capacity of a plant.

1–13 The New York Oil Company wants a dollar measure of its oil holdings. The company has the choice of the two procedures.

Procedure A

Possible observations: Just one, the assigned cost of $5,000,000.

Procedure B

Possible observations (all equally likely):

$ 5,000,000
8,000,000
9,000,000
10,000,000

Assume the true value of the oil is $8 million. (This would very rarely be known.)

Required: Compute the objectivity, the bias, and the reliability of the two measurement procedures. Which cost measure do you believe is more useful in decision making?

1–14 (Relates to Appendix IB). Prepare an analysis of cost variances from the following information:

Process	Workers	Standard Hours	Standard Costs per Hour	Total
1	Jones	1	$3.00	$ 3.00
2	Smith	3	4.00	12.00
				$15.00

During January, Jones worked forty hours and Smith worked 180 hours. Jones earned $130 and Smith $765. There were fifty units of product produced. All of Smith's and Jones' time was assigned to this product. Smith filled in and worked on process one for eight hours.

1–15 (Relates to Appendix IA). Prepare as complete an analysis of cost variances as possible from the following information:

Standard costs per unit	
Direct labor (5 hours @ $4)	$20.00
Material (20 pounds at @ $2)	40.00
Variable overhead ($1.50 × 5)	7.50
Fixed overhead ($3 × 5)	15.00
	$82.50

Budget information for the year

Variable overhead	$150,000
Fixed overhead	300,000
Normal activity for year	100,000 direct-labor hours
Practical activity for year	120,000 direct-labor hours

The normal activity for January is 9,000 direct-labor hours. The practical activity for January is 10,000 direct-labor hours. The actual results of January's operations were as follows:

Variable overhead	$11,000
Fixed overhead	$26,000
Actual activity	8,000 direct-labor hours
Actual production	1,450 units
Actual labor cost	$33,600
Actual material cost (30,000 pounds)	$66,000

The firm expected to produce 1,900 units in January but an expected slow-down at its major supplier necessitated a cutback in the possible level of activity to 1,700 units. Suppose the supply condition is expected to persist and no alternative sources are available. Is it possible to use idle capacity in the next period to counter the unfavorable effectiveness variance?

1–16 Consider the sets of variances to represent four different months that are essentially unrelated.

Variance	Month 1	Month 2	Month 3	Month 4
Material-price variance	$ 0	$ 0	$2,000 F	$1,500 F
Material-use variance	200 U	400 U	600 F	400 U
Labor-rate variance	0	7,500 F	8,000 U	0
Labor-efficiency variance	3,000 U	4,000 U	6,000 F	4,000 U
Variable-efficiency variance	100 U	100 U	200 F	80 U
Variable-spending variance	10 F	200 F	100 F	30 U
Fixed overhead-spending variance	800 U	1,000 U	200 F	750 U
Fixed overhead idle-capacity variance	700 U	300 U	300 F	1,000 U

The following general conclusions were made by the cost analyst
Month 1: The materials used are of inferior quality.
Month 2: The labor is of substandard ability.
Month 3: High-grade materials were purchased in an unsuccessful attempt to save money elsewhere.
Month 4: Production exceeded expectations.
Required: Do you agree or disagree with the conclusions of the cost analyst? Explain and justify your position.

SUPPLEMENTARY READING

A.A.A. *A Statement of Basic Accounting Theory*, The American Accounting Association, 1966.

ANTON, H. R., and P. A. FIRMIN, *Contemporary Issues in Cost Accounting*, Boston: Houghton Mifflin Company, 1966.

BENSTON, G. J., *Contemporary Cost Accounting and Control*, Belmont, Calif.: Dickenson Publishing Company, Inc., 1970.

DEMSKI, J. S., "An Accounting System Structured on a Linear Programming Model," *The Accounting Review*, October 1967, pp. 701–712.

DEMSKI, J. S., "Decision-Performance Control," *The Accounting Review*, October 1969, pp. 669–679.

DOPUCH, N., J. G. BIRNBERG, and J. DEMSKI, "An Extension of Standard Cost Analysis," *The Accounting Review*, July 1967, pp. 526–536.

FELTHAM, G., "The Value of Information," *The Accounting Review*, October 1968, pp. 684–696.

FRANK, W. and R. MANES, "A Standard Cost Application of Matrix Algebra," *The Accounting Review*, July 1967, pp. 516–525.

HORNGREN, C. T., "A Contribution Margin Approach to the Analysis of Capacity Utilization," *The Accounting Review*, April 1967, pp. 254–264.

HORNGREN, C. T., *Cost Accounting: A Managerial Emphasis*, 2d ed., Englewood Cliffs, N.J.: Prentice Hall, 1967, Chapters 1, 2, and 8.

IJIRI, Y., *Management Goals and Accounting for Control*, Amsterdam: North-Holland Publishing Company, 1965.

IJIRI, Y., and R. JAEDICKE, "Reliability and Objectivity of Accounting Measurements," *The Accounting Review*, July 1966, pp. 474–483.

SHWAYDER, K., "A Note on a Contribution Margin Approach to the Analysis of Capacity Utilization," *The Accounting Review*, January 1968, pp. 101–104.

SHWAYDER, K., "Relevance," *Journal of Accounting Research*, Spring 1968, pp. 86–97.

SORTER, G. H., "An Events Approach to Basic Accounting Theory," *The Accounting Review*, January 1969, pp. 12–19.

Chapter 2

Cost Control and
Statistical Techniques

Statistical methods are relevant and can be expected to find increased use in cost analysis and control procedures. This and the next chapter describe two particular applications. In this chapter statistical decision theory is used to decide whether or not to investigate cost variances. In the next chapter regression techniques are used to estimate cost relationships.

Particular attention should be paid to the limitations and assumptions explicit and implicit to each technique. As with any quantitative technique, the assumptions must be understood before the applicability of the technique in a given situation can be determined.

2.1   The Decision to Investigate Cost Variances

The conventional procedure in evaluating performance using budgeted or standard costs is to look at either the absolute size of the cost variance (the difference between actual and standard costs) or the percentage obtained by dividing the cost variance by the standard cost. Both these measures rely upon the intuition of management in deciding whether the variance should be investigated and whether the investigation should then lead to corrective action.

The analysis may be formalized by assuming that the expected value and variance of the probability distribution for the cost variance are known and the probability of an observation as unusual as the one observed is computed. If this probability is small, say 0.05, (depending on the importance the manager attaches to the cost in question), the particular cost variance is a candidate for investigation. This approach requires the manager to combine the probability of a cost variance as large or larger than the one obtained with the dollar amounts involved, and his feelings about the correctability of the situation, and to compare the results with alternative uses of the available resources. He may also consider the time trend of past observations (see Figure 2.2) in his analysis. There are difficulties in estimating the relevant data, and the procedure is limited by several factors including the complexity of balancing the cost and (opportunity) losses against alternative resource uses.

The statistical-decision procedure suggested in this chapter attempts to make the investigation decision more precise by incorporating the losses and gains as well as the probabilities directly into the decision-making process.[1]

2.1.1 Setting the Problem

The cost-variance investigation decision involves a multi-state process in which information about the states reaches the decision maker at discrete time periods. This information concerns the state of the process over which the decision maker has some, but not complete, control. The decision maker is in turn faced with the question of whether or not to intervene in order to exercise that control. Exercising control here means first deciding whether or not to investigate the process prior to the next stage, and secondly, if investigation takes place, deciding whether or not to correct the process.

Through time the process being reported on may change from being in control to being out of control or vice versa. Thus, the process can be described as one in which the state variable is subject to transformation during each stage. These transformations (from control to out of control and vice versa) are only partially under the control of the decision maker through the manipulation of decision variables (which are assumed here to remain constant within each stage of the process). Furthermore, knowledge about the process in a given stage is probablistic; that is, the information available about the process may or may not be indicative of the actual state of the process.

The description of the problem so far implies only a single process. In fact, at each stage the decision maker is monitoring several processes. His task is to select a subset of the processes for investigation given budget and other constraints and a desire to minimize costs. The constraints and cost minimization will usually prevent an investigation of all processes at each stage.

[1] The discussion in this section is influenced by R. M. Duvall, "Rules for Investigating Cost Variances," *Management Science*, June 1967, pp. 631–641; and R. S. Kaplan, "Optimal Investigation Strategies with Imperfect Information," *Journal of Accounting Research*, Spring 1969, pp. 32–43.

Furthermore, the investigation action can be dichotomized in practice so that either an exploratory investigation at a substantially reduced cost or a complete investigation may be undertaken.

The stochastic elements in the problem are several. First the process of transformation from an in-control to an out-of-control state (and vice versa) is in part probabilistic. The state of control shifts from stage to stage according to some random process as well as in response to the actions taken by the decision maker. Decisions to modify the process must be made on the basis of sample information which is also stochastic. Finally, an investigation once initiated may fail to disclose a situation requiring adjustment when one exists; and in addition, adjustment once undertaken may fail to restore the desired state.

Certain variables often included in a control system are not optimized in the present discussion but, rather, are treated as parameters (their levels are assumed fixed, although perhaps unknown). These parameters are the time interval between cost reports, the lag between measurement and control implementation, the cost of investigation and process of adjustment, and the accuracy of the information. Decisions are made only concerning the investigate decision and how information can be used to make this choice.

2.1.2 A Simple Investigate Decision Situation

Consider first a very basic problem in which monetary values are used to evaluate each state-action pair. The monetary values are assumed to reflect the consequences to the decision maker of each action under each state.

Decisions Using Prior Probabilities—The Case of Two States
Assume a two-state, two-action problem with states

θ_1: in control
θ_2: out of control,
    and possible actions
a_1: investigate
a_2: do not investigate.

There are several implicit assumptions. One of these is that the incurred costs are reported on a periodic basis. Thus a do-not-investigate action implies that the activity is continued at least until the next cost observation is available. An additional assumption made for this portion of the analysis is that an investigation always reveals the cause of an out-of-control situation which can and will be immediately corrected.[2]

---

[2] An interesting question not examined here concerns the effect on the analysis of investigations that last longer than the time between successive cost observations.

The cost of an investigation is assumed to be an amount C, the cost of correction is M, and the present value of the savings obtainable from an investigation when the activity is out of control is $L - M$ where $L - M > C$; if $L - M < C$, investigation would never be warranted.

Reliable estimates of the investigation and correction costs, C and M, should be reasonably easy to obtain. On the other hand, the benefits from an investigation are more difficult to determine with precision. In the first place the benefits may be in either of two forms. If the cost variance is caused by conditions that can be corrected, the benefit is in the reduction or elimination of the cause of the variance. Alternatively, if the variance is caused by a permanent change in the process, the benefits in this case result from a change in the decision process that may enable the firm to avoid similar situations in the future. For illustrative purposes, the discussion here will assume that the observed variance is of the correctable type.

It is assumed here that the relevant period over which the value of L is estimated is either the time until the process is expected to go out of control again or the time until the standards are expected to be revised. Under these conditions the present value of L depends on the future decisions that will be made. Hence, the present value of L depends upon following an optimal decision policy in the future. With these assumptions the problem becomes one amenable to discrete dynamic programming.[3] The difficulty in solving large realistic problems by this method suggests that a somewhat different approach using estimates of the value of L may be valuable.

For purposes of this discussion, the value of L is estimated as the present value of the cost savings over the planning horizon as defined in the previous paragraph. In the present example, assume an out-of-control process causes a cost of $2,500 per period over a fourteen-period planning horizon. Using a time value of money of 0.14 per period yields a value of $15,000 for L. Assume further an investigation cost of $2,000, and if an out-of-control situation is uncovered, it costs $3,000 to correct it.

Table 2–1 gives the general form of the cost payoff matrix associated with a two-state two-action problem. Typically the values will be of a small enough magnitude so that the decision maker is willing to act on the basis of the expected values.[4]

For the particular example under consideration the net present value of the

---

[3] See Kaplan, *op. cit.*, for an example of the discrete dynamic programming approach applied to this problem.

[4] This is even more likely to be a reasonable approach if the firm as a whole is considered. However, from the individual's point of view a utility analysis may be relevant thus producing a control problem. This is particularly likely to be the case if the cost-control procedures in use reward the manager in an asymmetric way. Furthermore, individual utility functions may be related to the size of the amounts with which the manager, rather than the firm, conventionally deals. See Chapter 16 for a further discussion.

cost savings if the process is out of control is $15,000, the investigation cost is $2,000, and the cost of correction is $3,000. Hence Table 2–1 can be transformed into Table 2–2 showing the costs for the present example.

Table 2–1 General Cost Payoff Matrix (Two-state Form)

	States: θ_j	
Actions: a_i	θ_1: In control	θ_2: Out of control
a_1: investigate	C	$C + M$
a_2: do not investigate	0	L

Assume now that the state probabilities are given by $f_n(\theta_j)$ in any period n ($n = 0, 1, \ldots$). Let $K(a_i, \theta_j)$ represent the payoff associated with action a_i if state θ_j obtains. Using the above notation in the present problem $K(a_1, \theta_1) = C$, $K(a_1, \theta_2) = C + M$, $K(a_2, \theta_1) = 0$, and $K(a_2, \theta_2) = L$ where the payoffs are in terms of costs and the firm wants to minimize expected costs. The expected payoffs for a given action are obtained by multiplying the payoffs

Table 2–2 Specific Cost Payoff Matrix (Two-state Form)

	States: θ_j	
Actions: a_i	θ_1 In control	θ_2: Out of control
a_1: investigate	$2,000	$ 5,000
a_2: do not investigate	0	$15,000

by their probabilities and summing across states for the given action. Therefore the expected cost of action a_1 in period n is given by $C[f_n(\theta_1)] + (C + M)[f_n(\theta_2)] = C + M[f_n(\theta_2)]$. The expected cost of action a_2 in the present problem is $0[f_n(\theta_1)] + L[f_n(\theta_2)] = L[f_n(\theta_2)]$.

Under these assumptions the investigate action should be taken at some stage n if its expected cost is less than the expected cost of not investigating; that is, where K is the payoff random variable and θ (without a subscript) is the state random variable, investigate if

$$E[K(a_1, \theta)] < E[K(a_2, \theta)].$$

Substituting, this means that

$$C + M[f_n(\theta_2)] < L[f_n(\theta_2)] \qquad \text{or} \qquad C - (L - M)[f_n(\theta_2)] < 0 \quad (2.1)$$

For the specific example suppose $f_n(\theta_1) = 0.82$ and $f_n(\theta_2) = 0.18$, then inequality (2.1) gives

$$\$2{,}000 - \$12{,}000\ [0.18] = -\$160 < 0$$

and investigation is the optimal action if the information and assumptions are accepted as presented.

It is assumed, further, that the decision maker can establish the prior subjective probability mass function over the states.[5] The probability mass function yields the values $f_0(\theta_j)$ required to use inequality (2.1) in period $n = 0$.

Two different situations involving this simplified example can be examined:

(a) In periods n ($n = 0, 1, 2, \ldots$), the process is either in control or out of control. Changes between states are not permitted and a process once corrected remains in the control state for the remainder of the planning horizon.

(b) In period n ($n = 0, 1, 2, \ldots$), the process is either in control or out of control. A change from the state in control to the state out of control may occur during any time period. The process is assumed to begin in the control state and at some future period it may change to the out-of-control state. It then remains in this state for the remainder of the planning horizon. For simplicity the change is assumed to occur at the start of the period. Furthermore, it is assumed that the transition occurs, if at all, prior to obtaining the cost observation.

SITUATION (a): Consider situation (a) first, involving a less realistic but more simple set of assumptions than situation (b). An investigation is immediately called for if $C - (L - M)[f_0(\theta_2)]$ is negative. But suppose that $f_0(\theta_2)$ is initially small enough that no investigate decision is indicated. Now suppose that in the next period ($n = 1$) a cost level, x, is observed that is more likely to occur when the process is out of control (see Figure 2.1). This observation increases the probability of state θ_2 and decreases the probability of state θ_1. If the probability attaching to state θ_2 (being out of control) is increased enough, then the expected cost from investigation is less than the expected cost from not investigating and action a_1 is preferred.

---

[5] This is perhaps a feasible task for someone familiar with the activity since only two states are involved. One merely needs to define the probability of the two states. Care is necessary, however, to provide for changes that may have taken place in the process. This implies that the prior probability should be based on relevant historical information adjusted for differences from past conditions by someone knowledgeable about the activity.

Using Bayes' theorem the revision of the state probabilities for a given cost observation, x (a value of the random variable X) in period 0 is given by

$$f_1(\theta_j) = f_1(\theta_j \mid x) = \frac{f_X(x \mid \theta_j)f_0(\theta_j)}{\sum\limits_{j=1}^{2} f_X(x \mid \theta_j)f_0(\theta_j)} \qquad (2.2)$$

where $f_X(x \mid \theta_j)$ is the probability (or probability density if continuous distributions for the cost observations are appropriate) of the observed cost x if θ_j is the true state. In order to use Bayes' theorem, the conditional probability of the cost observation under each state is required. If the expectation and the variance of the cost observations are known for both the case in which the cost is in control and when it is out of control, the data necessary to use Bayes' theorem can be obtained.[6,7] Suppose the facts in Table 2–3 are available (where X stands for the random variable cost observation).

Table 2–3   Cost Facts: Variance Analysis Problem

Parameters	General Situation		Specific Situation	
	θ_1: In control	θ_2: Out of control	θ_1: In control	θ_2: Out of control
Expected cost observation	$E(X \mid \theta_1)$	$E(X \mid \theta_2)$	$6,000	$8,000
Variance of cost observation	$\sigma^2(X \mid \theta_1)$	$\sigma^2(X \mid \theta_2)$	250,000*	250,000*

* Assumed to be independent of the state.

Suppose, further, that the cost-observation distributions in question are normal or approximately normal with the probability densities $f_X(x \mid \theta_1) = n_X(x \mid \theta_1)$ and $f_X(x \mid \theta_2) = n_X(x \mid \theta_2)$.[8] The probability densities of the cost

---

[6] It may be reasonable to assume that the variance remains unchanged whether the process is in control or not. This is assumed to be the case in this example.

[7] Formula (2.2) can also be used to revise the state probabilities using the sample mean as a sufficient statistic. Here $\bar{x} = [\sum(x)] \div n$; $E(\bar{X} \mid \theta_j) = E(X \mid \theta_j)$ is unchanged; $\sigma^2(\bar{X} \mid \theta_j) = [\sigma^2(X \mid \theta_j)] \div n$, and after n periods formula (2.2) is written

$$f_n(\theta_j) = \frac{f_{\bar{x}}(\bar{x} \mid \theta_j)f_0(\theta_j)}{\sum\limits_{j=1}^{2} f_{\bar{x}}(\bar{x} \mid \theta_j)f_0(\theta_j)}$$

[8] If the observed cost is determined by a large set of independent additive factors, no one of which is dominant, these distributions may be approximately normal. When this is not the case, some attempt may be made to estimate the relevant distribution. The letter n in the notation $n_X(x \mid \theta_j)$ is used to indicate the cost distributions are normal. Hence, in this case

$$f_X(x \mid \theta_j) = n_X(x \mid \theta_j).$$

observations can be obtained from a table of the ordinates of the normal density function. This is illustrated in Figure 2.1. All the information to compute the revised probabilities $f_1(\theta_1) = f_1(\theta_1 \mid x)$ and $f_1(\theta_2) = f_1(\theta_2 \mid x)$ is now available. These revised state probabilities can then be used to determine the expected cost from both actions (investigate and do not investigate) and thus provide a means for selecting between the two actions at stage 1.

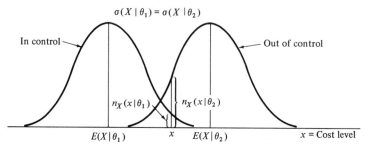

Figure 2.1   Normal cost observation distribution (two-state form)

In order to avoid making the expected-value calculations each time a cost value is observed, the break-even probability that equates the two actions can be obtained. To do so, let the revised-state probability for state θ_1 after n cost observations be given by $f_n(\theta_1)$, and thus $f_n(\theta_2) = 1 - f_n(\theta_1)$. Inequality (2.1) gives

$$C - (L - M)[f_n(\theta_2)] < 0. \qquad (2.1)$$

If this expectation is less than zero, the activity is a candidate for investigation; while if it exceeds zero, the activity is not. Setting the expectation given by inequality (2.1) equal to zero and solving gives

$$f_n(\theta_2) = \frac{C}{L - M} \qquad (2.3)$$

or alternatively

$$f_n(\theta_1) = 1 - \frac{C}{L - M} \qquad (2.4)$$

for the break-even value. Hence, if $f_n(\theta_1) < 1 - C/(L - M)$ an investigation should be undertaken, while if $f_n(\theta_1) > 1 - C/(L - M)$ no investigation is called for (at equality the manager is indifferent). For the specific probem introduced earlier, the break-even probability is $f_n(\theta_1) = 1 - 2{,}000/12{,}000 = 5/6 \doteq 0.83$. This implies that investigation is the preferred action even in cases for which the probability of being in control exceeds 0.5 so long as it is less than 0.83. If $f_n(\theta_1) < 1 - C/(L - M)$, an investigation is signaled, otherwise it is not. As soon as the revised probability of the in control state, state

θ_1, drops below $1 - C/(L - M)$, an investigation should be undertaken. The larger the cost savings and the smaller the costs of investigation and correction, the larger the break-even value.[9] Note that the break-even value is independent of the stage n and is therefore relevant to all time periods.

The revision process for the specific example, given a cost observation in period 1 of \$7,500 and $f_0(\theta_1) = 0.98$ would give[10]

$$f_X(7,500 \mid \theta_1) = n_X(7,500; 6,000, 500) = 0.0044$$
$$f_X(7,500 \mid \theta_2) = n_X(7,500; 8,000, 500) = 0.2420$$

and using formula (2.2)

$$f_1(\theta_1) = \frac{f_X(x_1 \mid \theta_1)f_0(\theta_1)}{f_X(x_1 \mid \theta_1)f_0(\theta_1) + f_X(x_1 \mid \theta_2)f_0(\theta_2)}$$

$$f_1(\theta_1) = \frac{0.0044(0.98)}{0.0044(0.98) + 0.2420(0.02)} = \frac{0.00434}{0.00918} \doteq 0.473.$$

The probability the process is in control is 0.473. Since 0.473 is less than 0.83 an investigation is signaled. The conclusion here depends on the priors, the observed cost level, and the conditional probability distributions. (The symbol $\doteq$ means approximately.)

Since a single observation, even when the likelihood ratio $f_X(x \mid \theta_2)/f_X(x \mid \theta_1)$ is large, may not trigger an investigation, and since successive observations may include observations that form a trend toward increasing the revised probability of state θ_1, it might be argued that it is reasonable to retain information about the sequence of information supplied by the cost observations. In other words, it could be maintained that a control-chart approach is relevant. Inspection of Figure 2.2 might suggest, for example, that even though the revised state probability has not yet dropped below the critical value, investigation may seem to be a reasonable action choice. This conclusion, however, is not valid from a Bayesian standpoint. The revision of probabilities using Bayes' theorem gives the proper weight to the sample evidence and the prior probabilities if the conditional probabilities have been correctly estimated.

---

[9] A limited budget for investigation could be allocated by ordering those cost differences to be investigated in the order of the expected saving to be obtained from the investigation. Since the cost of money is presumably incorporated into the computations as well as uncertainty, funds, ideally, should be made available to investigate any variance exceeding the critical ratio in equation (2.4). This is essentially part of the over-all capital allocation problem of the firm for the period.

[10] The notation $n_X(x; E(X), \sigma(X))$ stands for the value of the normal density function for the random variable X with mean $E(X)$ and standard deviation $\sigma(X)$ at the point x. $N_X(x; E(X), \sigma(X))$ gives the value of the normal distribution function at x; that is, the cumulative probability. See Tables I and II for these values.

SITUATION (b): Consider now case (b) in which the process is initially in a state of control but may move out of control with probability p at the start of any period. Assume the process cannot shift from the out-of-control state to

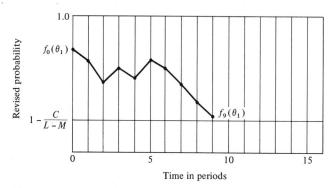

Figure 2.2   Control chart for the revised probability of the state in control, θ_1

the in-control state. This situation can be described as an absorbing Markov process with transition matrix

$$P = \begin{bmatrix} 1 - p & p \\ 0 & 1 \end{bmatrix} \tag{2.5}$$

where p is the probability of a change from the control to the out-of-control state. The transition is again assumed to take place before the cost observation is obtained.

The assumption is made at this point that the transition probability p remains constant from period to period. Since the transition probability is a conditional probability, this means that Prob. (θ_2 in period n given θ_1 in period $n - 1$) $= p$ for all n.[11]

If an out-of-control process would always be discovered in the period during which the transition took place, then the parameter p could be estimated from the fact that the mean number of periods before the process goes out of control is given by $1/p$. Even though it has been assumed that the investigation of an out-of-control process will always disclose this result, the approach adopted does not assume that such an investigation will always take place. Thus to use the mean number of periods when an out-of-control process is discovered tends to underestimate p.[12]

[11] The implications of a constant probability of transition to the out-of-control state is that the probability of moving to the out-of-control state n periods from the time the process starts is given by the geometric probability law to be

$$(1 - p)^{n-1}p.$$

[12] See T. R. Dyckman, "The Investigation of Cost Variances", *Journal of Accounting Research*, Fall 1969, pp. 215-244.

Assume a process starts in state θ_1 at time 0. The probability of being in state θ_1 at the end of period n given an observed cost of x in period n can be calculated. Using Bayes' theorem (2.2) for the nth period and assuming the process was not investigated previously, then the probability the process is in control (state θ_1) during period n (hence before the cost observation x) is given by $f_n(\theta_1) =$ Prob. (state θ_1 given state θ_1 in period $n - 1$, and the transition matrix P).

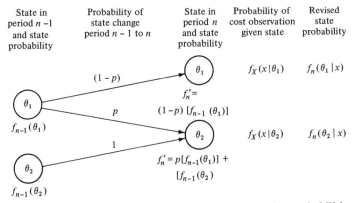

State in period $n-1$ and state probability	Probability of state change period $n-1$ to n	State in period n and state probability	Probability of cost observation given state	Revised state probability

$$f_n'(\theta_1) = (1-p)[f_{n-1}(\theta_1)]$$
$$f_n' = p[f_{n-1}(\theta_1)] + [f_{n-1}(\theta_2)$$

Figure 2.3   Data needed in Bayes' theorem to revise probabilities: situation (b) and matrix (2.5)

The situation can be illustrated by Figure 2.3. The model assumes all the data in the figure are known except the revised-state probabilities given in the last column. The adjustment process can be carried out by using the state probabilities modified to reflect the transition matrix effect (which is assumed to operate prior to obtaining the cost observation x). Let $f_n'(\theta_1)$ be the probability of state θ_1 in period n before the cost observation x. Then

$$f_n'(\theta_1) = (1 - p)[f_{n-1}(\theta_1)],$$
$$f_n'(\theta_2) = (p)[f_{n-1}(\theta_1)] + f_{n-1}(\theta_2),$$

and after the cost observation

$$f_n(\theta_j) = f_n(\theta_j \mid x) = \frac{f_x(x \mid \theta_j)f_n'(\theta_j)}{\sum_{j=1}^{2} f_x(x \mid \theta_j)f_n'(\theta_j)} \tag{2.6}$$

Note that state θ_1 cannot occur in period n if it did not exist in period $n - 1$. Further, an out-of-control state is assumed to be always discovered if an investigation is made.

The addition of the transition matrix P reduces the revised probability of remaining in state θ_1 at the end of period n from that given by equation (2.2) under situation (a). Equation (2.2) applies to a situation where there is no probability of moving from one state to the other. Equation (2.6) applies to a situation where there is a probability of moving from θ_1 to θ_2 and this probability is included in the revision process. If only the revision of probabilities at time n after adjusting for the transition matrix but before obtaining a cost observation were considered, the same equation (2.2) could be used for either situation. The inclusion of the transition matrix increases the probability of an investigation *ceteris paribus* at the end of period n over that in situation (a). Equations (2.3) and (2.4) can still be used to make action choices because $1 - C/(L - M)$ still gives the break-even probability.

Using the specific example, an investigation at the end of period 1 would be signaled for any p since the previous revised probability of the in-control

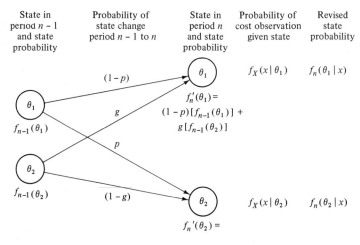

Figure 2.4   Data needed in Bayes' theorem to revise probabilities: situation (b) and matrix (2.7)

state is already less than the break-even probability. The effect of transition matrix (2.5) is to reduce the probability of being in the control state still further since after one period of operations the transition probability leads to a still larger probability of being out of control.

The problem can also be modified so that the process may not only go out of control but may also correct itself. This changes the transition matrix to the form

$$P' = \begin{bmatrix} 1 - p & p \\ g & 1 - g \end{bmatrix} \tag{2.7}$$

where g is the probability of a change from the out-of-control to the control state. This situation is illustrated in Figure 2.4.

Adjusting the state probabilities to the start of period n using matrix (2.7) yields $f_n'(\theta_1) = (1 - p)[f_{n-1}(\theta_1)] + g[f_{n-1}(\theta_2)]$ and $f_n'(\theta_2) = p[f_{n-1}(\theta_1)] + (1 - g)[f_{n-1}(\theta_2)]$. These adjusted probabilities can now be used in Bayes' theorem to obtain the revised-state probabilities. The equation form is identical to equation (2.6) although the numerical results will differ since the $f_n'(\theta_j)$ are not equal for the two separate transition matrices.

Once again equations (2.3) and (2.4) provide the necessary framework for the decision and $1 - C/(L - M)$ is the break-even probability. The effect of the small probability g, which is the probability of moving from θ_2 to θ_1 during the period, is to decrease the likelihood of an investigation decision from that in situation (b). In other words, if a change back to the control state occurs randomly, the probability of an investigation *ceteris paribus* decreases relative to that using matrix P [equation (2.5)]. The relationship to situation (a) depends on the matrix P' and the values of $f_{n-1}(\theta_j)$ and $f_X(x \mid \theta_j)$. However, the typical relationship would find the revised probability for the control state in the last situation [using the transition matrix (2.7)] to be greater than when only a shift out of control can occur [matrix (2.5)].[13] Suppose, for example, that $p = 0.2$; $g = 0.1$; $f_{n-1}(\theta_1) = 0.9$; $f_X(x \mid \theta_1) = 0.0941$; and $f_X(x \mid \theta_2) = 0.1295$.

Then for situation (a) where equation (2.2) applies

$$f_n(\theta_1) = \frac{0.0941(0.9)}{0.0941(0.9) + 0.1295(0.1)} \doteq 0.87,$$

for situation (b) using matrix P, and equation (2.6),

$$f_n'(\theta_1) = (1 - p)[f_{n-1}(\theta_1)] = 0.8(0.9) = 0.72$$

$$f_n'(\theta_2) = p[f_{n-1}(\theta_1)] + f_{n-1}(\theta_2) = 0.2(0.9) + 0.1 = 0.28$$

$$f_n(\theta_1) = \frac{0.0941(0.72)}{0.0941(0.72) + 0.1295(0.28)} \doteq 0.65;$$

for situation (b) using matrix P', and equation (2.6),

$$f_n'(\theta_1) = (1 - p)[f_{n-1}(\theta_1)] + g[f_{n-1}(\theta_2)] = 0.8(0.9) + 0.1(0.1) = 0.73$$

$$f_n'(\theta_2) = p[f_{n-1}(\theta_1)] + (1 - g)[f_{n-1}(\theta_2)] \doteq 0.2(0.9) + 0.9(0.1) = 0.27$$

$$f_n(\theta_1) = \frac{0.0941(0.73)}{0.0941(0.73) + 0.1295(0.27)} \doteq 0.66.$$

---

[13] Situation (a) using equation (2.2) implicitly assumes that p, the probability of shifting out of control, is zero, and that g, the probability of shifting into control, is also zero. Situation (b) with matrix P assumes that p is 0.2 and g is zero.

Smaller values of p would cause results more nearly like those in situation (a). Note that the important change is obtained by introducing the transition matrix. If g is small the additional refinement obtained by adding the probability g may be of little consequence.

2.2 Exploratory Investigations and the Value of Information

Suppose a firm has a choice of conducting two levels of investigation. The first level of investigation might be essentially exploratory in nature. It would cost less than a full investigation, but it might not disclose the cause of an out-of-control situation. The exploratory investigation should be conducted if the expected benefits from this action exceed those from both waiting and those from a full investigation. The investigation decision will be discussed using the value of perfect information.

Suppose perfect information were available concerning the actual state at stage n. Then if the state were θ_1, no investigation would be undertaken with cost 0. This is expected to occur $f_n(\theta_1)$ of the time. On the other hand, if the state were θ_2, an investigation would be made with cost $C + M$. This occurs $f_n(\theta_2)$ of the time. The expected cost for any given period n with perfect information is given by

$$E^* = 0[f_n(\theta_1)] + [C + M][f_n(\theta_2)].$$
$$= [C + M][f_n(\theta_2)]. \tag{2.8}$$

But without such information, the decision-maker's expected cost is the cost associated with the best action; the minimum cost is given by equation (2.9).

$$\min \begin{cases} C + M[f_n(\theta_2)]: & \text{investigate} \\ L[f_n(\theta_2)]: & \text{do not investigate} \end{cases} \tag{2.9}$$

Thus the expected value of perfect information, E_p, and therefore the maximum value of processing additional information, is equal to the value obtained from equation (2.8) subtracted from the minimum of equation (2.9). This gives

$$E_p = C[1 - f_n(\theta_2)] = C[f_n(\theta_1)] \text{ if investigate is minimum}$$

or $\tag{2.10}$

$$E_p = [L - M - C][f_n(\theta_2)] \text{ if do-not-investigate is minimum.}$$

For the specific problem introduced earlier and for period 1, assume $C = \$2,000$, $L = \$15,000$, $M = \$3,000$, $f_1(\theta_1) = 0.47$, $f_1(\theta_2) = 0.53$, and $(L - M - C) = \$10,000$.

With perfect information the expected cost would be

$$E^* = [C + M][f_1(\theta_2)]$$
$$E^* = \$5,000 \times 0.53 = \$2,650.$$

The expected cost without perfect information is

$$\min \begin{cases} 2,000 + 3,000(0.53) = \$3,590: & \text{investigate} \\ 15,000(0.53) = \$7,950: & \text{do not investigate.} \end{cases}$$

The better decision is to investigate with an expected cost of $3,590. Since the investigate decision gives the minimum expected cost, the expected value of perfect information is

$$E_p = C[f_1(\theta_1)] = 2,000 \times 0.47 = 940$$

Or equivalently $E_p = \$3,590 - \$2,650 = 940$

Additional information is worth no more than the difference between the expected cost of the best action and the expected cost with perfect information. This difference is $940.

Assume the records required for an exploratory examination are being kept, that the cost of such an investigation is C' where $C' < C$, and the probability that the cause of an out-of-control situation will be discovered when it exists is h. Therefore if the cost of an exploratory investigation is less than the expected value of perfect information, an exploratory investigation may be justified. In symbols

$$C' < E_p. \tag{2.11}$$

If C' is less, then the alternative of an exploratory investigation should be evaluated in terms of the expected cost associated with its use. The cost from the alternative of an exploratory investigation will amount to C' given state θ_1 and $C' + Mh + L(1 - h)$ given state θ_2 (where h is less than one). The value h is the probability that an exploratory investigation will lead to the discovery (and thus correction) of an out-of-control situation when it exists.

Three cases exist. The expected costs are given in Table 2.4

Table 2.4   **Expected Costs of Three Actions**

Case	Action	Expected Cost
a	Do not investigate	$L[f_n(\theta_2)]$
b	Exploratory investigation	$C' + [L(1 - h) + hM][f_n(\theta_2)]$
c	Full investigation	$C + M[f_n(\theta_2)]$

Setting case a equal to b and case b equal to c, two break-even probabilities, call them $f_b(\theta_1)$ and $f_c(\theta_1)$ can be determined. Typically, but not, necessarily, $f_b(\theta_1)$ will exceed $f_c(\theta_1)$. Using these break-even probabilities, the investigation decision can again be based on the revised probability $f_n(\theta_1)$. The choices are illustrated in Figure 2.5.[14]

Suppose that $f_c(\theta_1) < f_n(\theta_1) < f_b(\theta_1)$ at some stage n so that an exploratory investigation is made. Assume the investigation does not uncover any cause for the variance. The process may be either in or out of control at this point. However, before allowing the process to continue another period, the probabilities $f_n(\theta_j)$ should be revised for any information provided by this investigation and the full-investigation action should be compared to the action do not investigate. [This step need not be performed if the revision will increase $f_n(\theta_1)$.]

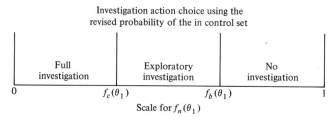

Figure 2.5   **Investigation action choice using the revised probability of the in control set**

These results bear directly on the extent of records to be maintained for control purposes. If $f_b(\theta_1) < f_c(\theta_1)$ for some process, a fact that may be ascertained in advance, an exploratory investigation will never be relevant and the necessary records to conduct one need not be kept. The likelihood of this situation increases as h decreases and as C' approaches C.

Budget Constraints and Cost Investigations

Consider now the imposition of a budget constraint on a period's investigation activities. Suppose that a firm budgets a fixed amount W per period for cost-control investigation purposes where the period is the same as that used to report cost observations. Then one means of selecting the optimal set of k processes to be investigated in any period would be to maximize the expected return based on the state probabilities for each process at the start of the period (recall that a process is assumed to change state only at the start of a

---

[14] For the example at hand and assuming $h = 0.4$ and $C' = 200$, $f_b(\theta_1)$ is approximately 0.96 and $f_c(\theta_1)$ equals 0.75.

period). In mathematical terms for period j and where Y and Y' are the decision variables:

$$\max \sum_{i=1}^{k} \{Y_i[(L_i - M_i - C_i)(1 - f_{ij}(\theta_1)) - C_i(f_{ij}(\theta_1))]$$
$$+ Y_i'[((L_i - M_i)h_i - C_i')(1 - f_{ij}(\theta_1)) - C'f_{ij}(\theta_1)]\}$$

subject to[15] (2.12)

$$\sum_{i=1}^{k} (Y_i(C_i + M_i) + Y_i'(C_i' + M_i)) \leq W$$

$$\sum_{i=1}^{k} (Y_i X_i + Y_i' X_i') \leq T$$

$$Y_i[(C_i - (L_i - M_i))(1 - f_{ij}(\theta_1)) + C_i(f_{ij}(\theta_1))] \leq 0 \quad (i = 1, 2, \ldots, k)$$
$$Y_i'[(C_i' - (L_i - M_i)h_i)(1 - f_{ij}(\theta_1)) + C_i'(f_{ij}(\theta_1))] \leq 0 \quad (i = 1, 2, \ldots, k)$$
$$Y_i + Y_i' \leq 1; \, Y_i, \, Y_i' = 0 \quad \text{or} \quad 1,$$

where k is the number of processes, W is the budget constraint, T represents restraints on physical resources X_i (of which there may be several), and $f_{ij}(\theta_1)$ is the probability that process i is in control after j periods.

A value of one for Y_i indicates a full investigation while a value of one for Y_i' indicates an exploratory investigation. The first constraint is the budget constraint. The second constrains real resources. The third and fourth constraint (written in terms of cost) assure that any investigation undertaken has a positive expectation. The fifth constraint assures that at most either a full or an exploratory investigation but not both will be initiated.

A more complete solution, not attempted here, would consider the use of funds for control purposes together with other fund uses as part of the overall capital budgeting cash-utilization problem. In such a formulation, the relevant planning period would probably differ from the cost-reporting period. The present solution also presumes an instantaneous adjustment by the firm.

2.3 Decisions Using Sample Information Alone

Suppose that the decision maker does not feel any information he has is useful in establishing a set of subjective probabilities over the states in control and out of control. (The expected costs and variances under the two states are assumed to be known.) Is there any way in which a rational

[15] There is a possibility in the budget constraint that the cost correction will not be incurred. It is included, without the factor h, to assure that the constraint will be met.

decision can be made? Consider this situation in the context of situation (a). Situation (b) is an extension involving the transition probabilities.

The likelihood, given by the probability densities of the first sample result under the two possible state situations, might be used to estimate the probabilities of the two states. Figure 2.1 is again relevant. The estimated probability of state θ_1 given an observed cost x is

$$f_1(\theta_1) = f_1(\theta_1 \mid x) = \frac{f_X(x \mid \theta_1)}{f_X(x \mid \theta_1) + f_X(x \mid \theta_2)} \qquad (2.13)$$

and

$$f_1(\theta_2) = 1 - f_1(\theta_1).$$

Using these probability estimates, the expected costs of the investigation action is again given by inequality (2.1), in this case for $n = 1$.

The statement that the decision maker does not feel any prior information he has is useful in establishing a set of subjective probabilities is somewhat misleading. A more accurate statement would be that he has no information that causes him to believe that one state is more likely than any other. In other words, the results in equation (2.13) implicitly assume prior subjective probabilities of $f_0(\theta_1) = f_0(\theta_2) = 0.5$. If this is not in line with the decision maker's beliefs, some means of determining his probabilities must be used.[16]

These probabilities can now be used as the prior probabilities for the next cost observation thus retaining the criterion of investigation given by equation (2.4).[17]

Alternatively, the results of n cost observations may be combined and treated concurrently by finding the conditional probability density given the mean cost. In this case

$$f_n(\theta_1) = f_n(\theta_1 \mid \bar{x}) = \frac{f_{\bar{x}}(\bar{x} \mid \theta_1)}{f_{\bar{x}}(\bar{x} \mid \theta_1) + f_{\bar{x}}(\bar{x} \mid \theta_2)}, \qquad (2.14)$$

where $\bar{x}$ is a sufficient statistic summarizing the first n sample results. Using the results of equation (2.14), the average cost for any set of n observations

---

[16] Several methods are available. See L. J. Savage, *The Foundations of Statistics*, New York: John Wiley, 1954; and R. L. Winkler, "The Assignment of Prior Distributions in Bayesian Analysis," *Journal of the American Statistical Association*, September 1967, pp. 776–800.

[17] Other possibilities also exist. For example, a maximum likelihood decision rule might be adopted. The decision maker would identify the state that maximizes the probability of the cost level. Then he chooses the action that minimizes the cost given that state. Using Figure 2.1, this state would be θ_2 and the decision maker would investigate.

can be found that will trigger an investigation. To investigate it is necessary that

$$C - (L - M)[f_n(\theta_2)] < 0$$

or

$$C[f_n(\theta_1) + f_n(\theta_2)] - [L - M][f_n(\theta_2)] < 0$$

which after some algebra implies

$$\frac{f_n(\theta_1)}{f_n(\theta_2)} < \frac{L - M}{C} - 1$$

or, substituting,

$$\frac{f_{\bar{x}}(\bar{x} \mid \theta_1)/[f_{\bar{x}}(\bar{x} \mid \theta_1) + f_{\bar{x}}(\bar{x} \mid \theta_2)]}{f_{\bar{x}}(\bar{x} \mid \theta_2)/[f_{\bar{x}}(\bar{x} \mid \theta_1) + f_{\bar{x}}(\bar{x} \mid \theta_2)]} < \frac{L - M}{C} - 1$$

and simplifying

$$\frac{f_{\bar{x}}(\bar{x} \mid \theta_1)}{f_{\bar{x}}(\bar{x} \mid \theta_2)} < \frac{L - M}{C} - 1.$$

Therefore, the break-even cost value $\bar{x}_c$, can be found from the equation

$$\frac{f_{\bar{x}}(\bar{x} \mid \theta_1)}{f_{\bar{x}}(\bar{x} \mid \theta_2)} = \frac{L - M}{C} - 1. \qquad (2.15)$$

Using normal density functions, equation (2.15) is

$$\frac{n_X(\bar{x} \mid \theta_1)}{n_X(\bar{x} \mid \theta_2)} = \frac{L - M}{C} - 1. \qquad (2.15b)$$

Since the values $L, M, C, \sigma^2(\bar{X}) = \sigma^2(X)/n$ are known for a given sample size n, tables of the normal probability density function can be used to find, through successive approximation, the value of $\bar{x}$ for which equation (2.15) is satisfied. Using the numerical example from the previous section and assuming $n = 4$ gives

$$L - M = 12{,}000 \qquad C = 2{,}000$$
$$\sigma^2(X) = 250{,}000 \qquad n = 4.$$

Therefore

$$\frac{L - M}{C} - 1 = 5, \qquad \sigma^2(\bar{X}) = \frac{\sigma^2(X)}{n} = \frac{250{,}000}{4} = 62{,}500,$$

and equation (2.15b) becomes

$$\frac{n_{\bar{x}}(\bar{x}; 6{,}000, 250)}{n_{\bar{x}}(\bar{x}; 8{,}000, 250)} = 5.$$

Using tables of the normal probability density function and applying trial and error methods indicates that $\bar{x}$ is approximately 6,950.

Since the density functions are assumed to be normal and since the variance of the density function for the sample mean is a direct function of the variance of X, the value of $\bar{x}$ that triggers an investigation will depend on the sample size.[18] If $C > (L - M - C)$, a necessary (but not sufficient) condition for investigation is that $f_{\bar{x}}(\bar{x} \mid \theta_1) < f_{\bar{x}}(\bar{x} \mid \theta_2)$; then, as n increases the sample mean must decrease in order to retain the critical ratio given by equation (2.15). A symmetrical argument holds when $C < (L - M - C)$.

2.4   Some Extensions

The next step would be to consider the cost-investigation problem when the state random variable is continuous rather than discrete. A second extension would examine multiple causes of cost variances, some, perhaps, uncontrollable. Further possibilities include relaxing the assumptions on the time interval between cost reports, introducing a lag between the investigation and the implementation of control, incorporating uncertainty into the cost estimates and the success of the control action, using dynamic programming as a solution technique, and developing techniques to estimate the transition probabilities. These tasks are considered by the authors to be important, but beyond the scope of this book.[19]

2.5   Summary

The problem of when to investigate a cost variance can be treated from a statistical decision-theory approach. This approach allows for the inclusion in the analysis of the costs from various actions and the subjective evaluations of the probabilities of the control and out-of-control states. The decision-theory approach can also be used to examine the value of information and hence the value of recordkeeping. The discussion extends to the value of exploratory investigations or other data-gathering systems. The

---

[18] Note that n is not large enough to assume that $\bar{X}$ is adequately approximated by a normal distribution if X itself is not.

[19] Many of these problems have not been resolved yet. For some insights on several the reader should consult the bibliography for this chapter.

chapter also suggests a math-programming formulation to select among alternative investigations given a budget constraint.

A major limitation of the analysis concerns the estimation of the relevant parameter values needed as inputs to the model. Of particular concern is the estimation of the savings, L, to be obtained from investigating an out-of-control situation. The attempt to examine the cost-variance investigation question from a decision-theory standpoint should lead to a more complete understanding of the more important variables (in terms of the sensitivity of the model to perturbations in the variables given their inherent variability) and their interactions even where the model's assumptions are not strictly met.

QUESTIONS AND PROBLEMS

2–1 Discuss the following questions. If a cost variance is investigated, will the cause of the variance be found? If the cause of the variance is found will the situation be corrected? If the situation is corrected, is the firm better off because the investigation was conducted? If it is not investigated will the variance continue in the future?

2–2 A process has an unfavorable variance reported of $7,600. It is estimated that these excess costs will continue if the process is allowed to continue without investigation and if the process is actually out of control. There is a 0.9 probability that the cause of the variance was a peculiarity of the one period and will not recur. This will be known at the end of the period if the variance does not recur.

The cost of conducting an investigation is estimated to be $1,000, and the cost of correction is an additional $1,200.

Assume that if there is something wrong, an investigation will reveal the problem and it will be corrected. If the variance is not corrected now, and if it recurs it will be investigated next period.

Required: Should the investigation be conducted? Assume a zero time-value of money.

2–3 The budgeted power cost is $20,000. The cost is budgeted at the expected amount when the process is in control. The expected cost when the process is out of control is $30,000. Management in charge of controlling the cost has indicated that there is equal likelihood of favorable and unfavorable variances and the standard deviation of the actual cost about the mean value is $6,000 for either state. Assume the cost is normally distributed. The actual cost for January is $27,000 and the cost for February is $26,000.

Required:

a. Compute the number of standard deviations the January and February costs are from the mean amount of $20,000 for both the in-control and out-of-control cases.

    b. Compute the probability of January's and February's costs being greater than $27,000 and $26,000 respectively if the in-control state exists (if the cost fluctuations are caused by random factors).

    c. Compute the probability density of each month's cost for both the case in which the process is in control and in which it is not.

2–4 Continuing problem 2–3 assume that the cost of investigation is estimated to be $4,000 and the cost of correcting is $1,000 for positive and negative variances. If the process stays out of control, the additional costs are estimated to be $7,000.

    Required: If the manager initially believes it is equally likely the process is in or out of control.

    a. Should the process be investigated at the end of January?

    b. Should there be an investigation of the variance in February if the costs of no investigation and being out of control are again estimated to be $7,000?

    c. Should there be an investigation in February if the costs of no investigation are estimated to be $6,500?

2–5 A process that is in control has an expected cost level of $100 with a standard deviation of $4. When the process is out of control the expected cost level is $112 with a standard deviation also of $4. The manager estimates that the net present value of the future savings from investigating an out-of-control variance is equal to $43.25, a five year annuity of $12 at 12 per cent. The cost of investigation is $38.90 for each variance investigated. An investigation will always be successful and there is no correction cost.

    Required:

    a. Assuming equal initial subjective state probabilities and normality, what cost level on any single observation should trigger an investigation? What assumption does this method implicitly make about the prior knowledge of the manager?

    b. Suppose equal probability is assigned to each state and assume that sample observations on the actual cost level can be obtained at a cost of $5 + 0.5n$ where n is the number of observations. What is the maximum (not the optimal) number of observations that should be taken? Assume no cost observations have been taken to date.

2–6 The classical statistical approach to problem 2–5, part a, would not specify the prior odds over the states. What problems does this raise? What prior knowledge about the states, if any, does it assume?

2–7 What can be done when the manager has very imprecise ideas about the prior state probabilities?

2–8 Suppose that over time, the revised probability of the out-of-control state has consistently risen until it is nearly, but not quite, equal to the break-even value. Suppose that unless the next revision leads to either a decline in the value or an increase smaller than any previous increase, an investigation will be indicated. Need the decision maker wait for the next observation or would he be prudent to begin an investigation immediately?

2–9 Is anything gained or lost by accumulating several cost observations before revising the state probabilities?

2–10 Return to problem 2–4 but assume the process initially starts in the control state (this is situation (b) in the text). Should an investigation be conducted in January or February using transition matrix (2.5) on page 42 and letting $p = 0.2$? (Assume these are the first two months.) Compare your answer with that of problem 2–4.

SUPPLEMENTARY READING

BIERMAN, H., JR., L. E. FOURAKER, and R. K. JAEDICKE, "A Use of Probability and Statistics in Performance Evaluation", *The Accounting Review*, July 1961 pp. 409–417.

BIRNBERG, J. G., "Bayesian Statistics: A Review," *Journal of Accounting Research*, Spring 1964, pp. 108–116.

DEMSKI, J. S., "Optimizing the Search for Cost Deviation Sources", *Management Science*, April 1970, pp. 486–494.

DUNCAN, A., "The Economic Design of $\bar{x}$ Charts Used to Maintain Current Control of a Process," *Journal of the American Statistical Association*, June 1956, pp. 228–242.

DUVALL, R. M., "Rules for Investigating Cost Variances," *Management Science*, June 1967, pp. 631–641.

DYCKMAN, T. R., "The Investigation of Cost Variances," *Journal of Accounting Research*, Fall 1969, pp. 215–244.

KAPLAN, R. S., "Optimal Investigation Strategies with Imperfect Information," *Journal of Accounting Research*, Spring 1969, pp. 32–43.

LEV, B., "An Information Theory Analysis of Budget Variances," *The Accounting Review*, October 1969, pp. 704–710.

LUH, F., "Controlled Cost: An Operational Concept and Statistical Approach to Standard Costing," *The Accounting Review*, January 1968, pp. 123–132.

OZAN, T., and T. R. DYCKMAN, "A Normative Model for Investigation Decisions Involving Multi-Origin Cost Variances," *Journal of Accounting Research*, Spring 1971.

PRATT, J. W., H. RAIFFA, and R. SCHLAIFER, *Introduction to Statistical Decision Theory*, New York: McGraw-Hill, 1965.

Chapter 3

Correlation-Regression Analysis and Cost Estimation

One of the more important elements in cost control is the determination of how costs change in relation to other measurable and controllable factors. The preparation of valid operating budgets, pricing decisions, establishing standard costs, developing performance reports, evaluating cost variances, and numerous other managerial activities often hinge on reliable cost estimates. The necessary estimates are frequently obtained through what might be called off-the-cuff or rule-of-thumb methods. These methods are at times somewhat formalized by the use of average data adjusted to reflect the plans of the organization and relevant economic or technological trends.

Lack of complete satisfaction with the results of such procedures combined with the improvement in mathematical, engineering, and management methods led to the development of several improved techniques for analyzing cost behavior. One of the more important techniques is represented by the application of industrial engineering methods, including efficiency, and time and motion studies, to the problem of estimating cost-behavior patterns. Such studies often involved an analysis of the underlying physical variables and conversion of the final results into cost estimates. The procedure works reasonably well for estimating the costs associated with direct materials, labor, and machine time. However, it is usually more difficult to estimate the costs of services, supervision, and the other indirect costs of operation.

These cost factors may be common to several products or departments and in addition there may be slack in one or more of the factors of production allowing an increase in output without an increase in the factor's cost. Alternatively, a small increase in output may result in a large increase in costs. Further, because of indirect relationships with the activity levels of other departments, it may not be feasible to use the same engineering methods for estimating costs that are usually employed on direct or easily traceable costs.

In addition to engineering approaches, accountants also attempt to understand cost behavior through the analysis of historical and standard-cost data. The technique used concentrates on the fixed-variable cost distinction discussed in Chapter 1. Although an improvement over *ad hoc* approaches, the fixed-variable approach makes several limiting assumptions that can substantially reduce the value of the subsequent analysis. First, the approach considers only one causal factor, typically an activity variable such as an output measure. Second, the technique assumes a linear relationship between output

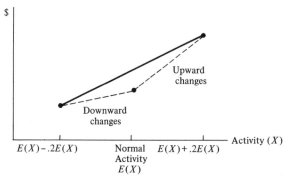

Figure 3.1   High-low method of cost estimation

and cost at least over the relevant range. (Using the semivariable-cost concept, this limitation can be mitigated.) Third, cost predictions can be obtained but the accuracy of these predictions is not known. Fourth, it tends to be insensitive to indirect cost allocations. Fifth, it relies heavily on the initial fixed-variable classification decision. Finally, even if the analysis is carried out for several periods, it is not clear whether the mean, the median, or some other summary cost statistic is the relevant measure.

One method in common use that illustrates these limitations is the so-called high-low method. Under this procedure two points are estimated. One of these represents the largest activity level anticipated, or, alternatively, it could be set at some per cent, say 20 per cent, above the normal activity level. The other point represents a symmetrically placed point equally far below the normal level of activity. A straight line connecting the two points is then used to estimate costs for any activity level. The procedure is illustrated by the solid line in Figure 3.1. The method is quick and easily applied and may provide inexpensive and useful approximations in cases where costs are closely related to the variability of a single activity measure. If costs exhibit sharper increases and smaller decreases as activity departs from the normal level at which the activity is designed to operate, the dashed-line function in Figure 3.1 will give better estimates in the most likely region of operation.

One technique that attempts to overcome some of the limitations inherent in the fixed-variable type of analysis involves the notions of multiple correlation and regression analysis. The statistical approach, it should be emphasized, is itself not free from limitations when applied in cost analysis and, for this reason, substantial attention is given to these limitations later in this chapter.[1]

In general, the dependent variable in the analysis is the cost of the activity being analyzed. Occasionally a physical measure such as units of material or labor hours may be used if the costs are a known function of the physical measure. The independent variables may include output, batch size, number of employees, number of products or product variations, weather, and so on.

For example, suppose the tasks performed in a service center consist of repair and maintenance of several common business machines; namely typewriters, desk calculators and adding machines.[2] The direct-labor costs of operating this department are considered by management to be a linear function of the time spent overhauling the various types of machines serviced during a given time period. Further, the overhaul time differs depending on the type of machine involved. In this example labor hours rather than labor cost is the dependent variable. The independent variables are the number of machines of each type worked on in a week. Once a relationship has been established between the total hours worked and the hours required on each type of machine, total direct-labor costs may be estimated by multiplying each term by the associated labor rate.

Suppose a linear relationship of the form

$$Y_i = b_0 + b_1 X_{1i} + b_2 X_{2i} + b_3 X_{3i} + U_i \tag{3.1}$$

is assumed where

Y_i = total direct labor hours in period i.
b_0 = constant of regression (places height of plane).
b_1 = estimated overhaul time for a typewriter.

---

[1] Some of the ideas in this section are developed further in G. J. Benston, "Multiple Regression Analysis of Cost Behavior," *The Accounting Review*, October 1966, pp. 657–672. See also J. Johnston, *Statistical Cost Control*, New York: McGraw-Hill, 1960; and R. Jensen, "Multiple Regression Models for Cost Control—Assumptions and Limitations," *The Accounting Review*, April 1967, pp. 265–272.

[2] This example may be found in P. R. McClenon, "Cost Finding Through Multiple Correlation Analysis," *The Accounting Review*, July 1963, pp. 540–547.

X_{1i} = number of typewriters overhauled in period i.
b_2 = estimated overhaul time for a desk calculator.
X_{2i} = number of desk calculators overhauled in period i.
b_3 = estimated overhaul time for an adding machine.
X_{3i} = number of adding machines overhauled in period i.
U_i = disturbance term (incorporates the net effect of other factors) in period i.

The weekly overhaul data in Table 3–1 are drawn at random from the last

Table 3–1   Hours Worked by Week and Machine

Week	Typewriters Serviced	Calculators Serviced	Adding Machines Serviced	Total Hours
1	5	8	7	64
2	7	6	9	64
3	9	5	5	53
4	9	4	7	54
5	8	3	8	51
6	9	3	10	57
7	9	2	10	53
8	9	1	10	49
	65	32	66	445

two years.[3,4] Before that time, this work was done by outsiders. Other conditions including technical abilities, labor intensiveness, and so on are assumed constant.

The estimated regression equation based on these data is (see Appendix 3A for the general means of deriving a regression equation)

$$Y = 8 + 1.456X_1 + 4.016X_2 + 2.047X_3. \tag{3.2}$$

The equation indicates that it takes 1.456 or about one and one-half hours on the average to overhaul a typewriter. This time differs substantially from that required for a calculator and estimates of future costs should reflect the differences in repair activity to be undertaken by the service center. Care should also be taken to recognize the uncertainty in the estimates resulting from, for example, errors in measuring the dependent variable, hours.

[3] Eight observations are used only to simplify the mathematics, in general much more of the available data would be used.
[4] The random selection may help reduce the serial correlation present because the level of activity in a week is likely to be related to that in the previous week.

Assuming one wage rate applies to all employees, the direct-labor cost could be predicted by multiplying the estimated hours by the rate. If other variable costs in the department bear a constant relationship to the wage rate, total variable cost can be estimated using an estimate of total hours obtained from the equation. On the other hand, if wage rates differ and an average rate is not relevant, the direct-labor cost cannot be determined using equation (3.2). A new analysis that uses cost as the dependent variable may be required.

The remainder of this chapter is subdivided into four sections. The first of these deals with the nature of the analysis and some of the fundamental data requirements needed to apply the mathematical correlation-regression model. The second major section examines the nonstatistical problems associated with implementing the analysis, and the third section discusses the inherent statistical difficulties. The fourth section discusses some issues in the use of statistical cost studies.

3.1   Nature of the Analysis

An early step in applying correlation-regression concepts to cost estimation is to think through the relationships between the variable to be predicted and the available independent variables. Typically the dependent variable is related to the independent variables through some unit of association such as output, input, or time. The concept of a unit of association is important because the validity of the regression equation and the numerical values emanating from the statistical analysis depend on the relevance and limitations that relate to the particular unit of association employed.

3.1.1 Unit of Association

Correlation-regression analysis may be adapted to either time series or cross-sectional data. Time-series data can be obtained from a single, stable process through time. Cross-sectional data are obtained from several homogeneous processes during a single time period. Because it is somewhat unusual for a firm to have a large enough number of homogeneous processes to provide sufficient cost data for cross-sectional analysis, time-series data will usually be more appropriate.[5,6] The example given in the previous section involves time series data.

[5] The problems and procedures discussed in the sections of this chapter are relevant to time-series or cross-sectional data.

[6] Situations such as parallel production lines and associated service facilities may provide situations where cross-sectional analysis is appropriate. Care must be taken to assure that the range of observations is large enough to include the expected variation in future activity.

In time-series analysis the unit of association that connects the values of the dependent and independent variables is the time period. The time period is a convenient but not necessarily ideal unit of association from a theoretical point of view.[7] If, as may often be the case, decisions concerning the dependent variable (such as direct-labor cost) and the impact of the independent variables (such as direct-labor hours) are time determined, then time is theoretically acceptable. On the other hand, the unit of association may in fact be output. In this case cost and labor hours are related because of output decisions and using time as the unit of association could produce misleading results.

For example, the output of the period may be 100 units and the labor costs incurred during the period may be $500. But there may also be labor costs related to these same units incurred in other time periods. Correlating the labor costs with output on the basis of a common time period under these conditions would not provide a meaningful predictive relationship.

There is an implication here that is pervasive throughout all of applied statistical analysis. Knowledge about the process under investigation is indispensable to obtaining meaningful statistical results. Only when the manager and the statistician work jointly and understand and appreciate one another's expertise and relative contributions are useful results likely.

In the machine-overhaul example, a week's time period is the unit of association. This implicitly assumes that all costs associated with accomplishing repairs are incurred in the same time period as that used to tabulate the repairs. Alternatively, if the overhaul decision is related to previous machine usage or expected activity levels (and hence the need for repairs in the overhaul period), then additional relationships can be developed that permit the value of the independent variables in equation (3.2) to be estimated.

3.1.2 Length of the Time Period

The time period used to obtain measures of the dependent and independent variable must be long enough to permit the bookkeeping procedures to record accurately the associated costs, output, labor hours, and other factors needed in the analysis. For example, if cost data were recorded hourly, significant differences related to the time of day could occur. Leads and lags in recording can be particularly troublesome. For example, if a cost relevant to one period's activity (a bonus for example) is recorded in a later period or if a cost relevant to several periods' activity is expensed in a single period (advertising is often treated this way), the resultant statistical relationships may turn out to be quite erroneous.

On the other hand, the time period must be short enough to avoid activity

---

[7] The fact that accounting records are, almost without exception, kept on a time-period basis, tends to lead to its use as the unit of association regardless of the underlying theoretical relationships.

variations within the time period that tend to average out the very cost behavior that is of interest. One of the major uses of the statistical analysis is
prediction. In order to increase the opportunity for and accuracy of predictions, the data should cover as wide a range of activity as possible. This, too,
suggests the value of short time periods, but what is a short time period
depends on the activity under consideration and the environment in which the
activity takes place.

The time period desired for predictive purposes can have an impact on the
period used for recording purposes. The analysis of cost behavior should be
one factor considered in the design of record-keeping procedures. Data lifted
directly from cost records as normally maintained may lead to misleading
results.[8] The manager must constantly examine the relevance of the data to
his problem. Furthermore, to assure the relevance of the statistical techniques
which rely on random-sampling techniques, the values of the unit of association should be selected randomly.

3.1.3 Type of Analysis

Multiple correlation-regression analysis attempts to determine the constants involved in a functional relationship between a dependent variable and
several independent variables. In general terms, such a relation can be written
as

$$Y = f(X_1, X_2, X_3, \ldots, X_k)$$
$$= b_0 + b_1 X_1 + b_2 X_2 + \cdots + b_k X_k + U. \tag{3.3}$$

Equation (3.1) is of this general form. The dependent variable, which may
be cost, is written as a function of k factors, called independent variables.
Rather than cost, the function could specify a relationship between output
and several independent variables such as hours worked or machines used.
This relationship formalized by equation (3.3) is called the regression equation. Determination of the regression coefficients, the b_j's, is the first task of
the analysis. Sample observations are collected. Each sample includes a value
for each of the independent variables and the dependent variable related by
the unit of association. For the machine-overhaul example, the unit of
association is the week and each week provides one sample set of observations
on each variable. The mathematical procedure by which the estimates of the
b_j's are determined is called least squares regression analysis and is described
in Appendix 3A for the general case.[9] The resulting regression equation can
be used to predict the values of the dependent variable, and hence cost, for
given values of the independent variables.

---

[8] The use of time periods as the unit of association can also lead to certain statistical
difficulties.

[9] Other methods which minimize absolute rather than squared deviations also exist.

A second task of correlation-regression analysis often involves estimating the reliability of the predictions. For this purpose several additional measures are required. These include estimates of the standard error of estimate, commonly written $S_{Y.12...k}$, the standard errors of the regression coefficients, written S_j, and the estimated correlation coefficient, written R.

Rewriting equation (3.3), the more complete form of the mathematical expression for the example discussed earlier is given by equation (3.4)

$$Y = 8 + 1.456X_1 + 4.016X_2 + 2.047X_3$$
$$(S_1) \qquad (S_2) \qquad (S_3)$$

(3.4)

where the S_j are the standard errors of the regression coefficients and R is the multiple correlation coefficient of the regression.

The use of a regression equation to predict values of the dependent variable and probabilistic statements concerning the error associated with any prediction depend on the validity of the assumptions of the model. In their strongest form, these assumptions are:

1. The expected value of the disturbance terms is zero.
2. The dependent variable has constant variance regardless of the values of the independent variables.
3. The disturbance terms are not correlated.
4. The variation in the dependent variable results from the variation in the disturbance term (the independent variables are measured without error and hence only the dependent variable is a random variable).
5. The number of sample observations exceeds the number of parameters to be estimated.

The manager usually wishes to predict or estimate costs for specific values of the independent variables. He would prefer to construct the predictive relationship on the basis of observations of the dependent variable (say, cost or output) for specific values (say, of direct-labor hours and machine time) of the independent variable. Usually, however, he is unable to assign values to the independent variables and then observe the resultant cost. More often he will be using the available historical data. Moreover, he may not wish to discard past data merely because it does not represent the exact combinations of values for the independent variables that he expects to prevail in the future or that he would select to observe if conditions permitted. Relevant data is usually too scarce for this type of behavior.[10] When both the independent variables as well as the dependent variable are the result of observation rather than predetermined, they are random variables and the assumptions

---

[10] This does not mean that all historic data will be used. Unusual circumstances surrounding past data may lead to its rejection. For example, data from a period in which output was restricted due to a supplier's strike should be omitted.

of the analysis apply to the joint probability distributions of the dependent and independent variables rather than to just the conditional distribution of the independent variable.

Fortunately the same computations can be made under either set of assumptions. Thus, for example, the regression equation can be determined regardless of whether the independant variables are considered to be random or not. Furthermore (subject to certain limitations described later), predictions of the relevant cost levels can be made using the estimated relationship. When all variables are random variables, the correlation coefficient can be interpreted either as a measure of the strength of association or, in squared form, as the proportion of variation in the dependent variable explained by the independent variables used in the analysis. When only the dependent variable is random the latter interpretation applies.

In the machine-overhaul example, values of the independent variables were not pre-selected, thus all variables are random variables. If the second and third assumptions listed earlier hold, then confidence intervals can be placed around the predicted value of the dependent variable.[11] This requires the value of the standard error. (Tests of the significance of the regression coefficients could also be conducted using their error measures.) Thus, if the standard error of estimate $S_{Y.123}$, were 2.112, the manager could be 99 per cent confident that in week 9 in which six typewriters, four calculators, and nine adding machines were overhauled, that the total number of hours, Y, would satisfy the relationship

$$43.223 - 2.58(2.112) \le Y \le 43.223 + 2.58(2.112)$$

or

$$37.774 \le Y \le 48.672.$$

The value 43.223 is obtained by solving equation (3.4) for $X_1 = 6$, $X_2 = 4$, and $X_3 = 9$, and then adding and subtracting 2.58 standard deviation units.

The correlation coefficient (assume it to be 0.9) indicates the closeness of the relation. One generally useful way to interpret it is to consider it in squared form. The coefficient of determination, as it is then called, indicates the per cent of the variability in total hours explained by the three independent variables used in the analysis. For the present case 81 per cent of the variation in total hours is explained by the repair activity on three types of machines.

---

[11] The prediction can be considered as the average value of Y for the given X's or as a predicted individual value of it. The confidence interval depends upon which interpretation is relevant and is larger for individual estimates than for averages. The confidence interval given here and the one usually given applies (although it omits several terms usually quite small relative to the standard error) to an individual value.

3.2 Problems in Applying Correlation-Regression Analysis

The problems in applying correlation-regression analysis can be examined under three headings:

1. Determining the relevant variables;
2. Specifying the form of the relationship;
3. Statistical difficulties.

3.2.1 Determining the Relevant Variables

The determination of the relevant cost-related factors is not an easy task. Variables may be overlooked because of a lack of recorded data on them. This fact makes it imperative that the accountant consult with those involved in the process before attempting to establish the relevant variables. Indeed such discussions could lead to a decision to change the information-processing system. An example of a variable that is often omitted from such studies is the external effect of an activity. For example, adequate maintenance and overhaul activity in one cost center may reduce repair costs of a second cost center because better quality products produced by the first cost center cause less wear and tear on the equipment in the second cost center.

The relevant variables typically depend on the activities of a given cost center and may differ widely among cost centers. It is therefore important to properly associate costs with the relevant cost center. Failure to do so may not affect plant-wide relationships but it can lead to poor decisions in the centers involved.

Care must also be taken to ensure that basic changes in the environment, such as a substantial increase in the skills and abilities of the labor force, either did not occur over the period studied or are represented in some way in the relationship. The dummy-variable technique might be used for this purpose. The method uses an extra variable that takes on the value of one for an observation when the condition exists and zero otherwise. In the machine-overhaul example a change in the type of calculator used could drastically alter the associated overhaul time. The change in the calculator could be represented by a dummy variable, by a separate independent variable, or a different equation might be used.

Specification of the relevant variables must be accompanied by specification of the crucial variables. Invalid relations can result from the omission of a key variable but it is usually both impossible and undesirable to attempt to incorporate all the cost-influencing factors into a single analysis.[12] Continuing

[12] Relevant variables that show no significant correlation with the independent variable may be dropped. Either they lack sufficient variability or their effect is subsumed by other variables.

relationships should be given particular attention since it is easy to assume incorrectly that no substantive changes in the relevant variables have occurred and thus the existing relationship is retained. Such may not be the case, however. For example, it may be that a previously near-constant factor, for example an input price, is now subject to substantial variation. If the cost of this factor were either omitted from the initial equation, or, alternately, included as one of the independent variables in the relationship and if, for example, high input prices are associated with high activity, then the actual relationship between physical input activity and output cost would be obscured if the previous relation were continued. Changing the type of calculator used or the overhaul procedure could produce similar effects.

One possible means of allowing for changes of this kind would be to incorporate a new variable to reflect the influence of the change in this factor. This alone would not be completely satisfactory for the price example because of the problems of multicollinearity created by the relationship between high input prices and high physical input activity; i.e., high activity might be generally accompanied by higher input prices. An alternative means of dealing with price factors is to use monetary measures for the variables involved and deflate them using a suitable price index. The interpretation of the results differs, however, depending on which approach is used. If, as is often the case, there is a desire to examine the effects of the price factor separately, or to use physical input measures, or unadjusted monetary measures, then there is reason to adopt the first approach or some variant of it.

Since time is often the unit of association, some attention should be given to influences that occur in different time periods. Perhaps the most common potentially cost-influencing factor associated with different calendar periods is the weather. This factor can be incorporated into the analysis using the dummy-variable method. Accomplishing this task may mean looking outside the firm's information system for relevant data, and this should be encouraged. Other examples of time-dependent variables involve seasonal factors such as holiday-season influences on production activity. Thus overhaul activity may be high in periods of otherwise slack activity.

A sharp change in activity is one result that may accompany seasonal patterns but which is also a function of other factors such as strikes and maintenance policy. It is often the case that cost behavior is asymmetric to large increases and decreases in activity (being sluggish on the downside) and this should be recognized, if costs are to be adequately estimated, again perhaps through the use of a dummy-variable or by a separate relationship for each type of period.

3.2.2 Specifying the Form of the Relationship

Cost relationships are not smooth, well-defined functions. Usually several functional forms fit the data equally well. Relationships are continuously undergoing change, and observations of these relationships are subject to multiple measurement errors. Relationships may also change over time either as a result of changes in economic conditions, technology, or learning (see Chapter 4). Such factors need to be considered in any attempt to forecast cost behavior. It is assumed in this chapter (perhaps unrealistically) that learning is not an important variable.

Under these conditions what is known about the underlying technological or economic basis of the relationship is critical. The manager (with expert assistance) is the one to provide this information, not the accountant or the statistician. Typically, the simplest relationship consistent with the theoretically determined cost-behavior pattern would be selected. In the final analysis, however, it is not whether the relationship selected perfectly represents the actual situation but whether it yields useful results that is critical.

Relationships can often be subject to transformations in order to make them easier to use. Logarithmic (the logarithms of the variable values are used) and square-root (the square roots of variable values are used) transformations represent just two of several possibilities. For example, a multiplicative cost relationship of the form $Y = b_0 X_1^{b_1} X_2^{b_2}$ is transformed into the linear expression $\log Y = \log b_0 + b_1 \log X_1 + b_2 \log X_2$ by taking logs.[13]

The traditional regression equation, and the one discussed here, is obtained by finding the equation that minimizes the squared residuals. The implicit assumption is that the importance of the estimation error is a function of the squared prediction error. There is no implicit reason why it should necessarily be the case that doubling the prediction error quadruples the effect of that error. It is possible, for example, that the absolute errors better reflect the importance of the estimation error to the manager. If so, techniques that minimize absolute errors should be used. In some cases the fact that the necessary computer programs do not exist can prevent a more appropriate analyses. The manager must then hope the approximation achieved is adequate.

3.2.3 Statistical Problems

Any formal statistical analysis involves assumptions and the impact of the failure of these assumptions to be fulfilled on any probabilistic statements made constitutes the subject matter of this subsection. The least-squares (or graphical or any other method) method of fitting an equation that is used to

---

[13] Transformations are typically accompanied by implicit assumptions concerning the form of underlying probability laws and hence have important implications for any probabilistic statements made. For example, if a logarithmic transformation is made and, say, confidence-interval statements are to be made concerning predicted cost levels, the assumption must be made that the conditional probability laws (if regression analysis is relevant, or the joint probability laws if correlation analysis is called for) are log normal rather than normal in the untransformed values.

predict cost behavior can, however, be computed regardless of the probabilistic statements under discussion.

Several problem areas are explored here including:

1. Measurement errors;
2. Correlations among the explanatory variables and between the disturbance term and the explanatory variables;
3. The distribution of nonspecified factors as they are reflected in the error term.

Measurement Errors

Errors in measurement can occur in either the dependent or independent variables. Errors in the latter are more critical.

Independent measurement errors in the dependent variable only increase the disturbance term (assuming a linear relationship, at least after transformation). The increase in the error term means an increase in the standard error of estimate, and simultaneously a decrease in the correlation coefficients. The regression coefficients, the b_i, themselves are unbiased when measurement errors in the dependent variable exist. Measurement errors in the machine-overhaul example are most likely to be of this type.

Measurement errors in the independent variables are more serious. Such errors result in the disturbance term being correlated with the particular variable or variables to which the errors relate. Unfortunately, shorter time periods that seem to be desirable for several reasons stated earlier tend to increase the chance of this kind of measurement error. This may happen, for example, by recording an event or the measurement of the event in a period other than that in which the related cost was recorded. Measurement errors in the independent variables are unlikely in the machine-overhaul example.

If the error is constant and a linear functional relationship holds, then the effect is entirely on the constant term and, thus, of minimal interest. (Relative errors also affect only the constant term if a logarithmic formulation is appropriate.) Errors in the independent variable that cannot be considered in this or a similar fashion result in underestimates of the regression coefficients involved. This is one reason "activity" measures are often preferred to "cost" measures for the independent variables. Furthermore, the larger the relative measurement error, the larger the understatement. Thus, for example, the omission of a relevant variable such as omitting a machine type, if it is correlated with one or more of the independent variables, produces such a downward bias. Least-squares predictions are, however, still appropriate.

Correlations Among the Explanatory Variables

The existence of a correlation among the independent variables (intercorrelation) makes it difficult to separate the effect of these variables. The production of two complementary products where the output of each is treated as an independent variable provides an example. Intercorrelation does not affect the validity of the predictions of the dependent variable provided it is expected to continue in the future. However, the regression coefficients can no longer be used to estimate the marginal change in the dependent variable for a unit change in a given independent variable holding the other independent variables constant. This is true because the lack of independence among the independent variables prevents the availability of sufficient information to determine the regression coefficients. Intercorrelation also causes an increase in the standard errors of the regression coefficients.

This situation is especially likely to be a serious problem in cost-behavior studies since several of the independent variables often move together; they exhibit near constant ratios.

In the machine-overhaul example estimates of the regression coefficients are possible because the work was done in different ratios. Suppose instead that there was a constant ratio (2-1-3) of the time required on the three types of machines. That is, if it took six hours in a given week to overhaul a typewriter it would take three hours to overhaul a calculator and nine hours for an adding machine.

The independent variables now move together. Activity on each is high at the same time and low at the same time. The independent variables are all perfectly correlated and the estimated standard error, $S_{Y \cdot 12 \cdots k}$, and the standard errors of the regression coefficients, the S_j, will be infinite implying low reliability for the individual regression coefficients. Estimates can still be made of the total hours associated with overhauling combinations of two typewriters, one calculator, and three adding machines in a given time period if the intercorrelations are not perfect, but the estimates of the regression coefficients will have unnecessarily large standard errors.

This example is an extreme one but it serves to suggest the problem whenever two or more of the independent variables are correlated. The situation is most common in cost centers with a relatively stable activity mix regardless of changes in total activity. Fortunately, most computer programs provide the correlations among the variables so that the problem can be recognized at that stage even if it is not expected on the basis of knowledge concerning the process.

Several means of dealing with this situation exist. Activities being examined that involve intercorrelation might be broken into subactivities that are analyzed separately. The accounting function can be of substantive assistance here. Another alternative is to find a common measure into which the intercorrelated variables can be converted. An example might be labor hours. Thus the physical output of two or more different activities can in this way be converted to a single output measure. The resultant relationship measures the collective impact of a set of activities on cost.

The accountant can also be helpful in the process of cost allocation and his subjective decisions are important. It is not whether judgment will be used but whether the judgments that must be made will increase or decrease the value of the output from the decision model.

Assumptions Concerning the Disturbance Term

When time is used as the unit of association there is a danger that successive observations will be dependent. The cost (or time required) of some activity in period n is likely to be related to the cost (or time required) in period $n - 1$. This situation produces serial correlation among the disturbance terms. Serial correlation does not bias the regression coefficients but it causes serious problems in using the standard error and the standard errors of the regression coefficients. Under the assumptions of the model, probability statements concerning deviations from the regression line should be independent of the unit of association, usually the time period for the particular observation in cost studies. When serial correlation exists this is not true. The problem can be handled using the generalized least-squares technique.

The tendency for costs to be sticky when activity declines is one cause of serial correlation. Expanding activity often leads to increased employment of men and machines. When activity ceases to expand or declines, these factors of production are not easily reduced to reflect the new levels. A period's cost is heavily influenced by the level of cost in the previous period.

A plot of the data may reveal serial correlation if the time of each observation is included with the point. Most, if not all, computer programs for regression analysis have standard tests for serial correlation. Here again, the manager should consider the activity and determine logically whether serial correlation is likely to be inherent to the data. If so, he should attempt either to avoid it or, at least, to recognize the limitations to the methodology caused by its presence. In terms of the machine-overhaul example, the presence of serial correlation prevents management from making valid probabilistic statements concerning estimated costs.

Resort is sometimes successfully made to first differences to avoid the problem of serial correlation. A problem is that measurement errors are magnified and hence the problems associated with these errors are more severe.

A second problem arises if the disturbance term is not independent from one or more of the explanatory variables. Such situations are not uncommon in cost studies and typically arise from bookkeeping procedures. For example, if repairs are not considered as an independent variable and if they are typically made when the activity of one or more of the independent variables is low, then a negative correlation between these variables and the disturbance term will exist. Under this condition the regression coefficients are both biased and inconsistent.

Another statistical limitation concerns the assumption of normality for the distribution of the disturbance term. The use of the normal probability law to make probabilistic statements is conditional on this assumption of normality.

Perhaps it is more appropriate to state that the distribution of the disturbance term should be "close enough" to normal. If reasons exist for suspecting nonnormality or statistical tests suggest that normality is doubtful, probability statements concerning the analysis should be made with caution. It is important to recall that transformations of the variables also affect the disturbance term and it is the transformed variable that is relevant.

The estimation technique used in nearly all cases assumes further that the variance of the distribution of the disturbance term is constant over the range of values for the variables. In other words, the variance of the disturbance term is assumed to be independent of the dependent and of the independent variables. This situation is known as homoscedasticity (nonconstant variance is called heteroscedasticity). When this is not the case, that is, when heteroscedasticity exists, the standard errors of the regression coefficients are not correctly estimated. Furthermore, the standard error is a function of the independent variables causing probability statements to be inaccurate.

Heteroscedasticity is difficult to test for since a large number of observations is required. Again, resort may be made to a nonempirical analysis. For example, accounting data are likely to exhibit heteroscedasticity if the activity range is large, since at higher activity levels higher costs with inherently more room for variability are present. Numerically, if enough observations are available, heteroscedasticity may be indicated by plotting the squared differences between the estimated value from the regression line and the actual observation to determine if there is a relationship between the variability and the activity level. The existence of heteroscedasticity is usually countered by transformation of the data using logs, square roots, or other transformations.

3.3 Problems in the Use of Statistical Cost Studies

The early stages of cost-behavior studies are often characterized by a search for relationships using both what is presumed to be known about the situation and by working with the available historical data. Variables are plotted against one another and possible forms for meaningful relationships re examined. From this work emerge hypotheses concerning the relevant variables and the functional form of the relationship. Such hypotheses should be confirmed using new data. But new data is generally not available. One way to circumvent this problem is to develop the hypotheses from a randomly selected subset of the available historical data. These hypotheses could be tested using the remaining data. Once the final relationships are established all the relevant data should be used to estimate the statistical parameters. Anticipated changes in the environment must be considered in light of their impact on the relevant data to be used.

The interpretation of the results of the cost-behavior analysis are much the same as those for any other statistical analysis of this type. The slope coefficients which measure the marginal impact on cost of a unit change in the independent variable are useful only for recurring decisions in which the future can be assumed to be like the past (unless a means for incorporating additional information is appended). Furthermore, for predictive purposes an independent variable is useful only if it can be measured more easily than the dependent variable it is supposedly being used to predict.

The slope coefficients in a cost-behavior study measure the change in the average cost for a unit change in the independent variable. If a correlation analysis is relevant, they also give the average change in cost per unit change in the independent variable.[14]

The functional relationship should be used for prediction with caution. Two types of predictions are important—those that extrapolate the relationship and those that interpolate from the relationship.

Generally, predictions based on extrapolating the relationship outside the range of data points studied can be done only when the functional form of the relationship is well established by theory and the general magnitude of the parameters can be verified from other studies. One of the problems, especially when several independent variables exist, is that the range of data is difficult to determine. Thus a given prediction may involve values of two independent variables within the observed range of each taken alone, but not within their joint range of occurrence.

The problem of extrapolation extends immediately to the constant term. Unless the comments on the known form of the relationship are valid, the constant term should not be viewed as a measure of fixed cost. Typically, there are no data points for all variables at zero levels simultaneously.

Interpolation, which is more common, may also be questionable in given circumstances. First there is the question of whether the joint values of the independent variables result in interpolation or extrapolation. Second there is the question of the validity of the interpolation. For example, if a product is typically made in batches of say 1,000 and if the functional relationship is derived thereon, then it may not lead to useful predictions involving odd-lot batches that require special handling of other processing costs.

In general, if it can be assumed that the relationships hold not only for the data points used to derive them but also for the new ones being examined, then predictions can be made. Probability statements in turn can be made if the statistical assumptions are also met. Nevertheless, sometimes predictions

---

[14] The importance of each independent variable depends on the regression coefficient and the variability of that variable. The beta coefficients can be used to establish the relative importance of the independent variables. The beta coefficient for a particular variable can be obtained by multiplying the regression coefficient for that variable by the ratio of the standard deviation for that variable to the standard deviation of the dependent variable.

are required when one is not certain of the validity of the assumptions. In such cases it is often necessary to forge ahead. It is important to remember, however, the tenuous nature of these necessary decisions.

Equation (3.3) is valid only for the range of data used to estimate the parameters in it. Thus, if the cost for overhauling nine typewriters, eight calculators, and ten adding machines in one week is desired, the relationship expressed by equation (3.3) may not be useful. Each of these activity levels has been experienced individually, but the three have not been experienced concurrently. Thus the suggested level of activity might require substantial overtime, or it might disrupt normal operating activity in some way. The point is that care should be taken in extrapolation and interpolation using such relationships.

Multiple regression and correlation analysis is not generally used in cost-behavior studies. In part this results from the disfavor in which simple regression and correlation is held because it relates cost behavior to a single independent variable. In part it also results from the general distrust of statistical methods not widely understood and often misused. For these and perhaps other reasons, it is difficult to get management to use the technique.

And yet the more meaningful data that this technique can yield coupled with the existence of ready-made computer programs to handle the input data quickly and relatively cheaply should provide strong arguments in its favor. Nevertheless, the marginal cost of obtaining the data and the predictions desired (including the opportunity costs of delay) must not exceed the marginal benefits from increased revenues or reduced costs achieved through improved decisions.

Finally, the accountant should be sure that he collects data relevant to implementing such procedures. The final form of the functional relation is only as good as the data used to derive it. The accountant's role in cost behavior studies is a central and critical one to their success.

3.4 Summary

Multiple correlation-regression analysis provides an important and powerful technique for estimating and predicting costs. If the proper assumptions are valid, probability statements can also be attached to predicted cost levels. Moreover, the sensitivity of the predictions to errors in estimation can be investigated.

The technique is subject to several limitations resulting from errors in the data and the techniques presently used by accountants to record cost information. The effects of these limitations on the estimating equation and the cost predictions should be borne in mind both in the design and in the use of cost-information systems. The more important cost predictions are, the more attention should be given to the length of the time period used to record costs, the establishment of cost centers, the assignment of costs to periods and centers, and so on.

The methods described are only as effective as the model and the data. For this reason it is imperative that the managers and the statisticians work with the accountant if they are to avoid applying highly sophisticated techniques to relatively naive data.

APPENDIX 3A
THE GENERAL LINEAR REGRESSION MODEL

The material in this appendix assumes that the reader knows matrix algebra.[15] If n observations are available on each of k variables, n equations can be written of the form

$$Y_i = b_0 + b_1 X_{1_i} + b_2 X_{2_i} + \cdots + b_k X_{k_i} + U_i \tag{3A.1}$$
$$i = 1, 2, \ldots, n$$

where U_i represents a disturbance term to allow for the variables explicitly omitted from (3A.1). Using matrix notation,

$$Y = XB + U \tag{3A.2}$$

where Y is an n by 1 column vector of the n observations on the dependent variable.
X is an n by k matrix of the n observations on each of k independent variables.
B is a k by 1 column vector of the unknown coefficients.
U is an n by 1 column vector of the disturbances.

What is desired are estimates of the $b_j, j = 1, 2, \ldots k$. If it can be assumed that[16]

1. The expectation of the disturbance term is 0 for all i, $E(U) = 0$.
2. The dependent variable has constant variance regardless of the associated set of values for the independent variables.
3. The disturbance terms are pairwise uncorrelated.
4. The source of variation in repeated observations results only from variation in the disturbance term (the independent variables are measured without error).

[15] For a discussion of the matrix algebra necessary to understand the development in this Appendix, see J. Johnston, *Econometric Methods*, New York: McGraw-Hill, 1960, Chapters 3 and 4.
[16] Under certain conditions these assumptions may be relaxed in part without violence to the method.

5. The number of observations exceeds the number of parameters to be estimated;

then an estimate of Y is given by equation (3A.2)

$$\hat{Y} = X\hat{B} \tag{3A.3}$$

where $\hat{B}$ is a column vector of estimates of the b_j. The estimated errors are given by

$$Y - \hat{Y} = Y - X\hat{B}. \tag{3A.4}$$

The least-squares technique minimizes the sum of the squared residuals. Since the residuals are given by equation (3A.4), the sum of the squared residuals is given by

$$(Y - X\hat{B})'(Y - X\hat{B}) \tag{3A.5}$$

where the prime indicates the transposed matrix. Multiplying out and taking the partial derivative with respect to $\hat{B}$ in order to minimize equation (3A.5) gives

$$-2X'Y + 2X'X\hat{B}. \tag{3A.6}$$

Setting this result equal to zero and solving gives[17]

$$\hat{B} = (X'X)^{-1}X'Y \tag{3A.7}$$

where the exponent -1 indicates the inverse matrix. The values of the b_j appearing in equation (3.2) are derived using equation (3A.7) where the X matrix consists of the second, third, and fourth columns of Table 3–1, and the Y-column vector is the last column of Table 3–1.

QUESTIONS AND PROBLEMS

3–1 For what purposes might an organization want to know how costs react to changes in the level of activity?

3–2 Suppose the true unit of association between cost and labor input measured by direct-labor hours is the output-level decision. Why might a misleading relationship result if time were used as the unit of association?

3–3 Cost and related data that might be used in multiple correlation-regression analysis are available for given-length time periods. Usually these time periods are established for purposes other than cost analysis (tax purposes for example). What problems can be encountered because of the failure

[17] The computation of an inverse is illustrated in Johnston, *ibid.*, pp. 82–85.

to consider the analysis function in the design of the firm's information system?

3–4 The accompanying graphs illustrate three different cost-volume relationships. Assume the diagonal lines represent the least-squares regression line

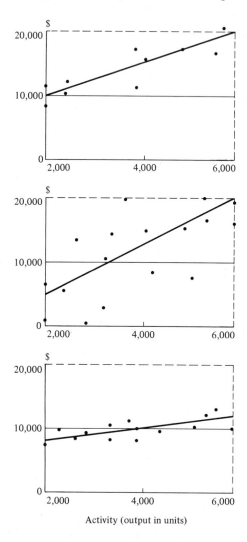

Activity (output in units)

determined mathematically from the underlying data in each case. Note that the data range from activity levels of from about 2,000 to 6,000 units.

    a. Using the top graph, what might the manager estimate fixed costs to be? Would you be satisfied with his estimate? Why?

    b. In which of the three cases does a change in activity have the greatest impact on cost?

c. In which case does the relationship permit the smallest error in prediction? What does this suggest about the value of the analysis?

d. In which case is cost most closely related to changes in output? Defend your choice.

3–5 Consider the inventory control model which leads to the following formula for the economic order quantity

$$EOQ = \sqrt{\frac{2QP}{S}}$$

where

EOQ is the economic order quantity.

Q equals the annual quantity used in units.

P equals the cost of placing an order.

S is the annual cost of storing one unit.

What portion of the data necessary to estimate the relevant future values needed to use this model is available in the accounting records or in the firm's records in general? How is correlation-regression analysis relevant to the problem of determining the EOQ?

3–6 In the machine-overhaul example discussed in this chapter, suppose that during a week in July of a given past year one half of the calculators were replaced by a new and more complex type of machine. What should be done at the time of installation and now to assure a more meaningful cost analysis? Are there any special factors that might need consideration?

3–7 Suppose a correlation-regression analysis in a service department uses two independent variables, namely, direct-labor hours and dollar value of materials. What effects on the estimates of future cost levels (the dependent variable) might be expected?

3–8 In a given cost analysis, data was gathered for each bimonthly period over the last four years. Plotting all the data available suggested a relationship between the activity and total employment that gave a very close estimate of total activity. On the basis of this preliminary investigation, the organization hypothesized that cost was a function of the total employment level and used that data for the previous four years to test the hypothesis.

What conclusion concerning the hypothesis do you suppose they reached? What comments can you make concerning their methodology?

3–9 Three independent variables are used in a correlation-regression analysis. The ranges of observations on each are given below.

$$X_1: 15 - 83, \qquad X_2: 25 - 52, \qquad X_3: 6 - 11.$$

a. Assuming that each independent variable has the same regression coefficient, which one is most important in explaining changes in the dependent activity variable?
b. Would it be appropriate to use the regression equation to predict the activity level for values of $X_1 = 70$, $X_2 = 50$, and $X_3 = 10$?

3–10 If the regression equation for two independent variables and one dependent has the form

$$C = 20 + 4X_1 + 2X_2$$

where C = weekly cost for the activity.

X_1 = direct-labor hours/week.

X_2 = number of orders processed/week.

$S_{c.12}$ = 5 (the standard error of estimate).

S_c = 6 (the standard deviation of weekly costs).

a. Explain the exact meaning of the numbers 20 and 4.
b. Explain the exact meaning of the value for $S_{c.12}$ and S_c.
c. Assuming normality, estimate the probability that the cost of the activity will lie between 46 and 50 if $X_1 = 4$ and $X_2 = 5$.
d. Assuming normality, estimate the probability that the cost will lie between 40 and 50 if $X_1 = 4$ and $X_2 = 5$.
e. Under what conditions would you be willing to use these estimates?

3–11[18] The time spent adjusting and the setup cost required on a piece of machinery depends on the experience and training of the machine operator. For this reason a ten week training program has been set up. After ten weeks there will be a class of machinists in each week of the program. The manager of the department wishes to estimate the setup time (and cost) based on the number of weeks of training. Two machinists are selected at random from each of the ten classes and the setup time on a typical job is measured. The results follow on next page.

Required:
a. The manager cannot decide whether model A or model B is appropriate.
   Model A: $T = b_0 + b_1 W + U_A$
   Model B: $T = b_0 + b_1 X + U_B$
   He is willing to assume U_A or U_B is normally distributed with zero mean and constant variance. Using scatter diagrams (T vs W and T vs X) and whatever else you think is reasonable choose between the models.

[18] Adapted from N. Dopuch and J. Birnberg, *Cost Accounting*, New York: Harcourt, Brace and World, 1969.

Weeks of Training W	$1/W$ X	Setup Times (minutes)*	
		Machinist 1 T	Machinist 2 T
1	1.00	9.5	10.2
2	0.50	9.0	6.4
3	0.33	5.5	7.1
4	0.25	5.8	6.8
5	0.20	6.6	5.3
6	0.17	5.5	7.3
7	0.14	5.2	5.4
8	0.12	4.9	7.6
9	0.11	5.9	4.2
10	0.10	4.5	6.3

* A different pair of machinists are observed for each week.

b. Suppose the manager selects model B. Obtain estimates of b_0, b_1, and the standard error of estimate $S_{T \cdot X}$. The following data may be helpful $S_{T \cdot X}$. The following data may be helpful

$$\Sigma X = 5.84, \quad \Sigma T = 129, \quad \Sigma X^2 = 3.0928;$$
$$\Sigma TX = 44.439; \quad \Sigma T^2 = 882.34;$$
$$\Sigma T = nb_0 + b_1 \Sigma X; \quad \text{and} \quad \Sigma TX = b_0 \Sigma X + b_1 \Sigma X^2.$$

c. Suppose that the statistician asserts that model B is more reasonable than A because A implies a machinist with no experience (or training) can set up the equipment in a finite expected time while a machinist with a great deal of time will be able to set up the equipment in a negative expected time. Model B, on the other hand, implies that a machinist with no experience cannot set up the equipment and that the machinist with a great deal of experience needs a finite amount of time at least of b_0.
  1. Do you agree? Why or why not?
  2. If you agree would you be willing to use Model B to estimate setup time for a machinist with fifteen weeks of training?
  3. If you disagree would you be willing to use model A for this estimate?
d. Suppose the study was made by observing the same two machinists in each of the ten weeks. What problems are created? Do any problems result if two different men for each week are used at a point in time when the program is 10 weeks old?
e. A machinist with five weeks of training set up the equipment in 3.8 minutes. Using the results of the study would you say:
  1. He was unusual? Why or why not?
  2. If so, what might explain this result?

f. What interpretation can be given the correlation coefficient in this problem?

3–12 What does the least-squares criterion implicitly assume about the importance of the prediction error to the manager?

3–13 "If historically valid data on another variable is available, it should be included in the regression equation since predictions will be improved." Evaluate this statement.

3–14 Describe the effects on the results of a correlation-regression analysis caused by

a. Serial correlation;
b. Measurement errors in an independent variable;
c. Intercorrelation between two independent variables.

3–15 A method regularly used to establish the fixed and variable fractions of a cost is the so-called high-low method. The approach relies on the two extreme outputs to reflect the change in cost resulting from a change in activity. What limitations are present in this method?

SUPPLEMENTARY READING

BENSTON, G. J., "Multiple Regression Analysis of Cost Behavior," *The Accounting Review*, October 1966, pp. 657–672.

DEAN, J., *Managerial Economics*, Englewood Cliffs, N.J.: Prentice-Hall, 1951, Chapter 5.

JENSEN, R., "Multiple Regression Models for Cost Control—Assumptions and Limitations," *The Accounting Review*, April 1967, pp. 265–272.

JOHNSTON, J., *Econometric Methods*, New York: McGraw-Hill, 1963.

JOHNSTON, J., *Statistical Cost Control*, New York: McGraw-Hill, 1960.

SPENCER, M. H., and L. SIEGELMAN, *Managerial Economics*, Homewood, Ill.: R. D. Irwin, 1964, Chapters 5–9.

TROXEL, R. B., "Variable Budgets Through Correlation Analysis—A Simple Approach," *National Association of Accountant's Bulletin*, February 1965, pp. 48–55.

Chapter 4

Learning Curves and Cost Behavior

Conventional economic theory assumes that both the average-variable cost and the marginal cost per unit of product are concave-downward functions. Furthermore, the marginal-cost curve intersects the average-variable cost curve at its minimum. These classic relationships are illustrated in Figure 4.1.

The shape of the marginal-cost curve reflects initially increasing efficiency with increasing output followed by increasing marginal costs resulting from inefficiencies. Constant efficiency, a condition often assumed in accounting analyses, would be reflected by a horizontal marginal-cost curve.

The analysis as traditionally made mixes together two factors that should be considered separately. These include the time rate of production and the total number of units produced.[1] The marginal cost per unit might, on an *a priori* basis, be expected to increase as the time rate of production increases or, perhaps, to exhibit a cost-behavior pattern similar to that in Figure 4.1 with the horizontal axis relabeled in terms of the units produced per unit of time.

In many situations, such as the production of a new product, however, the learning phenomenon tends to reduce the marginal cost as the cumulative output increases. If the rate of production is increased so that the incremental unit cost is increasing

[1] See J. Hirshleifer, "The Firm's Cost Function: A Successful Reconstruction?", *The Journal of Business*, July 1962, pp. 235–255 and A. Alchian, "Costs and Outputs," in M. Abramovitz, *The Allocation of Economic Resources: Essays in Honor of B. F. Haley*, Stanford, Calif.: Stanford University Press, 1959.

(decreasing efficiency) but learning is also taking place simultaneously, it is difficult to predict the shape of the marginal cost curve.[2] This in turn has implications for decision making and for accounting.

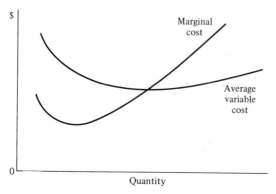

Figure 4.1   Average-variable and marginal-cost curves: traditional economic analysis

That average labor time per unit of output declines, at least in the early stages of a new process, has been generally known for many years.[3] The observation that the rate of improvement exhibited regularities for similar activities even across firms and repeated itself for new but similar projects was an important factor in making the effects of the learning phenomenon predictable.

4.1   The Learning-Curve Model

Industrial analyses indicate that the nature of the learning phenomenon can be described as a constant percentage reduction in the *average* labor input time required per unit as the cumulative output doubles. For example, assume a reduction rate of twenty per cent and that the first unit takes 125 hours. Then the average for two units should be 100 hours, 0.8(125); a total of 200 hours for both. The second unit takes seventy-five hours to produce. Four units would take an average of eighty hours each, 0.8(100), or a total of 320 hours. This means that 120 hours, 320 − 200, must be expended in total to produce the third and fourth units. One minus the percentage

---

[2] If a steady state has been reached or the learning effect is exhausted, the more conventional analysis applies.

[3] Initial applications were made in the airframe industry on the basis of regularities observed as early as 1925. See M. A. Requero, *An Economic Study of the Airframe Industry*, Wright-Patterson Air Force Base, Ohio, Department of the Air Force, October 1957, p. 213, and T. P. Wright, "Factors Affecting the Cost of Airplanes," *Journal of Aeronautical Science*, February 1936, pp. 122–128.

reduction is known as the learning rate. The learning rate in the present example is $1 - 0.2 = 0.8$ or 80 per cent.

Mathematically, the learning-curve effect can be expressed in exponential equation form as

$$Y = aX^b \tag{4.1}$$

where

Y is the *average* number of labor hours required for X units.

a is the number of labor hours required for the first unit.

X is the cumulative number of units produced.

b is an index of learning equal to the log of the learning rate divided by the log of 2.[4] For the present example, $b = -0.322$.

Since Y is the average number of labor hours required for X units, the total number of hours required for X units is given by

$$YX = aX^{b+1}. \tag{4.2}$$

The learning effect can be graphed. The average number of labor hours required for X units as expressed by equation (4.1) is graphed on arithmetic

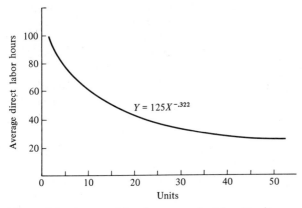

Figure 4.2   Average labor hours required for X units

scales in Figure 4.2 and on log scales in Figure 4.3. Equation (4.1) is linear on the log chart since

$$\log Y = \log a + b \log X. \tag{4.3}$$

---

[4] This can be shown as follows. If the first unit takes a hours then the average for two units is $0.8a$ hours according to the model. Since $X = 2$, equation (4.1) gives $0.8a = a(2)^b$.

Taking logs (all to the base 10) $\log 0.8a = \log a + b \log 2$. Simplifying $\log (0.8a/a) = b \log 2$ or $b = (\log 0.8)/(\log 2)$.

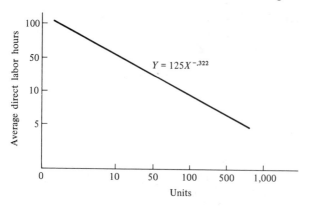

Figure 4.3   Average labor hours required for X units

An appealing alternative but equivalent mathematical description of the learning-curve model given by equation (4.1) is obtained by altering the form of the formula to incorporate the learning rate explicitly. The result for the present example is

$$Y = a(0.8)^{\log_2 X} \qquad\qquad (4.4)$$

where the symbols retain their same definitions.[5] The problem with the model in this form is that it is necessary to recompute the exponent at each step.

The learning model described so far defines Y in terms of the average number of labor hours required for X units. It is also possible to define learning in terms of the improvement in the time required to produce the *individual* unit rather than the improvement in the *average* time. When this alternate interpretation of learning is relevant, equation (4.1) may again be used but Y must be redefined as the required labor time for the Xth unit.[6] Suppose that instead of the average time decreasing by 20 per cent for doubled quantities, the manager believes that it is the time required to produce the Xth unit that declines by 20 per cent. Under this interpretation, if the first unit again requires 125 hours, the second unit would now require 0.8(125) or 100 hours, and the fourth unit would require 0.8(100) or eighty hours. Then using equation (4.1) with Y' substituted for Y gives

$$Y' = aX^b \qquad\qquad (4.5)$$

[5] Mathematically, using equation (4.3), and the fact that
$$b = \log 0.8/\log 2$$
$$\log Y = \log a + (\log X)(\log 0.8)/(\log 2)$$
$$= \log a + \log 0.8 \exp (\log X/\log 2)$$
$$= \log a + \log 0.8 \exp (\log X \log_2 10)$$
$$= \log a + \log 0.8 \exp (\log_2 X)$$

[6] See J. E. Howell and D. Teichroew, *Mathematical Analysis for Business Decisions*, Homewood, Ill.: R. D. Irwin, 1963, pp. 159–163.

where Y' is the number of labor hours required to produce the Xth unit, and all other terms are defined as before. Using this model the total number of hours required for n units is given by integrating equation (4.5) and the average time by dividing this integral by n. Hence the average time for n units using this model is

$$\frac{1}{n} \int_0^n aX^b \, dX = \frac{1}{n} \left(\frac{a}{b+1} \right) n^{b+1} = \frac{a}{b+1} n^b. \tag{4.6}$$

The equations are similar but the interpretation of the results is markedly different. The appropriate model to use depends on what the manager knows about the learning process under the existing conditions. If the data is plotted on log-log paper, the only difference in the plots is that, for the average model, the average direct-labor hours for X units are plotted on the vertical axis, whereas for the marginal model, equation (4.5), the marginal direct-labor hours for the Xth unit are plotted on the vertical axis. The analyst will look for a linear pattern to be suggested by the data.

4.1.1 Determining the Parameters of the Model

In order to use the model as defined by either equations (4.1) or (4.5), it is necessary to estimate the parameters a and b. The data gathered may be plotted on log-log paper and estimates made of the constants a and b.[7] It is useful in this stage to collect data on subactivities since the subactivities may often be involved in future production.

The manager is well advised to be skeptical of the applicability of the slope coefficient obtained from the data. Significant variations are common in empirical studies.[8] Previous work suggests that the learning rate and, thus, also the slope, are directly related to the initial ratio of machine to labor input hours. Where this ratio is three machine hours to one labor hour, the learning rate tends to be near 90 per cent. When the ratio is one to one, the learning rate is around 85 per cent, and when it is one to three, machine to labor, the rate is about 80 per cent. The decline in these figures is intuitively appealing since as the relative amount of labor in an activity increases, the opportunities for learning increase. The effect is reflected in a declining learning-rate percentage and a decline in the slope coefficient (that is, a larger negative slope).

As an example, consider a company that acts as a subcontractor for parts used in the space program. Assume the company has been requested to bid on a contract for 750 units required in the assembly of the re-entry mechanism

---

[7] The value of a is the intercept on the verticle axis, the value of Y (or Y') when X is zero. The value of b is the slope of the line.

[8] See N. Baloff, "The Learning Curve—Some Controversial Issues," *Journal of Industrial Economics*, July 1966, pp. 275–282.

of a new space capsule. Thus the firm is interested in the expected cost of the contract. The company had recently produced 250 of the items at the following costs as indicated by the accounting records.

Direct materials	$10,000
Direct labor (5,000 hours @ $5)	25,000
Tooling (can be reused)	3,000
Variable overhead	5,000
Fixed overhead (billed on the basis of one fourth of direct-labor cost)	6,250
Total cost	$49,250

The company has retained a partial record of the total time required to produce the 250 units. The data are first unit, 122 hours; fifteen units, 735 hours; 100 units, 2,724 hours; 250 units, 5,000 hours.

The learning effect applies only to the direct-labor time and perhaps to the variable overhead time if it is a direct function of the direct-labor time. Plotting the labor-time data on a log-log scale after converting it to averages suggests a straight line with an intercept of approximately 120 hours. Since the relationship appears to be linear using averages, the model of learning suggested by equations (4.1) or (4.4) can be used with b established by solving equation (4.1) for $Y = 20$ when $X = 250$ and $a \doteq 120$. (A least-squares technique could also be used.) This gives:

$$Y = aX^b$$
$$20 = 120(250)^b;$$

hence

$$\frac{\log 20 - \log 120}{\log 250} = b$$

or

$$b = -0.325.$$

Assume that from this analysis and what the manager knows about the labor intensity of the process he concludes that an 80 per cent learning rate is appropriate. (Recall that the b value for an 80 per cent learning rate is -0.322.) With this data he may use equation (4.2) to estimate the total direct-labor hours required for the additional 750 units or he may reason as follows. Given an 80 per cent learning rate for the time required for the average unit, a doubling of the quantity produced results in a 20 per cent reduction in the average time per unit. Hence the average time for 500 units is 0.8(20) = sixteen hours and the average time for 1,000 units is 0.8(16) equals 12.8 hours. The total time required for the 750-unit contract would be 1,000(12.8) equals 12,800 hours less the 5,000 hours put in on the initial 250 units, a requirement of 7,800 hours. Assuming that the hourly rate remains constant, variable overhead remains at 20 per cent of direct labor, and other costs change proportionally, the marginal costs of the new contract would be

Direct materials	$30,000
Direct labor (7,800 hours @ $5)	39,000
Tooling	0
Variable overhead	7,800
Total marginal cost	$76,800

The firm may still choose to incorporate a fixed-overhead element but the anticipated marginal costs of the 150-unit order are $76,800. This is less than twice the cost of the initial 250 units though the present contract would be three times as large.

4.1.2 An Example of the Use of Learning Curves in Decision Making

An additional example of the use of learning curves in estimating costs for decision making is useful at this point.[9] An aircraft company was faced with a cutback in orders resulting from a stretch-out procurement program by the Air Force. Its reaction was to consider canceling various subcontracts and doing this work in its own plant.

One such subcontract involved 372 landing-flap assemblies. However, before canceling the subcontract the aircraft company wished to consider the costs of the two alternatives.

The aircraft company had already produced 165 similar assemblies, the last of which took 445 hours. This put the company well along its learning curve. Extrapolating the curve indicated a total labor input of 111,000 hours for the 372 additional units. In contrast, the subcontractor, while apparently a more efficient producer of this item in the long run, was just getting started on its learning curve. Extrapolating its curve indicated that the subcontractor would be able to produce its one hundred sixth-fifth assembly with only 402 hours, forty-three hours less than the aircraft company had needed. Nevertheless, since at the decision time its curve was much higher the total hours required to produce 372 assemblies by the subcontractor was predicted to be 164,000 hours, or 53,000 more than required by the aircraft company.

[9] The example is adapted from one in an article by Andress: F. J. Andress, "The Learning Curve as a Production Tool," *The Harvard Business Review*, January–February 1954, pp. 87–97.

The short run, lower cost choice was to cancel the subcontract and to do the work internally. In the long run, assuming future cost characteristics are known with certainty and there is enough additional work of an identical nature, it would be cheaper to continue the contract since the subcontractor can do the job with less labor after getting out as far as the aircraft company on its learning curve. The decision hinged on the expected future demand for this type of landing flap assembly. (Note that a change in assembly type probably takes both firms back to the start of their learning curve.) In the case described, the future demand was uncertain and difficult to predict. Hence the aircraft company elected to cancel the subcontract and take advantage of the present savings which amounted to over $300,000.

4.1.3 Difficulties in Obtaining the Data

Perhaps the most serious limitation to using learning curves is in obtaining valid data on which to base their computation. For example, suppose a firm decreases the planned labor input into a product by increasing the use of purchased parts. The result may be a decline in the actual labor used per unit, but it would not be due to learning. There is a shift of the required labor input to the supplier. Indeed, the effect of ignoring such facts may simultaneously give an apparently declining learning curve coupled with increasing unit cost. A given learning curve relates to one manufacturing process and if the process is changed the learning curve may no longer apply.

The learning curve phenomenon measures only direct labor. Thus, if more time is spent in, say, designing the product or process, there may again be an apparent increase in learning as reflected by the curve without a decline in total cost. The direct labor is merely shifted to indirect labor or overhead. A similar effect occurs if supervisory labor or new equipment replaces direct labor.

Declines in the labor input can also occur when there are changes in the materials used. Better materials can reduce labor input without necessarily lowering cost. A similar result can be obtained if there is a change in the labor mix. Better but more expensive labor can cause an artificial learning effect. These factors can work in the opposite direction as well. For example, a tight labor market may lead to poorer labor quality. Both the effect of new and poorer labor diminishes the learning effect yet costs may decline if the wages are sufficiently low. Changes in labor mix, overhead, and the associated factors of production, then, can considerably confound the learning-curve effect.

One additional example is worthy of comment. It is unusual but increased production rates can lead, at least initially, to increased effectiveness. As effectiveness (or efficiency) rises the labor input per unit falls as a response to greater efficiency. Further increases in the rate of production may reverse this phenomenon. Changes in the rate of production can affect the data used to plot the learning curve and develop its parameters. Great care and skill is necessary to either eliminate or correct for these data limitations. Further, changes contemplated in future processes should be considered before relationships derived from historical data are applied to new situations.

4.2   Learning-Curve Applications

The applicability of learning curves is, as has been previously indicated, more important in cases where the labor input in an activity is large and the activity is complex. Since the curve is steepest at its start and since new projects cause recycling, the learning effect is also more pronounced where the rate of product or process innovation is high. Finally, if learning is expected and planned for, greater use of this phenomenon can be made. Indeed, if learning is encouraged and expected, a climate may be created where it can and will occur. An interesting example was supplied by Conway and Schultz who showed that when a new group of workers were put on a task already far down its learning curve, the fresh approach brought by the new group produced a new learning cycle.[10]

Andress suggests that conditions conducive to learning are ideal in the electronics, home appliance, construction, shipbuilding, and machine shop areas.[11] On the other hand he suggests that industries which are capital intensive such as petroleum refining "would find the learning curve of little value."[12] Hirschmann finds, however, that a significant learning effect also exists, although to a lesser degree, in heavily capital intensive industries.[13] He attributes this to the removal of bottlenecks, relaxing preset safety margins, and technological resourcefulness generally.

4.2.1 Pricing

Since learning curves permit better cost predictions, it seems that they should be employed in pricing decisions. In some cases involving government contracts, consideration of learning-curve effects is required. The question is not whether learning curves will be used but what are the appropriate parameters.

An extension of the pricing use of learning-curve data is in buying from a supplier. Sometimes a supplier will experience high initial outlays resulting in

[10] R. W. Conway and A. Schultz, "The Manufacturing Process Function," *Journal of Industrial Engineering*, January–February 1959, p. 48.

[11] Andress, *op. cit.*, pp. 95–97.

[12] *Ibid.* p. 96.

[13] W. B. Hirschmann, "Profit from the Learning Curve," *The Harvard Business Review*, January–February 1964, pp. 125–139.

part, from the fact that the supplier is at the early stages of its learning curve relative to the job. A purchasing firm might be willing initially to pay a higher price if the supplier agrees to and subsequently lowers the price per unit.[14]

4.2.2 Work Scheduling

Learning curves increase a firm's ability to predict their required labor input and make it possible to forecast labor needs. They also allow the development of production and delivery schedules with greater accuracy. These in turn permit the firm to do a better job of scheduling maintenance and overhead activity, quality control, material purchasing, and promotion. Better forecasting and scheduling result in lower costs through better cost control and improved customer relations.

4.2.3 Capital Budgeting

One of the more important aspects in capital-budgeting problems is the timing of cash flows. The learning effect suggests that unit costs are likely to begin high and taper off. This is in contrast to the steady state, constant unit cost usually assumed in capital-budgeting analysis. Furthermore, the learning curve permits improved estimates of production levels that can be attained and thus has implications for cash flows. These modifications can be particularly important where the project start-up period is large relative to the life of the project.

4.2.4 Motivation

Costs are often controlled using standards and variances from standards. If these standards are set without regard to the learning phenomenon, meaningless initial and unfavorable variances may occur with resulting motivational impact. Performance reports that show large unfavorable variances about which the manager can do nothing and which he may even expect, can lead to a deleterious effect on his aspiration level and thereby his performance. Sometimes this is resolved by admitting the learning effect through arbitrary adjustments or allowances or by making no evaluations until the process "settles down." It would be an improvement to recognize the learning effect in the standard where possible.[15]

The same problem arises when the investigation of an out-of-control process leads to corrective action. The time over which the corrective action takes

---

[14] See Andress, *op. cit.*, pp. 94–95, for an example.

[15] Even such decisions as establishing piecework incentive rates should be made considering the learning effect.

effect often covers several cost-reporting periods. During this period, costs may even rise for a while before the learning effect takes hold. Simultaneously, management will be keeping close tabs on the reaction of costs to new procedures. Hence it is necessary for management to be cognizant of the influence of learning during this period and to use standards, if at all, that consider it.

A similar effect is apparent in evaluating divisional performance. Large activities in early phases of activity will experience relatively higher costs and lower output than at later stages. This should be considered when a division manager's performance is evaluated.

4.2.5 External Reporting

Learning influences profits through its effects on cost and output. When these effects are important some attention should be given to them on the firm's annual report. For example, the *Wall Street Journal* in early 1967 reporting on the consolidation of all subsidiaries by the Phillips Petroleum Company in which it held over a 50 per cent interest stated that "the effect of this [consolidation] will be to reduce earnings from what they would be without such consolidation, because most of the companies being consolidated are ones that are under construction or in the start-up stage, and which therefore are expected to show losses this year."[16]

Assume a situation where these early losses were expected when the decision to undertake the construction was made. If financial reports are to be an aid in evaluation and are to be consistent with decision making, some attempt should be made to separate nonrecoverable losses from costs that are incurred as part of the learning process. Where there is good reason to believe that learning will take place, it is appropriate to capitalize some or all of a firm's early losses as assets rather than mislead investors into believing that the financial situation is unfavorable. Admittedly this procedure could be misused by managers wanting to defer losses that are likely to be nonrecoverable. It would have to be applied with care.

4.3 Summary

The concepts of learning curves have many applications. They should be used in cost control, labor planning, and even financial reporting. The true nature of the learning curve associated with a new product or process will never be known *a priori*. However, a reasonable assumption of its shape is better than the implicit assumption of no learning at all.

---

[16] Reported in N. Baloff and J. N. Kennelly, "Accounting Implications of Product and Process Start-ups," *Journal of Accounting Research*, Autumn 1967, p. 142.

QUESTIONS AND PROBLEMS

4-1 Modify the following statement so that it is more accurate: "Marginal costs will tend to increase as more units are produced."

4-2 What conditions may cause the average variable cost to decline as
   a. Output per unit of time increases?
   b. Cumulative output increases?

4-3 Accept as a premise that the average labor hours required per unit is reduced 20% as the quantity produced doubles. Is it correct to say that "This implies a situation where the second unit requires about 80 per cent as much direct labor as the first; the tenth 80 per cent as much as the fifth, and so on?"

4-4 If an 80 per cent learning model is assumed to apply to the individual time for the Xth unit and labor costs $5 per hour, how much should it cost in direct labor to produce 100 units if the first unit takes eighty hours?

4-5 In plotting learning-curve data why is log-log paper particularly useful?

4-6 "Learning curves are relatively easy to estimate, however, their influence tends to be of very marginal value." Evaluate this statement.

4-7 Suggest ten decisions where the learning effect may be important.

4-8 The Sharp Company subcontracts some aircraft parts to the Doit Company because of the greater familiarity of the latter with the task. The manager of Sharp notes that Doit has an 85 per cent learning curve while Sharp has an 80 per cent curve. However, Doit is far down the curve. Since Sharp would start its own curve if it made the part; it would incur large initial costs. Since it would also not need to pay freight or profit to Doit, the manager believes that Sharp, at least from a learning-curve viewpoint, should not subcontract. Do you agree? Why?

4-9 The Boxer Company makes parts for ship navigation systems. It has previously made about 10,000 parts exactly like the type ordered by the government for a new type of submarine. A new government order calls for 10,000 parts. The company's records yield the following cost data for the 10,000 parts made to date.

Direct materials	$ 1,000,000
Direct labor (800,000 hours @ $8)	6,400,000
Setup costs (no labor)	60,000
Variable overhead ($4.00/DLH)	3,200,000
Fixed overhead (allocated at $1.00/DLH)	6,400,000
Total costs	$17,660,000

Assuming an 80 per cent learning rate on the average time required and no change in unit-of-labor costs per hour, estimate the company's additional costs from accepting the order.

4–10 What is the most significant feature about the learning curve that makes it useful?

4–11

Assume a learning rate of 80 per cent; that is, the average number of labor hours required per unit is reduced 20 per cent as the quantity produced doubles.

Required:
a. If the first 100 units require 100 hours, how many total hours will be required to produce 200 units? How many additional hours are required for the second 100 units?
b. Suppose the firm has an opportunity to bid on a contract that will raise its total output from 200 to 500 units. How many labor hours will be involved?

4–12 Discuss how learning curve techniques may be used in setting standards for control.

SUPPLEMENTARY READING

ANDRESS, F. J., "The Learning Curve as a Production Tool," *The Harvard Business Review*, January–February 1954, pp. 87–97.

BALOFF, N., "The Learning Curve—Some Controversial Issues," *Journal of Industrial Economics*, July 1966, pp. 275–282.

CONWAY, R. W., and A. SCHULTZ, "The Manufacturing Progress Function," *Journal of Industrial Engineering*, 1959, pp. 39–53.

HIRSCHMANN, W. B., "Profit from the Learning Curve," *The Harvard Business Review*, January–February 1964, pp. 125–139.

JORDAN, R. B., "Learning How to Use the Learning Curve," *N.A.A. Bulletin*, January 1958, pp. 27–40.

TAYLOR, M. L., "The Learning Curve—A Basic Cost Projection Tool," *N.A.A. Bulletin*, February 1961, pp. 21–26.

TEICHROEW, D., *An Introduction to Management Science*, New York: John Wiley, 1964, pp. 159–163.

WYER, R., "Learning Curve Techniques for Direct Labor Management," *N.A.A. Bulletin, Conference Proceedings*, July 1958, pp. 19–27.

Chapter 5

Cost-Price-Volume Decisions

Decisions involving price, volume, and cost can be split into two classifications: those decisions made after the capital assets necessary for production have been acquired, and those made in connection with the acquisition of the necessary capital assets. It is important to distinguish between the two situations, since considerations which are relevant for one may not be relevant for the other. Applying the same procedures in both situations can lead to incorrect decisions. This chapter reviews the pricing and output decisions in the case when the capital assets are already owned. The problems of decision making when the capital assets have not yet been acquired are capital-budgeting decisions. These decisions are examined in Chapters 13, 14, and 15.

5.1 Price-Volume Decisions

Assume that the Scot Company owns a new plant which is fully equipped with the latest model machinery to make lawn mowers. What price should it charge? At what output should it produce? What cost and profit decisions can it make? These decisions are examined in reverse order.

What profit decisions can be made? The answer is none. The company decides on a price and an output; it attempts to produce the goods efficiently. If the planning process is effective and is efficiently carried out, then a profit may result. But management does not "plan" profits. In this situation it cannot say that it

94

needs a profit of 20 per cent on the investment of $1 million and therefore must have a profit of $200,000. The profit is a result of planning and the execution of the plans, but it is a residual of these plans and not the result of a "profit decision."

The cost decisions of the Scot Company are somewhat less limited. The firm can budget costs for various levels of output, can attempt to control costs and improve efficiency, and can use inventories to stabilize production. However, the basic cost structure is determined by the characteristics of the machinery and plant purchased. Whether overtime is necessary is a decision to be made in each period, but to some extent the decision was made when the plant was built. If the demand for the product is high enough, it will be necessary to incur overtime; but the decision that determined the size of the plant and in turn resulted in the necessity to incur overtime was made in a previous period.

The pricing decision is one of the most important decisions made by management, and one of the most misunderstood. Two pricing methods commonly used which are subject to criticism are the *cost plus* and the *desired-return-on-investment* methods of pricing.

5.1.1 Cost-Plus and Return-on-Investment Pricing

With the cost-plus method of pricing, the cost of the product is computed and a "reasonable" or "fair" profit is added to obtain the price. If a government cost-plus contract is in hand, this is a justifiable procedure; but in a competitive situation (as in bidding for a government contract) it may lead to undesirable results.[1] One difficulty is in computing unit cost and involves deciding on the level of activity which should be used to absorb fixed costs to product. A second problem is in determining unit price and involves deciding on what constitutes a "reasonable" profit. But perhaps of most importance is the fact that the entire cost-plus procedure is not theoretically sound.

To illustrate the problem of determining unit cost, assume that the Scot company can produce 10,000 lawn mowers per month when operating at capacity. The monthly fixed costs are $200,000, and the variable costs are $30 per lawn mower. What is the cost of one lawn mower? One reasonable answer is $50 (the variable costs of $30 plus fixed costs of $20). The absorption of fixed costs is based on capacity. But suppose the company expects to produce and sell only 5,000 lawn mowers during the month. Are the unit costs to be used for pricing then $70 (the variable costs of $30 plus fixed costs per unit of $40)? Carrying this issue to its illogical conclusion, if only one unit is to be produced, the total cost per unit would be $200,030, or at the opposite extreme $30, if the fixed costs are not considered as part of the unit cost.

---

[1] For some results in this area see S. Colantoni, R. Manes, and A. Whinston, "Programming, Profit Rates and Pricing Decisions," *The Accounting Review*, July 1969, pp. 467–481.

With cost-plus a reasonable profit is added to the unit cost. The desired-return-on-investment pricing method focuses attention on return on investment instead of income. It has no advantage over the cost-plus procedure, and retains the disadvantage of requiring the computation of unit cost. There is no objection to a company attempting to recover all costs and to earn as much profit as it can in a competitive environment. But this desire does not necessarily mean that all costs will be recovered, or that the company will earn a profit.

5.1.2 Standard Price

One method of handling the pricing problem is to base. The absorption of fixed costs on normal activity without regard to the expected or actual level of operations. This procedure is better than adjusting the cost per unit and the price upward as the output decreases. In fact, it can be used to set a sort of "standard" price which must be obtained in order to maintain the productive facilities and earn a selected return on the capital employed. Nevertheless, it is not always desirable to set a standard price. In some situations the firm may be able to charge more than the standard price (for example, if it is introducing a new product for which there is little if any competition as yet), while in other situations it may be desirable or necessary to set a price less than the standard price. Competition, for example, may prevent the use of the standard price. In fact, a complementary product may be priced below its direct-variable costs. An example is the pricing of razors by a company which also manufactures razor blades.

5.1.3 Determining Price and Output—Theoretical Solution

The theoretical solution to the problem of output and price is an exercise in the application of economic theory. For this reason it is useful to digress for a moment to examine the major differences in assumptions between the behavior of costs as economists see them and as accountants generally consider them. Figure 5.1 plots total variable, total fixed, and total costs first from the economist's point of view (Figure 5.1a) and then from the accountant's point of view (Figure 5.1b). Figure 5.2 represents the same breakdown for unit costs, assuming a single measure of activity.[2] Both figures are simplified in order to highlight the major differences.

A substantive difference involves the range of activity graphed. The economist graphs a broader range of possible activity and changes in efficiency. The accountant, on the other hand, is usually concerned only with a limited range of activity. Over this range fixed costs are constant except perhaps for occasional discrete upward jumps. Furthermore, within a wide

---

[2] A failure to specify whether total or per unit costs are under consideration can lead to useless discussions and often to erroneous conclusions.

range the accountant's assumption of linearity for the variable-cost activity relationship is usually an adequate approximation.

The differences in the curves are a function of different assumptions and they need not be considered as conceptual differences. Given an identical problem, there would be essential agreement among them on the relevant-cost

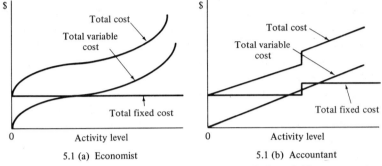

5.1 (a) Economist   5.1 (b) Accountant

Figure 5.1   Total cost curves from (a) an economist's and (b) an accountant's viewpoint

curves involved (one remaining difference would be that the economist includes the cost of equity capital as a cost but the accountant excludes it.)

With these distinctions in mind, the discussion now turns to the resolution of the price-output decision from the vantage point of economic theory. There is a tendency to dismiss the analysis which follows by suggesting that the solution is akin to determining the number of angels that can dance on

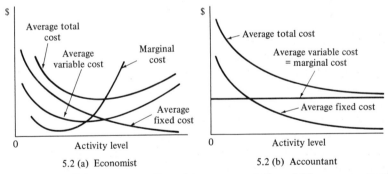

5.2 (a) Economist   5.2 (b) Accountant

Figure 5.2   Unit-cost curves from (a) an economist's and (b) an accountant's viewpoint

the head of a pin. Rather than pretend to present a procedure that permits the determination of the exact price that will maximize profits, this section develops a theoretically sound guide for determining price and output. The principles are correct, even though in many situations they can not be applied with exactness because of incomplete information: the procedure then is a normative one.

Before the cost curves of economic theory can be very useful, it is necessary to add the revenue function to the analysis. The economist typically assumes that units sold (and therefore output activity indirectly) increase as price decreases (accountants often assume a constant price over the expected or relevant range of activity), and that the number of units of product that can be sold at different prices is known. Usually it is assumed that the lower the price, the more units will be sold. Although this is not always a valid assumption, it will be useful in the illustration to follow. (The assumption is, however, not necessary for the theory being developed.)

It is possible to plot the number of units that can be sold at all feasible prices. This curve is called the average-revenue or price curve. It shows the price or average revenue per unit necessary in order to sell the associated number of units. The average-revenue curve (AR) in Figure 5.3 slopes downward to the right because it is assumed that the number of units sold increases as the price decreases.

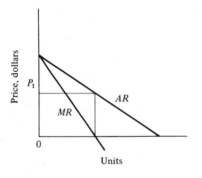

Figure 5.3   Revenue curves

A marginal-revenue curve (MR) is also plotted in Figure 5.3. This curve shows the amount of revenue added by the sale of one more additional unit. It slopes downward to the right since it is necessary to reduce the price to sell an additional unit. It is below the average-revenue curve since every time the sales price is reduced the price of all previous units also has to be reduced.

No useful decisions can be made with just the revenue curves, but it is interesting to note that when the price is P_1 (Figure 5.3) the marginal revenue is zero, and that with a lower price the marginal revenue becomes negative. This means that a further reduction in price results in a reduction in total revenue. With zero costs, a price of P_1 constitutes the minimum price that the firm could charge without losing money on the next unit of product sold.

If the marginal-cost curve is added (see Figure 5.4), additional conclusions can be drawn. This curve shows the amount of cost that is added by the production and the sale of one additional unit of product. For example, if it costs $300 to produce and sell 100 units and $305 to produce and sell 101 units, the marginal cost of the 101st unit is $5. The accountant is accustomed to talk of variable, or incremental, costs. In this case the incremental cost of one more unit is $5. The shape of the marginal-cost curve indicates that the firm is at first operating under increasing efficiency (the marginal-cost decreases) and then reaches a point where the efficiency decreases (the marginal-cost increases). If constant efficiency is assumed, the marginal-cost curve becomes a horizontal line.

The point where the marginal-cost curve intersects the marginal-revenue curve (point B in Figure 5.4) is very important. This intersection determines the optimal output (Q units) and optimal price (P).

If the company is producing less than this level of output, one more unit of production and sale results in additional revenue greater than the additional cost (the marginal revenue is greater than the marginal cost). Thus, as long as the value of the marginal-revenue curve is greater than the value of the marginal-cost curve, it is profitable to increase output. The point where the two curves intersect is the optimal level of output. But assume a decision is made to increase production by still another unit. Figure 5.4 shows that if

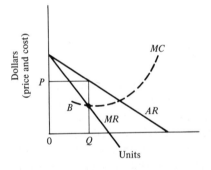

Figure 5.4   Determining output and price

production is increased beyond Q units, the additional cost is greater than the additional revenue. Thus there is no profit incentive to increase output and sales beyond Q units.

What price will maximize profits? To sell Q units it is necessary to charge a price P. This is determined by constructing a vertical line through the point B where marginal cost equals marginal revenue until it intersects the average-revenue line and then horizontally to the vertical axis. This determines the price necessary to sell Q units and thus maximize profits. If a lower price is charged, more than Q units are purchased, but the additional revenue earned by these additional units is less than the additional costs. If a price greater than P is charged, the number of units sold is less than Q, and marginal revenue is greater than marginal cost. Only an output of Q units sold at a price of P maximizes profits.

Several additional remarks can be made. The optimal output is determined directly by the intersection of the marginal-cost and marginal-revenue curves. The price necessary to achieve this optimum is determined indirectly by this same intersection. The marginal-revenue curve in Figure 5.4 implies the average-revenue curve in the same figure and hence once point B is known, the optimal price can be determined. Also, the only costs that entered into the decision were those costs which vary with output. This is a difficult thought to digest; but it is true that costs which are constant in total and do not vary with output should not enter into the pricing decisions. They are used to set the standard but not the selling price.[3]

Since the logic of the above analysis is correct, why is it not more commonly used in practice? The reasons are related to the fact that the required information is often incomplete. Seldom can the average-revenue, the marginal-revenue, and the marginal-cost curves be known with certainty. If these curves are not known, then the solution to the problem of output and price cannot be solved with absolute accuracy. For example, it might be argued that if prices were reduced, competitors would also reduce prices and output would not be increased. When plotting a firm's average-revenue curve the actions of competitors should be taken into consideration. If this is not done, the curve is meaningless. If it is done, the objection just mentioned is not applicable.

5.2   Break-Even Analysis

The break-even point is located where the total cost curve intersects the total revenue curve or equivalently where total revenue equals total cost. Conventional break-even analysis represents total revenue and total cost with straight lines. This assumes that output and sales can be increased without changing price (at least, the effect of price changes are not shown) and that the firm operates at the same efficiency at all levels. Thus, to increase profit it is necessary merely to increase the number of units sold. The conventional analysis is illustrated in Figure 5.5.

Several comments might be made concerning Figure 5.5. First, fixed costs are assumed to have two step increases over the relevant output range. It is common for the accountant to assume that the total-expense line can be approximated by a straight line between these steps. The point X represents the break-even point and the activity level Q_b the break-even activity level.[4] The curves are drawn down to zero activity even though the nature of the relationships are suspect in this region. These relationships may be established using the correlation-regression techniques discussed in Chapter 3. The regression line is of limited value over ranges where no data points exist. A very low activity level is an example of such a region.

---

[3] Recall that the standard price is that price needed to cover both variable and fixed costs and yield a selected profit margin.

[4] Note that when fixed costs jump, it may be possible to have more than one break-even point.

If the firm relaxes the requirements that the quantity sold can be increased with the price remaining unchanged and that the efficiency be constant, the plottings of total revenue and total costs are no longer straight lines. This

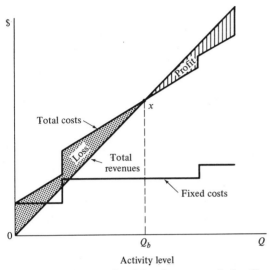

Figure 5.5 Conventional break-even analysis: Constant selling price

type of break-even chart is illustrated in Figure 5.6. Figure 5.6 is useful in explaining why the firm should produce at the level where marginal cost equals marginal revenue, since it shows that at this point profit is maximized. It also shows that there may be two break-even points. This phenomenon results from the fact that in order to increase output, price must be reduced, but if the price is reduced sufficiently total revenue ultimately decreases. Thus, the total-revenue curve slopes downward and recrosses the total-expense curve.

The horizontal axis of the conventional break-even chart (Figure 5.5) showed the number of units sold (the price is constant). The horizontal axis of the revised break-even chart (Figure 5.6) shows that the net result of the number of units sold and the price necessary to sell that number of units. Thus, the break-even chart of Figure 5.6 shows the revenues, costs, and profits for different levels of units sales and different prices (though for only one level of sales at each price).

Beneath the break-even chart of Figure 5.6 is a chart of marginal costs, marginal revenues, and average revenues. If the two charts are drawn correctly, they are interrelated in the following ways. The output where marginal cost equals marginal revenue, Q_m, is the output where the difference between the total-revenue and total-cost curves is the greatest (the profit is maximized and the slope of the total-cost curve equals the slope of the total-revenue

curve). The price at which the income is greatest on the break-even chart is
the price determined by the intersection of the vertical line through the point
where marginal cost equals marginal revenue, point B, and the average-revenue curve. The point where total revenue reaches a maximum, point A, is
where the marginal revenue is equal to zero. The marginal-cost curve reaches
a minimum at the point where the total-cost curve changes from concave
downward to concave upward. Finally, the two break-even points, Q_{b_1} and

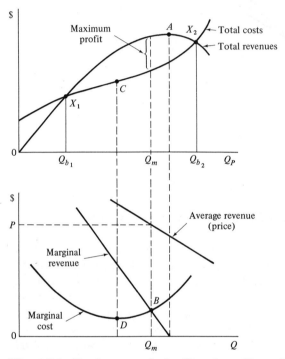

**Figure 5.6   Break-even analysis: Changing selling prices. Units sold and the prices
at which they are sold (moving to the right the price decreases and the units sold
increase)**

Q_{b_2}, (neither of which appears in the lower graph), bracket the optimal level
of activity.

The presentation of a break-even chart with changing prices is not meant
to suggest that the conventional break-even chart with its assumption of
constant prices is not useful. In many cases it is useful. However, if the need
is for a chart showing the results of using different possible price-quantity
relations, a figure similar to Figure 5.6 should be used.

A common practice of managers is to draw a break-even chart assuming
the present price and to show that a decrease in price requires greater sales in
order to break even. There is no question that the lower the price, the higher

the break-even point in terms of units sold and total revenues. The lowest conceivable break-even point is a price equal to the sum of the variable costs of one unit and the total fixed costs. Thus only one unit would have to be sold to break even. But would that unit be sold?

A careful look at Figure 5.6 shows that the optimal price and output are determined by reference to the marginal-cost, marginal-revenue, and average-revenue curves. The effect on the break-even point is not considered, nor should it be. The conventional break-even analysis is inadequate for deter-mining the optimal price and output. For example, Figure 5.7 shows a break-even chart with two possible revenue lines, R_1 and R_2, which are the result of two prices, P_1 and P_2. All other things being equal, the price that leads to the revenue line R_1 appears more desirable since it gives a lower break-even point and higher profits at every point of output. However, it is impossible to determine the better of the two prices until the probable revenues to be earned

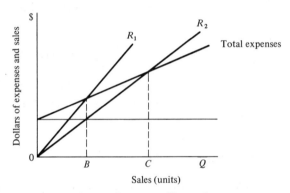

Figure 5.7 Comparing two selling prices

following each of the two suggested price policies are inserted. Assume that with price P_1, which results in the revenue curve R_1, the firm operates at the break-even point B; but with price P_2 the firm sells an amount equal to capacity, Q. In this case, price P_2, which results in line R_2, is the more desirable, even though the indicated break-even point with that price is higher. The fact that a larger dollar amount of sales (or of units sold) is needed to break-even does not indicate that the break-even point is harder to attain. Again, a price equal to the sum of the variable cost per unit and the total fixed costs gives the lowest break-even point, but it may be difficult to sell that one unit necessary to break even.

It is also important to recognize that break-even analysis is essentially an *ex ante* static analysis. The initial *ex ante* diagram cannot easily be used to explore changes in the activity levels over time. This is the result of the irreversibility of efficiency changes and the sticky nature of costs to decreases in activity levels.

5.2.1 Break-Even Analysis and Changes in Costs and Sales Price

If the firm is selling its product at an optimal price (marginal revenue equals marginal costs) prior to a change leading to increased efficiency (in the form of decreased marginal costs), then the profitable action is for the manager to decrease his price and increase his output. This is not done altruistically to share the increased profits with the consumer but rather to increase the profits of the firm. Inspection of Figure 5.6 (particularly the lower portion) shows that any lowering of the marginal-cost curve results in the optimal output being increased, and in a lower price in order to sell these extra units. The profits of the firm are increased by the amount of the increase in the area between the marginal-revenue and marginal-cost curves from the origin to their intersection.

The same result can also be derived from the upper portion of Figure 5.6. A decline in the marginal cost due to an increase in efficiency results in a decrease in the slope of the total-cost curve at all points and a lowering of the curve. (The marginal cost is the slope of the total-cost curve.) The slope of the cost curve now equals the slope of the total-revenue line at a point above Q_m. Thus the optimal output is increased and a lower price is required to sell the larger output.

If a change is made in selling expenditures, it can be expected that the break-even chart will change. For example, increased advertising expenditures may enable the firm to increases its prices without decreasing sales.

5.2.2 Break-Even Charts, *Ex Post* Analysis, and Cost Control

Break-even charts are used extensively in reviewing and analyzing past results, since they show at a glance when favorable or unfavorable variances exist. Frequently it is easier to get executives to look at charts than at tabular presentations.

One popular type of break-even chart used for this kind of analysis is shown in Figure 5.8. Instead of revenues and budgeted costs, just the difference between the two (budgeted profit) is plotted for different levels of sales. The actual profit for the period (a month here) is marked on the graph; the location of the actual profit in relation to the budgeted profit determines whether the budgeted profit for the actual level of activity was attained. In Figure 5.8 the profit for January is more than budgeted and the profit for February is less than budgeted. One explanation could be that expenses were not reduced rapidly enough as sales declined. The expected variability around the line as determined perhaps from a correlation-regression analysis would be useful in evaluating the significance of the observed deviations.

An alternative presentation would show only the budgeted costs for the different levels of sales and the actual expenses for the different time periods. Such a graph is shown in Figure 5.9.

In addition to showing the budgeted and actual total costs, it is desirable to break down the totals by types of cost, by departments, and by product lines. Charts may be prepared for any of these breakdowns, so that the budgeted and actual results may be compared for any level of operations.

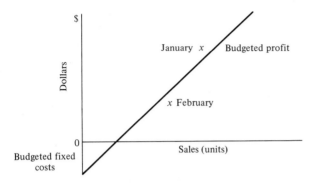

Figure 5.8   Budgeted and actual income

Also for many costs, measures of activity other than sales are more appropriate as explanatory variables. Indeed, several variables may be employed using the correlation-regression techniques described in Chapter 3. Graphs can then be constructed to illustrate the net effect of each independent variable. Thus the direct-labor costs incurred might be plotted against number of

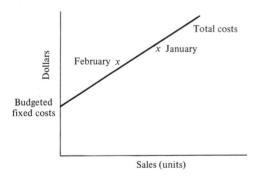

Figure 5.9   Budgeted and actual costs

units of product actually produced and/or machine hours, while the wage costs of accounts payable clerks are plotted against invoices processed and/or hours worked. For each cost classification one or more appropriate measures of activity should be determined. An examination of these charts can direct efforts toward areas where possible savings can be achieved.

5.2.3 Break-Even Analysis and Uncertainty

Assume two different break-even charts as shown in Figure 5.10. The slope of the line gives the contribution margin per unit. Situation (b) may be interpreted to be the same as situation (a) except that the profit line results from a higher price or lower variable cost. Is the higher price in situation (b) more desirable than the price in situation (a)? The break-even point is lower, but this is an inevitable result of a higher contribution margin; however, it assures nothing about the likelihood of occurrence of the different possible profits following either pricing policy. The change in the break-even point cannot be used as the criterion in making the decision.

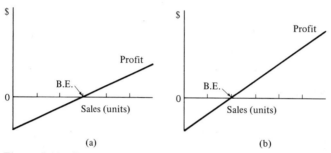

(a)   (b)

Figure 5.10   Break-even charts for two different prices for the same product

A more reasonable decision-making process would first establish for a given price policy the probability density function, showing the likelihood of selling different amounts of product.[5] See Figure 5.11 where such a distribution is superimposed on a break-even chart. The left-hand vertical axis still records dollars while the right-hand vertical axis gives the probability density of sales at that point. The distribution is assumed to be continuous and unimodal but it is not assumed to be normal or even symmetrical.[6]

The probability density function for demand (and thus sales) shows the relative likelihood of each level of sales. The total area under the curve is equal to one and the area over any sales interval is equal to the probability that sales will be in that interval. Such a curve could be developed from historical data and it might be substantially modified for circumstances the

[5] In this chapter the probability distribution of the number of units sold is assumed to be the same as the number of units demanded. The possibility of the firm's being unable to fill an order because demand is in excess of the number of units on hand, with the result that the customer buys elsewhere, could be allowed for but the solution to this problem then becomes more complex because it combines pricing, production, and inventory decisions. The separation of pricing, production, and inventory decisions is unrealistic, but it is helpful in understanding one segment of the decision. Also, while optimizing a segment of the firm may not be the ideal solution, it is frequently an important feasible solution.

[6] Normality is introduced later but it is not required for this step of the analysis.

decision maker believes now exist which are not adequately reflected by the historical data.

If the choice is made to produce, the profit, Y, for a given price policy is $Y = a + bx$, and the expected profit is obtained by taking the expectation:[7]

$$E(Y) = a + bE(X).$$

The term a is equal to or less than zero and measures the negative of the fixed costs. If the decision maker chooses not to produce, the return is zero in all

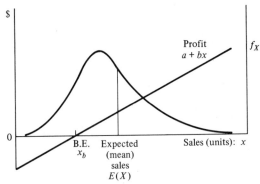

Figure 5.11   Break-even chart with a probability distribution over demand super-imposed

cases. Thus he need only compute the expected profit associated with the decision "produce" and take the action to produce if the expected profits exceeds zero. He is basing his decision on the expected profits.[8] It is assumed that the fixed cost represents the opportunity costs of using the production facility in the best alternative manner.

A decision can be made on the basis of the expected state (such as expected demand) value whenever the payoff functions for the actions are linear

----

[7] Equivalently, the expected income is equal to the product of the income at each level of sales and the probability density of that level of sales integrated over all sales levels; that is, by

$$\int_0^\infty (a + bx)f_X(x)\,dx. \tag{5.1}$$

Sometimes the evaluation of the integral given by this expression becomes rather complex and it is therefore useful to know that the decision can be made on the basis of the expected level of sales when the payoff function is linear.

[8] The assumption is implicitly made that the monetary values represent relevant measures of the impact of the outcomes on the manager (in more technical terms, the decision maker's utility for money is linear).

functions. For example, suppose the payoffs for two different decisions involving linear payoffs are given by

Action	Payoff
1:	$a_1 + b_1 x$
2:	$a_2 + b_2 x$

where $b_1 > b_2$ and $a_1 < a_2$ to assure that the two lines cross, and the actual value of x is independent of the two actions. Then the break-even sales level, x_b, is found by setting the two equations equal and solving. This yields

$$x_b = \frac{a_2 - a_1}{b_1 - b_2}. \tag{5.2}$$

Action 1 is more desirable than action 2 if

$$E(a_1 + b_1 X) > E(a_2 + b_2 X)$$

or

$$a_1 + b_1 E(X) > a_2 + b_2 E(X)$$

or

$$b_1 E(X) - b_2 E(X) > a_2 - a_1.$$

Thus action 1 is more desirable if

$$E(X) > \frac{a_2 - a_1}{b_1 - b_2} = x_b. \tag{5.3}$$

Equation 5.3 indicates that if the expectation is greater than the break-even, the expected payoff from action 1 exceeds that from action 2. Action 2 is more desirable if the expected value of X is below the break-even. This result is independent of the shape of the distribution; it depends only on the value of the expectation. For the present example, the payoffs from the decision to produce are represented by the equation for action 1 with slope greater than zero while the payoffs for the decision not to produce are represented by a line coincident with the X-axis and a slope of zero.

The expected level (the mean) of sales may not, however, always be easy to determine. The modal value of sales is the most likely level, and the median value is that level of sales for which the odds are equal that it will or will not be exceeded. These two values are perhaps relatively easy to visualize and discuss with the manager. Mean sales has no such simple interpretation or visualization. Furthermore, for skewed distributions such as the one in Figure 5.11, the mean tends to be slightly larger than the median. If median sales exceed the break-even in this case, the decision to take action 1 is still best since the mean exceeds the median. But if median sales are less than but close to the break-even, the best decision may not be clear. Experience with moderately skewed distributions indicates that as a general rule of thumb the median falls about two thirds of the distance from the mode toward the mean.[9] Using this general relationship, the mean can be estimated for moderately skewed distributions by the formula $E(X) = \text{mo} + \frac{3}{2}[\text{med} - \text{mo}]$. If the probability distribution can be assumed to be symmetrical then the mean, median, and mode are identical and the decision process is again simplified.

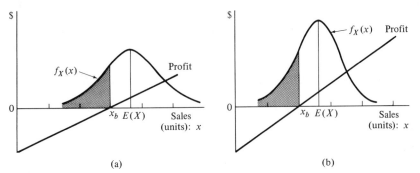

(a) (b)

Figure 5.12 Break-even charts for two different prices for the same product and different demand distributions

Turning now to the choice between the two prices whose profit functions are graphed in Figure 5.10, a decision is obtained by examining the expected profits since both payoff functions are linear. However, a different probability distribution applies to each price decision because price influences demand. The distributions for the example illustrated in Figure 5.12 assume that a lower price, case (a), increases the likelihood of larger sales levels. In this situation both distributions are assumed to have different means and variances. Since expected sales exceed the break-even level in both cases, a choice should be made between the two prices based on expected profits. Thus a solution can be obtained by evaluating expression (5.1) for both price situations and selecting the price that yields the larger expected income. Equivalently, the expression for the expected profit given by equation (5.4) can be used.[10]

$$\text{Expected profit} = E(Y) = b[E(X) - x_b] \qquad (5.4)$$

[9] This is a result of using Pearson's coefficient of skewness.
[10] If $Y = a + bX$, then $E(Y) = a + bE(X)$. At the break-even point $Y = 0$ and $a = -bx_b$. Therefore $E(Y) = -bx_b + bE(X) = b[E(X) - x_b]$.

where b is the slope of the profit function (the contribution margin per unit); $E(X)$ is expected sales; and x_b is the break-even sales volume in units.

Equation (5.4) states that the expected profit associated with any price is given by the product of the contribution margin with the amount by which expected sales exceed the break-even sales volume.

Example

Assume that the contribution margin per unit is $2 in case (a) and $2.50 in case (b), fixed costs are $100,000, and expected sales are 60,000 units in case (a) and 46,000 units in case (b); then the break-even sales level (x_b) is 50,000 in case (a) and 40,000 in case (b). The expected profits are $E(Y) = 2(60,000 - 50,000) = \$20,000$ in case (a) and $E(Y) = 2.50(46,000 - 40,000) = \$15,000$ in case (b). The lower contribution margin is preferred.

If $E(X) < x_b$, equation (5.4) would be negative (i.e., an expected loss would be indicated).

In most practical problems there are other uncertainties (although typically of a lesser magnitude). Thus there is uncertainty concerning the various costs that will be experienced (even if suitable measures could be agreed on), the performance of the employees, the lives of the equipment, and so on. Introduction of these complexities is considered by the authors to be beyond the scope of this volume.[11]

The probability distributions can be used to obtain measures of riskiness associated with each price distribution. The shaded areas in Figure 5.12(a) and (b) represent the probability of failing to achieve the break-even level of sales. If the previous example is used, and now assuming normality, and that the standard deviation of the sales distribution $\sigma(X)$, is known, then this area can be obtained from a table of the normal probability distribution function.[12,13] Assuming $\sigma(X) = 10,000$ and using Table I in the appendix.

$$P(x < x_b) = P\left(\frac{x - E(X)}{\sigma(X)} < \frac{x_b - E(X)}{\sigma(X)}\right)$$

$$= P\left(z < \frac{50,000 - 60,000}{10,000}\right) = P(z < -1) = 0.1587.$$

[11] The interested reader is referred to R. K. Jaedicke and A. Robichek, "Cost-Volume-Profit Analysis Under Conditions of Uncertainty," *The Accounting Review*, October 1964, pp. 917–926.

[12] An alternative and theoretically superior means of incorporating riskiness into the analyses is to use utility theory to determine the payoffs. The analysis so far assumes the utility function is linear with money and that decisions can therefore be made using expected values. If true, the risk measures derived here are not relevant. Determining and using utilities is still, however, more of an art than a science.

[13] If $E(X)$ and $\sigma(X)$ are known or can be estimated and are finite this probability can be estimated using Tchebychev's inequality for cases where the probability density function is not normal.

The choice between alternatives might be based on the size of these probabilities where expectations were considered inadequate. It is not clear, however, just how much of a difference in these probabilities is needed to compensate for a larger expectation. It is a matter of judgment on which most managers would experience some difficulty.

Another indication of riskiness is the expectation associated with only the negative portion of the profit function; that is, for values of $x < x_b$. This partial loss expectation is given by

$$\int_{-\infty}^{x_b} (a + bx)f_X(x)\, dx. \tag{5.5}$$

In Appendix 5A the negative of this integral is shown to be equal to[14]

$$b\sigma(X)[n_Z(z_b) + z_bN_Z(z_b)] \tag{5.6}$$

where

$$z_b = [x_b - E(X)] \div \sigma(X) \qquad \text{and} \qquad x_b < E(X).$$

For the continuing example, the partial loss expectation is given by (note that $z_b = (50{,}000 - 60{,}000)/10{,}000 = -1$).

$$\text{Expected partial loss} = \$2(10{,}000)[n_Z(-1) - z_bN_Z(-1)]$$
$$= \$20{,}000[(0.2420) - 1(0.1587)] = \$1{,}666.$$

Although the expected partial loss is part of the total expected value, it may be weighed separately by the manager in selecting among alternatives when the total expectations are considered inadequate measures.

Still a third measure of riskiness is supplied by the ratio of the expectation associated with the negative portion of the profit function, the partial loss expectation given by equation (5.6), to the partial gain expectation associated with the positive portion of the profit function (that is, for values of $x > x_b$) given by equation (5.7) derived in Appendix 5A where $x_b < E(X)$:

$$b\sigma(X)[n_Z(z_b) - z_bN_Z(-z_b)]. \tag{5.7}$$

In the present example, equation (5.7) yields

$$\$2(10{,}000)[n_Z(-1) + 1N_Z(1)] = \$20{,}000[0.2420 + 1(0.8413)] = \$21{,}666.$$

The ratio is then $\$1{,}666/\$21{,}666 \doteq 0.077$. Where the total expectation, $\$21{,}666 - \$1{,}666 = \$20{,}000$, is not an adequate measure of the impact of the separate possible outcomes on the manager, this is perhaps the best of the three risk measures offered since it includes the positive as well as the negative possibilities. Presumably, the larger the value of this ratio the less

[14] The expectations given by equations (5.6) and (5.7) assume a normal density function for sales. Also $n_z(z_b)$ is the value of the standardized normal-density function at $\pm z$ and $N_z(z_b)$ is the value of the standardized normal-distribution function at z_b.

attractive the investment. However, it is possible for an alternative to have a larger ratio but also for the partial gain expectation to have increased more than the partial loss expectation. Suppose, for example, that the denominator for a second alternative is $25,000 and the numerator is $2,000. This gives a ratio of 0.080 and a total expectation of $23,000. If the manager rejects the second alternative in favor of the first, he rejects the net increase in the total expectation because of the larger ratio. Care must be taken to be sure the manager wishes to behave in this way.

5.2.4 Nonlinear Profit Functions

In the previous example profit is assumed to be a linear function of unit sales; that is, profit plotted against sales is a straight line. In this situation the profit resulting from expected (mean) sales could be used in decision making since it is equal to the expected profit. Whenever the profit plotted against sales is a straight line, mean sales can be used in computing expected profit, or, equivalently, the profits of the different possible sales weighted by the probability of their occurrence could be used.

The following example assumes that profit is not a linear function of sales.

Example
Assume the probability mass function for sales is given in Table 5–1

Table 5–1   Probability Mass Function for Sales

Sales (units)	P (sales)	Column 1 × column 2 (units)
1,200	0.30	360
700	0.50	350
0	0.20	0
		Expected unit sales = 710

The expected profit is computed in Table 5–2

Table 5–2   Expected Profit

Sales (units)	Profit*	P (sales)	Column 2 × column 3
1,200	$20,000	0.30	$6,000
700	0	0.50	0
0	(35,000)	0.20	(7,000)
		Expected profit =	($1,000)

* The profit figure for different levels of sales are assumed to be the result of economic analysis and are not given by a linear function of sales.

There is an expected loss of $1,000; thus the decision being considered is not desirable. The mean sales of 710 units cannot be used to make the decision because profit is not a linear function of sales in this example. Also, the sales distribution is skewed. The risk measures described earlier could again be used but the calculations are more difficult when normality cannot be assumed.

Example

For another example suppose that the sales distribution is continuous and can be approximated by the probability distribution $f_X(x) = r - \dfrac{r^2}{2} x$ where sales are between 0 and $2/r$. Furthermore, assume that the profit function is quadratic of the form $a + bx^2$, then the expected profit is given by (where $a \leq 0, b > 0, r > 0$)

$$\int_0^{2/r} (a + bx^2)(r - \frac{r^2}{2} x) \, dx. \tag{5.8}$$

Equation (5.8) can be integrated to yield equation (5.9). (The steps in the integration are omitted here.)

$$arx - \frac{ar^2}{4} x^2 + \frac{br}{3} x^3 - \frac{br^2}{8} x^4 \Big]_0^{2/r} = a + 2b/3r^2. \tag{5.9}$$

Expected profit is a function of the fixed costs, a, the contribution per unit, b, and the constant r in the probability function. But the relationship is not a simple function of the expected level of sales.

5.2.5 Break-Even Analysis and Changes in Product Mix.

Break-even analysis is at its best when there is a set price and only one product is being sold. The problems of price changes have been discussed and a reasonable solution suggested. The problem of product mix is more complex. Not only may the total output vary, but also the amount of each product sold may change from period to period. If the different products have different profit margins the profit per dollar of sales will differ for each product and the break-even point becomes a function of the mix of sales.

One possibility is to draw break-even charts by product lines. The costs that can be identified directly with the product line are plotted to obtain a break-even point of direct costs (direct in terms of the product line). On top of these costs, in order to obtain another break-even point, the costs that are assigned to the product as the result of indirect-cost allocations may be plotted.

If one break-even chart is desired for a company that produces several different products, the assumption of a normal product mix might be made

and this assumption clearly indicated on the chart. In any event, the usefulness of a break-even chart for the company as a whole decreases as the
number of products made by the firm increases.

5.2.6 Break-Even Analysis and Changes in Inventory

A break-even chart implicitly assumes that the fixed costs incurred by the
firm are charged against the revenues of the period. This is consistent with a
variable-costing procedure which charges only variable costs to product but
is not consistent with normal cost-accounting procedures (except when there
are no changes in inventory and cost variances are charged against the
income of the period).

Assume that a firm is using a cost-accounting system with overhead
absorption based on normal activity. If there is an increase in inventory during the period, then some of the fixed costs incurred during the period are
applied to the goods in inventory and are not deducted from the revenues of
the period. If this income is compared to the budgeted income (the amount
the firm expects to earn according to the break-even chart), the reported income is greater, all other things assumed to be equal. There are two solutions
to this problem. One would be to use variable-costing procedures in computing the income of the period. The second would be to adjust either the
budgeted income of the break-even chart or the income which is a result of the
cost-accounting system for such changes in the inventory.

5.2.7 Break-Even Analysis and Uniform Cost Control

Break-even analysis assumes that constant attention is given to cost control
over the range of activity considered. This may not, in fact, be the case. For
example, in times when business is expanding rapidly, management may tend
to emphasize volume with a resulting decrease in attention to cost control.
Poorer materials and workers with marginal skills may be used at the same
time that prices and wages are rising. Labor turnover increases. Simultaneously, selling prices may increase together with a shift of the entire demand schedule to the right. It is also not uncommon for selling expenses per
order to decline although total selling costs may rise. The net result is likely to
change. An increase will occur if variable costs increase more than the selling price.

5.2.8 Break-Even Analysis and Fixed Costs

The break-even sales volume is determined in part by the level of fixed
costs. The question arises as to how these costs should be measured. Many
possibilities exist including historical cost allocations, adjusted historical
costs, current costs, replacement costs, and so on. The choice may be viewed

itly as an approximation of the opportunity costs of using the fixed
tors of production. In the conventional analysis historical costs are used.
Thus a given percentage change in the fixed-cost factor changes the break-even
level of activity by the same percentage. This is true if

$$bx_b = a. \tag{5.10}$$

Where b is the unit contribution margin per unit, x_b the break-even sales
level, and a the fixed cost, a change of y per cent in fixed costs yields a new
fixed-cost level of $(1 + y)(a)$. If equality is to be maintained in equation
(5.10), then

$$(1 + y)bx_b = (1 + y)(a)$$

or

$$b[(1 + y)x_b] = (1 + y)(a).$$

This means that the break-even level of activity also increases by y per cent,
given b constant.

5.3 The Profit Value Ratio (PV Ratio)

Break-even analysis is closely related to capital-budgeting decisions involving expansion of capacity or changes in the production function. For example, should a company produce aluminum if it is currently in
the chemical industry, or, alternatively, should it expand its productive
capacity for aluminum if it is currently in the aluminum industry but finds its
productive capacity too small?

Before expanding the productive facilities for a present product, or adding a
new product, management must decide as to the relative desirability of the
different profit possibilities of the different product lines. These are normal
capital-budgeting decisions, and the discounted cash-flow capital-budgeting
procedure is a proper method of analysis for this type of problem.[15]

Some companies, however, prefer to use a different technique in deciding
which product is worthy of additional sales effort and productive capacity.
The procedure makes use of the ratio of the variable margin to sales (the excess of revenues over variable costs, divided by sales). This ratio is called by
various names, but the exact title is unimportant. The terminology PV ratio
(PV standing for profit value) is used here.

[15] Capital-budgeting decisions and the associated cost implications are discussed in
Chapters 13, 14, and 15.

The PV ratio fails as a guide to the type of decision being considered for two reasons. First, it relies on the excess of revenues over variable costs for the present manufacturing process. The manufacturing process being considered for the additional productive capacity may make use of a different degree of automation and thus may have a different PV ratio. The PV ratio fails to take into consideration the capital outlays required by the additional productive capacity and the additional fixed costs that are added (for example, the additional accountants, quality-control personnel, and foremen who will be required for the operation and whose salaries become fixed costs). Secondly, the PV ratio fails to consider the number of units sold, or which can be sold.

Inspection of the PV ratios of products can suggest profitable product lines that might be emphasized and unprofitable lines that should be re-evaluated and possibly eliminated from the company's offerings. But until the analysis is broadened to take into consideration all incremental costs incurred because of the expansion, a decision cannot be made as to whether or not to expand the line.

The PV ratio is a questionable device for decision making, but it does give an indication of the relative profitability of the different profit lines, if all other things are equal. For example, an automobile manufacturer may make ten different models of his low-priced car. Should a car be pushed by salesmen because of the high PV ratio? If the fixed costs connected with producing additional cars are truly fixed the car with the highest PV ratio may be the most desirable car to sell. But even here the conclusion may not be correct, for the PV ratio generally uses average revenues and average-variable costs. The decision is one which should be made using marginal analysis.

The use of PV ratios defined in terms of marginal profits per marginal dollar of costs can lead to reasonable decisions. But even this ratio should not be used in decisions that are of a nonmarginal nature (such as one involving plant expansion). The PV ratio as generally computed is useful for forming impressions, not making decisions.

5.4 Summary

It is possible to arrive at a standard price of a product by computing the cost of product and adding a reasonable profit. The cost of product should include fixed-overhead elements determined using normal activity to compute the overhead rate. A standard price is a reasonable target. In the long run the price of the product must be close to the standard price in order to attract additional investment to the industry. With incomplete knowledge as to the characteristics of the demand curve (because of uncertainty as to the reaction of competitors and customers to price changes), it may be sensible for a firm to charge a standard price for its product. A "fair" profit resulting from the use of a standard price may be more attractive to management than the dangers accompanying a price reduction justified using the argument that the firm is attempting to find the sales volume which equates marginal cost and marginal revenue. Failure to predict correctly the firm's demand curve (average-revenue curve) can result in a situation where the additional costs are greater than the additional revenues. Why was the price reduced? Because it was thought that the increase in the number of units sold would be greater than actually resulted (the elasticity of demand was overestimated). Thus, keeping the present price may be an economically valid decision if the element of uncertainty which accompanies any price change is taken into consideration. The theoretical solution to the problem of determining the optimal price requires a knowledge of the number of units likely to be sold at different prices and the marginal costs for different levels of output. The theoretical solution does not prevent the selling price from being greater than the marginal costs, but it does mean that the fixed costs do not enter into the decision.

Frequently prices are set with reference to other factors than those mentioned in this chapter. Long-run considerations may enter into the decision; for example, the effect a price may have on customer goodwill, or the possibility of competitors entering the market if the price is too high. These factors may lead to setting a price lower than the price which would maximize short-run profits.

Break-even analysis can be broadened from its conventional use to take a variety of factors into account. Methods are suggested in the chapter for dealing with uncertainty about demand, changes in product mix, and so on. Nevertheless, the method often makes substantive assumptions, such as constant-cost efficiency and no change in inventories, both of which limit its application.

The output and pricing decision may be made to maximize profits, but a firm does not know if it is going to make a profit. It may very well be that it will be minimizing a loss. To determine whether a profit will be made, it is necessary to compare the average cost and average revenue, or total cost and total revenue. But the pricing and output decisions may still be made without knowing whether or not a profit will be earned.

APPENDIX 5A
DERIVATION OF THE EXPRESSIONS FOR
THE EXPECTED PROFIT AND
PARTIAL EXPECTATION EQUATIONS

This Appendix derives the equation for expected profit (5.4), the expectation associated only with the negative portion of the income line (5.6), and the portion associated with the positive portion of the income line (5.7). The following assumptions are made and the following notation is used:

Assumptions and notation
1. The decision maker's utility function for money is linear.
2. The sales distribution is normal with mean $E(X)$ and standard deviation $\sigma(X)$; i.e. $n_X(x; E(X), \sigma(X))$ or more simply $n_X(x)$.
3. The profit function is linear of the form $a + bx$ where b is the contribution margin per unit and a is nonpositive.
4. The expected sales level, $E(X)$, exceeds the break-even, x_b, otherwise the case will be one with an over-all expected loss.

The situation is illustrated in Figure 5A.1.

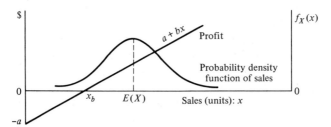

Figure 5A.1   Break-even chart and sales distribution

The vertical axis on the left is in dollars and applies to the profit line. The vertical axis on the right gives the height of the normal-probability density function for sales. The area under the normal-probability curve to the left of any point x is given by

$$N_X(x; E(X), \sigma(X)) = N_X(x) = \int_{-\infty}^{x} \frac{1}{\sigma(X)\sqrt{2\pi}} \exp\left[-\frac{(x - E(X))^2}{2\sigma^2(X)}\right]$$

and is illustrated in Figure 5A.2. (This is called the normal distribution function or the cumulative normal-probability function.)

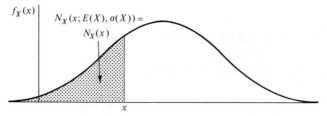

Figure 5A.2   Cumulative normal-probability function

After standardizing, the normal-density function has mean zero and variance one and the expressions for the normal-density function and the normal-
distribution function can be written as $n_Z(z)$ and $N_Z(z)$ respectively.

From Figure 5A.1, the total expected value is given by

$$\int_{-\infty}^{+\infty} (a + bx)n_X(x; E(X), \sigma(X))\, dx \tag{5A.1}$$

or, breaking this integral into two pieces,

$$\int_{-\infty}^{x_b} (a + bx)n_X(x)\, dx + \int_{x_b}^{+\infty} (a + bx)n_X(x)\, dx \tag{5A.2}$$

Since the value $a + bx$ at any sales level can be written as $b(x - x_b)$, expression (5A.2) becomes

$$\int_{-\infty}^{x_b} b(x - x_b)n_X(x)\, dx + \int_{x_b}^{\infty} b(x - x_b)n_X(x)\, dx. \tag{5A.3}$$

Now let $z = (x - E(X))/\sigma(X)$. Then $x = z\sigma(X) + E(X)$, and $x_b = z_b\sigma(X) + E(X)$. Consider now only the first integral in expression (5A.3)

$$\int_{-\infty}^{x_b} b(x - x_b)n_X(x)\, dx. \tag{5A.4}$$

Adding and subtracting $E(X)$ gives

$$b\int_{-\infty}^{x_b} ((x - E(X)) + (E(X) - x_b)n_X(x)\, dx. \tag{5A.5}$$

Separating the integral and factoring out the constant $(E(X) - x_b)$ yields

$$b\left[\int_{-\infty}^{x_b} (x - E(X))n_X(x)\, dx + (E(X) - x_b)\int_{-\infty}^{x_b} n_X(x)\, dx\right] \tag{5A.6}$$

Now using the fact that

$$n_X(x) = \frac{1}{\sigma(X)\sqrt{2\pi}} \exp\left[-\frac{(x - E(X))^2}{2\sigma^2(X)}\right]$$

and $z = [x - E(X)]/\sigma(X)$ so that $x = \sigma(X)z + E(X)$, then $dx = \sigma(X)\, dz$ and substitution into equation (4A.6) with a suitable change in the limits of integration yields

$$b\left[\int_{-\infty}^{z_b} \frac{z\sigma(X)}{\sigma(X)\sqrt{2\pi}} \exp\left[-\frac{z^2}{2}\right]\sigma(X)\,dz\right.$$

$$\left. - z_b\sigma(X)\int_{-\infty}^{z_b} \frac{1}{\sigma(X)\sqrt{2\pi}} \exp\left[-\frac{z^2}{2}\right]\sigma(X)\,dz\right]. \qquad (5A.7)$$

Simplifying and collecting terms gives

$$b\sigma(X)\left[\underbrace{\int_{-\infty}^{z_b} \frac{z}{\sqrt{2\pi}} \exp\left[-\frac{z^2}{2}\right]dz}_{\text{1st integral}} - z_b\underbrace{\int_{-\infty}^{z_b} \frac{1}{\sqrt{2\pi}} \exp\left[-\frac{z^2}{2}\right]dz}_{\text{2nd integral}}\right] \quad (5A.8)$$

The second integral in expression (5A.8) is the probability $z < z_b$, which is the value of the normal-distribution function at z_b; $N_z(+z_b)$. This is the area illustrated in Figure 5A.1 for $x = z_b$ and $z_b < 0$. To evaluate the first integral, make the substitution $v = z^2/2$. Thus $dv = z\,dz$. Then the integral

$$\frac{1}{\sqrt{2\pi}} \int ze^{-z^2/2}\,dz$$

becomes

$$\frac{1}{\sqrt{2\pi}} \int e^{-v}\,dv.$$

Integrating the latter gives

$$\frac{1}{\sqrt{2\pi}}(-e^{-v} + c)$$

or, substituting

$$\frac{1}{\sqrt{2\pi}}(-e^{-z^2/2} + c)$$

and for the present problem, using the limits of integration $-\infty$ and z_b this is

$$\frac{1}{\sqrt{2\pi}}(e^{-z_b^2/2} - e^{-\infty 2/2}) = -\frac{1}{\sqrt{2\pi}}e^{-z_b/2}.$$

This gives the negative of the value of the normal density function at z_b which by symmetry is $-n_Z(z_b)$. Thus the partial expectation associated with the negative portion of the profit function when $E(X) > x_b$ is given by

$$-bo(X)[n_Z(z_b) + z_b N_Z(z_b)]. \tag{5.6}$$

(Note that z_b will be negative when $E(X) > x_b$ and that the result of this computation is the partial expected loss if the minus sign is ignored).

By a similar line of argument not reproduced here, the partial expectation associated with the positive portion of the profit line and thus with the second integral in expression (5A.8) is given by

$$\int_{x_b}^{\infty} b(x - x_b)n_X(x; E(X), \sigma(X)) \, dx = bo(X)n_Z(z_b) - bo(X)z_b N_Z(-z_b)$$
$$= bo(X)[n_Z(z_b) - z_b N_Z(-z_b)]. \tag{5.7}$$

The total expectation is given by the sum of equations (5.6) and (5.7),

$$E(Y) = bo(X)[n_Z(z_b) - z_b N_Z(-z_b)] - bo(X)[n_Z(z_b) + z_b N_Z(z_b)]$$
$$= -bo(X)z_b[N_Z(-z_b) + N_Z(z_b)] = -bo(X)z_b \tag{5A.9}$$
$$= bo(X)\left[\frac{x - E(X)}{\sigma(X)}\right]: \quad \text{since } z_b < 0 \text{ in the present case:}$$
$$= b[E(X) - x_b]. \tag{5.4}$$

APPENDIX 5B
THE USE OF VALUES IN RESOURCE ALLOCATION DECISIONS

Accounting has traditionally turned to historical cost to evaluate the sacrifice associated with the use of fixed factors of production. The modern method however is to use values. This can be illustrated in the context of the solution to the dual of a linear programming formulation involving the allocation of fixed production resources.

Example
Assume there are two pieces of equipment (instead of equipment they could be identified as any fixed factors of production) with excess capacity of six and four hours. There are two products with the characteristics given in Table 5B–1.

Table 5B–1   Data for Linear Programming Problem

Product	Time Required on Equipment		Profit Contribution per Unit
	1	2	
X_1	3	$\frac{1}{2}$	12
X_2	2	1	4

The above situation may be described in terms of a linear programming formulation as: Maximize $P = 12X_1 + 4X_2$ where P is profit contribution, subject to

1. $3X_1 + 2X_2 \leq 6$ for equipment 1.
2. $\frac{1}{2}X_1 + X_2 \leq 4$ for equipment 2.
3. $X_1, X_2 \geq 0$.

The optimum solution is to produce two units of X_1 and no units of X_2. This is indicated by the lower tableau in Table 5B–2 obtained using the simplex method (X_3 is the slack variable for equipment 1 and X_4 is the slack variable for equipment 2). The total profit is given in tableau 2 to be $24 = 12(2) + 0(3)$, or it can be found directly using the objective function to be:

$$P = 12X_1 + 4X_2$$
$$P = 12(2) + 4(0) = 24.$$

Table 5B–2   Simplex Solution

			Tableau 1			
			$C_1 = 12$	$C_2 = 4$	$C_3 = 0$	$C_4 = 0$
Basis	C	Solution	X_1	X_2	X_3	X_4
X_3	0	6	3	2	1	0
X_4	0	4	$\frac{1}{2}$	1	0	1
$C_j - z_j$		0	-12	-4	0	0
			Tableau 2			
X_1	12	2	1	$\frac{2}{3}$	$\frac{1}{3}$	0
X_4	0	3	0	$\frac{2}{3}$	$-\frac{1}{6}$	1
$C_j - z_j$		24	0	-4	-4	0

Equipment 1's time is fully utilized but equipment 2 has three hours of free time as indicated by the solution value 3 for the variable slack X_4.

The dual to this problem can be obtained by letting U_1 equal the "cost" or value of one unit of equipment 1's time, U_2 equal the "cost" or value of one unit of equipment 2's time.

This gives: Minimize $C = 6U_1 + 4U_2$ where C is "cost" or value of the scarce resource, equipment time, subject to

1. $3U_1 + \frac{1}{2}U_2 \geq 12$ for product X_1.
2. $2U_1 + 1U_2 \geq 4$ for product X_2.
3. $U_1, U_2 \geq 0$.

The problem can again be solved using the simplex method or, since only two variables are involved, a graphical approach is possible. The graphic approach is illustrated in Figure 5B.1.

Inspection of Figure 5B.1 and the equation being minimized $(6U_1 + 4U_2)$ indicates that $U_1 = 4$, $U_2 = 0$ is the optimal solution since this is the feasible point that minimizes the objective function.

From a decision standpoint this means that an hour of time on equipment 1 has a value of $4 and an hour of time on equipment 2 has $0 value.[16] Note that the historical costs of equipment 1 and equipment 2 do not enter into the solution. The above solution indicates the firm could afford to pay $4 for one hour of equipment 1's time.

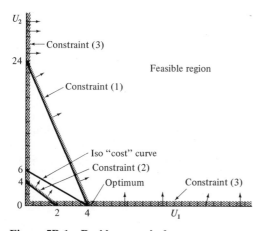

Figure 5B.1   Problem graphed

It is also possible to use the values in the solution to the linear programming problem to examine the sensitivity of the solution to changes in the profit-contribution figures. The simplex method indicates that the given solution holds so long as each $C_j - z_j$ term in the final tableau is nonpositive. The two $C_j - z_j$ terms for the variables not in the solution are calculated by the expressions

$$C_2 - z_2 = -4 = 4 - [(12)(\tfrac{2}{3})] \qquad\qquad (5B.1)$$

and

$$C_3 - z_3 = -4 = 0 - [12(\tfrac{1}{3}) - 0(-\tfrac{1}{6})]. \qquad\qquad (5B.2)$$

[16] For a more complete explanation of linear programming and the dual see H. Bierman, Jr., C. P. Bonini, and W. H. Hausman, *Quantitative Analysis for Business Decisions*, Homewood, Illinois: R. D. Irwin, 1969, pp. 320–341.

If a change in $C_1 = 12$ takes place, say to some new value, call it C_1', the solution will remain optimal if both the expressions (5B.1) and (5B.2) remain nonpositive. Consider first an increase in C_1; that is, suppose $C_1' > C_1$. This would cause both expressions (5B.1) and (5B.2) to be larger negatively. The solution would not change. However, a decline in C_1, if large enough, could alter the solution. The optimal solution will change if either expression (5B.1) or (5B.2) becomes positive. So long as C_1' remains nonnegative, expression (5B.2) will be nonpositive. Hence, by setting expression (5B.1) equal to zero and solving for C_1', the value at which there is a change in the optimal solution can be obtained. Solving

$$0 = 4 - [C_1'(\tfrac{2}{3})]$$

yields

$$C_1' = 6.$$

For the present problem, the solution given in tableau 2 is optimal so long as $C_1 > 6$ assuming no change in C_2.

A similar analysis can be made for changes in C_2 holding C_1 constant. In this case only increases in C_2 can affect the solution. This effect is again observed by examining expression (5B.1) since C_2 does not enter into expression (5B.2). Setting expression (5B.1) equal to zero and solving yields

$$0 = C_2' - [12(\tfrac{2}{3})]$$

or

$$C_2' = 8.$$

The present solution is optimal so long as $C_2 < 8$ assuming no change in C_1. The problem of concurrent changes in C_1 and C_2, resulting perhaps from a dependence between them, is more complex and is not illustrated here.[17] The limits developed can be used to determine when a new solution is required and the new solution will indicate the marginal advantage to be obtained from changing over to the new optimum compared to the value of the objective function if the nonoptimal solution is continued. This marginal advantage should then be compared to the cost of changeover.

A similar analysis can also be applied to changes in the technological coefficients. However the analysis is more complex. In fact, sensitivity analysis becomes a difficult task in a large organization engaged in many activities.

[17] See S. I. Gass, *Linear Programming*, New York: McGraw-Hill, 1964, Chapter 8.

QUESTIONS AND PROBLEMS

5–1 In a situation where a corporation desires a 20 per cent return on the plant assets it owns, would it be correct to start the budgeting process by computing the necessary profit and then conceiving decisions which will lead to the desired profit?

5–2 Assume the cost-accounting system produces a cost per unit of $50. What questions may be raised relative to this cost measure?

5–3 In establishing an optimal price should the firm take into consideration fixed costs of production?

5–4 The conventional break-even analysis shows total cost and total revenues as straight lines. What are the assumptions and limitations of using straight lines in this type of analysis?

5–5 Explain how the following curves are interrelated:
  a. Total revenue and marginal revenue.
  b. Total cost and marginal cost.

5–6 Discuss the following statement, "If you lower your price the break-even point will increase."

5–7 Assuming a firm is currently pricing its product optimally, should it change its price if it is able to shift its average variable-cost curve downward? Assume the average revenue curve slopes downward.

5–8 An automobile executive wants to expand the sales of his deluxe model since its ratio of gross margin to sales is higher than that of any other model. This expansion would require additional plant facilities. Discuss.

5–9 A corporation has fixed costs of $250,000 and variable costs of $2 per unit. The company is attempting to choose the best of three possible prices. The prices, mean sales, and the standard deviations of sales are as follows:

Prices	$2.50	$3.00	$3.50
Mean sales (units)	600,000	280,000	100,000
Standard deviations	40,000	30,000	20,000

Required: Based on expected monetary values, what price should be charged? (Compute the effected profit for each of the three prices and choose the price with the highest expected profit.) What is the break-even volume and what choice of price is best using expectations?

5–10 (Reference to problem 5–9).

Required:

a. For each possible price, what is the probability of operating at less than break-even?

b. For each possible price, what is the partial loss expectation?

c. For each possible price, what is the ratio of the partial loss expectations to the partial gain expectation (equation 5.7)?

d. Using these risk measures which alternative price is best?

5–11 The ABC Corporation is about to market a new product which has fixed costs of $100,000 and variable costs of $3 per unit at a level of production of 100,000 units. (There are changes in efficiency for different levels of sales.) The company is considering selling at a price of $4 per unit. The probability distribution of sales and the expected profit for the different levels of sales are:

Sales	P (sales)	Profit Given Sales
50,000	0.10	(25,000)
100,000	0.50	0
150,000	0.30	40,000
200,000	0.10	75,000

Required:

a. Compute the mean sales.

b. Compute the expected profit.

5–12 The demand for a product is said to have an elasticity greater than one if a decrease in the sales price of the product will result in an increase in total revenues. The Roger Corporation has hired an economist who has come up with the following schedule which shows that the elasticity of the product being sold by the Roger Corporation is greater than one (the demand is relatively elastic). The capacity of the plant is 150,000 units per year.

	Present Policy	If Price Is Reduced 10%	If Price Is Reduced 20%
Price per unit	$ 1.00	$ .90	$ .80
Unit sales (per year)	100,000.00	120,000.00	150,000.00
Fixed manufacturing costs (per year)	15,000.00	15,000.00	15,000.00
Variable manufacturing costs	.50 (per unit)		

Required:

a. Compute the total revenues following the three alternatives.

b. What are the break-even points?

c. Which price should the firm charge?

5–13 A corporation has fixed costs of $250,000 and variable costs of $2 per unit. The company is attempting to choose the best of three possible prices. The prices, mean sales, and the standard deviations of sales are as follows:

Price	$ 2.50	$ 3.00	$ 3.50
Mean sales (units)	500,000.00	280,000.00	200,000.00
Standard deviation	20,000.00	30,000.00	40,000.00

Required: Based on the expected monetary values, what price should be charged? Compute the break-even points for the three prices.

5–14 The Akron Company has two plants producing the same product and wants to know how the production decision should be made if it wishes to continue to split production between the two plants. Assume the product of the plants is sold in a perfectly competitive market.

An economist has been hired as a consultant. He suggests that each plant should produce so that their marginal cost equals marginal revenue (which in turn is equal to the price of the product).

Required: Comment on the recommendation.

5–15 The Akron Company has two plants producing the same product on a government order for 1,000 units. It wants to know how to split production between the two plants.

Required: How should the decision to split the production be decided?

5–16 In August of 1965 Ford of England slowed its production of automobiles and shifted to a four-day work week. It was suggested that the company increase its export of cars. The company stated that a good export position required a strong home market, since large production reduces unit costs. If the sales in the home market slow down, unit costs rise putting pressure on export sales prices (for a more complete report see *The New York Times* of August 24, 1965).

Required: Comment on the company's point of view.

5–17 The following diagram combines a traditional break-even analysis with a probability density function for demand.

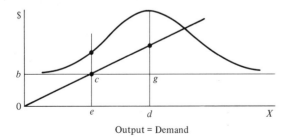

Output = Demand

a. Give an expression using the letters in the graph for the unit contribution margin.
b. Give the break-even output.
c. Should this firm produce? Why or why not?
d. Assuming the density function is normal, give an expression for the expected profit, i.e., the total expectation considering both the possible losses and gains.

5–18 The graph in this problem illustrates several average-cost curves and a revenue curve under the condition of perfect competition.

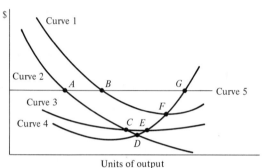

a. Name the five curves.
b. Indicate the break-even point.
c. Indicate the maximum profit point.
d. What area represents the total profits of the firm when it is producing at its optimal output level?

5–19 "Costs are a function of output increasing when output increases and decreasing when output decreases." Comment.

5–20 The American Dynamics Company experienced an increase in its break-even volume as sales expanded sharply over the period 1962–1968. This occurred despite the fact that their prices were increased enough to cover the direct increases in unit variable cost resulting from increases in direct material prices, wage rates, and related items. Can you suggest a reason for this occurrence?

5–21 One way to estimate fixed-cost levels is to fit a regression equation to the cost data and use the intercept term (the constant in the equation) as a measure of fixed costs. Is this a good procedure?

SUPPLEMENTARY READING

CHARNES, A., W. W. COOPER, and Y. IJIRI, "Breakeven Budgeting and Programming to Goals," *Journal of Accounting Research*, Spring 1963, pp. 16–43.

COLANTONI, S., R. MANES, and A. WHINSTON, "Programming, Profit Rates and Pricing Decisions," *The Accounting Review*, July 1969, pp. 467–481.

DEARDEN, J., *Cost and Budget Analysis*, Englewood Cliffs, N.J.: Prentice-Hall, 1962.

JAEDICKE, R. K., and A. ROBICHEK, "Cost-Volume-Profit Analysis Under Conditions of Uncertainty," *The Accounting Review*, October 1964, pp. 917–926.

MANES, R., "A New Dimension to Breakeven Analysis," *Journal of Accounting Research*, Spring 1966, pp. 87–100.

SAMUELS, J. M., "Opportunity Costing: An Application of Mathematical Programming," *Journal of Accounting Research*, Autumn 1965, pp. 182–191.

VICKERS, D., "On the Economics of Break-even," *The Accounting Review*, July 1960, pp. 405–412.

Chapter 6

Some Behavioral Aspects of Cost Control

The traditional approach to cost control has involved the comparison of actual results with budgeted or standard amounts that represent goals for management. For many years considerable attention has been given to improving the means by which such analyses could be used. Standards and the analysis of variances were used to increase the ability of management to exercise control over performance. The development of cost centers and the decentralization of decision making were in large part responses to the need for subcomponents within a firm that had control of specific resources and could therefore be evaluated in light of their utilization of these resources. Central to these developments was the assumption that the more sophisticated the system the greater the likelihood of success in controlling costs and improving performance. Indeed, there was perhaps a tendency for many firms to expect desirable results merely from the use of the techniques alone.

The importance of measuring and maintaining performance has not diminished. But in recent years attention has focused on a new dimension that has had and will continue to have a profound impact on the activity of the accountant. Although the importance of interpersonal relationships and individual behavior is not a new area of study and its impact on organizations and groups has been under examination for many years, it is only recently that the results have begun to have an impact on managerial accounting theory and practice.

There has developed an increased recognition of the importance of the organizational—and human—resource assets of the firm.[1] If management uses only conventional measures of revenues, expenses, profits, cost variances, and output, it is possible that short-run economic gains may be achieved at the expense of long-run goals. Failure to consider the impact of control techniques on the individuals responsible for the activity of the firm may adversely affect employee morale, loyalty, trust, and motivation.

Present methods of evaluation often fail to consider how people are motivated. Cost control and other reports measuring performance are often used primarily for punitive purposes. Several authors have found that there is a strong asymmetrical reward system connected with performance reports.[2] The fact that the budget is exceeded is more important than how much it is exceeded. Equally important, reports may be required and investigations conducted when there are unfavorable variances; these investigations are frequently followed by reprimands and recommendations for corrective action to be taken, while favorable reports do not elicit an offsetting favorable response. Control systems may lead to reports of losses but fail to show the opportunity costs of ventures foregone. The result is conservative behavior on the part of managers, often substantially more conservative than top management desires. These comments suggest that the design of control techniques should include the motivational aspects of human activity as a paramount consideration.

Organizations arise from the needs of individuals to cooperate to achieve personal goals otherwise unattainable or reached with less difficulty by organizations. These personal goals usually include social and psychological goals as well as economic ones; in fact, the former are often more important than the latter. Each individual is in turn expected to contribute toward the realization of the organization's goals; often the goals of its dominant members.

Since many of the managers will have goals that differ substantially from the goals of the organization and since these goals will be multidimensional, it is imperative that means be found to obtain goal congruence. Means must be found by which a diverse set of individuals with a diverse set of goals can be motivated to seek the goals of the organization.

6.1 The Budget

The budget consists of a set of specific goals. Even if the budget is to be adjusted for unanticipated events, it gives the appearance of inflexibility. It is a source of pressure that can, if it becomes too great, create

---

[1] See R. Likert, *The Human Organization*, New York: McGraw-Hill, 1967.

[2] For an example see D. H. Woods, "Improving Estimates that Involve Uncertainty," *The Harvard Business Review*, July–August 1966, pp. 91–98.

mistrust, hostility, and may eventually lead to declining performance. Research suggests that there is a great deal of distrust of the entire budgetary process at the supervisory level.[3] There are several reasons for this distrust by supervisors. These reasons are based on the beliefs that

1. Budgets tend to oversimplify the real situation and fail to allow for variations in external factors.
2. Budgets do not adequately reflect qualitative variables.
3. Budgets simply confirm what the supervisor already knows, or alternatively distorts the true situation.
4. Budgets are too often used to manipulate the supervisor and therefore the indicated performance measures are suspect.
5. Budget reports emphasize results not reasons.
6. Budgets interfere with the supervisor's style of leadership and are thus unwelcome.

Budgets may also produce unwanted side effects.[4] One of these is the formation of small informal groups to combat pressure and reduce tension. Such informal groups usually have their own goals and these may conflict with those of the organization. Pressure is most acute on supervisors who are compelled to accept responsibility for meeting budgeted goals. In addition to forming informal groups, they may try to shift responsibility to other departments or to question the validity of the budgeted data. Such a situation makes it difficult for the accounting staff functions to be discharged effectively.

Sometimes a supervisor may even be able to distort successfully the measurement process. This might be done by overt manipulation of the data or by actions which improve his immediate performance but harm the firm; for example, a foreman might delay needed maintenance.

A second undesirable side effect that can develop from the budgeting process is the overemphasis on departmental performance as compared with firm performance. Important interdepartment dependencies and economies may be ignored or overlooked in a quest for optimization of the performance as reported.

A third effect is the perhaps undue publicity given to individual performance, particularly to "failure." The extensive exposure given to performance reports across departments for comparative purposes may increase friction among supervisors as well as between supervisors and the accounting staff.

A fourth and particularly noxious consequence of the budget and performance evaluation process can be a stifling of initiative. Individuals are

[3] C. Argyris, *The Impact of Budgets on People*, New York: The Controllership Foundation, 1952. The study is admittedly old but there is no more recent evidence that would cause its conclusions to be suspect.

[4] On these and related issues see M. E. Wallace, "Behavioral Considerations in Budgeting," *Management Accounting*, August 1966, pp. 3–8.

often discouraged from trying something new when the established ways have a large chance of success and new methods portend a greater degree of uncertainty. Churchill, Cooper, and Sainsbury found that workers who were audited conformed more closely to company policy than those who were not. Furthermore, they did so even when there were more efficient alternatives available.[5]

The problems associated with the budgeting process do not mean that the process should be scrapped, but rather that careful consideration is required if it is to have the desired effect. Ideally the budget provides a plan for achieving a goal or goals that have been accepted by the participants. If the budgeted amounts are reasonable, the projected achievement levels may then become the aspiration levels of the supervisors who must also obtain acceptance of the budget by members of their activities. If the goal aspired to is reached, the manager will experience subjective feelings of success, and if it is not reached, he will experience subjective feelings of failure.[6] The manager, according to the aspiration literature, will extend a disproportionate amount of energy to achieve his aspiration level.[7] It seems, then, useful to investigate various proposals for securing conformance between aspiration levels and firm goals as expressed in budgets.

6.2   Variable Budget Standards

One of the early empirical studies dealing with the interactions of budgets, aspiration levels, and performance in an accounting context was conducted by Stedry.[8] His pioneer study, although subject to question in several areas, highlighted the importance of the acceptance of the goals or standards and the relationship between the level of difficulty implied by the standard and the resulting performance.

Stedry used several groups in controlled experimental situations. Some of these were given budgets and some were not. Among those given budgets, some were asked to set their own goals prior to receiving the budgets and some were given the budget first. Finally budget levels were varied; high, medium, and low budgets were used.

The groups that were told a goal existed but were never told its amount

[5] N. C. Churchill, W. E. Cooper, and T. Sainsbury, "Laboratory and Field Studies of the Behavioral Effects of Audits," in *Management Controls*, edited by Bonini, Jaedicke, and Wagner, New York: McGraw-Hill, 1964.

[6] See K. Levin, T. Dimbo, L. Festinger, and P. Sears, "Level of Aspiration," in *Personality and the Behavioral Disorders*, edited by J. M. Hunt, New York: Ronald Press, 1944, pp. 333–378.

[7] On this and several points here see S. W. Becker and D. Green, "Budgeting and Employee Behavior," *The Journal of Business*, October 1962, pp. 392–402.

[8] A. C. Stedry, *Budget Control and Cost Behavior*, Englewood Cliffs, N.J.: Prentice-Hall, 1960.

performed better than those who were told their budgeted amounts initially. Of those told their budgets first, those groups with attainable (medium at best) goals performed better than those given high (difficult to attain) goals. Stedry also found an interaction effect between the setting of the individuals' aspiration levels and the imposed budgets.[9] A high budget led to the best performance in those groups setting their aspiration level after receiving the budget, and it led to the lowest performance when given to those groups that set their aspiration level first.

The level of the budget also had an impact on aspiration levels. Groups given budgets with goals less than their aspiration level tended to lower their aspiration level. Such behavior may have led to performance substantially below the abilities of the individuals and the level that was attained without a goal being set. The report on actual performance also influenced the aspiration level: the aspired level tending toward the actual level.

Stedry concluded that budgets should be developed consciously considering the motivational effects. By properly adjusting the budget given to an individual in light of his past performance, he could be motivated toward better performance. He recognized that it would be necessary to consider each individual separately and that it would be necessary for the manager to achieve his aspiration level part of the time.

While perhaps intuitively appealing, the use of individual budgets to motivate individual managers suffers from several limitations. In the first place this approach would require a dual record system. Records must be kept of actual performance and expected performance for evaluation and decision making. Simultaneously a separate set of records must be kept in order to provide the manager with budget levels and performance reports that would achieve the desired motivational results. Since actual results affect aspiration levels, and budgets would be expected to exhibit certain relationships to one another over time, it would seem that two sets of records would be necessary.

Not only is this dual reporting system an additional cost, but it could lead to undesirable results in terms of trust, morale, and performance if it became general knowledge.[10] In addition there is the problem that develops if two individuals with similar tasks under similar conditions discover that they are being measured against different standards. This would be a particularly touchy subject with labor unions which are not sympathetic toward techniques that hint of manipulation. It appears doubtful that the dual reporting system would remain privy to top management alone.

[9] Stedry, however, defined aspiration level in terms of the goal hoped for rather than the goal aimed for. There is also a question as to the long-run validity of his essentially short-run study.

[10] Another cost would involve hiring trained psychologists to establish workable means of measuring accurately each employee's aspiration level, assuming it could be done at all.

Hence, one could accept the basic hypothesis advanced by Stedry and even prefer a motivational system such as he proposes, yet find the problems of implementation insurmountable.

6.3 Participatory Budgeting

The theory behind participatory budgeting is that if there is participation in the setting of goals as defined in the budget, the established levels of accomplishment and the required sacrifices to achieve it will be accepted as the goals of the participants.[11]

Participation by itself will not necessarily lead to better performance, however. One problem with the participatory technique is that it may be quite difficult to realize in practice. Argyris describes what he calls pseudo-participation on the part of the supervisor.[12] The supervisor must first perceive that his input is desired and then he must supply his knowledge and expertise to the questions at hand. He must really become involved, not just go through the motions.

Consider, for example, the following comment. "We bring them in (supervisors of budget areas), we tell them that we want their frank opinion, but most of them just sit there and nod their heads. We know they're not coming out with exactly how they feel. I guess budgets scare them."[13] Here is a case where the supervisors do not perceive that their opinions are really desired. The result is a failure of the budget and control process before it begins. Knowledge of this attitude should be a signal to the accounting department of a possibly serious breakdown in the trust and respect of the supervisors for the accounting function. If true it will almost certainly impair the effectiveness of that department.

6.4 Other Methods

There are other means of obtaining goal congruence. Mention has already been given to the idea of independently auditing the performances of supervisors and others (examined by Churchill, Cooper, and Sainsbury). An appealing suggestion is the use of an audit technique to evaluate the means by which decisions are made. In other words, managers could be evaluated, at least in part, on the basis of the principles and techniques used in decision making rather than on the consequences of the decisions alone. Quite often a good procedure can lead to a poor result when decisions must be made under uncertainty. Moreover, poor decision making can occasionally work

[11] Becker and Green, *op. cit.*, p. 397.
[12] Argyris, *op. cit.*
[13] *Ibid.*, p. 28.

out for the best. The firm that did not construct a plant in downtown San Francisco just prior to the great earthquake because the payback period was seven years rather than an arbitrarily imposed limit of five years should congratulate itself on its good fortune not on its decision making.

Still another means of motivating employees is through incentive plans. Several firms have gone so far as to adopt group plans that reward the entire group for gains achieved by a member of that group.[14] Some observers believe this may provide a means of circumventing the problems of isolating individual performance in an age characterized by technological dependence.[15] In the opinion of these observers, individual standards may increasingly give way to group standards.

Group standards could be one means of treating the very real problem of goal congruence among technologically oriented employees. These individuals often preceive their goal as recognition among those of similar talents in professional organizations. They may be more interested in securing a position in a firm composed of men with similar talents than in working toward the goals of the firm for which they presently are employed.

6.5   The Future of Behavioral Theory in Cost Control

The history of cost control has been marked by the views that the primary incentive for employees is an economic one. Furthermore, employees have been implicitly viewed at best, as indifferent and, at worst, as wasteful, lazy and purposefully inefficient. Modern behavioral theory, on the other hand, recognizes a whole host of goals in addition to the economic one. It recognizes that individual behavior is essentially adaptive, problem solving, and decision oriented; that this behavior is constrained by limited knowledge, limited cognitive ability, and changing value structures. Hence individuals tend to adopt "satisficing" behavior (or constrained optimization behavior) patterns.[16]

Managerial accounting has traditionally been viewed as the primary means of controlling and reducing costs. Yet organization theorists have argued for some time that this traditional view with its emphasis on cost variances and the budgeted income, and the implied behavioral implications, produces or reinforces the responses of indifference, inefficiency, hostility, and conflict

---

[14] The individual may be rewarded separately as well.

[15] A well-known example here is the Scanlon Plan. See F. C. Lesieur (ed.), *The Scanlon Plan*, Cambridge, Mass.: MIT Press, 1958.

[16] See E. H. Caplan, "Behavioral Assumptions of Management Accounting," *The Accounting Review*, July 1966, pp. 496–509; and "Behavioral Assumptions of Management Accounting—Report of a Field Study," *The Accounting Review*, April 1968, pp. 342–362.

which management wishes to avoid.[17] In this regard Katz *et al.* found that management may be more effective when it concentrates on the organizational needs of the firm rather than directly on profit requirements.[18] Although a conclusive statement that a reduction in undesirable responses by employees can be attained by moving toward approaches more consistent with a modern behavioral model cannot be made because of the lack of reliable empirical data, there is a strong presumption that this may be the case.[19]

6.6 Summary

This section contains a list of suggestions for improving the goal congruence and hence the control function. No claim for originality is made here (or elsewhere in this chapter for that matter). The ideas have been borrowed liberally from the numerous sources, some cited here or on previous pages.

1. Continued attention should be given to the problem of accounting for human resources.[20] Measures are available by which aspects such as trust and loyalty can be measured. Changes in these measures may provide indications of the effects whose measurements are desired.

2. Communication and feedback devices need re-examination. It is important for individuals to learn about their success or failure. More frequent feedback is required than is generally now supplied.[21,22] If performance equals or exceeds expectations, aspirations will improve and increased efficiency can be obtained. If performance is slightly below expectations, feedback is needed so that employees will continue to work for the budgeted goals. If performance is substantially below expectations, budgetary revisions downward may be in order to prevent the frustrations associated with failure to reach aspiration levels which in turn leads to lower future performance. These comments suggest that the feedback and budget cycle

[17] See Argyris, *op. cit.*; M. Haire, *Psychology in Management*, New York: McGraw-Hill, 1956; R. Likert, *New Patterns of Management*, New York: McGraw-Hill, 1961; and D. McGregor, *The Human Side of Enterprise*, New York: McGraw-Hill, 1960.

[18] D. Katz, N. Maccoby, and N. Morse, *Productivity, Supervision and Morale in an Office Situation*, Institute for Social Research, University of Michigan, 1950; and D. Kats, N. Maccoby, G. Gurin, and L. G. Floor, *Productivity, Supervision and Morale Among Railroad Workers*, Institute for Social Research, University of Michigan, 1951.

[19] See Caplan, "Behavioral Assumptions of Management Accounting—Report of a Field Study," *op. cit.* for a similar conclusion.

[20] For example see R. L. Brummet, E. G. Flamholtz and W. C. Pyle, "Human Resource Measurement—A Challenge for Accountants," *The Accounting Review*, April 1968, pp. 217–224.

[21] See Becker and Green, *op. cit.*, pp. 399–400.

[22] The problem of data abundance, an outgrowth of EDP., and the increased likelihood of mistakes, omissions, and a decline of skepticism of the data provide related problems.

should be tied to aspiration levels and their changes rather than to an arbitrary time cycle where economically feasible.[23] The time dimension is important, however. In the short run factors may not be controllable by the manager that are under his control over the long run.

A related point concerns the matching of the input and output data with the period budget. This suggests that time periods be used for which useful input and output figures can be developed. The figures must be valid not only from a measurement point of view but in addition they must be related. In other words, the input-activity measures must be related to the output-activity results if the resulting feedback is to be of any value. The problem of measurement and reporting time lags is one that needs attention on this score. The accounting function has a significant role to play in creating believable data.

3. Accountants should work more closely with behavioral scientists. Furthermore, they should learn more of this area themselves. Encouragement should be given to those on the job to obtain this training. Such an approach will accelerate a total-system's view of the accounting function; a step that will facilitate more goal-oriented control techniques.

4. Participation schemes should be introduced into organizations with due consideration for the psychological problems entailed. Where such plans exist, consideration should be given to improving their effectiveness. When this is done a system of participation with some goals imposed will improve the setting within which effective control can be exercised. This, it should be emphasized, is a necessary but not sufficient condition for effective control. The accounting department still needs to develop and cultivate the trust of the line positions through better measurement techniques if it is to help the line managers do a better job.

QUESTIONS AND PROBLEMS

6–1 Should decisions be made to optimize the well-being of a segment of an organization as a whole?

6–2 Are quantitative measures of dollars of expected profit (or rate of return or present value) good and sufficient bases for making business decisions?

6–3 Is cost accounting the best means of implementing a cost-reduction program?

6–4 Who has responsibility for repair department costs?

6–5 Of the several possible objectives of a cost-accounting system, which are most likely to be successfully achieved?

---

[23] *Ibid.* Also see J. L. Child, and J. W. M. Whiting, "Determinants of Level of Aspiration: Evidence from Everyday Life," in *The Study of Personality*, edited by H. Brand, New York: John Wiley, 1954, pp. 145–158.

6–6 Should cost standards be hard or easy to attain?

6–7 Are people more motivated by threats of punishment or by the offer of rewards for accomplishment?

6–8 Assume you have been directed by the president of your firm to improve profits by 10 per cent. What alternatives do you have?

6–9 What methods might be used to motivate development and research department personnel toward achieving the firm's objectives?

6–10 How should a class in, say, cost control, tackle its own motivation problem?

6–11 Every six months the production manager, I. Makit, and the purchasing manager, D. LeGrump, decide the raw material and other input needs of the production department. LeGrump knows that he is responsible for meeting the general purchasing schedule once it is set up and agreed to by Makit and himself.

Eight weeks ago Makit advised LeGrump that he noticed the supply of one essential input was running low and that he would need the next batch of raw material on time (in accordance with the original production schedule) in four weeks. LeGrump found that the regular supplier could not make delivery in accordance with this schedule. He called a number of places and finally found a supplier who accepted the four-week commitment.

LeGrump followed up by mail and was assured by the supplier that he would receive the material in time. The matter was so important, LeGrump called again a week in advance and was again assured the material would arrive in time.

The day before the material was to be used LeGrump checked once again and found the shipment had not been received. Inquiry revealed the shipment had been misdirected by the railroad and was still in Chicago, 500 miles away, and would not be received for 2 days.

The material was finally obtained but only after considerable extra expense (only a part of which is recoverable) and substantial down time.

Where do you believe the responsibility lies and who should bear this cost?

6–12 The Spede Manufacturing Company owns a trucking fleet, has its own utility services, and maintains a repair shop. These are all operated as profit centers.

The trucking division had been complaining to the utility division that its wires at one point in the road were too low and they did not give the larger trucks enough clearance. The repair shop agreed to make the changes, but wanted to know whether the costs of the adjustment were to be charged to the utility division or the truck division. Both the divisions refused to accept the $1,500 cost of making the adjustment, and the repair shop refused to perform the task unless it could charge the costs of making the adjustment to one of the two divisions.

One day the top of a truck caught the wires and ripped them down. The cost of repairing the lines was $2,500, and there was an additional cost to the firm of $4,000 because of the disruption of service.

Investigation disclosed that the truck had failed to clamp down its top properly and the extra two inches of height caused the catching of the wire.

The trucking division and the utility division both refused to accept the $2,500 repair charges.

Required: Assume you are the controller in charge of the accounting for the three service divisions (repair, trucking, and utility). What would be your next step? What is the proper role of responsible accounting in determining the blame for this situation?

6–13 The following letter was received by a new controller. Write a reply.

THE KROCKS AND POTTS COMPANY
(MAKERS OF FINE DINNERWARE)
SCURRY, OHIO

Controller   Today
13 Morningside Avenue
Sashay, Ohio

Dear Controller:

I hesitate to write to you even before your arrival, but a problem has come up in the controller's division about which you should be informed.

As you know we have just recently overhauled our entire organization and brought in a number of new people. One of these new people is Ben Pole, who has taken over our Putter, Pennsylvania activities. Ben is a good man and well suited to our decentralized activities.

About the same time we hired Ben, U. U. Pusher, one of our extremely bright and young staff members, took over our new performance analysis staff. This staff operates out of the controller's office.

It is Pusher's duty to prepare reports showing budgeted performance, actual performance, and explanations for any differences for both divisions of the plant. Pusher has a staff of two men, one for each division, who operate out of our main plant. They have consulted and are acquainted with their respective division's line and staff executive personnel as well as with the operation.

Until yesterday we thought all was going well. Yesterday afternoon, however, Ben Pole stormed into my office quite unhappy about the whole setup.

I can't recall his exact words but the gist of his comments indicate that he feels Pusher's staff is usurping his responsibilities. He feels they snoop around asking too many questions and generally waste his staff's time. Ben feels it is his job to analyze and explain his division's performance.

From your experience can you think of any reason for Ben's position and what would you suggest we do, if anything, about his complaint?

Sincerely,
I. M. Thebos
Manager

6-14[24]

Memo

To: Controller
From: Thebos
Subject: Budgets

Ben Pole has sent me the following budget report that applies to his manufacturing supervisor.

Period	1	2	3	4	5	6
Budget	$39,000	$40,000	$39,500	$38,000	$38,500	$38,500
Actual	41,000	39,500	38,000	39,000	38,500	38,250
Variance	2,000U	500F	1,500F	1,000U	0	250F

The supervisor has a substantial number of men and a large amount of equipment under his control. He is paid a "base" salary which is actually somewhat low for his type of work. However, we have a rather liberal bonus plan which pays him an additional $1,000 per month each time he makes his budget and two per cent of the saving (amount below budget).

We have been quite pleased so far with the continued improvement in the supervisor's performance and wonder if this might not be a model for the rest of our operations. What do you think?

I. M. Thebos

Required: Write a reply.

SUPPLEMENTARY READING

ARGYRIS, C., "Human Problems with Budgets," *The Harvard Business Review*, January–February 1953, pp. 97–110.

ARGYRIS, C., *The Impact of Budgets on People*, New York: The Controllership Foundation, 1952.

BECKER, S. W., and D. GREEN, "Budgeting and Employee Behavior," *The Journal of Business*, October 1962, pp. 392–402.

BENSTON, G., "The Role of the Firm's Accounting System for Motivation," *The Accounting Review*, April 1963, pp. 347–354.

BRUNS, W. J., "Accounting Information and Decision Making: Some Behavioral Hypotheses," *The Accounting Review*, July 1968, pp. 469–480.

BRUNS, W. J., and D. T. DeCOSTER, *Accounting and its Behavioral Implications*, New York: McGraw-Hill Book Company, 1969.

CAPLAN, E. H., "Behavioral Assumptions of Management Accounting—Report of a Field Study," *The Accounting Review*, April 1968, pp. 342–362.

---

[24] This problem as well as 6–11 and 6–13 was suggested by problems in C. T. Hongren, *Cost Accounting A Managerial Emphasis*, Englewood Cliffs N. J.: Prentice-Hall, 1962.

CAPLAN, E. H., "Behavioral Assumptions of Management Accounting," *The Accounting Review*, July 1966, pp. 496–509.

MARCH, J. G., and H. A. SIMON, *Organization*, New York: John Wiley, 1958.

STEDRY, A. C., *Budget Control and Cost Behavior*, Englewood Cliffs, N.J.: Prentice-Hall, 1960.

WALLACE, M. E., "Behavioral Consideration in Budgeting," *Management Accounting*, August 1966, pp. 3–8.

Chapter 7

Inventory Valuation and Decisions

Inventory valuation is somewhat complex because management wishes to accomplish two quite separate purposes: to make inventory-level decisions and to provide data for financial reporting to internal and external parties. The objective of decisions concerning inventory levels is to minimize the cost associated with inventories. One relevant cost in this connection is the opportunity cost of lost sales. A second relevant cost is the inventory carrying cost, which can be determined using the average inventory value and the per dollar cost of carrying inventory.

Financial reporting, on the other hand, requires not only useful measures of inventory values at the beginning and end of the period but also data that lead to meaningful income figures. The dual information requirement for external reporting makes the attainment of meaningful figures for both inventory values and income measures difficult. A theoretical approach to this problem and a practical alternative are suggested. Much conventional accounting information is not needed for inventory-level decisions.

Management also has the task of measuring performance for evaluation purposes and to control costs. Here the question of inventory values is joined by the question of determining the responsibility for cost incurrence. Because of the need for more detailed information, the approaches offered for external reporting are not necessarily useful for internal performance measurement and cost control.

7.1 Inventory Costs and Internal Decision Making

The establishment of optimal inventory levels is one part of determining the current asset portfolio and is one of the more important decisions the firm must make on a continuing basis in relation to its operations. Recent years have seen the development of several formal models for inventory control.

Implementing these models requires a good deal of data that the accountant should be in position to supply. Unfortunately, however, accountants have frequently lacked familiarity with the models and hence have failed to accumulate the relevant data.

The number of companies using formal and sophisticated inventory models is not nearly so large as the recent deluge of writing on the subject might indicate. Nevertheless, the simple economic-order-quantity model, the EOQ model, with some of its extensions, has been used with success by a number of companies. Furthermore, the future will no doubt see increased use of the simple models as well as an introduction of more complex models. The range of models is extensive and it is not the task of this book to develop the theory of inventory control. Fortunately, however, the data requirements of the simpler models are reasonably constant across situations. It is these general data requirements that are examined here.

7.1.1 Reasons for Holding Inventories

Inventories are held for essentially three reasons: transactions, precautionary, and speculative. If a firm knows the demand for its products, the output of its productive process, and the availability of the factors of production with certainty, and if input prices will not change, then it will have only a transactions reason to hold inventory. If, on the other hand, uncertainty exists concerning demand, the output of the productive process, or the supply (and timing) of the input factors, then a precautionary motive for holding inventory arises. This motive occurs when, for example, there are opportunity costs associated with stock-outs.

When input prices can be expected to change, the opportunity to speculate on the expected increase or decrease in prices exists. In general, formal inventory models do not include this possibility. Nevertheless, management should be aware of the fact that optimal inventory levels do depend to some degree on expected input price movements. For example, if prices of input factors are expected to fall a firm should consider allowing its inventory to decline in the expectation of replacing it at a lower price later. The firm would, however, be limited in its actions by inventory needs for both transactions and precautionary purposes. The savings arising from lower prices would be augmented by the carrying costs avoided with a lower inventory and decreased by the increased likelihood of stock-outs.

7.1.2 Inventory Costs

The relevant inventory costs are suggested by the equation for the economic order quantity, EOQ, for the inventory model involving stock-out costs for inventory items that can be back ordered.[1]

$$EOQ = \sqrt{\left(\frac{2C_1 D}{C_2}\right)\left(\frac{C_2 + C_3}{C_3}\right)} \qquad (7.1)$$

where

C_1 = order cost (per unit per order).
C_2 = storage cost (per unit per time period T).
C_3 = stock-out cost (per unit per time period T where the unit can be back ordered).
D = total demand (during time period T).

The costs associated with inventories arise from the processes of acquiring and carrying them, and from being out of stock. The costs of acquiring inventories include the incremental costs of placing and receiving orders as well as the incremental costs of setting up production. These costs also include inspection, shipping, handling, returning inferior goods, set-up costs and paying bills. Carrying costs are composed of storage costs such as rent, insurance, costs of spoilage and obsolescence, taxes, and the opportunity cost of the funds tied up in the inventory. Stock-out costs include the costs of lost goodwill during the stock-out.

It is, or should be, the accountant's task to supply the cost data suggested above. He must be cognizant not only of what data are needed but also of the likely measurement errors associated with his figures. If this information is available, the sensitivity of the optimal solutions can be examined.

The data relevant to stock-out costs is difficult to obtain with accuracy. Permanently lost sales and the declines in goodwill are very difficult to estimate, and hence the figures used are usually very unreliable. Bias and lack of objectivity are both present in most cases. The costs of special orders, while somewhat easier to obtain, also present problems since they are often influenced by the time when the order is made and the conditions, such as the required delivery time and size, which surround the order.

The determination of acquisition costs is also difficult. In part this is true

[1] See C. W. Churchman, R. L. Ackoff, and E. L. Arnoff, *Introduction to Operations Research*, New York: John Wiley, 1957, pp. 205–206. The basic EOQ model is $EOQ = \sqrt{2C_1 D / C_2}$

because these costs are common to other activities as well. Inspectors may inspect output as well as input, for example. Furthermore, several variables usually influence the incremental level of these costs, and hence some technique such as a multiple regression analysis is required to obtain adequate estimates of these costs.

Carrying costs are perhaps the easiest to estimate although even here the opportunity-cost measure of holding inventories is subject to a wide estimation range. Typically, carrying costs are estimated as a percentage rate per dollar of average-inventory investment based on actual, estimated, or expected figures for the component costs.

But how should the average-inventory investment be measured? In theory it should represent the funds tied up in the inventory investment. Two alternative measures of this value would be the replacement cost or net sales value of the inventory. Raw materials and often finished goods have reasonably active markets from which replacement or net sales values respectively can be estimated. This is not generally the case for partially finished items which typically constitute the largest segment of inventories for most manufacturing oriented firms. In this case the inventory values may be estimated by using the cost of the resources committed to the goods in process. A question arises concerning the inclusion of fixed costs in these inventory values.

7.1.3 Fixed Costs and Inventory Values

The adherents of including only variable costs argue that fixed costs would be incurred in any event, and thus they are period costs and not inventoriable. This argument has some validity but falls short of proving the case for using only variable costs. A fixed cost may not be as inevitable or as nonrelevant as the statement suggests.

Consider the wages of a plant manager and the depreciation of the plant. These are fixed costs, but it is possible that if there were no intention of producing the product the plant could be sold or diverted to producing another product. The plant manager could be switched to another job. The fixed costs are relevant costs of product when there are opportunity costs connected with factors of production which in turn give rise to the fixed costs. Thus the value of the plant manager's services, if he were performing other tasks, represents the opportunity cost of the plant manager working on the present product. In like manner, the funds which would result from the sale of a plant or the net revenue that would result from other uses of the plant are the opportunity costs of using the plant to make the present product. It may be reasonable to substitute the wages of the plant manager and the depreciation of the plant for the opportunity costs of these factors of production, and to consider these costs as inventoriable.

In many cases the factors of production that give rise to fixed costs do not have alternative uses; their opportunity costs are zero. These fixed costs are time-period costs and are not inventoriable: they would be incurred even if production ceased. The variable (or incremental) costs incurred in producing the units of product are the only inventoriable costs in this case. Under these conditions the fixed costs are not inventoriable.

An alternative approach to inventory valuation would abandon the concept of cost entirely in favor of a present value or present benefit basis. Using this approach the value of an inventoriable item would be the smaller of the item's net sales value or its replacement cost.[2] This approach can be summarized by the relationship:

$$I = \text{Min}[C, S] \tag{7.2}$$

Where I is the inventory value, C is the replacement cost, measured using incremental, opportunity, or avoidable cost, and S is the net sales value of the item to be inventoried; and I is equal to the minimum of C or S.

The inventory value cannot exceed the net sales value although it may be less. Similarly, the inventory value cannot exceed replacement cost.

For an example, assume the variable cost of an item in stock is $80, the cost (in economic terms) of replacing the item in the next period is expected to be $85, and the net sales values is $100. Under these assumptions, the inventoriable value would be $85. If to alter the assumptions slightly, the net sales value remains at $100 but the replacement cost is $110, the inventory benefit is $100. On the other hand, if the replacement cost is $60, then $60 is the inventory value of the item. Finally, if there is no opportunity to replace the item during the next period but it could be expected to be sold, then the net sales value of the item, $100, would be the inventory value of the item.

Since the inventoriable cost is likely to exceed variable costs, it could be said that fixed costs are being inventoried. However, using the present benefit procedure for inventory valuation purposes, there is no need to know the actual cost since valuation is based on future benefits not past costs.

The discussion can also be related to the reasons for holding inventories. If future variable costs are expected to increase, the replacement cost of the item rises and hence so does the inventoriable value (assuming the net sales value exceeds the higher replacement cost). This is the speculative reason for holding inventory. Also if failure to produce today is expected to result in lost future sales because of limited capacity and if replacement cost is higher than net sales value, the inventoriable value is the net sales value. This is the precautionary motive for holding inventory. Finally, inventory held for

[2] The approach is similar but not identical to that proposed by G. H. Sorter, and C. T. Horngren, "Asset Recognition and Economic Attributes—The Relevant Costing Approach', *The Accounting Review*, July 1962, pp. 391–399; and C. T. Horngren, and G. H. Sorter, "Direct Costing for External Reporting," *The Accounting Review*, January 1961, pp. 84–93.

transaction purposes would also lead to a direct application of expression (7.2).[3]

It is important to emphasize that the present value approach rests on subjective judgments and hence is unlikely to receive wide acceptance. Yet it can be argued that procedures presently being used to estimate the value of goods-in-process inventory are also subjective. Any procedure adopted must find its justification in the fact that it leads to reasonable estimates of the relevant figures at acceptable cost.

7.1.4 Additional Factors

As the basic EOQ model is extended, the effect of lead times in ordering and quantity discounts on purchases are two of several complications that are introduced. The incorporation of lead times and an uncertain demand rate creates the need for a safety stock. Safety stocks add to expense and it becomes necessary to balance this cost against the cost of stock-outs.

7.1.5 Inventory Cost Changes and Control

The inventory EOQ formula and the associated total cost equation also provide the manager with the means of evaluating the sensitivity of costs to the decision. For example, if a different value for one of the cost variables is inserted, the new total cost can be computed. It is also possible to compute the total cost if the inventory policy is adjusted to reflect the expected change in the cost variable. The adjusted cost can be compared to the original cost (less the cost of revising the decision) to determine the net advantage to revising the optimal order quantity. Where several costs vary at once and probability distributions for these changes can be estimated (perhaps several distributions would be required for one or more of the cost variables to take dependencies into account), computer simulation techniques can be used to estimate the total cost and make the comparisons suggested in this paragraph.

7.2   Inventory Costing and Financial Reporting

Recent years have witnessed an increasing application of marginal analysis to decision making and the reporting of only variable costs on income statements for internal-performance evaluation. The increased attention to variable costs has produced a continuing argument among accountants concerning the appropriateness of valuing inventories on the basis of variable

---

[3] Alternatives to producing inventory would be to acquire additional productive facilities and employees or, possibly, to subcontract. The least cost alternative should be chosen.

costs alone for financial reporting and hence influencing external decision making. The approach can be referred to as variable costing.[4]

The term *variable costing* is used in two different ways. First, it can refer to a method of accounting that considers fixed costs as costs of the time period and treats only variable costs as inventoriable costs. Second, variable costing may refer to a system of internal reporting and analysis for decisions which differentiates between fixed and variable costs. The distinction is central to an important issue in cost accounting: whether costs are being computed for the purpose of inventory valuation for internal decision making and control or for the purpose of reporting to outsiders.

In this book the term *variable costing* is used only when the discussion concerns inventory valuation for reporting financial position and income. The distinction between fixed and variable costs is useful for decision making, but the necessity to determine the nature of costs for purposes of decision making is not dependent on, although it may be influenced by, the method of accounting for fixed costs for financial reporting purposes. The additional problem in reporting is that the inventory value is a variable in the computation of period income.

Under generally accepted methods of financial accounting, all or a portion of the fixed costs are absorbed as costs of product, and the financial income reported for a period is affected not only by sales and efficiency but also by the amount of production and by the change in inventory. Thus the reported income of a period may be increased not only by more sales or better efficiency but merely by producing more and putting the excess into inventory. This can be illustrated with an example.

Example

Assume a company sells 5,000 units at $8 each in both March and April. The production costs are identical for both months. They are:

Fixed costs $90,000 (per month)
Variable costs $1 (per unit)

Production for March was 10,000 units and for April 20,000 units. The normal activity for both months is 15,000 units.

A variety of income statements (see Table 7.1) are possible for the two months, depending on the policy regarding the accounting for the absorption of the fixed costs.

It is important to note that the "actual" cost procedure and the normal-costing procedure give the same reported income if the unabsorbed overhead is allocated back to the product sold and to the ending inventory and a

---

[4] The terms *direct costing* or *marginal costing* are frequently used instead of variable costing. They all refer to a procedure that considers fixed costs an expense of the time period and only variable costs as a cost of product.

LIFO cost flow is assumed. Both procedures result in the reported income of the period being a function of the level of production as well as of sales.

Frequently, activity variances in financial reporting are handled as expenses of the period in which they are incurred instead of being considered as costs of product to be allocated to the costs of goods sold and to the ending inventory. In the first procedure they are included with other expenses of the period and allowed to affect the reported income. In the second procedure they are

Table 7–1   Income Statement Using Actual Costs and Normal Activity Costing

| | "Actual" Costs | | Normal Activity Costing (overhead variance allocated to product) | |
	March	April	March	April
Sales	$40,000	$40,000	$40,000	$40,000
Less: Variable costs	5,000	5,000	5,000	5,000
Fixed costs	45,000*	22,500†	45,000**	22,500††
	$50,000	$27,500	$50,000	$27,500
Income (loss)	($10,000)	$12,500	($10,000)	$12,500

* The fixed cost per unit produced was $90,000/10,000 or $9 per unit. There were 5,000 units sold; thus the fixed costs charged to expense were $45,000. The remainder are inventoried.

† The fixed cost per unit produced was $90,000/20,000, or $4.50 per unit. There were 5,000 units sold; thus the fixed costs charged to expense were $22,500. This statement assumes a LIFO cost flow.

** On the basis of normal activity the fixed cost per unit was $90,000/15,000, or $6 per unit. There were 10,000 units produced in March; thus the fixed cost absorbed by product was $60,000 and the unabsorbed fixed cost was $30,000. Half of the unabsorbed overhead, $15,000, is charged to inventory and half to expense since 5,000 units were sold and 5,000 units remain in inventory. Thus the total fixed cost charge to expense was $15,000 of allocated, unabsorbed overhead and $30,000 of normal overhead (one half of the absorbed fixed costs of $60,000).

†† During April production was 20,000 units; thus there was $120,000 = $6(20,000) of fixed overhead absorbed to product. There was a favorable idle-activity variance of $30,000 = $6 (20,000 − 15,000). The fixed cost charged to expense was the number of units sold times the normal-overhead rate of $6 (this assumes a LIFO flow of costs), minus 5,000/20,000 of the $30,000 idle-activity variance.

subtracted from the reported operating income so that it is not affected by the level of activity. The results are shown in Table 7–2.

The second normal-costing procedure gives equal reported incomes for the two months if attention is focused on a subtotal before the deduction of the activity variance. However, this might result in the reporting of income for each of twelve months, but then a reported loss for the year when the idle-activity variance is taken into consideration.

Table 7–2   Income Statements with Different Treatment of the Idle-Activity Variance

	Normal-Activity Costing (idle-activity variance included as an expense)		Normal-Activity Costing (idle-activity variance subtracted from the reported operating income)	
	March	April	March	April
Sales	$40,000	$40,000	$40,000	$40,000
Less: Cost of goods sold*	35,000	35,000	35,000	35,000
Idle-activity variance	30,000	(30,000)		
	$65,000	$ 5,000		
Operating income (loss)	($25,000)	$35,000	$ 5,000	$ 5,000
Less: Idle-activity variance			30,000	(30,000)
Income (loss)			($25,000)	$35,000

* The $35,000 is equal to $5,000 variable cost and $30,000 fixed overhead.

The last procedure illustrated for these facts is variable costing (see Table 7–3). When this process is followed, all fixed costs are accounted for as expenses of the period in which they are incurred, and only variable costs are considered to be inventoriable.

Table 7–3   Income Statement: Variable Costing

	Variable Costing	
	March	April
Sales	$40,000	$40,000
Less: Variable costs	5,000	5,000
Excess of revenues over variable costs	$35,000	$35,000
Less: Fixed costs	90,000	90,000
Income (loss)	($55,000)	($55,000)

Under variable costing the reported incomes of the two periods are the same. This is consistent with the fact that the sales and efficiencies of the two periods were exactly the same, and that the only difference in the two periods was the level of production. While the other methods all arrived at a reported income for one period and a loss for the other, the variable-costing procedure shows the same loss for both periods.

Accounting theoreticians generally feel that income should not be a function of production or of the level of inventory that is carried (especially where the higher the inventory the higher the resulting income). They do not wish to recognize revenue at the production stage except in special cases where the sale is certain and the production period is long (ship building and extractive industries offer examples). Generally they hold that a completed legal sale is necessary to justify the recognition of revenue. It is paradoxical that these accountants, who are so careful about when to recognize revenue, often allow income and asset values to be distorted by procedures which indiscriminantly permit the inclusion of fixed costs in inventory values. If fixed costs are included in inventory, under conventional accounting procedures, then the income is affected by changes in inventory and changes in production, as well as by the level of sales and efficiency.

The primary advantage of variable costing is that reported income is not directly affected by changes in inventory and changes in production. To increase reported income, either total sales must increase or some meaningful change must be achieved in the cost-revenue relationship. The fixed costs of production of the period are not inventoried but are charged to expense. Thus the final reported income figure is not influenced by fluctuations in inventory levels. This is desirable since an increase in inventory may indicate increased efficiency, but, on the other hand it may cause inefficiency since excess inventory gives rise to additional handling, storage, and carrying costs which are undesirable. Also, increasing inventory levels may suggest the existence of marketing problems. Unfortunately the inventory values obtained by omitting fixed costs may give little indication as to the real value or even the inventory's cost (when the value excludes the opportunity costs of fixed factors of production). Hence, such values are unlikely to be useful in the models discussed in Section 7.1, or as indicators of the true asset values.

A policy of including only variable costs as a cost of inventory biases the valuation of the inventory in the direction of being less than the actual value of the inventory either in terms of net sales value, value in use, or replacement cost. This conclusion is based on the assumption that some fixed factors of production are in scarce supply and have alternative uses; thus, they have opportunity costs. The allocation and absorption of fixed costs to inventory may be incorrect because they are based on historical costs, but the inclusion of fixed costs can be considered as an attempt to include an estimate of the opportunity costs of the factors of production that conventionally result in fixed-cost charges.

Another argument advanced in favor of inventorying fixed costs is the concept of matching expenses with the revenues which they help earn. If the fixed costs are a valid cost of product (as is indicated above), it is argued that they should not be considered an expense until the product is sold. The accounting treatment of the variable- and fixed-cost factors identified as costs of product should be the same.

The question of the better method of valuing inventory for financial statement purposes remains. Does the generally accepted accounting practice of absorbing fixed overhead to product result in situations where an outsider basing his decision on a widely distributed annual report may be misled?

7.2.1 Criteria for Judging Financial Reporting Procedures

What is good financial reporting? The decision whether or not to use variable costing for financial reporting must be decided by whether or not it is good reporting. There follow four criteria that can be used in deciding what shall constitute good financial reporting. These are:

1. Is it in accordance with generally accepted accounting practice and conventions as set forth by professional organizations and governmental bodies?
2. Is it in accordance with good accounting theory as described in accounting literature?
3. Is it good accounting theory?
4. Is it useful for decision making?

Too frequently the first three criteria are cited as the determining factors in choosing the proper method. The fourth criterion is neglected or assumed to be automatically covered by accounting practice or basic accounting theory. This assumption is unwarranted.

If accounting practice is to be the determining criterion, then change is impossible since by definition what is being done is correct. The accounting practice in effect today is of interest, but a statement of convention should not be used as evidence that a procedure is correct or incorrect. The fact that an official pronouncement approves absorption costing does not help determine whether variable costing is a reasonable procedure or not.

The criterion of accounting theory should not be discarded lightly. The authors of the past seventy years have contributed tremendously to raising the level of accounting practice. The fact that thought-provoking writings have been produced by such men as Cole, Hatfield, Paton, and others makes accountants reluctant to modify time-honored concepts. But it must be recognized that these men changed accounting practice, advocated further changes not accepted, and certainly did not intend to freeze accounting thought. To quote an accounting authority as a justification for an accounting procedure is meaningful only to the extent that the logic of the authority continues to be applicable. It does not actually show one or another position to be sound. Even when a logical argument can be presented in favor of a given position it does not follow that yet another position is unsound.

The arguments presented so far suggest that there are times when it is useful to inventory fixed costs and that there are other times when these costs should be excluded. One means of achieving this result is to use the present-benefit approach discussed in Section 7.1.3. However, the same factors of subjectivity and complexity that work against its use for valuing work-in-process inventories also make its acceptance for financial reporting unlikely.

The accountant typically has only three alternatives available in practice. They are:

1. Dividing the total costs incurred during the period by the number of units produced to obtain the unit cost (absorption costing).
2. Using a standard-overhead rate based on a predetermined level of activity, for example normal activity, and considering any idle-activity variance as a cost of the period. (To distribute the variance to product would make this procedure the equivalent of the first procedure.)
3. Inventorying only variable costs.

All three procedures give the same inventory and income results if, in every period, all of the product produced were sold. However, these assumptions seldom describe the actual situation, for some of the product produced is usually not sold. The problem is made even more complex by the fact that production as well as the amount sold changes from period to period.

Since whichever method is used makes no attempt to judge fixed costs in terms of their applicability to future cost reduction or incremental revenue production, none of the choices is optimal. Recognizing the limitations imposed by restricting the set of alternatives, the better choice at least for determining income is the third one. The first two procedures suggested result in the incomes of successive periods being affected by the changes in production and the changes in inventory. With the second procedure, not only is income affected by changes in production, but by using a predetermined overhead rate based on normal activity, the company can show a deceptively high-income figure with very low sales. (If the overhead is overabsorbed to product, and the idle-activity variance is favorable, this reduces the expenses and increases the income of the period assuming inventories increase.)

If variable costs alone are inventoried, the unit value of the inventory is unaffected by fluctuating productions levels. This is the variable-costing solution. Under variable costing the inventory presented in the position statement would include only variable costs. An additional advantage of this procedure is that, in the absence of input price changes or changes in efficiency, the inventory reported in the position statement would reflect changes in the physical units on hand. This may be preferred over fluctuations in the cost per unit caused by variations in the level of production. This fluctuation occurs if the cost per unit is determined by dividing the actual costs by actual production, or by distributing the idle-activity variance back to inventory and the cost of product sold. The disadvantage of variable costing for financial reporting is that the inventory figures are usually meaningless indicators of actual value.

How important is the fact that inventory figures do not represent actual values? What decisions would be made differently because of the exclusion of fixed costs from the inventory position? Even in the computation of financial position, variable costing often gives information that is generally as useful for decision making as absorption costing. But the present-benefit argument that fixed cost should sometimes be included as a cost of product still remains.

7.2.2 An Alternative

A paradoxical situation may often exist where inventory values may best be approximated by absorption costing which includes fixed costs, while income is best measured by variable costing so that fluctuations in productive activity are eliminated. This section suggests a means by which both objectives can be accomplished. Income is measured by an accounting procedure that considers all fixed costs as expenses of the time period. Thus the fluctuations in income caused by changes in production and inventory are eliminated.

To avoid an understatement of inventory values, the often unwanted by-product of a variable-costing procedure, the inventory is presented at full cost, using the methods of absorbing overhead to product.[5,6] The fixed overhead in the inventory of the present period is compared to the amount of fixed overhead in the inventory of the previous period, and the change is recorded in the retained-earnings account. The change in fixed costs included in inventory at the end of the period appears in the reconciliation of retained earnings, but does not affect the reported income of the period.

A reconciliation is needed, however, since both absorption and variable costing assume that income is being measured in terms of the difference between revenues and expenses of the period. If income were to be redefined in terms of the change in the stockholders' equity at the beginning and end of the accounting period, excluding new capital and capital distributions, the need for the special adjustment to retained earnings would be eliminated. If production is treated as increasing the well-being of the stockholders, this fact would then be reflected in the income statement. However, as long as accountants consider realization of income to be accomplished only by a completed sale, and cost to be the basis of asset accounting, then the basic inconsistency between absorption and variable costing will continue to exist, and with it a need for reconciliation of the two conventions.

A possible objection to the suggested procedure is that it makes use of the retained-earnings reconciliation to adjust the amount of fixed costs remaining in inventory and considers the fixed costs an asset after they have been expensed. Against this objective can be balanced an improved measure of in-

---

[5] Understatement here implies that the variable cost of production is less than the market value or reproduction cost of the inventory.

[6] The method need not be restricted to valuing inventories at full cost. Some other figure could be used to obtain the desired inventory value.

come compared with that of generally accepted accounting procedures, as well as an improved valuation of inventories and presentation of financial position compared with that under variable costing. The following example shows how the suggested procedure works. The results from the suggested procedure are also compared with those from conventional accounting and variable costing.

Example

The AC Company produces one product. The budgeted and actual fixed-manufacturing costs of each year are $10,000. The standard and actual-variable manufacturing costs are $2 per unit. The company has normal capacity of 10,000 units and uses normal capacity to absorb fixed overhead to product (the fixed-overhead rate is $1 per unit). Assume no work-in-process inventories.

At the beginning of the year the company had the position statement given in Table 7–4.

Table 7–4   Position Statement as of January 1: AC Company

Other assets	$40,000	Capital stock	$20,000
Finished goods		Retained earnings	20,000
	$40,000		$40,000

During the year the company finished 10,000 units of product and sold 4,000 units for $3.10 per unit. During the following year the company finished 2,000 units and sold 4,000 units also at $3.10 per unit. Assume the only expenses are costs of manufacturing.

Under the suggested procedure the reports in Tables 7–5, 7–6, and 7–7 could be prepared.

Table 7–5   Income Statements: AC Company

	Year 1		Year 2	
Sales revenues (4,000 × $3.10)		$12,400		$12,400
Manufacturing costs				
Variable costs (4,000 × $2)	$ 8,000		$ 8,000	
Fixed costs	10,000	18,000	10,000	18,000
Operating loss		($ 5,600)		($ 5,600)

The fixed costs are charged to expense in the period in which they are incurred. However, generally accepted accounting principles consider the cost of manufactured goods to include a *pro rata* share of the fixed manufacturing

Table 7–6 Position Statement: AC Company

	Dec. 31 Year 1	Dec. 31 Year 2		Dec. 31 Year 1	Dec. 31 Year 2
Other assets	$22,400	$20,800	Capital stock	$20,000	$20,000
Finished goods	18,000	12,000	Retained earnings	20,400	12,800
	$40,400	$32,800		$40,400	$32,800

Table 7–7 Retained Earnings Reconciliation: AC Company

	Dec. 31 Year 1	Dec. 31 Year 2
Retained earnings, January 1	$20,000	$20,400
Less: Operating loss for year	5,600	5,600
	$14,400	$14,800
Plus: Adjustment for changes in amount of fixed costs in inventory	6,000	(2,000)
Retained earnings, December 31	$20,400	$12,800

costs incurred. Thus the inventory and retained earnings are adjusted for the amount of fixed costs considered to be associated with the goods in inventory (six tenths of $10,000 in year 1 and four tenths of $10,000 in year 2).

Since the second year begins with $6,000 of fixed costs in inventory and ends with $4,000, a credit of $2,000 to inventory, and a debit of $2,000 to the retained-earnings account is required. The accounting entries would be

	Year 1		Year 2	
Retained earnings—Adjustment for amount of fixed costs in inventory		$6,000	$2,000	
Finished goods—fixed costs	$6,000			$2,000

These entries adjust the amount of fixed costs included in inventory to be consistent with the number of units in inventory as of December 31. They do not affect the income of the period or future periods.

This procedure accomplishes several goals. The inventory is stated at full cost, thus satisfying the concern with the omission of fixed costs often needed for meaningful inventory values that results from using variable costing. On the other hand, the incomes of the two periods are equal, as would be expected for two accounting periods where the revenues were equal, where the total number of units sold were the same, and where there were no changes in efficiency. Under the conventional variable-costing procedure, the income statements would be exactly the same as above, but the inventories would include only the variable costs. The income statements under absorption accounting are given in Table 7–8.

Table 7–8   Income Statements Using Absorption Accounting: AC Company

		Year 1	Year 2
Revenues		$12,400	$12,400
Manufacturing costs			
Standard cost of product		12,000	12,000
Activity variance—Loss		0	8,000
Total expenses		$12,000	$20,000
Net income (loss)		$ 400	($ 7,600)

Generally accepted accounting procedures lead to the interesting (though misleading) conclusion that there is an income of $400 in year one, and a loss of $7,600 in year two, when the only difference between the two years is the level of production.

7.2.3 Variable Costing and Internal Reporting

It is not unusual for firms to prepare financial reports for purposes of evaluating performance in divisions, departments, cost centers, or for other activities. Often these reports are prepared to focus attention on the contribution of the activity and hence use a variable-costing approach. The method is most appropriate when a department's performance goal is profitability.

As will be discussed in Chapter 10, not all segments of a firm should have profitability as a goal. For some, cost minimization subject to an assigned output goal (in terms of quantity and quality) is more appropriate. In these cases cost control is the primary long-run objective of internal reporting. The variable costs, however, may only approximate the controllable costs. Differences occur to the extent that expenditures that are fixed in relation to the level of activity are nevertheless under the control of the department manager.

Internal reports can create problems in performance evaluation and thereby in motivation if they are prepared to reflect inappropriate goals or if they include costs over which the manager is not able to exercise control. Dependencies between cost centers and fuzzy lines of responsibility for decisions and expenditure authorization contribute to the difficulties. Although not ideal for this purpose, variable costing is an improvement over full-costing methods. Problems in motivation are more subtle and the reader is referred to Chapter 6 for a discussion of the issues involved.

A common error is to assume that a method of reporting on performance for external purposes is equally relevant to internal performance measurement and cost-control needs. The two objectives must be considered separately.

7.3 Summary

Developments in inventory decision models suggest new areas for cost accumulation and analysis. Typically, the accountant can do more to understand these models and to provide the necessary cost data.

One of the data requirements for determining optimal inventory levels is the cost of holding inventories and this is based on the value of resources tied up in inventories. While net realizable values and market-replacement cost data are often available for finished goods and raw materials respectively, work-in-process inventories are harder to value. Often some cost approach is used. The present-benefit approach is one alternative to the use of cost. Problems of implementing this technique stem, however, from its subjectivity. However, the present-benefit approach would be more useful if it could be implemented.

Similarly, inventory values are also necessary inputs to external decision making because of their relevance to asset values and reported income for financial statements. The subject is a separate one from internal decisions involving inventory control but involves many of the same elements. Inventory valuation for financial reporting deals with the dual problem of establishing useful inventory and income figures.

One problem here is to separate the cost of product and the cost of idleness as the use of productive facilities fluctuates. The concept of present benefits is again a possibility but implementation problems exist. It is likely that either a variable-costing or absorption-costing technique will generally be used. The use of variable-costing creates a problem in that inventories are undervalued and income is distorted by the level of production using absorption costing. A method is suggested in the chapter to mitigate the inventory valuation problem created by using variable-costing techniques to determine income.

QUESTIONS AND PROBLEMS

7-1
   a. What three fundamental data needs exist affecting the problem of inventory valuation? What data are necessary for financial reporting but are not needed for inventory-level decisions?
   b. How should reports be prepared for internal performance evaluation?
   c. Why are there differences between inventory-cost data for (1) inventory-level decisions, (2) financial reporting to outsiders, and (3) internal performance measurement?

7–2 Suppose cash and cashlike assets (short-term securities for example) are considered as an inventory. Using the *EOQ* equation (7.1) what would the symbols mean?

7–3 In decisions involving the level of cash and cashlike assets to hold, what related decisions involving cash must be considered?

7–4 Three important inventory costs C_1, C_2, and C_3 (ordering costs, storage costs, and stock-out back-order costs, respectively) are usually treated as linear functions of the inventory quantity (i.e., as constant per unit per time period over a rather wide range). Consider now several components of these costs and decide how they vary with inventory quantity over the relevant range. Also suggest methods of estimating each.

A. Order Costs
  1. Clerical processing labor
  2. Inspection labor
  3. Forms and materials
  4. Transportation

B. Storage Costs
  1. Insurance
  2. Taxes
  3. Obsolescence and breakage
  4. Warehouse costs(light, heat, labor)
  5. Interest in investment

C. Stock-Out Costs
  1. Special order filling
  2. Lost goodwill

7–5 Three names (variable costing, direct costing, and marginal costing) are used for the accounting procedure which for financial reporting purposes expenses all fixed costs and considers only variable costs to be inventoriable. Which name do you consider most appropriate and why?

7–6 What advantages for financial reporting does the use of absorption costing using normal activity have over the use of actual costs and actual activity as the basis of overhead absorption?

7–7 When does the use of normal activity and overhead absorption result in a distortion of the measure of income? How can this be corrected?

7–8 Is the use of variable costing reasonable from the point of view of financial accounting?

7–9 May cost factors which are conventionally classified by the accountant as being fixed ever be considered a cost of product from an economic point of view?

7–10 Should revenues be recognized as the production takes place or when the product is sold? Should income be a function of the level of production rather than sales? Should the cost per unit for reporting inventory levels and determining income for products be a function of the level of production?

7–11 Company Y produces one product which it sells for a price of $4.80 per unit. The production costs are as follows:

Fixed costs per year	$150,000
Variable costs per unit	$1

Normal activity is 100,000 units per year. At the beginning of 1968 the company has the following position statement.

Position Statement January 1, 1968

Other assets	$50,000	Capital stock	$30,000
Finished goods*	25,000	Retained earnings	45,000
	$75,000		$75,000

* Represents 10,000 units ($10,000 of variable costs and $15,000 of fixed costs).

The information for the years 1968–1970 is as follows:

	Sales (units)	Sales (dollars)	Production (units)
1968	50,000	240,000	80,000
1969	50,000	240,000	40,000
1970	50,000	240,000	120,000

The manufacturing costs of each year were as indicated previously.

Required:

a. Prepare income statements for the three years using normal activity as the basis of overhead absorption.

b. Prepare income statements for the three years using variable costing as the basis of overhead accounting.

c. Prepare retained earnings reconciliations for the three years assuming that inventory is presented on the position statements using normal activity as the basis of overhead absorption while variable costing is used for measuring the income of the period.

d. Prepare a position statement as of December 31, 1970.

7–12 Company Y produces one product which it sells for $5.00 per unit. The production costs are as follows:

Fixed costs per year	$200,000
Variable costs per unit	$1

Normal activity is 100,000 units per year. At the beginning of 1970 the company has the following position statement:

Position Statement January 1, 1970

Other assets	$45,000	Capital stock	$30,000
Finished goods*	30,000	Retained earnings	45,000
	$75,000		$75,000

* Represents 10,000 units ($10,000 of variable costs and $20,000 of fixed costs).

The information for the year 1970 is as follows:

Year	Sales (units)	Sales (dollars)	Production (units)
1970	50,000	250,000	140,000

The manufacturing costs were the same as specified above. The company uses a LIFO inventory procedure.

Required:

a. Prepare an income statement using normal activity as the basis of overhead absorption. Allocate idle-activity variances to inventory and cost of goods sold. Assume a LIFO flow of costs.

b. Prepare an income statement using variable costing as the basis of overhead accounting.

7–13 Explain the difference between the reported income and the incomes of $100,000 budgeted for sales of 10,000 units (see the accompanying break-even chart).

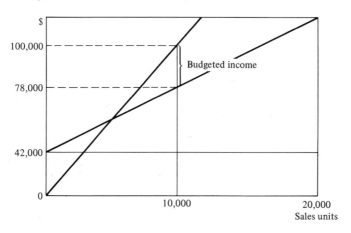

THE GRIPPER COMPANY
INCOME STATEMENT
FOR MONTH ENDING JULY 31, 1970

Sales (10,000 units sold for $10 apiece)		$100,000
Expenses:		
Manufacturing cost of sales (see note 1)	$60,000	
Selling expenses		
Variable $10,000		
Fixed 15,000	25,000	
Administrative expenses	5,000	
		90,000
Income (before taxes)		$ 10,000

Note 1:
  Standard cost:

Material	$ 8,000	
Labor	15,000	
Variable overhead	3,000	
Fixed overhead (based on a fixed overhead rate of $2 per direct-labor dollar)	30,000	
Material usage, price and labor efficiency and wage-rate variances	$19,000	$56,000
Idle-activity variance (favorable)	15,000	4,000
		$60,000

Note 2: The budgeted-fixed costs for the month were

Manufacturing overhead	$25,000
Selling	12,000
Administrative	5,000
	$42,000

The budgeted-variable selling expense is 10 per cent of sales.

7–14 The Capable Company includes the idle-activity variance based on normal capacity in its cost of sales. The income statements for January and February were as follows:

Sales	January	February
Sales	$900,000	$900,000
Less: Manufacturing cost of sales	750,000	950,000
Manufacturing margin	$150,000	$(50,000)
Less: Selling and administrative expenses	25,000	25,000
Net income	$125,000	$(75,000)

During the month of January the company produced 500,000 units of product and sold 300,000. During the month of February the company produced and sold 300,000 units.

The variable costs of manufacturing are $1.50 per unit. There were no spending (expense) or efficiency variances during either of the two months. The fixed costs budgeted and incurred for each of the two months were $500,000. The normal capacity of the plant is 500,000 units (used for determining the fixed-overhead rate).

Required: Present comparative income statements for the two months which would be more useful in appraising the results of operations for the two months.

a. Using direct costing.

b. Using absorption costing.

SUPPLEMENTARY READING

BRUMMET, R. L., "Direct Costing: Should It Be a Controversial Issue?" *The Accounting Review*, July 1955, pp. 439–443.

CHURCHMAN, C. W., R. L. ACKOFF, and E. L. ARNOFF, *Introduction to Operations Research*, New York: John Wiley, 1957, Chapters 8, 9, and 10.

DOPUCH, N., "Mathematical Programming and Accounting Approaches to Incremental Cost Analysis," *The Accounting Review*, October 1963, pp. 745–753.

HADLEY, G., and T. M. WHITIN, *Analysis of Inventory Systems*, Englewood Cliffs, N.J.: Prentice-Hall, 1962.

HEPWORTH, S. R., "Direct Costing: The Case Against," *The Accounting Review*, January 1954, pp. 94–99.

HORNGREN, C. T., and G. H. SORTER, "Direct Costing for External Reporting," *The Accounting Review*, January 1961, pp. 84–93.

SHILLINGLAW, G., "The Concept of Attributable Cost," *Journal of Accounting Research*, Spring 1963, pp. 73–85.

SORTER, G. H., and C. T. HORNGREN, "Asset Recognition and Economic Attributes—The Relevant Costing Approach," *The Accounting Review*, July 1962, pp. 391–399.

Chapter 8

Joint Costs and Joint Products

This chapter is concerned with two similar but basically different types of cost: joint costs and indirect costs. Joint costs relate to a situation where the factors of production by their basic nature result in two or more products. The jointness results from there being more than one product, and these multi-products are the result of the method of production or the nature of the raw material and not of a decision by management to produce both (though management may find the production of one of the resulting products uneconomical and drop the "finishing" process). An example of a joint cost is the cost of a barrel of crude oil purchased by a refining company. Several products, including gasoline, fuel oil, tar and chemicals, result from the processing of a barrel of crude oil, and these products all have a common cost, namely, the cost of oil. By the nature of the raw material (or the productive process) several products result; thus the costs are "joint" to these products. Frequently, in joint cost situations, it would be uneconomical to produce a single product.

Indirect costs, on the other hand, result from the production of more than one product, but the decision to use the factors of production to produce several products is a decision of management. Any indirect cost factor could be directed to the production of one product instead of several products. A railroad is an example of a productive process which may lead to indirect costs, with the cost of the rails being an indirect cost to both freight and passenger travel. Unfortunately, the distinction between joint and indirect costs is often blurred since both may be involved at once.

165

Another example of indirect costs occurs if a plant produces beer cans and soda pop cans, since some of the same equipment may be used to produce both products yet both need not be produced. Another example is the machinery used in processing timber: the cost of logs is a joint cost.

There are, then, two types of costs (joint and indirect) that cannot be directly identified with the end products when two or more types of products are being made. It might be said that these costs are common to all products; in fact, the term "common costs" is sometimes used to describe both of these types of costs.

Products resulting from joint costs are called joint products if they are approximately of equal importance to the firm. Products of relatively small importance to the business are called by-products. The by-product may be of considerable absolute value but it is still a by-product so long as it results from the production of the main product. An example of a by-product is the scrap metal resulting from the production of an airplane. This scrap has considerable value in absolute amount, but compared to the value of the primary product, airplanes, it is of small value. The scrap results from the air-plane production process and hence is also a by-product. If the value of the end product were nearly equivalent to the value of the scrap produced, the scrap metal would be considered a joint product by accountants, though common usage might still refer to it as a by-product.

In practice, the distinction between a joint product and a by-product is primarily a result of accounting convention and of minimal use to management in decision situations. The remainder of this chapter deals with the problems of determining output decisions for joint products and establishing their inventory values. Some interesting results for the accounting problem of inventory valuation can be developed by considering the decision problem first.

8.1 Joint Costs and Decision Making

Suppose a firm makes two products, call them A and B, from a raw material that costs $2 per pound and that weighs ten pounds. The ten pounds of raw material yields one unit of A at four pounds and one unit of B at six pounds. The direct-finishing costs are $1.25 per pound of A and $0.50 per pound of B. Indirect-finishing (joint-processing) costs that apply to both A and B amount to $0.70 per pound of the raw material. These facts are summarized in Table 8–1.

Both the direct- and indirect-finishing costs indicated above are of an incre-mental nature. (Any purely fixed costs have been omitted since they do not affect the production decision to be made.)

Neither cost, that of A or of B, can be determined with certainty since they have common costs of $20 for material and $7 for processing costs. However,

Table 8–1 Summary Statistics: Products *A* and *B*

	A	*B*
Weight of product resulting from 10lb. of raw material (cost $20.00)	4 lb	6 lb
Direct-finishing costs	$1.25 per lb	$0.50 per lb
Indirect-finishing costs $7 (applies jointly to *A* and *B*)		

the cost of making both *A* and *B* can be determined. It costs $35 to manufacture four pounds of *A* and six pounds of *B*.

Also, if the company made just *A* and did not finish *B*, the costs would be $32 (made up of $20 plus $7 plus $5). If it made just *B* and did not finish *A*, the costs would be $30 (made up of $20 plus $7 plus $3).

Raw material	$20
Joint-processing costs	7
Direct costs of *A* ($1.25 × 4)	5
Direct cost of *B* ($0.50 × 6)	3
	$35

From the above information several initial conclusions can be drawn that do not depend on an allocation of joint costs and yet are theoretically sound:

1. If the revenues from the sale of *A* plus *B* are in excess of $35, the firm should produce. (It does not follow that if the revenues are less than $35 it should not produce.)
2. If the revenues from the sale of *A* are greater than $32, the firm should should produce *A*. It should not finish *B* unless the revenues arising from the sale of *B* are in excess of $3, the direct cost of finishing *B*.
3. If the revenues from the sale of *B* are greater than $30, the firm should produce *B*. It should not finish *A* unless the revenues arising from the sale of *A* are in excess of $5, the cost required to finish *A*.
4. If the revenues from the sale of *A* and *B* are both less than $30, then the firm should not produce either *A* or *B*.

Although products *A* and *B* are joint products, since that they are made from a common raw material, the manufacturer may choose not to produce one or the other or both. Thus, a chemical company may find that it is commercially sound to produce one joint product, but that the use for another of the joint products has decreased, with a resulting decrease in price, so that production is no longer economically sound.

8.1.1 Determining the Price of Joint Products

It is frequently assumed that the pricing policy for joint products requires a cost allocation of an arbitrary nature. This is not true. It is possible to establish a theoretically sound framework for determining price and output decisions for joint products.

The example of the preceding section dealing with products A and B produced in fixed proportions may be used. These products will be assumed to have independent demand curves (average-revenue or price curves). (See Figure 8.1.) The demands for the two products may be independent or

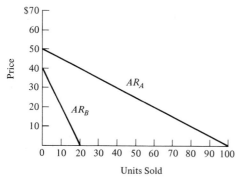

Figure 8.1   Demand curves for two joint products

mutually dependent, but for simplicity it is assumed here that the prices and total sales at different prices of the two products are independent of each other. The only assumptions made are that the demand curves slope downward to the right (the number of units sold increases as the price is decreased), and that the output of product B depends on how many units of A are produced. If the demand curves are flat, the conclusions in items 1 through 4 on page 167 are relevant and the firm should maximize output subject to these conclusions and any other constraints it faces.

To continue the numerical example (recall that each unit of A weighs four pounds and each unit of B weighs six pounds), let

$$Q_A = 100 - 2P_A \tag{8.1}$$

and

$$Q_B = 20 - 0.5P_B \tag{8.2}$$

be the demand equations where Q and P stand for quantity and price respectively and the subscripts designate the product. Solving equations (8.1) and (8.2) for P_A and P_B yields

$$P_A = 50 - 0.5Q_A \tag{8.3}$$

and

$$P_B = 40 - 2Q_B. \tag{8.4}$$

Using equations (8.3) and (8.4), the total-revenue equations, R_A and R_B, are obtained by multiplying price by quantity.

$$R_A = P_A Q_A = 50Q_A - 0.5Q_A^2 \tag{8.5}$$

$$R_B = P_B Q_B = 40Q_B - 2Q_B^2. \tag{8.6}$$

Since, economically, optimal solutions are a result of equating marginal revenue with marginal cost, the next step is to obtain the marginal-revenue expressions for each product. This is done by differentiating equations (8.5) and (8.6) with respect to Q_A and Q_B respectively. This yields

$$MR_A = dR_A/dQ_A = 50 - Q_A \tag{8.7}$$

$$MR_B = dR_B/dQ_B = 40 - 4Q_B. \tag{8.8}$$

Equating marginal revenue with marginal cost however is not so easily accomplished since the joint raw material and processing costs are not allocatable to the products and yet they increase with output. Instead of separate

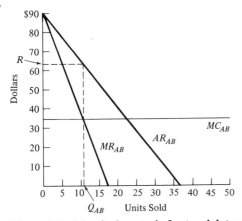

Figure 8.2   Marginal analysis for two joint products

demand curves for the two products, then, consider the ten pounds of raw material as making one product, namely, four pounds of A and six pounds of B. Average-revenue and marginal-revenue curves for this new product can then be obtained. The average-revenue curve for one unit would consist of the price necessary to sell four pounds of A plus the price necessary to sell six pounds of B. This is illustrated in Figure 8.2.

Several complications should be noted. When the marginal revenue of B falls below \$3 per unit of B (that is, marginal revenue is \$3 for six pounds or one unit of B), then B should not be finished, and the marginal-cost curve for the product A plus B should take this into consideration by elimination of the \$3 of finishing costs. This occurs, using equation (8.8), when B equals $9\frac{1}{4}$ units (or 55.5 pounds). In like manner, when the marginal revenue of A falls below \$5 per unit of A (that is, marginal revenue is \$5 for four pounds or one unit of A), then A should not be finished, and the marginal-cost curve should take this into consideration. This occurs, using equation (8.7), when A equals forty-five units (180 pounds). For simplicity in drawing the curves, it is assumed that the relevant parts of the graph occur before either of these possibilities takes place.

The only cost curve shown in Figure 8.2 is the marginal-cost curve. The curve is assumed to be a horizontal line; thus, it also serves as an average variable-cost curve.

Figure 8.2 shows that the optimal solution to the problem of setting the output level is OQ_{AB} units, where the units are expressed in terms of four pounds of A and six pounds of B. At that output, the prices charged result in average revenues of OR. Note that OR is not the price, since OQ units are not sold, but rather units of products A and B are sold. To find the prices at which the units are sold, it is necessary to return to Figure 8.1 and find the prices for A and B that clear the market of the number of units that will be produced. The price of A times the number of units of A, plus the price of B times the number of units of B, is equal to OR times OQ_{AB} (the number of units) from Figure 8.2.

The solution can also be obtained using equations (8.7) and (8.8). Again, consider a single unit of A (four pounds of A) and a single unit of B (six pounds of B) to be the result of processing one unit of raw material (ten pounds). Then the marginal revenue of the joint product AB is given by the sum of equations (8.7) and (8.8), namely

$$MR_{AB} = 90 - 5Q_{AB}. \tag{8.9}$$

Equating the marginal revenue to the marginal cost of completing both product yields

$$90 - 5Q_{AB} = 35. \tag{8.10}$$

Both the joint costs and the direct costs of finishing are incorporated in the \$35 marginal cost figure of equation (8.10). Solving equation (8.10) yields eleven for Q_{AB}. In other words, the initial solution is to produce eleven units of both A and B. The prices to be charged are obtained from equations (8.3) and (8.4) using $Q_A = Q_B = 11$. The prices are

$$P_A = 50 - 0.5Q_A = \$44.50 \qquad (8.11)$$

$$P_B = 40 - 2Q_B = \$18.00. \qquad (8.12)$$

It might appear that the problem is solved. Marginal revenue equals marginal cost for the production level found and the determined prices. This need not be the case. Since the direct costs of finishing are not common to both products, to have an optimal solution the marginal revenues for each product separately must exceed their marginal-finishing costs. Using equations (8.7) and (8.8), the marginal revenues are

$$MR_A = 50 - Q_A = 50 - 11 = \$39 \qquad (8.13)$$

$$MR_B = 40 - 4Q_B = 40 - 44 = -\$4. \qquad (8.14)$$

The marginal revenue of B is less than its finishing cost of $3 and, indeed, here it is negative. If the marginal revenue of each product had equaled or exceeded its finishing cost the solution given by solving equation (8.10) would have been optimal. But this is not the case.

Equating the marginal revenue of product B to its finishing cost yields

$$40 - 4Q_B = 3 \qquad (8.15)$$

and solving indicates that only $9\frac{1}{4}$ units of B should be finished. The rest should be sold for whatever can be obtained for them (possibly as scrap) at the split-off point.[1] The $9\frac{1}{4}$ finished units of B should be priced, using equation (8.4), at $40 - 2Q_B = 40 - 2(9\frac{1}{4}) = \$21.50$.

Equating the marginal revenue of B with its marginal-finishing cost means that the costs of the joint raw material and processing costs of the last unit must be recovered by product A. Therefore, the marginal cost of producing a unit of A is $\$20 + \$7 + \$5 = \$32$. Now, equating marginal revenue and marginal cost for product A yields

$$MR_A = MC_A, \qquad 50 - Q_A = 32, \qquad Q_A = 18. \qquad (8.16)$$

---

[1] It is interesting to note that in this case the same product may be both a by-product and a joint product. However, if B can be sold at a profit as a by-product, this would reduce the number of units finished. For example, if the incremental profit from the sale of one unit of B at split off is $5, only eight units of B would be finished. $40 - 4Q_B = 3 + 5$ and $Q_B = 8$.

The optimal quantity of product A is eighteen units, and, using equation (8.3), it should be priced at $50 - 0.5Q_A = \$41$ a unit.

Summarizing, the optimal solution is to produce and sell eighteen units of product A at \$41 a unit (or $\$41/4 = 10.25$ per lb.). The production will yield eighteen units of product B of which $9\frac{1}{4}$ units should be finished and sold for \$21.50 per unit (or $\$21.50/6 = \$3.58$ per lb.). The remaining $8\frac{3}{4}$ units of B should be disposed of at the split-off point without finishing them. If an integer solution is required, 9 units should be finished.

Summarizing, the steps necessary to solve this joint price-output problem for any number of products are:

1. Derive the total- and marginal-revenue functions for each product.
2. Add the marginal-revenue functions to obtain a single marginal-revenue function which assumes equivalent units of all products will be sold (four pounds of A and six pounds of B are made equivalent units in the example).
3. Set the joint-marginal revenue equal to the joint-marginal cost (where the joint-marginal cost equation is obtained in the same way) and solve for the quantity of the joint product.
4. Determine the marginal revenue for each separate product using the equations determined in step 1 and the quantity determined in step 3.
   (a) If the marginal revenue for all separate products is equal to or greater than the direct-finishing costs, the solution obtained in step 3 is optimal.
   (b) If the marginal revenue less finishing costs for a product is negative, equate the marginal-revenue function for that product to its finishing costs to determine the optimal output. Steps 1 through 4a must be repeated for all products with nonnegative marginal revenues using the relevant costs.

   The analysis given here includes the case where the production involves by-products since the same dependencies in output and profits exist.

The reader may object to a pretense of accuracy in the solution offered since all the information necessary for this solution is seldom known in practice. The objection has merit, but the importance of the presentation is not in terms of its being applied exactly as illustrated but rather in terms of a method of reasoning. This reasoning shows that the allocation of joint costs is not essential to a clear and definite solution to the problems of output and pricing of joint products.

8.2   Inventory Valuation and Joint Costs

The first fact to note concerning the accounting for joint costs is that the joint costs cannot be split up and identified with certainty to several joint products. There is no single right way to split the cost of a barrel of crude oil among the products made from it. The total cost of a barrel is known, but the costs of the several products processed from it cannot be known with certainty. The same is true of the indirect costs.

Having recognized the impossibility of the job, the accountant is still faced with the necessity of determining inventory values. As Chapter 7 on inventory costs and values showed, these figures are required for external and internal decision making. They may also affect performance evaluation through their effect on the computed contribution of the several products. Thus, procedures must be established for determining reasonable values for reporting joint-product inventories.

8.2.1 Net Revenue and Cost Allocation

One possible method of joint-cost allocation is to take the expected sales value of each component product and compute the costs so that they are proportionate to the gross sales value. An objection to this procedure arises since different products may require different finishing costs to prepare them for the market. If the finishing costs are subtracted from the sales value, then it would also be reasonable to charge each product with an amount of the common cost in proportion to those amounts. The assigned cost would then be in proportion to the net sales value of the products to the firm.

For an example of these two methods, suppose that a raw material costs $200 per unit and that three joint products are made from each unit. The characteristics of the three products are given in Table 8–2.

Table 8–2   Product Characteristics: Three-Product Example

Product	Pounds	Sales Revenue	Per Cent of Total	Finishing Costs	Net Sales Value	Per Cent of Total Value
A	70	$130	26.5	$30	$100	25
B	20	210	43.0	50	160	40
C	10	150	30.5	10	140	35
		$490			$400	

Using the net sales value to prorate the $200 of costs, product A would be charged with 25 per cent, or $50; product B with 40 per cent, or $80; and product C with 35 per cent, or $70. A different allocation of the common costs results if the gross sales revenue of each product is used.

If the units are sold for the predicted prices, it is interesting to look at the income statements resulting from the use of net sales value to prorate the $200 of costs. The results are given in Table 8–3.

**Table 8–3   Unit Income Statements: Net Sales-Value Method;
            Unequal Finishing Costs**

	Product *A*	Product *B*	Product *C*
Sales	$130	$210	$150
Finishing costs	30	50	10
Cost of raw material	50	80	70
Total expenses	$ 80	$130	$ 80
Gross profit	$ 50	$ 80	$ 70
Gross profit as per cent of sales	38.5	38.1	46.7

The percentage of gross profits to sales for all three products differs. Now assume that there were no unequal finishing costs, but that the net sales value
was actually the sales price and that all finishing costs were common to both
and were included in the $200 figure. The income statements are given in
Table 8–4.

**Table 8–4   Unit Income Statements: Net Sales Value Method;
            Equal Finishing Costs**

	Product *A*	Product *B*	Product *C*
Sales	$100	$160	$140
Less: Raw material and finishing costs	50	80	70
Gross profit	$ 50	$ 80	$ 70
Gross profit as per cent of sales	50	50	50

Note that the ratio of gross profits to sales is now the same for all three
products, a result of the method of computing the allocation of the common
costs. The percentages will be different only where there are finishing costs
which can be directly identified with the end product, and where those finishing costs are not in proportion to the net sales value of the product. The
tendency of the joint-cost allocations to result in an equal ratio of gross profit
to net sales values warns against placing excessive faith in profit figures for
product lines resulting from arbitrary joint-cost allocations.

Where the gross sales value method is used for the information presented
in Table 8–2, the income statements in Table 8–5 result. There is an increase
in the apparent contribution per unit of product *C*.

Both methods make implicit assumptions about the importance of finishing costs in generating a contribution to fixed costs and profits. The gross
sales value method assumes all costs are equally effective in generating a
contribution to fixed costs and profits. The net sales value method, on the

other hand, assumes that the finishing costs generate sufficient revenues to cover themselves only: they are implicitly assumed to contribute nothing toward fixed costs and profits. Neither assumption is likely to be in accord with the facts.

Table 8–5   Unit Income Statements: Gross-Sales-Value Method

	Product A	Product B	Product C
Sales	$130	$210	$150
Finishing costs	30	50	10
Costs of raw materials	53	86	61
Total expenses	$ 83	$136	$ 71
Gross profit	$ 47	$ 74	$ 79
Gross profit as a per cent of sales	36.2	35.2	52.7

The preceding methods of cost allocation are probably the most reasonable methods, but there are many other methods used in practice.[2] One common method is to allocate the costs on a physical measure. For example, the pounds of product in the above illustration could be used. This would result in product A receiving 70 per cent of the $200 common costs despite the fact that its net sales value is only $100. This does not seem to be a reasonable procedure, since the allocations are made on a basis completely unrelated to the value of the product.

8.2.2 By-Products

Assume that in addition to the products, A, B, and C, there is another product, Z, which is relatively small in value (perhaps scrap metal that is accumulated and sold to scrap dealers). Assume that fifty pounds of Z are generated from each unit of raw material, that Z sells for $0.40 a pound, and that it costs $0.10 a pound to dispose of it.

Each unit of raw material results in $50 \times \$0.40$, or $20 of the sales value of Z. But preparing Z costs $0.10 a pound, or $5. The net value of the scrap is $20 less $5, or $15. One reasonable accounting procedure for by-products

---

[2] A. A. Walters has described a joint-cost model where demand is in the form of a joint-probability distribution for a given price. (Up to this point the amount demanded for different prices was assumed known.) The specific model presented by Walters is limited by his assumptions that price is fixed at the beginning of the marketing period and held throughout the period and that product is impossibly expensive to store; but he does show that under certain conditions the allocation of fixed cost based on *expected* sales is reasonable. See A. A. Walters, "The Allocation of Joint Costs," *American Economic Review*, June 1960, pp. 419–432.

is to remove from the total manufacturing costs the net value of the by-product (the sales value less the finishing and disposal costs) and set it up in a by-product inventory account.

The by-product inventory is priced at its sale price (net of preparation cost). This procedure results in the by-product showing neither a profit nor a loss unless there is a change in the price of the by-product after it has been transferred to inventory. It does, however, implicitly recognize revenue prior to sale. Decisions on the disposition of by-products should not be made on the basis of this information.

If the dollar value of the by-product becomes significant in size, then the procedure described above can distort the relative performance of the by-product compared to the primary products since it now tends to show no profit for the by-product. It could then be treated as a joint product.

A common practice is not to assign any material costs to the by-products. If the amounts are small, this procedure can be excused since the errors are not material. However, the procedure is not theoretically sound.

8.2.3 An Alternative Determination of Common-Cost Allocation

An alternative method of allocating common costs is suggested by the use of such costs in a decision-making context (this method is, however, not presently in use). Consider again the products A and B discussed in Section 8.1. The marginal revenues of the individual products can be used to obtain the

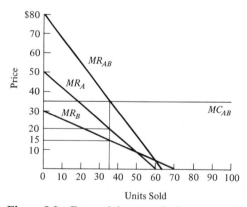

Figure 8.3   Determining marginal revenue of product

inventory values. Suppose, in harmony with Figure 8.2 (but not the numerical example), that the marginal revenues of both products are equal to or exceed their finishing costs.

Figure 8.3 shows the marginal-revenue curves of product A and product B as well as the combined marginal-revenue curves. The marginal-cost curve includes finishing costs. The total marginal cost of the two products at the point of optimal output is equal to $35. It is reasonable to divide the marginal cost into two parts based on the marginal revenue of each product. At the optimal level of output the marginal revenue of A is $15 and the marginal revenue of B is $20; the marginal revenue and the marginal cost of the joint product is $35. Dividing the $35 of cost between A and B results in $15 being allocated to A and $20 to B. This procedure is somewhat different from earlier methods of allocation, which based the allocation on the price (average revenue) less any finishing costs. The two procedures would be equivalent if the average-revenue curve were horizontal since the average-revenue and marginal-revenue curves would then coincide.

If a firm has one unit of A and one unit of B in inventory at the end of a period, and if these units would otherwise be produced next period, then the value of these units is the cost that can be saved (less holding costs) from not making these units in the next period. The value of these units is the marginal cost of the units to be produced in the next period. But since marginal revenue will be equated to marginal cost, the marginal-revenue figures can be used to split the marginal costs. If the productive facilities are not available in the next period, or if the demand will expand so that without the existing inventory of finished products the total demand would not be met then the value of the units in the inventory would depend on the revenues they could earn and not on their costs of replacement. (The actual costs are sunk and are not relevant to the decision to sell.)

The numerical example given previously led to a marginal revenue for A of $32 and for B of $3. These would become the unit inventory values for any marginal units of product.

Two final points might be made:

1. Suppose the raw material has been purchased, and all of product A has been sold while some product B is still on hand (A and B are joint products). If the firm could not economically store any more B nor sell B, then the cost of product A is the entire cost of the raw material. The cost (and value) of B's raw material is zero.

2. If the firm has purchased a small amount of raw material, and the analysis is similar to that presented in Figure 8.3, then it is reasonable to split the cost of the raw material between A and B, using the expected marginal revenues of the products. These costs would be relevant for decision making (though the price would be set by reference to the average-revenue curves) since they give a reasonable estimate of both the cost and value of the last units made.

8.3 Summary

Common costs arise when the factors of production lead to two or more products. Although it is not possible to determine a precise cost for each product, it is possible to make economically sound price and output decisions.

The decision-making techniques also suggest an additional means of valuing inventories. The procedure uses the marginal revenue of the joint products to allocate costs. It does not make the unrealistic implicit assumptions, concerning the revenue-generating ability of specific costs, that are made by the gross sales-value and net sales-value methods. However, since it uses marginal revenues it can only be used for small amounts of product.

QUESTIONS AND PROBLEMS

8–1 It is sometimes said that joint-cost allocations are worthless since they cannot be used for decision making. Comment.

8–2 The costs of operating and maintaining a building are common costs with several products resulting. Do you think that it is useful to allocate building-department costs to operating departments and to product lines?

8–3 Distinguish between joint costs and indirect costs.

8–4 Distinguish between joint products and by-products from an accounting point of view.

8–5 Assuming the presence of joint costs, what type of decisions may be made using cost-revenue information?

8–6 A firm makes two products which are normally of equal value. Because of a temporary overabundance of one product it is sold for scrap at a net of $0 per unit. How should the cost of the raw material be allocated during that period of overabundance?

8–7 Is it reasonable for the accountant to allocate joint costs to different products despite the fact that it is acknowledged that it is an impossible task to prove the allocation is "the" correct allocation?

8–8 The Fidler Company has an accounting problem resulting from the production of joint products. How much of the raw material and other joint costs of $3,000 should be assigned to each of the joint products A, B, and C?

Joint Products	Pounds*	Sales Value (price × units)	Direct- Finishing Costs
A	150	2,000	400
B	50	3,000	900
C	200	4,000	1,700

* Product resulting from one unit of raw material and joint cost of $3,000.

Required: Compute a reasonable allocation of the $3,000 to the three joint products, using the net sales values.

8–9 Referring to problem 8–8, assume that there is a by-product produced which has a value of $100 (per $3,000 of joint costs) and processing costs of $20. Compute the allocation of the $3,000 to the joint products and to the by-product.

8–10 Referring to problem 8–8, assume that the market prices of the factors of production remain unchanged, but the sales prices of the joint products A, B, and C change to $2,500, $2,000, and $1,000 for A, B, and C, respectively. What would be your decision relative to producing and selling each type of product?

8–11 The Capital Corporation stamps a component part, which shall be called X. From a roll of steel 100 feet long it is expected that fifty units of X will be obtained. The cost of 100 feet of the steel is $25, and the standard material cost of a unit of X has been set at $0.50. X utilizes approximately 90 per cent of the total metal.

In April 1970, an engineer found that by cutting the metal scraps from the production line of X into easily handled shapes a product Y could be made. For the remainder of 1970, Y's were made from this scrap. It is estimated that one unit of Y could be obtained per foot of steel. Y utilized approximately one tenth of the total metal; the cost per unit was established at $0.025. To record the manufacture of one million units of Y from 1,000,000 feet of steel the following journal entry was made for the material component of Y (a standard-cost system was in use for material):

Inventory—Y	25,000	
Material		25,000

To record the manufacture of 500,000 units of X the following entry was made:

Inventory—X	250,000	
Material		250,000

Required: Comment on the procedure followed.

8–12 The AC Company has an extensive scrap operation since the pieces of metal resulting from stamping operations have a high value on the scrap market. Total scrap sales amount to approximately $4,000,000 per year. The total sales of the corporation are approximately a billion dollars per year. The expenses of operating the scrap-processing center (where the scrap is sorted and baled), are approximately $300,000 of direct costs.

The controller has argued that the scrap operation should be charged with part of the cost of raw material; the production manager, who is in over-all charge of the scrap operation, argues that it should not be charged since there is no reasonable method of assigning material costs to the operation.

Required: Comment on the positions of the controller and the production manager. What, if any, are the accounting problems?

8–13 A raw material is used to produce two products. One unit of raw material costing $8.50 is turned into one unit of A and one unit of B. Additional information is as follows:

Joint cost of processing raw material	$ 4
Direct cost of finishing product A	8
Direct cost of finishing product B	12

The price-quantity relationships of the two products are:

$$Q_A = 40 - \tfrac{1}{2}P_A, \qquad Q_B = 80 - 4P_B,$$

where Q is the number of units demanded in one day with price P.

Required:

a. How many units of raw material, product A, product B, should be processed daily?

b. If there were one unit each of A and B remaining in the finished-goods inventory, what would be the inventory value of those units?

c. Suppose $P_A = 16$, $P_B = 18$ regardless of the firm's output and either product can be sold for $7 at the split-off point. What should the firm do?

8–14 The Auston Company purchases a raw material for $50 per unit that is turned into two different products A and B. The joint costs of processing are $30. After the two products are separated it costs $14 to finish A and $6 to finish B. One unit of A and one unit of B are obtained from each unit of raw material.

The following quantity-price relationships are expected to continue into the future. (They relate the units of demand for a month.)

$$P_A = 200 - \tfrac{1}{2}Q_A, \qquad P_B = 150 - 2Q_B.$$

a. What price and what output for each of the two end products would maximize profits?

b. Assuming one unit of unfinished A and twenty units of unfinished B are on hand at the end of a month, how should these be valued?

8–15 The following summary is from W. J. Baumol *et al.*, "The Role of Cost in the Minimum Pricing of Railroad Services," *The Journal of Business,* October 1962.

Summary

1. In the determination of cost floors as a guide to the pricing of particular railroad services, or the services of any other transport mode, incremental costs of each particular service are the only relevant costs.
2. Rates for particular railroad services should be set at amounts (subject to the regulation of maximum rates and to legal rules against unjust discrimination) that will make the greatest total contribution to net income. Clearly, such maximizing rates would never fall below incremental costs.
3. Pricing which is not restricted by any minimum other than incremental cost can foster more efficient use of railroad resources and capacity and can therefore encourage lower costs and rates. This same principle applies to other modes of transportation.
4. The presence of large amounts of fixed costs and unused capacity in railroad facilities makes it especially important that railroad rates encourage a large volume of traffic.
5. Reduced rates which more than cover incremental costs and are designed by management to maximize contribution to net income do not constitute proof of predatory competition.
6. "Fully distributed" costs derived by apportioning unallocable costs have no economic significance in determining rate floors for particular railroad services. The application of such a criterion would arbitrarily force the railroads to maintain rates above the level which would yield maximum contribution to net income and would deprive them of much traffic for which they can compete economically. For similar reasons, restriction of railroad minimum rates according to the "full cost of the low-cost carrier" is economically unsound.

Required: Comment on the conclusions.

8–16 The following argument can be found in the source for problem 8–15.

"Fully Distributed" Cost, An Invalid Basis for Minimum
Pricing

The relevant incremental costs constitute all the cost information pertinent to the determination of floors in the pricing of particular railroad services. "Fully distributed" cost, measured by some kind of arbitrary statistical apportionment of the unallocable costs among the various units or classes of traffic, is an economically invalid criterion for setting minimum rates, from both a managerial and a regulatory standpoint. No particular category of traffic can be held economically responsible for any given share of the unallocable costs. Whether any particular rate is above or below some fully distributed cost is without real economic significance for minimum pricing.

Stated differently, the appropriate aim of the railroads is to determine that margin above incremental costs, traffic volume considered, at which a rate produces the maximum total contribution toward fixed costs and net income. Fully distributed costs cannot serve this vital economic purpose. They present an entirely false picture of traffic profitability. Their use would drive away great quantities of profitable, volume-moving traffic now handled at rates below fully distributed costs.

Required: Is the statement valid for a manufacturing firm?

SUPPLEMENTARY READING

BAUMOL, W. J., *et al.*, "The Role of Cost in the Minimum Pricing of Railroad Services," *The Journal of Business*, October 1962, pp. 1–10.

MANES, R., and V. L. SMITH, "Economic Joint Cost Theory and Accounting Practice," *The Accounting Review*, January 1965, pp. 31–35.

National Association of Cost Accountants, *Research Series No. 31, Costing Joint Products*, 1957.

PFOUTS, R. W., "The Theory of Cost and Production in the Multi-Product Firm," *Econometrica*, October 1961, pp. 650–658.

SHUBIK, M., "Incentives, Decentralized Control, the Assignment of Joint Costs, and Internal Pricing," *Management Science*, April, 1962, pp. 325–343.

WALTERS, A. A., "The Allocation of Joint Costs," *The American Economic Review*, June 1960, pp. 419–432.

WEIL, R. L., "Allocating Joint Costs," *The American Economic Review*, December 1968, pp. 1342–1345.

Chapter 9

The Analysis of Nonmanufacturing Costs

Traditionally, cost accountants have primarily concerned themselves with manufacturing costs. In recent years an increasing amount of attention has been directed to the control and analysis of distribution and other nonmanufacturing costs. This has occurred partly because of the increased relative importance of these costs as a per cent of total costs and partly because of the introduction of formal decision-making models in this area.

This chapter examines several types of nonmanufacturing costs including distribution costs, administrative costs, and research costs. Attention is also given to the impact of the Robinson-Patman Act on cost record keeping in this area.

The techniques used for decision making and control of manufacturing costs are, in large part, also relevant to nonmanufacturing costs. Thus the notions of cost-variance analysis, cost-volume-profit analysis, budgeting, and performance reporting are all appropriate in some degree to the present subject material. However, the benefits are more difficult to measure in the area of nonmanufacturing costs than they are with manufacturing costs.

9.1 Distribution Cost Analysis and Control

The distribution function generally begins before the manufacture of the product and continues after the cash is collected. Under this broad time horizon, distribution costs typically include:

183

1. The costs (including advertising costs) of promoting customer goodwill and obtaining sales.
2. The costs of handling and storing the completed product and of shipping it to the customer.
3. The costs of recording and collecting the amounts owed to the company by its customers.
4. Handling the returns and servicing guarantees (a more generous guarantee being a way to enhance the saleability of the product).

The purpose of the distribution function can be taken as maximizing the long-run contribution to fixed costs and profits.[1] Thus the analysis of distribution costs should be directed toward decisions that can be made to improve the over-all contribution. This implies that such costs should be broken down by product line, customer type, salesmen, geographical location, and so on. The classification in Table 9–1 suggests some of the possibilities:

Table 9–1   Possible Breakdowns of Distribution Costs

Sales Outlets (customer type)	Methods of Selling
Wholesalers	Mail order
Retailers, independent	Company salesmen, outside
Discount houses	Company salesmen, inside
Chain stores	

Product Line	Graphical Location
	Cities over 1,000,000
Product A	Cities over 100,000
B	Cities over 10,000
C	Cities under 10,000
	or
	Sales districts, counties, states, countries

Historical cost figures should be regarded with suspicion. In the first place, the data may reflect arbitrary cost allocations and costs that would not be altered by the decision being contemplated (the contraction or expansion of some activity, for example). Second, future costs are relevant and historical data only provide reliable indications of the future when conditions remain essentially unaltered. In the determination of future costs, the use of modern

---

[1] Short-run goals may include market penetration and establishing markets for new products. Performance evaluation should take cognizance of these short-run goals when they are operative and considered consistent with long-run profit maximization.

statistical techniques of experimentation and decision making can be particularly helpful.

Distribution costs are usually common to several functions and, therefore, allocation must often be made on a relatively arbitrary basis. In decision making and control, it is important to recognize the common nature of these costs and the effect of this commonality on decisions.

9.1.1 Decision Making and Distribution Costs

Many decisions in the distribution area are made intuitively, and it is unlikely that distribution cost analysis will completely eliminate the necessity of making such decisions in this manner. For example, it will probably never be possible for the accounting department using historical cost to tell the marketing staff that they are spending too much or too little on advertising and prove that an alternative amount is optimal. On the other hand, the accounting department can tell top management that the revenues of a product are not recovering the manufacturing and distribution costs—including advertising—directly associated with the product. This may lead indirectly to a decision concerning advertising.

In the type of cost analysis being considered it is useful to think of three layers of costs:

1. Direct costs are costs that can be directly identified with the product, division, geographical unit, etc.
2. Allocated costs with traceable benefits are costs that cannot be directly identified, but which have a close correlation with, the activity of a unit. For example, costs of writing bills may be allocated on the basis of the number of lines on an invoice.
3. Allocated costs with indirect benefits are costs that cannot be directly identified and that have little correlation with the activity of a unit. For example, the benefits derived from the sales manager's salary may not be closely identified with any one product line and thus must be arbitrarily allocated to several product lines.

In addition to the above three distinctions it is often useful to know if the cost is fixed or variable. These classifications take on a different meaning in the analysis of distribution costs from that of manufacturing costs. In manufacturing-cost analysis, interest centers on how costs react to changes in manufacturing activity. With distribution costs, interest centers on how costs react to changes in sales or a given type of promotional effort. An example of a variable-distribution cost is a salesman's commission. An example of a fixed cost is the salary of the sales manager. The problem is complicated, however, by the fact that costs may be fixed in one sense, but not in another. Thus advertising costs may be fixed by a managerial decision, but in order to increase sales it may be necessary to increase the amount spent on advertising.[2] On the other hand, a given amount of advertising may result in increased sales if the sales price is lowered. Thus advertising may be considered fixed when the firm is considering a change in sales price, or the firm may vary both advertising and sales price at once.

The decisions made with the help of distribution-cost analysis are varied. Among some of the more important are:

1. Setting prices of the product.
2. Expanding, contracting, or abandoning product lines or sales effort.
3. Expanding, contracting, or abandoning specific customer outlets or geographical locations.
4. Establishing warehouses and supply points.
5. Determining the relative merits of different sales efforts (including performance of salesmen).
6. Media selection.

The above decisions require cost and revenue information classified in several ways. For example, where possible, each cost must be identified as to product line and geographical location. Also of interest is the relation of the cost to any particular type of sales outlet, its functional classification (delivery, warehousing, billing, collecting, sales, etc.), and its natural classification (labor, supplies, utilities, etc.). Costs that cannot be directly identified with product lines, geographical locations, and so on, present a problem. Should they be allocated? All costs may be allocated, but the manager should carefully distinguish among the direct costs, the allocated costs with traceable benefits, and the allocated costs that have no close relation with the unit to which the cost is being allocated.

For example, assume a situation where the Tall Bottle Company makes four different types of bottles. Management is reviewing the profitability of the milk bottle line. The income statement for the most recent period is given in Table 9–2.

Assume further that all the fixed costs are unavoidable and would be incurred even if the product were abandoned, and that the $2,500 of allocated costs includes $1,000 of costs that are variable and closely related to the sale of milk bottles (these include delivery expense, which is allocated by weight, bulk, and mean distance of the deliveries).

What action, if any, should management take? If the income statement is rearranged, management will find that the sale of milk bottles is contributing $2,500 to the recovery of common and fixed costs, and should not be abandoned. This is shown in Table 9–3. Allocated costs in the amount of $1,000 are considered relevant to this decision.

---

[2] Advertising is often treated as a residual factor in budgeting. This treatment implicitly assumes advertising is a function of sales and does not acknowledge the effect of advertising on sales.

The fact that the product is recovering more than the variable costs does not mean that no action is required. A company may recover variable costs every day right up until it has to file bankruptcy papers. The analysis does

Table 9–2   Milk Bottles Income Statement

For year ending December 31		
Sales	$30,000	
Less: Manufacturing costs of goods sold		
(includes fixed costs of $3,000)	25,000	
Gross margin		$5,000
Less: Distribution costs		
Directly identified with product		
(includes fixed costs of $2,000)	$ 6,500	
Allocated costs	2,500	
		9,000
Net loss		($4,000)

indicate, however, that assuming the fixed costs are unavoidable, the company is better off with the milk bottle business than it would be without it. It is possible that more or less selling effort is required or that the price should be raised or lowered. The income statement presented shows that management should not be complacent. It does not indicate the nature or the direction of managerial action.[3]

Table 9–3   Milk Bottles Income Statement: Revised

Sales		$30,000
Variable costs		
Manufacturing	$22,000	
Distribution ($1,000 + $4,500)	5,500	$27,500
Contribution to recovery of fixed costs		$ 2,500
Fixed costs		
Manufacturing	$ 3,000	
Distribution	3,500	$ 6,500
Net loss		($ 4,000)

In recommending a decision not to drop the product, neither the unavoidable fixed costs nor the allocated costs not closely related to the product were considered. If some of the fixed costs could be avoided by the dropping of the product, these costs become relevant to the decision.

If the problem were changed so that there were the option to sell the milk

[3] The possibility of allocating effort in other directions should also be considered.

bottle portion of the business, then most of the fixed costs could be avoided. The price that could be obtained for the business becomes a type of opportunity cost. The problem might then be solved by implementing the theory of capital budgeting (see Chapter 13). The procedure would be to compare the present value of the cash flows resulting from retaining the business to the present value of the cash flows that would result from the sale of the business.

Recent years have also witnessed the introduction of operations research models to distribution decisions. The advertising function is one of several in the distribution area in which formal mathematical models have been used.[4] For example, programming and statistical decision-theory models have been applied to the media selection and message effectiveness problems. Typically the models attempt to minimize cost subject to a constraint on the minimum total service provided. While a substantial portion of the costs, such as the cost per unit of an advertising medium, are externally set, there is a tendency to ignore the associated internal costs. This is particularly true for the cost of supportive activities which can be allocated only to the advertising function on relatively arbitrary bases. The allocation should include even the fixed costs of providing service, accounting for example, where such costs may be considered as opportunity-cost approximations for using the committed resources.

Formal mathematical models have been used to make other distribution decisions as well. The location of warehouses and the establishment of supply centers provide examples. Costs play a central role in all of these decisions. Hence it behoves the managerial accountant to understand these models and the cost-information requirements they entail.

There are a variety of decisions and they often require different arrays of cost information. Not all costs are relevant for all decisions. Costs to be especially watched are costs that are fixed but avoidable, and costs that are common to many products or other units. The inclusion or exclusion of these costs depends on the exact nature of the decisions. Neither the inclusion nor exclusion of allocated and fixed costs should be automatic.

9.1.2 Distribution Cost Control

The control of distribution costs is especially difficult since, in contrast with many manufacturing type operations, there is no easily measurable and assignable output. Also standards of performance are much more difficult to set. Nevertheless it is sometimes possible to set standards that are effective enough to assist in the control of distribution costs.

For purposes of cost control, it is useful to separate distribution costs into those involved with obtaining sales and those involved with filling orders. The techniques of control are somewhat different.

[4] See D. W. Miller and M. K. Starr, *Executive Decisions and Operations Research*, Prentice-Hall, Englewood Cliffs, N.J., 1964, Chapter 9.

Control of Order-Filling Costs

Order-filling costs include the costs of order processing, storage, packing and shipping, billing, credit, and collection. The use of task analysis and work measurement techniques can be valuable in setting standards for budgeting and controlling costs of this type.

Where the action is repetitive and of a uniform nature and the benefits easily measured, the setting of the standards is relatively well defined. Thus the billing department may be judged on how much it costs to turn out invoices, with due consideration for the characteristics of the invoices. The shipping and receiving departments may be judged on the number of items handled and the weight of the items. The credit and collection departments may be effectively controlled in a manner similar to that used in the control of manufacturing costs.

Consider the situation in a billing department. Suppose a firm employs twenty individuals in the billing department. Each can handle (the standard at normal activity levels) 500 billings per week. The twenty employees are all paid $200 per week. Suppose that in a given week, 9,700 billings were made. If the twenty employees had worked at the standard rate, the expectation would be that 10,000 billings would have been made. What is the explanation of the difference of 300 billings?

An analysis similar to that of Chapter 1 is relevant. In the first place, it is necessary to know how the standard was determined since this affects the interpretation of the variance. Suppose the standard was established on the basis of normal activity. Under these conditions the actual sales level may explain some of the variance. For example, there may have been 9,700 billings requiring processing. Alternately, the employees may have been inefficient in performing their jobs (assuming that more than 9,700 billings required processing). Or, alternately, the bills may be more complex than the average bills. The idle-capacity variance in this case is 10,000 − 9,700 or 300 billings. An analysis of these factors can assist in week-to-week activity evaluation and hopefully lead to better performance.

It should be noted that the approach, or attitude, taken by management toward cost control can influence cost reduction programs. Cost savings are not likely to be achieved in areas where costs are considered uncontrollable by management.

Suppose that in the above example 9,700 billings actually required processing. Even when activity and expectations match, there may still be valuable information available for cost control. Since the work force could process 10,000 billings there is presently over capacity in the billing task—at least for the week in question. But this may represent only a necessary safety factor to handle variable-activity levels. It would be useful to know the standard-activity level and the activity's variability. The cost of the difference between the normal capacity, 10,000 billings, and the actual output level in this case, 9,700 billings, is $120: $200/500 (10,000 − 9,700), or, alternately, the cost of billing is $4,000/10,000 or $0.40. Since 300 billings less than 10,000 were processed, the cost of the idle capacity is $0.40(300) or $120. This amount might represent the investment required to maintain a stable work force necessary to meet fluctuating activity levels. On the other hand, it might indicate opportunities for cost savings over the longer run. Management must decide the employee level for each task and whether it wishes to meet peak activity levels by hiring part-time employees, by overtime, by delays, or by shifting employees from other tasks. Each reasonable alternative should be examined in terms of its cost considering a full cycle of activity and the frequency associated with the various activity levels. If this has not been done previously, large cost variances suggest that it may be profitable to consider the alternatives.

The process (controlling the cost of billings) would involve the concept of work measurement. It should be mentioned that work measurement may often be a difficult task. In distribution-cost control, the difficulties may center about the diversity of tasks performed by individuals of a group or, instead, on the difficulty of isolating an output measure (such as the number of billings). Sometimes work measurement is difficult because of the nature of the output. For example, how should the output of the market research staff be measured for cost-control purposes? These comments are also generally applicable to the control of administrative costs. For example, how should the output of the legal or economic-analysis staff be computed?

Control of Order-Getting Costs

Controlling the costs of selling is complicated by the fact that the effectiveness of the costs in gaining sales is affected by variables beyond the control of the sales department, such as general business conditions, the action of competitors, the design of the product, the price of the product, and changing habits of consumers. In the control of selling costs, the quantitative measures must sometimes be tempered by qualitative judgments as to whether the sales department or a particular salesman is doing a "good" job. Furthermore, the measurement and control of costs becomes more complex as advertising becomes more general, selling more personal, products more interrelated, and as economic conditions change more quickly. Thus, control of institutional advertising cost is not facilitated by allocating it to specific products.

Companies frequently use measures such as selling cost per order, or selling cost per call, or calls per day, as control devices. But there is a danger in comparing salesmen where the geographical and economic characteristics of the different sales areas differ considerably. Used with discretion, however, these measures can be useful in forming impressions of how effectively a salesman is performing.

Control of order-getting costs is more effective in the cost planning stage than in the implementation stage. Still, *ex post* implementation analysis is important as a step in improving resource allocation. Analysis can highlight those areas (product line, selling method, advertising medium, etc.) where the contribution is large, either on a unit basis or in total, and thus identify possibilities that may deserve greater (or less) effort on the part of the firm. A comparison of actual costs to the figures used in decision making can help determine the limitations of the decision model or provide cost information for future decisions.

9.1.3 Distribution Costs and Financial Reporting

The greatest portion of the distribution costs are considered expenses of the time period in which they are incurred, and little attempt is made to assign these costs to the periods which benefit from their incurrence. Thus advertising costs are generally considered an expense in the period in which the advertising medium appears, rather than a cost allocated over the periods that benefit from the advertising. In like manner, the selling costs connected with obtaining unfilled orders are only infrequently carried over to the period in which the order is filled. These are considered to be conservative accounting procedures and thus desirable. But, in part, the accounting treatment reflects the impact of taxes. Since such expenses are deductible for tax purposes, they are usually treated as tax expenses in the earliest period permitted by law. For simplicity and consistency this treatment is then typically used in the firm's financial records regardless of its effect on the data supplied to external decision makers.

9.2 Administrative Costs

A distinction between administrative and distribution costs is somewhat artificial, at least from an analysis and control point of view. All of what has been said concerning distribution costs is relevant, at least in part, to administrative costs. Those distinctions that can be drawn are essentially ones of degree and not of substance.

Administrative costs are basically fixed in the short run (some authors would refer to them as "programed"). In this sense they are similar to promotional expenditures. Few of these costs exhibit any variability with short-run changes in the physical activity of the firm.

As was true in the case of distribution decisions, formal models have also been applied in recent years to several problems in the administrative area. These include problems of the optimal sized work force, the related problems of absenteeism, pay incentive plans, vacations, and so on. Once again these decisions usually center on cost considerations since the contribution of administrative activity to profit and fixed costs is extremely difficult to establish. The decisions, when formalized, are often based on minimizing the expected cost to perform some given level of service.

Often an analysis of cost behavior is important since management needs to know what improvement in costs can be obtained by the introduction of some corrective action: Management needs a cost-benefit analysis. For example, if the relationship between the absentee rate and total-period costs were known, and if the effect of various strategies (such as a bonus for a good employment record) on the absentee rate could be estimated, then decisions among several strategies to lower absenteeism would be facilitated.

The accountant can assist in these decisions if he recognizes problem areas, often a result of cost analysis, and understands the types of formal and informal analysis that could be applied. He is then in a position to analyze cost behavior, predict the effect of strategic variables on costs, and thereby assist in the initiation and implementation of administrative cost-reduction programs.

Control is again usually achieved in the planning stage through the use of budgets based upon the type and amount of service anticipated for the period in question. However, some tasks, including clerical activities, lend themselves to the use of standards based on some measure of task activity. Where this is the case, the control methods found in the production area can be applied. Generally, however, administrative services are rendered indirectly to many different departments and in addition it is practically impossible to establish input-output relationships that permit over-all evaluations. These facts make the control and evaluation of administrative costs one of the more difficult areas.

The tendency of new administrative services, regardless of their actual value, to become permanent once initiated argues strongly for a full analysis of suggested new activities. The same types of stringent criteria should be applied to the benefits associated, or alleged to be associated, with new administrative services before they are adopted, as are applied to other more easily evaluated activities in the firm. However, objective measures of the benefits may not always be available.

9.3   Research and Development Cost Analysis and Control

Once again much of what has been said about distribution and administration costs is relevant to the research and development area. Nevertheless there are additional factors that call for some discussion.

The difficulty of measuring the results or output of an activity are perhaps most pronounced in this area. Usually it is only over an extended period of time involving several years, that some indication of the success of research and development activities can be obtained. Further, bench marks against which to measure the effectiveness of research and development activities are not easily established. Conditions may change appreciably over time and the difficulty of disentangling a research department's contribution from that of sales, production, and so on make it difficult to use historical data. Also, information concerning similar activities in other firms is neither easily obtained nor adjustable to permit comparisons.

The use of budgets as a control mechanism is common but suffers from several shortcomings. First, there is usually a strong incentive built into the control system to stay within budgeted levels. Such budgets, however, reflect an amalgamation of research activities and are therefore unrelated to specific projects or the advantages to be obtained therefrom.

Second, department managers are often moved up to higher positions. Hence they may be motivated more by the easily seen short-run budget controls than by the long-run, and more difficult to evaluate, research contribution to the firm. Finally, research and development budgets, like many promotional expenditures, have an indirect impact on the level of sales and thereby on cash flows. Thus they interact with the very factors that often determine the budgeted level for research. This interrelationship, although indirect, is nevertheless important. Research and development expenditures (like promotion expenditures) should not usually be treated as residual budget allocations made after production and similar outlays have been determined. Indeed, in most industries the single most important activity affecting the future prosperity of the firm is the success of its research and development activities.

Given the importance of research and development and the unreasonableness of short-run evaluations, the emphasis should be placed on creating a climate where research has an optimal chance of success. In accomplishing this objective, it is important to consider the unusual character of the creative individual, the frustration of delays resulting from inadequate facilities or lack of adequate assistance, the need for praise that such individuals possess, their desire for some pure (or free) as well as specific-objective research, the importance of minimizing paper work and reports, as well as the tendency for many creative individuals to be unconcerned with time and cost considerations.

A useful approach to control and, indirectly, also for analysis, is to organize the research department by projects. Each project should be under the supervision of someone in the department. The supervisor then takes responsibility for administration and personnel evaluation. Cost control is achieved through the comparison of periodic reports listing percentage completion, expenditures of time and resources, as well as estimates of time and resources needed to finish the project, with initial project estimates. Typically it will be necessary to subdivide projects into well-defined subtasks in order to maximize the effectiveness of this control procedure.[5] Even the mere fact that

---

[5] The ability to form projects and to divide them into distinct and ordered subtasks suggests that the techniques of PERT and PERT-Cost might be applicable at least to certain specific-object research. See Chapter 12.

control is considered important, if attempted in a reasonable way, can often encourage real savings in both costs and time.

9.4   The Robinson-Patman Act

The Robinson-Patman amendment to the Clayton Act concerns itself with unlawful price discrimination.[6] Price discrimination is considered unlawful where the effect "may be to substantially lessen competition or tend to create a monopoly in any line of commerce." The law is administered by the Federal Trade Commission.

The primary purpose of the act is to make it easier to establish a violation and more difficult to achieve a defense than was the case under the Clayton Act. For a firm to be subject to the act, several conditions must be satisfied. These conditions are that the prices "must

1. Occur in interstate commerce.
2. Be related to 'commodities of like grade and quality'.
3. Have the requisite effect on competition.
4. Be other than price changes occurring because of market conditions such as seasonal clearances.
5. Not be justified as a means of meeting an equally low price of a competitor.
6. Not be justified by cost differences of equal or greater magnitude."[7]

Defenses by firms faced with suits under the Robinson-Patman Act have attempted to show that one or more of these six conditions are not satisfied. In general, this has been very difficult to do. The concept of interstate commerce has been expanded until this section of the law offers little if any defense. Goods can be considered of like grade and quality even though they are not identical. Once price differences have been established, the presumption of at least a potentially undesirable effect on competition is nearly automatic, and it has been extremely difficult to rebut this charge by the defense of meeting an equally low competitor's price.[8]

Complaints involving distress merchandise have been rare, and thus this

[6] For a more complete description of the Robinson-Patman Act, see H. E. Taggart, "Cost Justification: Rules of the Game," *Journal of Accountancy*, December 1958, pp. 52–60; and H. E. Taggart, *Cost Justification*, Michigan Business Studies, Vol. XIV, No. 3, Ann Arbor: University of Michigan, 1959; and supplements No. 1 and 2, 1964 and 1967.

[7] Taggart, *Cost Justification, op. cit.*, p. 548.

[8] The meeting-of-competition defense has been used successfully by only one firm in public proceedings, and this defense took seventeen years.

sort of activity is unlikely to bring action by the Commission. This is important since, contrary to normal legal proceedings, a defendant under the Robinson-Patman Act is presumed guilty unless he can successfully establish a defense. Furthermore, if the firm is unable to establish a successful defense, it may be subject to treble damages. These facts suggest that it is desirable not to come under the investigatory scrutiny of the Commission.

In fact, the most successful defense against a complaint brought by the Federal Trade Commission under the Robinson-Patman Act has been by cost justification of the price differences. Even in this area success is an elusive goal. While about 50 per cent of the cost defenses made in public proceedings have been at least partially successful, there have been relatively few cases that have reached the stage of public proceedings.[9] Most of the complaints have been settled by informal hearings before the Commission's staff. The number of successful cost defenses in informal hearings, however, is not known since the results of such hearings are not available to the public.

The reasons for the limited use of the cost defense stem in part from the time-consuming nature of the work involved and the expense of making cost-justification studies. Perhaps even more important is the difficulty anticipated in convincing the Commission or, more accurately, the Commission's accountants, that adequate cost justification exists. Nevertheless, the fact that cost calculations have been accepted in both formal and informal proceedings is evidence that this defense is not completely illusionary.

An analysis of the cases that have been open to the public suggests several basic principles that are valuable for firms faced with potential complaints by the Federal Trade Commission. Perhaps most important in this list is recognition of the fact that any cost-justification defense must convince the Commission's accountants. One important means of accomplishing this objective is to provide evidence of having considered the price differentials in light of the related costs prior to offering the prices to customers. Cost analyses prepared in advance and, perhaps, if possible, after consultation with the Commission, could provide evidence of this good faith. Since the effect of the Commission's actions can be severe, the best talent available should be put on the job. This is not a place for the second team.

Several additional points can also be gleaned from the public cases.[10] They include:

1. Time has been the only satisfactory means of allocating labor services.
2. Sales dollars cannot be used to allocate overhead.
3. Differential costing is not acceptable.

---

[9] Taggart, *Cost Justification, op. cit.*, pp. 544–545. Only twenty-two defendants pleaded this defense in twenty-two years, while in the year 1957 alone the Commission issued twenty-two complaints.

[10] The reader is referred to Taggart, *Cost Justification, op. cit.*, particularly Chapters 20 and 21.

4. Cost methods and classifications already in use by a firm need not be accepted by the Commission.
5. Management cost estimates are not acceptable.
6. Sampling methods may be used but samples must be demonstrably representative. (Small samples are suspect.)

The generally acceptable principles enumerated above are few in number. Several additional principles also are relevant to the treatment of specific cost items. The interested reader is referred to the materials authored by Taggert (see footnote 6) and the report of the Advisory Committee (Appendix A to the Taggert book) for specific examples.

Perhaps the best summary of this section is given by Taggert when he writes that "the cost defense, with all its complexities and uncertainties, is the most practical and available [defense against a complaint under section 2(a) of the Robinson-Patman Act]. And the conclusion to be derived from studying the recorded cost-defense cases is that the best time to prepare to offer the cost defense is before a complaint is issued."

Example

Ten thousand units of a product are being produced and sold at a price of $10. The product costs $5 per unit (variable costs are $3, and fixed costs are $2 per unit and $20,000 in total). An order for 10,000 more units can be obtained if they are sold at a price of $8 per unit.

Should the order be taken, from the point of view of economic considerations (assuming the order will not reduce the present sales)? Since the price per unit of $8 exceeds the variable cost per unit, the additional business is desirable from an economic point of view.

Should the order be taken, from the point of view of legality under the Robinson-Patman Act? Can the $2 difference in price be explained by a "saving" of $2 in fixed costs? The answer is no. The defense would be rejected. If the company wants to accept the business, it will have to change its basic price to all customers to $8 per unit, or change the price for the order to $10 per unit, or find another defense. One possible defense would be to show that the fixed costs of $20,000 should reasonably be allocated to the other sales. For example, assume the $20,000 is related to packaging equipment which will not be used with the new order since there is going to be bulk shipment. In this case a price difference might be justified by real cost savings.

9.5 Summary

If X dollars are expended for direct labor, it is not difficult for the accountant to suggest that Y units of product should be forthcoming. The benefits of the expenditures are concrete and relatively easy to measure. If significantly less than Y units of product results, there is cause for suspecting some type of inefficiency.

With costs of the kind treated in this chapter the cause-and-effect relationship is not as easily measured. Two salesmen may be doing equally good work, but one has a better territory and so is making more sales. Or, the automobile traffic in one city may be heavier than in another, resulting in fewer calls per day for one salesman than another. In one year the advertising campaign may be considered a big success, but in the second year sales decrease and it is a complete failure. Are sales declining because of changes in the quality of advertising, changes in styling of the product, changes in prices, changes in actions of competitors, or because of a general business recession? Is a salesman efficient if he reduces his selling expense, or is he just making fewer telephone calls and traveling less?

There are too many variables connected with distribution and administration costs for the accountant to offer definitive advice in this area. He can report magnitudes of expense and sales and break these down in various ways, but it is generally rash to draw conclusions and recommend decisions about performance on this information. It would be better for the accountant to obtain the assistance of a statistician and by the use of experimental and statistical techniques attempt to determine the impact of the several types of costs on sales and profits. For example, by varying the advertising expenditures in one market area while not changing the expenditures in other areas, management may obtain some insight into the effectiveness of the advertising. It would seem desirable for the accountant to supplement his skills in this field.

The accountant should be alert to the relationship of nonmanufacturing costs to activity variables and to other variables that can be manipulated by the firm. An example involving the relationship of total cost to the absentee rate is discussed in Section 9.2. The accountant is in an excellent position to observe cost behavior and analyze alternatives for cost reduction. Further, the accountant should be familiar with the cost requirements of formal models that have been subject to increasing use in decision making involving nonmanufacturing activities. In particular, he should be cognizant of the importance and subsequent difficulties associated with measuring the relevant indirect costs required by these models.

In some cases cost control may be achieved by the same methods that are used in the area of production costs. Generally, however, output measures and standards are not easily established. Therefore, control tends to be exercised more through comparing budgeted and actual costs. Management must also be particularly alert to the necessity of designing the elements of these indirect-control systems so that they motivate employees toward achieving the goals of the firm.

QUESTIONS AND PROBLEMS

9–1 It has been said that the primary function of the accountant relative to distribution costs is to record the costs so that the information is available for analysis. Comment on this proposition.

9–2 Why is distribution-cost analysis more difficult than manufacturing-cost analysis?

9–3 Is it possible for fixed-distribution costs to be avoidable?

9–4 How would you allocate billing department costs to different product lines?

9–5 How would you allocate shipping department costs to different product lines?

9–6 Are advertising expenditures properly considered expenses in the period in which the advertising is distributed?

9–7 Would it ever be reasonable to consider costs associated with selling to be an asset at the end of a period rather than an expense?

9–8 As a business manager would you want an income statement for a product line which included allocations of joint distribution and manufacturing costs not controllable by the manager in charge of the product line?

9–9 Stenographic pools that handle all dictation and typing required by executives are common. On the one hand, they save money by cutting down the total number of typists and/or stenographers required. On the other hand, a pool eliminates private secretaries, and executives generally dislike pools in part for convenience reasons and in part because private secretaries are often considered status symbols. How would you analyze the problem of whether or not to have a stenographic pool? Assume the pool does not presently exist.
   a. How would you estimate the costs and savings?
   b. What other factors should be considered?

9–10 The Elson Company is considering a suggestion to allocate national magazine advertising costs to sales territories on the basis of circulation of the media weighted by an index of relative buying potential in each territory. Is this a good method for decision making involving:
   a. Whether to discontinue an unprofitable territory?
   b. Measuring the performance of a district sales manager?
   c. Controlling advertising costs?

9–11 A firm is considering the purchase of a special type of duplicating machine. Two of the costs that must be estimated are service and operating costs (other than materials used in duplication). Service is supplied at a fixed monthly fee but operating costs are not. How would you estimate the total of these costs?

9–12 The Automated Tank Company reports the following results for operations in the past two years:

	19X0	19X1
Sales Revenues	$3,000,000	$3,300,000
Cost of sales	1,500,000	2,250,000
Gross margin	$1,500,000	$1,050,000
Operating expenses	900,000	300,000
Net profit	$ 600,000	$ 750,000

During 19X1, $675,000 of depreciation expense on manufacturing equipment was transferred from operating expense to cost of sales since management felt the decrease in the value of manufacturing equipment should be considered a cost of the manufactured product. There has been no essential change in either the manner in which operations are conducted or in prices.

The Company is considering two alternatives:

1. An intensive sales campaign expected to increase sales by $750,000. This effort will necessitate nine additional salesmen at a salary of $12,000 each.
2. Opening a new branch which is expected to increase sales by $675,000. The operating costs for the new branch include rent, $4,500, office employees, $30,000; branch manager (who is presently employed at the home office and whose present duties would be allocated to other present employees), $25,000, and other expenses, $10,000. All figures are yearly.

Required: Which alternative do you favor and why? Assume the figures are accurate as given.

9–13 How should service department costs be treated from a cost-control and decision-making viewpoint?

9–14 The Winter Company is considering offering one of its customers a quantity discount, but the president of the firm is concerned about the possibility of the government bringing action under the Robinson-Patman Act. The usual method of shipment for the Winter Company is to pack its product individually in boxes and ship by truck. If a customer would be willing to buy in larger quantities (such as 1,000 units), larger containers could be used. In fact, it would be possible to ship the product loose in a railroad freight car. The estimated packing saving would be $0.20 per unit.

Required: Would the cost savings described be acceptable grounds for having price differentials for customers who ordered in 1,000-unit lots?

9–15 The Fall River Paper Company sells to two different customers. One customer is charged a price of $2 per unit and the other customer is charged a price of $3 per unit. In defense of its pricing policy, the following schedule was prepared by the company.

	Unit Revenue and Cost Schedules for Selling to:			
	Company A		Company B	
Net margin*	$1.00	100%	$2.00	100%
Distribution Costs (allocations based on net margin)	.60	60%	1.20	60%
Net income	$ .40	40%	$ .80	40%

* Net margin is after deducting the cost of product sold, $1.

Since the profit per dollar of net margin was the same for sales to both companies, the Fall River Paper Company argued that it was reasonable to charge Company A a price of $1.00 and Company B a price of $2.00.

Required: Comment on whether the price differentials are justified. What additional information would you want to know?

9–16 Since the cost defense against a charge of illegal price discrimination provided by Section 2(a) of the Clayton Act as amended by the Robinson-Patman Act has proved largely illusory in practice, the prudent company would be well advised to charge the same price on commodities of similar grade and quality. Do you agree with this statement? If so, why? If not, why not?

SUPPLEMENTARY READING

Antitrust Laws, Report of the Attorney General's Committee, 1955, Washington, D.C.: U.S. Government Printing Office, particularly pp. 155–186 and pp. 170–176.

CHARNES, A., W. W. COOPER, J. K. DEVOE, D. B. LEARNER, and W. REINECKE, "A Goal Programming Model for Media Planning," *Management Science*, April 1968, pp. 423–430.

EDWARDS, C. D., "20 Years of the Robinson-Patman Act," *Journal of Business*, July 1956, pp. 149–159.

JONES, R. L., and H. J. TRENTIN, "Budgeting General and Administrative Expenses: A Planning and Control System," *Management Bulletin* 74, New York: American Management Association, 1966.

KING, W. R., "Performance Evaluation in Marketing Systems," *Management Science*, July 1964, pp. 659–666.

TAGGART, H., *Cost Justification*, Bureau of Business Research, University of Michigan, Ann Arbor, particularly Chapters 20, 21 and Appendix A.

Chapter 10

Measuring Performance

The ability of management to react optimally to change is limited by the timing and the nature of the amount of information available, the continuous nature of change, lack of familiarity with operations of other units, and by the difficulty of predicting with certainty the ripple effects of decisions made and actions taken. As a partial solution many firms resort to some degree of decision decentralization. It is inefficient to attempt total decision control from the top level of a large firm. Decision making is delegated from top management to lower level personnel to take advantage of the familiarity with operations and the availability of information at different activity levels. This delegation may involve the authority to make nearly all the operating decisions (including buying materials externally) or, alternately, the authority may be limited to a small range of decisions.

Concurrent with decentralization of control and decision making there arises a need to control these decision-making subunits to assure that their actions are consistent with the goals of the total entity. Subactivities, if left on their own, tend to suboptimize by failing to consider economies and diseconomies external to their own activity.

Control may be achieved through goal setting and performance evaluation. The type of goal set and the manner in which performance is evaluated should depend on the degree of decision making delegated. As decentralization increases, the measures used to evaluate the performance should become more general. Thus, where authority is delegated to determine the complete mix of inputs toward production and the sale of a product, as might be true of a division, the evaluation of performance is characterized by focusing on a measure such as net contribution or perhaps return on investment. Where this is not the case, cost may often be used.

The evaluation and control mechanism is influenced by the organizational structure of the firm. The specification of the firm's organizational structure and its accounting system must both be considered when designing an evaluation system. The accounting system should provide performance measures that reflect the consequences of decision making for the activity and hence allow top management to evaluate these decisions in light of the firm's goals. There should be incentives for subactivity managers to improve their performance.

How can the performance of a member of management be measured? The first step is to establish the objective or objectives of the activity over which he has authority. The second step is to see how well these objectives are met. The prime objective of the firm is assumed here to be maximization of profits. Perhaps a more realistic way to phrase the objective is to describe it as profit maximization subject to constraints (for example, continuity of existence). Profit in this definition includes the opportunity cost of invested funds as a cost.

The extent of success in attaining objectives may be assessed quantitatively or qualitatively. The qualitative criterion includes such things as relations with superiors and subordinates, training of subordinates, professional attainments, civic activities, and ability to get things done. The qualitative factors are relevant in judging performance, but are traditionally more the province of the industrial psychologist than of the accountant. It should be recalled, however, that the means used to evaluate an individual affects his motivation and, thereby, his attainment of corporate objectives. Thus it is important for the accountant to understand and work with the behavioral scientist in designing control reports and performance-measuring techniques. This chapter considers, however, only quantitative measures of performance. The reader interested in a further examination of the qualitative factors is referred to Chapter 6. Quantitative factors that provide useful information include:

1. Costs and cost variances.
2. Physical production (quantity and quality).
3. Sales.
4. Income.
5. Return on investment.
6. Investment turnover.
7. Income per dollar of sales (operating rate).
8. Share of market.
9. Rate of growth.
10. Changes from period to period of any of the above measures.

10.1   Single Measures of Performance

There is danger in seeking out the one best measure of performance and using it to the exclusion of all other measures. Frequently, a
single measure cannot do the job satisfactorily, since a measure that is useful
for one purpose is not useful for another. The fact that a golf drive went 250
yards is useful in judging the force with which the ball was hit, but knowledge
of the total distance covered is not sufficient to conclude whether the drive was
good or bad. Information relating to the starting point and to location and
distance of the hole is needed before this type of evaluation can be made.

Most of the quantitative measures just listed are not above unintended distortion or manipulation. The manipulations may be a product of figure
juggling or the result of managerial actions designed to obtain the result
looked for by superiors, even though the end result may not be consistent
with the end objectives of the corporation. It is important to ensure, to the
extent possible, that the measure of performance being used does improve
performance and that the measure of performance is consistent with the basic
objectives of the firm. To obtain a valid measure of performance, several
measures may be needed and then judgment should be applied to weighing
the importance of each measure. If this is not done, the result may not
measure performance but rather the ability of a clever manager to obtain a
favorable report on his performance.

The measures of performance used should be influenced materially by the
nature of the responsibilities of the manager (or organization) whose performance is being measured. Where possible, items which are not controllable
by the manager should be excluded from the measure. This concept implies
that the methods used by a manager in decision making and control rather
than the actual results should be evaluated since the results are often a product, in part, of factors over which he has no control or influence. Uncertainties can cause excellent decision making to yield unsatisfactory results and
vice-versa.

The performance measure adopted should indicate how well the man or the
organization is meeting predetermined objectives. To accomplish these objectives more than one measure of performance will usually be required, and
different measures will be needed for different situations, firms, and organization levels.

The subsections of Section 10.1 discuss some of the limitations of several
of the measures listed earlier. Section 10.2 considers the task of developing
appropriate measures for different organizational levels.

10.1.1 Investment Turnover

Investment turnover may be defined as the sales of a period divided by the average investment.

$$\text{Investment turnover} = \frac{\text{sales}}{\text{average investment}} \qquad (10.1)$$

The investment turnover gives an indication of how intensively the investment is being used. If more sales are generated, the turnover increases. Taken by itself, the investment turnover is not a good measure of a manager's performance since total sales and turnover can be increased by increasing selling effort, lowering selling price, or by a random change in general economic conditions. An increase in turnover may not reflect more efficient use of resources by the manager whose performance is being measured: it may reflect factors beyond his control. However, when used in conjunction with other measures, investment turnover may be helpful in pointing out a cause of decreased profits, namely, less intensive use of the resources committed to the operation.

10.1.2 Operating Rate

The operating rate is the operating profit per dollar of sales.

$$\text{Operating rate} = \frac{\text{operating profit}}{\text{sales dollars}} \qquad (10.2)$$

The operating rate gives an indication of the efficiency of operations, but only an indication since in addition to efficiency the profit per dollar of sales is affected by:

1. Changes in the level of sales.
2. Changes in the product mix sold.
3. Changes in the price of the products sold.
4. Changes in the costs of materials and services used to produce the products sold.
5. Accounting methods of determining operating profit.

If each of the above influences is isolated and the effect of each computed, then the operating rate is useful. The inclusion or exclusion of income taxes for performance measurement is not crucial so long as the same procedure is followed for the different operating localities being compared. If attention is focused on the operating rate, without proper analysis, incorrect conclusions may be drawn as to the causes of the changes in the rate. For example, assume the following situation:

	Period 1	Period 2
Sales	$1,000,000	$1,500,000
Income	50,000	300,000
Operating rate	5%	20%

Here the operating rate increased from 5 per cent to 20 per cent. Does this reflect increased efficiency?[1] To answer this question it is first necessary to know what the income should be for sales of $1,500,000. It may be that the income should be $400,000 for sales of that level, and instead of being "good," the operating rate of 20 per cent for sales of $1,500,000 reflects inefficiency. The increase in the operating rate may have occurred merely because of the increase in sales, for which the sales manager should receive primary credit. Moreover, assuming increased, even maximum, efficiency at this output, the increase in income could still have been attained at the expense of future periods. In other words, a good case can be made for the argument that to maximize profitability (a long-run notion) the firm cannot maximize accounting income in any single period. For example, research and development tends to reduce short-run profit measures. The effects of the changes responsible for the change in the operating rate should also be examined for their long-run effects. Taking advantage of short-run opportunities can have adverse long-run consequences.

In another situation, sales may not have changed at all, but the operating rate may change because different products are sold. For example:

	Period 1	Period 2
Sales	$1,000,000	$1,000,000
Income	100,000	200,000
Operating rate	10%	20%

Does this situation reflect increased efficiency? Maybe not; it may indicate merely a change in the composition of sales from low-margin items to high-margin items. This may or may not reflect on management's efficiency in production. It may, for example, indicate increased efficiency on the part of a

---

[1] The term *efficiency* is used here to describe a situation where the assets of the firm are being employed to maximize, on a long-run basis, the contribution for a given level of output.

manager responsible for sales-promotion decisions (a change in sales mix). On the other hand, it may merely reflect a fortuitous market phenomenon.

Discussion of these and similar problems arising with the use of the operating rate could be expanded. But the problems cited, and other problems which could be cited, must be given attention and must enter into any analysis of the operating rate.

10.1.3 Return on Investment (ROI)

The return-on-investment method of measuring performance is said to have several desirable features. First, it provides a single, comprehensive figure that incorporates the impact of a large number of events on the division or other activity unit. Thus it is useful for comparing different divisions. Furthermore, since it measures how effectively the division's assets are used to generate profits, it compels managers to acquire only those investments that improve the expected return. To attain these advantages ROI must be used carefully.

The return on investment may be computed by dividing income by average investment or by multiplying the investment turnover (sales divided by average investment) by the operating rate (income divided by sales).

$$ROI = \frac{sales}{average\ investment} \times \frac{income}{sales} = \frac{income}{average\ investment} \qquad (10.3)$$

Just how important these three percentages (investment turnover, operating rate, and return on investment) are considered to be by management is difficult to guess. There are indications that they are thought to be important devices for measuring efficiency of utilization of resources. Dearden, for example, writes that "... nearly every major decentralized company in the United States today uses some adaptation of return on investment for measuring division performance."[2]

The return on investment as a measure of performance is only as good as the numbers used to compute it. It should not come as a surprise to anyone familiar with accounting that the problems of measuring sales, income, and average investment are numerous.

Measuring sales is often spoken of as the problem of revenue recognition. Is revenue to be recognized when the order is received, the product made, the product shipped, or the cash received? Since most companies are on the accrual basis of realizing revenue, the revenue is recognized when the goods

---

[2] J. Dearden, "The Case Against ROI Control," *The Harvard Business Review*, May–June 1969, p. 124.

are shipped or the services performed. Only in relatively rare cases does this method of accounting cause difficulties in computing the investment turn-over. For example, a shipbuilding firm that uses the accrual method and recognizes revenue only on a completed sale might have a low investment turnover in a period of great activity if no ships were delivered during this period. This specific difficulty might be readily solved by shifting to a produc-tion basis (percentage of completion basis) of revenue recognition, but the general problem of revenue recognition does exist.

The problems of measuring the income of a corporate entity are many, and they increase when attention is focused on the component parts of an organization. The main problems are the pricing of transfers and the splitting of common costs. These problems become important when the component parts of the company are compared to each other. Accounting procedures, which are generally accepted from a financial reporting point of view, may result in a report of income that is worth little from the point of view of comparing different operating units. The report of income can be qualified by footnotes, but these qualifications tend to be lost when attention is focused on the return on investment.

Some of the problems of income measurement that are particularly relevant for the purpose of measuring return on investment are:

1. Revenue recognition and the matching of expenses with revenues.
2. Treatment of repairs and maintenance costs.
3. Accounting for inventory. (During periods of fluctuating prices income will be affected by the choice of inventory valuation basis, FIFO, LIFO, average cost, and so on, as well as by changing inventory levels.)
4. Treatment of nonproductive supplies. (Should they be expensed when purchased or should they be inventoried?)
5. Choice of depreciation procedure. (Are subunits using depreciation procedures that permit meaningful comparisons of their calculated return on investment?)
6. Adjustments for changes in price level.
7. Allocation of common cost, especially central office expenses.
8. The effect of changes in the level of production on income (caused by absorption costing combined with changes in production).

Fortunately, theories and techniques have been developed to handle all the above problems. Unfortunately, the theories and techniques are frequently not applied uniformly to all plants and all divisions of a company. Thus, one plant may use LIFO and another FIFO. One plant may use straight-line depreciation, another may use some method of accelerated depreciation. For any of the eight items listed above, examples can be presented showing two plants or divisions (assumed to have the same physical characteristics) that will have different returns on investment, the differences caused entirely by the accounting methods, not by variations in efficiency.

Measuring Average Investment

Many of the problems of measuring average investment are directly related to the problems of income measurement. The list is shortened here in order to focus attention on the three primary problems.

1. Valuing long-lived assets.
2. Valuing inventories.
3. Allocation of assets administered directly from the central office.

There are three problems associated with the valuation of long-lived assets. First, what items should be capitalized and what items charged to expense? This is particularly troublesome with repairs, maintenance charges, and any large expenditures for developing new procedures or products. For example, in the oil industry, should the costs of digging dry wells and producing wells be treated as assets or as expenses?

The second problem is to decide what to do about depreciation. Should the accrued depreciation be subtracted in computing the average investment? This is a troublesome question, to which there is no one simple answer. There are, however, several observations which may be made. With constant revenues and maintenance charges, an asset will have an increasing return on investment through the periods of use if either straight-line depreciation is used (and the accumulated depreciation is subtracted), or any one of the decreasing-charge methods of computing depreciation is used (and the accumulated depreciation is subtracted). With the above assumptions, the depreciable asset has an equal return on investment through the periods of use only if a compound-interest method (an increasing-charge method) of computing depreciation is used. But this method complicates the analysis of income (revenues of the later periods are charged with larger and larger depreciation charges), and is not generally used by industrial firms (see Chapter 17 for an alternative).

If straight-line depreciation is used, a common result is for the investment to show a low initial return and an increasing return over time as the investment base declines. This phenomenon tends to discourage new investments that might decrease the rate of return simply because they are new.

Return on investment as conventionally computed does not provide a reliable check on investment performance. Discounted cash flow techniques and portfolio considerations are involved in selecting investments. The accounting measures of profit (even ignoring tax problems) are not generally designed to be consistent with investment decision methods. Thus, for example, there is only one depreciation schedule that would be consistent with a given investment's cash-flow pattern. This schedule differs from investment to investment and may not resemble any traditional accounting depreciation pattern (straight-line, sum-of-the-years digits, etc.). As a result the calculated return on investment differs from the projected rate of return even though actual cash flows are precisely as estimated.[3]

Nearly all firms use some measure of book value for the fixed assets included in the investment base. Market values, although theoretically more correct, seem to present too many implementation problems for practical use. Some firms use gross book values rather than the net figures suggested here. When gross book values are used the return on investment is more likely to be increased by scrapping old assets. Moreover, if group depreciation methods are in use, no loss is recognized on retirement.

The third problem of valuing long-lived assets for purposes of determining the average investment is possibly the most important. What should be done about the fact that the unit used to measure the investment in long-lived assets is the dollar when the dollar has different meanings in different years? The purchasing power of the dollar has changed significantly over time. Ignoring this fact means that assumptions are being made concerning the relationship between the rate of increase of inflation and technology. If the return-on-investment measure is to have significance, the effect of unexpected changes in the price level has to be resolved.

The problem of measuring the value of inventories is related to the fact that LIFO is accepted for accounting purposes. Under this procedure the oldest goods purchased are the last goods to be charged as an expense. This means that if LIFO is used, the inventory value often represents goods dating back to the moment of introducing LIFO. In any event, the inventory resulting from the use of LIFO rarely gives an indication of the actual cost of the inventory, nor does it give an indication of its present value.

Other problems of measuring inventory include writing down obsolete or spoiled items, taking a meaningful physical inventory, and in the case of a manufacturing firm, deciding what costs are inventoriable.

When assets are administered directly from the central office, should these assets be allocated for purposes of computing the return on the investment of a division or plant? This is the cousin of the familiar problem of common costs and could be termed the problem of common assets. If there are some reasonable grounds for allocating the asset, then it should be allocated. For example, if the payroll is paid out of a centrally administered payroll fund, then the cash held in this fund should be considered an asset assignable to the individual plants. In this example the take-home pay of the workers of each plant would seem to be a reasonable basis for allocation.

Some companies do not allocate cash administered by the central office. This is not harmful if all the operating units being compared have like characteristics, but if they are unlike (one plant having a large amount of long-lived assets, another a large number of workers), then the failure to allocate cash may give misleading results.

[3] Also see Chapters 13 and 17.

Return on Investment and Decision Making

The usefulness of return on investment for decision making or performance evaluation is limited. Among the more questionable uses of the return on investment approach are:

1. Capital budgeting decisions (including equipment replacement, capacity expansion, research, buying versus leasing, making versus buying, introducing new product lines or other new activities).
2. Pricing decisions.

The objection to return on investment as a guide for capital budgeting decisions results from the fact that the procedure ignores the time shape of earnings and the discounting of future earnings back to the present. The present-value approach to capital budgeting is not perfect, but it is to be preferred over the return-on-investment method (see Chapter 13).

It is sometimes suggested that pricing decisions should be made with one eye on the return on investment, and that an "optimal" return on investment should be the goal. It is well to keep economic principles in mind. A company may set a price, but the buyers determine how much is purchased; that is to say, each product has a demand curve. The fact that a set return on investment is desired does not mean that it will be attained by changing the price. The successfulness of a change in price depends on the demand curve, which in turn depends on the degree of competition to be found in the industry and among industries as well as the preferences of consumers. Theoretically, a price should be established that equates marginal revenue and marginal cost. If profits can be increased by raising or lowering prices, this decision can be reached without looking at the return on investment.

10.1.4 Return on Investment and Measuring Divisional Performance

A very difficult and interesting problem is caused by the use of return on investment to measure the performance of a division. Assume a high return on investment is considered desirable, and that division A has a return on investment of 35 per cent and division B a return on investment of 20 per cent. Division B may actually be the better managed division. If division A is rejecting all investment proposals of less than 35 per cent, this leads to a high return on investment but a less than optimal amount invested in the division from the point of view of the firm as a whole, assuming the firm has a cost of money of less than 35 per cent. It is not desirable for a division to employ a very high cutoff rate for investments while the home office has a great quantity of idle cash which it wants invested.

The conflict of interests created by the use of a single measure of performance is not unique to return on investment. For example, a grocery chain might employ profit per dollar of sales as a measure of a store manager's efficiency. Since certain items in the store have profit margins below the "standard required" margin, some store managers would stock a small amount and allow these items to run out on busy days so that the profit per dollar of sales figure would not be decreased. Although this would decrease the profit of the store, it may still be done since the major emphasis is on the objective of earning the required profit per dollar of sales. The significant ratio for decision making here should have been the total contribution per unit of floor (or shelf) space if, as is likely, floor space represents the scarce resource of the firm.

One method of counteracting the distortions just described is to include the rate of growth among the measures of performance. Since growth for growth's sake is not desirable, growth in income rather than in sales is suggested. If income is growing at the same time that return on investment is maintained at the desirable level (or even increased), then, at least according to the quantitative measures, the manager is doing a reasonable job. Including the rate of growth in the performance measures puts the spot-light on the manager who is willing to be satisfied with the status quo. Balancing growth against return on investment ensures that the manager will not be obsessed with growth in sales at the expense of profits, or return on investment at the expense of growth.

Example

Assume the income and investments of successive years are as follows:

Year	Operating Profit	Average Investment
1965	$10,000	$100,000
1966	11,000	110,000
1967	14,300	125,000

The growth rates in operating profits are:

$$1965\text{--}1966 \qquad \frac{1,000}{10,000} = 10\%$$

$$1966\text{--}1967 \qquad \frac{3,300}{11,000} = 30\%$$

$$1965\text{--}1967: 14,300\,(1 + r)^{-2} = 10,000$$

$$(1 + r)^{-2} = \frac{10,000}{14,300} = 0.6993$$

$$r \doteq 19.5\%$$

The returns on investment are:

$$1965 \quad \frac{10,000}{100,000} = 10\%$$

$$1966 \quad \frac{11,000}{110,000} = 10\%$$

$$1967 \quad \frac{14,300}{125,000} = 11.4\%$$

The manager is accomplishing growth and an increase in the return on investment simultaneously. It is still possible, however, that the investment decisions being made may not be taking full advantage of the individual opportunities available or may not be making adequate allowance for the interrelationships among the existing and proposed investments. Investment policies, which are based on "portfolio" considerations need to be examined in light of the return and risk goals of the firm as a whole remembering the constraints within which both the firm and the division must operate.

All assets should not be expected to earn the same return since the required profitability may well differ among assets even in a single division. The return appropriate to different divisions need not be the same nor need it be identical to the average rate earned across the entire company. If performance is measured using a single rate, decisions that are inconsistent with the over-all goals of the firm are likely.

10.2   Measuring Performance on Different Levels of Organization

The proper measures of performance are related to the degree of decentralization present, and are a function of the level of organization under consideration. Several organizational levels are considered in this subsection. They include

1. Department or cost center.
2. Plant.
3. Division.
4. Company.

10.2.1 The Department

The term *department* is used here interchangeably with cost center or burden center. Assume that the performance of a manager such as foreman or a department head is to be measured.

A manager's task is to accomplish his set objective with a minimum of cost. Recognizing that he could accomplish his task with more dispatch with the incurrence of more cost, he compromises between cost and time. Thus a controller might be able to prepare his reports two days sooner by hiring ten more accountants or using a more powerful computer but still not hire the additional accountants or use the computer because the costs would be greater than the value of the expected benefits. To say that costs are too high must mean either that there is gross inefficiency and waste of resources or that the benefits to be obtained are less than their cost even if the costs are administered effectively.

In a research and development department, the quantitative measurement of costs is reasonably accurate while the measurement of the benefits is very inaccurate. Hence it is very difficult to control or measure the performance of this type of department with purely quantitative measures (see Chapter 9). On the other hand, both the direct costs and the benefits of a production department may be determined with relative accuracy, the indirect costs with less accuracy. The benefits in this case are the units produced. Generally the costs are measured in terms of the labor, material, and overhead which are used by a department. The physical product may be converted into the amount of labor, material, and indirect costs which should have been used (the standard costs of the product) and the cost-control techniques suggested in Chapters 1 and 2 can then be used.

It is also necessary to control the scrap or spoilage that results from the manufacturing process. A large production with low costs per unit may be desirable, but not if it results in large amounts of rework or unusable product. This undesirable outcome may be prevented by excluding bad units in computing the production of the period (if the bad production was caused within the department) and by carefully controlling the amount of spoilage.

The main pitfall in measuring the performance of a foreman is one that applies to all levels of management, namely, the inclusion of items not controllable by the person whose performance is being measured. The foreman should be held accountable for costs that can be directly identified with his department and when he can exert control over the total amount of costs incurred. But the measure of performance, for example, for the foreman of an operating department should not include the insurance on the machinery used in the department. While this cost may be directly identified with the department, it is not a cost item controllable by the foreman.

10.2.2 The Plant

The discussion of performance measurement for the plant manager assumes that he has no control over the sale of the product but that he is concerned with all phases of its production.[4] When attempts are made to compute a

---

[4] Even though the production manager does not control sales, he can indirectly influence the level of sales. Availability of a product of good quality will lead to satisfied customers, which in turn will influence the demand schedule. While the production and inventory control policies of the plant manager can influence sales, it is not desirable to measure his efficiency on the basis of sales, or a figure which is influenced to a great extent by the level of sales.

profit and a return on investment for the plant under these conditions, it is quite likely to be the case that this computation will be dysfunctional and may even be misleading. The profit of the plant is a function of the level of sales, the sale price, and the cost of product. If the plant manager has control over the last item only, his performance should be measured only by the cost of product, or perhaps better, by the costs incurred in relation to the level of production.

Computing a profit for a plant is generally thought to supply both a measure of performance and an incentive. It may approximately accomplish this goal during prosperous periods, but in periods of slack activity it supplies an excuse for the plant manager. He can blame the poor showing on low unit sales or a low sale price. While these two items are probably the more dramatic of the causes of low profits, there may also be inefficiencies that should be corrected.

A suitable measure of the performance of the plant manager is similar to the measure of performance of the foreman. His task is to complete a good product at as low a cost as possible. Thus, the same measures used at the department level are also appropriate at the plant level. A desirable situation is one in which the costs of production of one plant may be compared to the costs of similar plants.

In addition to the quantitative measures centering around the costs of production, the over-all evaluation of performance should include the quality of the work performed and the timeliness of production; that is, ability to meet production schedules. While sometimes difficult to quantify, these factors can be extremely important in relation to the maintenance of the firm's profits. Evaluation should also consider any geographic and time differences involved in profit figure comparisons.

Since the authority of the plant manager is broader than that of the department head, more costs incurred in the plant are controllable by him. In fact any out-of-pocket expenditures originating in the plant are usually subject to his control, and thus should be used in measuring his performance. Should expenses such as depreciation of plant and equipment be included in the computation of the cost of product? While the plant manager may not have had a voice in the original purchase of these assets, he does control their use, and the opportunity costs of these assets may well be included perhaps as a separable item. The measure of the opportunity cost would be the incremental revenues that would have resulted from the best alternative use of the assets.

10.2.3 The Division

The measurement of the performance of the division manager who does not control sales is exactly analogous to that of the plant manager. The use of costs of production is a better measure of performance than a fictitious profit figure. Where the division manager is also in charge of the sales force, the problem of measuring performance is broadened. The division then becomes an entity very similar to a small corporation and many of the measures of performance relevant for corporate organizations can be used. These may include total sales, profits, return on investment, investment turnover, operating profit per dollar of sales, share of market, and changes in any of the above items.

Two problems that are encountered with a division but not with a separate corporation are the problem of common costs (costs of the central office incurred in servicing several divisions), and the problem of pricing transfers to and from other divisions. Chapter 11 treats this subject.

In measuring the performance of a division, the allocations of central office costs should be excluded. The division manager has no control over these costs, and while the division may benefit from the incurrence of the expenses, it may do more harm than good to include these costs in divisional income statements and computations of return on investment. On the other hand, it may be desirable to inform the division that it is billed a standard amount for central office services and that in order for the corporation to be profitable these costs must be recovered.

10.2.4 The Company

The measures of performance used in the case of a division that controls its sales force can also be used for the company. Several problems are eliminated, such as transfer pricing and allocation of overhead costs, but the many problems of financial accounting remain. For example, should variable costing be used so that effects of changes in inventory are eliminated? In computing the return on investment, should the investment be net of depreciation? What methods of inventory flow and depreciation should be used? There are no shortages of accounting problems.

There are other problems as well. If, for example, decreased sales are a result of general business conditions, does this absolve the company president from the blame of having a bad year? The president is responsible for how well the company does, but he cannot control the business cycle.

10.3 Measures for Improving Performance

Good performance measures provide the manager with figures he can use to control operations. However, performance measures often represent the combined results of many subsidiary variables. Where possible it is helpful to provide the manager with indicators of the economic value of the scarce resources to the subactivity; the opportunity costs of the scarce resources.

These measures of opportunity cost provide the means by which the manager can make better decisions concerning which activities to push and which resources are in short supply. In some cases the opportunity cost of resources can be obtained by noting the increase in contribution that can be achieved by switching one unit of a scarce resource to its best alternate use. The opportunity cost of other factors can be estimated by determining the contribution obtainable if another unit of the resources were available. Shadow prices resulting from the solution of mathematical programming formulations are measures of opportunity cost and may facilitate resource allocation decisions.[5]

Results of mathematical programming formulations are also relevant to control. If decisions are made using a linear programming model, the original solution adopted before the operating plan is implemented may be compared with a revised solution based on changes occurring in the data input to the model during the operating period. The value of the objective function using the now nonoptimal activity-level solution with the new data can be determined and compared with the value of the objective function under the new optimal solution. The difference represents the gain from altering the program. If this difference exceeds the change-over cost, consideration should be given to altering the activity levels.

If it is too late to make the adjustments, the revised solution compared to the initial solution provides a rough measure of the forecasting error and the maximum amount that might be expended on improving this activity. The difference between the actual results and the revised or *ex post* solution is an estimate of the opportunity cost associated with the actions taken. The differences or variances can be examined using the methods described in Chapters 1 and 2.

10.4   Summary

The quantitative measures of performance may assist in measuring performance, but they are not the complete answer. If enough measures are used, always in reference to trends and changes, and with such factors as general business conditions considered, then a reasonable indication of the performance of the management team can be obtained. For example, the use of share of market can be a measure of performance when business conditions change, but this has to be supported by an analysis of changes in prices and selling expenditures to make sure the market gain did not result in

[5] Using the dual of the profit-maximization form of the problem, the optimal value of each ordinary or structural variable represents the increase in contribution if the associated activity is increased by one unit. The optimal value of each slack variable shows the decline in contribution if that activity is expanded by one unit. See the references to Chapter 11.

decreased profits. In addition to the record of performance, an analysis of the decision-making technique used by the manager would be extremely useful in evaluating management.

QUESTIONS AND PROBLEMS

10–1 From the annual reports of three companies in the same industry, compute the
  a. Operating rates;
  b. Investment turnover;
  c. Return on investment.
Describe the difficulties of using the computations. Would the same difficulties persist if you had access to the corporate records?

10–2 What additional measure is required for evaluating performance in a profit center that is not required in a cost center?

10–3 To what extent can quantitative measures reflect the performance of a manager? Would it be reasonable to rely exclusively on qualitative measures?

10–4 What factors may affect the investment turnover, operating rate, and return on investment?

10–5 Should accumulated depreciation be deducted in computing the investment for purposes of computing return on investment?

10–6 What are the difficulties of measuring the performance of a research and development department?

10–7 In a manufacturing firm, how would you measure the performance of the departmental foreman, department head, plant manager, division manager, personnel manager, sales manager, and the president of the firm?

10–8 *The Deep Well Machine Company*
  The Deep Well Machine Company has twenty divisions and is highly decentralized. Each division makes its own decisions as to price, output, and investments.
  One of the primary means of measuring performance used by the company is the return-on-investment chart. Using a series of these charts the performance of each division through time is noted as well as the comparison of each division with each other division.
  Top management is very enthusiastic about the charts since they show the relationship of profit to sales (operating profit per dollar of sales), sales to investment (the investment turnover), and the return on investment (profit divided by average investment).
  The charts are relatively easy to construct since each return-on-investment curve is a smooth curve. Thus only three or four points have to be plotted for each return-on-investment value and a curve drawn to connect the points.

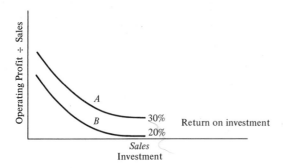

Required: Comment on the effectiveness of these charts as control devices. Is division A more efficient than division B if the cost of money to the firm is 0.15? Explain.

10–9 The ABC Company has a policy of accepting only investments that have yields equal to or in excess of 0.10. It also pays out as dividends 60 per cent of its earnings. Assuming that investments are financed entirely with stock equity funds generated from operations, at what minimum average rate would you expect the earnings of this firm to grow? Assume further that there are many investments available that yield 10 per cent.

10–10 Managers are usually evaluated on their actual performance. What alternatives are there and what is your evaluation of them?

SUPPLEMENTARY READING

BIERMAN, H., JR., "A Further Study of Depreciation," *The Accounting Review*, April 1966, pp. 271–274.

COUGHLAN, J., "Contrast Between Financial-Statement and Discounted-Cash Flow Methods of Comparing Projects," *N.A.A. Bulletin*, June 1960, pp. 5–20.

DEARDEN, J., "The Case Against ROI Control," *The Harvard Business Review*, May–June 1969, pp. 124–135.

DEMSKI, J. S., "Predictive Ability of Alternative Performance Measurement Models," *Journal of Accounting Research*, Spring 1969, pp. 96–115.

DEMSKI, J. S., "The Decision Implementation Interface: Effects of Alternative Performance Measurement Models," *The Accounting Review*, January 1970, pp. 76–87.

FURLONG, W., "Risk Income and Alternative Income Concepts," *N.A.A. Management Accounting*, April 1967, pp. 25–29.

MAURIEL, J., and R. ANTHONY, "Misevaluation of Investment Center Performance," *The Harvard Business Review*, March–April, 1965, pp. 98–105.

SHWAYDER, K., "A Proposed Modification to Residual Income—Interest Adjusted Income," *The Accounting Review*, April 1970, pp. 299–307.

SOLOMONS, D., *Division Performance: Measurement and Control*, New York: Financial Executive Research Foundation, 1965.

Chapter 11

Transfer Pricing

Since the end of World War II two interesting business pheno-
mena which are in many respects contradictory have accrued. One
is the large number of business combinations (mergers and
acquisitions) which have resulted in an increase in the complexity
of business organizations. The other is the increased use of
decentralization or divisionalization as a means of controlling
large corporations. Many of these corporations are the result of
business combinations. Thus firms seek the advantages of being
large and small, simultaneously.

The desirability of decentralization arises in part from a
planning point of view. The underlying rationale stems from the
limitations on human cognitive ability. This position has been
advanced by Hayek and Von Mises in their defense of the price
system, and later by March and Simon as the principal of bounded
rationality.[1] The desirability of decentralization was eloquently
expressed by Hayek in describing the role of the price system:

> As decentralization has become necessary because nobody can
> consciously balance all the considerations bearing on the decisions of
> so many individuals, the coordination can clearly not be affected by
> "conscious control", but only by arrangements which convey to each
> agent the information he must possess in order effectively to adjust
> his decisions to those of others. And because all the details of the
> changes constantly affecting the conditions of demand and supply of
> the different commodities can never be fully known, or quickly enough
> be collected and disseminated, by any one centre, what is required is
> some apparatus of registration which automatically records all the
> relevant effects of individual actions, and whose indications are at the
> same time the resultant of, and the guide for, all the individual
> decisions.

[1] F. Hayek, *The Road to Serfdom*, Chicago: University of Chicago
Press, 1944; L. Von Mises, *Bureaucracy*, New Haven: Yale University Press,
1944; and J. G. March, and H. A. Simon, *Organizations*, New York: John
Wiley, 1958.

The advantages of decentralization have also been advanced from a motivational prospective. Argyris and Likert among others maintain that decentralization permits factors that motivate middle and lower management to play a more important role.[2] Others, including Dean, emphasize improved control through better knowledge of the strength and weakness of specific company activities.[3] Regardless of the reasons for decentralization, the existence of several divisions with interrelated activities creates a need for performance evaluation. Often one division sells to another and this complicates the evaluation process since the arm's length transaction found between firms in the market is lacking.

11.1 The Need for Transfer Prices

If an automobile company buys its glass from an independent glass company, the price is set by market forces. The automobile executives can determine the cost of glass by looking at purchase invoices. If the automobile company creates a glass division to manufacture all its glass, a transfer-pricing problem is created. The assembly division "buys" from the glass division. The prices of the units sold is set by management and this price is not usually a market price.

The price has an important effect on the glass division's profits (since it affects revenues) and the profits of the assembly division (since it affects its costs), but it does not directly affect the profits of the company as a whole, though there may be indirect effects via the decisions made from the accounting information which incorporates the transfer prices.

11.2 Conflict of Interests

It is assumed that the basic goal is profit maximization for the corporation as a whole. Decentralization attempts to gain that goal by having division managers act in the interest of their own divisions. To the extent possible, the intracompany pricing method should be consistent with the goals of maximizing the profits of the company and the division.

It does not always follow that a division manager acting to maximize the profits of his division will be acting to maximize the profits of the corporation. Hirshleifer and Cook have both supplied illustrations where the rational

[2] C. Argyris, *Personality and Organization*, New York: Harper & Row, 1957; and R. Likert, "Measuring Organizational Performance," in *Studies in Personnel and Industrial Psychology*, edited by E. A. Frishman, Homewood, Ill.: The Dorsey Press, 1961.

[3] J. Dean, "Decentralization and Intercompany Pricing," *The Harvard Business Review*, 1955, pp. 65–74.

actions of the division manager (consistent with maximizing the profits of the division) are not consistent with maximizing the profits of the company.[4] In part this is because one division may be able to act as a monopolist in its dealings with other divisions. A division may also attempt to alter activity decisions made in the central office by modifying its cost structure. Furthermore, it is possible for one division to affect external economies (by using up an overabundant resource or encouraging a cost-benefiting technological change) or diseconomies (by using a scarce corporate resource or changing the reward structure) in other divisions.[5]

Do the gains arising from simulated competition and decentralized authority exceed the losses arising from decisions aimed at maximizing division profits rather than corporate profits? The answer to this question is avoided here by assuming there is agreement that an intracompany pricing scheme should be used and that it should facilitate the maximization of corporate profits rather than divisional profits. Nevertheless, many executives would object to the weakening of decentralization by a procedure that overrules decisions made at the division level because of the claim that the decisions were not consistent with the maximization of the profits of the company. In some firms, at least, the degree of decentralization is limited. For example, Whinston found in two firms that little authority was decentralized when it came to output and type-of-product decisions although substantial authority for cost control was delegated.[6] Division managers are rarely if ever given the option to acquire or dispose of large segments of the division's capital assets, nor are they able to control the disposition of their earnings. In such a situation it is not clear that a manager can be held responsible for the profitability of current operations since he is not responsible for the methods of production and sale.

11.3 Transfer Prices Available

The intracompany prices may be established in several ways. These include:

1. Market price (determined by printed price lists, invoices, price quotations, or other evidence).

---

[4] J. Hirshleifer, "On the Economics of Transfer Pricing," *Journal of Business*, July 1956, pp. 172–184; P. W. Cook, "New Technique for Intracompany Pricing," *The Harvard Business Review*, July–August 1957, pp. 74–80; also see J. R. Gould, "Internal Pricing in Firms Where There Are Costs of Using an Outside Market," *Journal of Business*, January 1964, pp. 61–67.

[5] See Appendix 11A for a further discussion of these points.

[6] A. Whinston, "Price Guides in Decentralized Organizations," in *New Prospectives in Organization Research*, edited by W. Cooper, H. Leavitt, and M. Shelly, New York: John Wiley, 1962, pp. 409–417.

2. Marginal cost.
3. Variable costs (perhaps used as a substitute for marginal costs because of the difficulty of determining the marginal-cost curve).
4. Full cost (either actual or standard and including or excluding an amount of "reasonable" profit).
5. Negotiated price.
6. Prices determined by the central office.

The transfer-pricing problem has frequently been approached from the point of view that only one procedure is correct. This chapter attempts to show that any of the above alternatives may be reasonable and that the choice of method can be made only after determining the purpose for which the information is to be used. At its best, accounting information is raw material, which, to be useful to management, must be processed. Without analysis, any intracompany pricing scheme may lead to faulty information and decisions.

11.4   Uses of Divisionalized Data

What are the uses of the accounting data of the decentralized operating units? The intracompany prices are the basis of the revenues of one division and the costs of the other; thus the pricing method directly affects the basic reports of the operating units. These reports may be used for:

1. Measuring the performance of division management.
2. Decision making including:
   (a) Make-or-buy decisions.
   (b) Pricing policy for the end product.
   (c) Output decisions of components and end product.
   (d) Capital-budgeting decisions and decisions to drop products.
3. General financial information including:
   (a) Determination of income of the corporation.
   (b) Determination of financial position of the corporation.

The use of the report dictates which one or more of the intracompany pricing methods best fills the needs of management.

11.4.1 Measuring Performance

The best method of intracompany pricing for purposes of evaluating the divisional management of the selling division is market price. In the absence of an easily determined market price, it may be necessary to use negotiated prices or a combination of market and negotiated prices. The use of market price simulates the market conditions which the divisions would face if the divisions were separate corporate entities rather than subdivisions of one business organization.

While market price may be the most desirable method, it cannot always be easily applied. For one thing, there is the problem of determining the market price. Anyone who has purchased an automobile knows that market price is not always equal to list price. Industrial prices are also confused by special terms of payment, freight absorption, quantity concessions, and so forth.

Even if it can be assumed that the market price can be determined, the question still remains as to whether it is a fair price for internal purposes. For example, the manufacturing division may have a more or less captive market, and so have less selling expense than the firms setting the market price. Should the manufacturing division get the entire benefit of these savings?

A troublesome problem also exists when there is no market price. For example, if one division conducts research that is applicable to another division, at what price should the research be sold? Here the sale price must be negotiated or possibly, arbitrated. In a research type of operation there is frequently no market price, and costs incurred are not relevant in setting the value of the research.

In the absence of market price, any reports or measures resulting from the intracompany price are even more arbitrary than the normal accounting report. Do such reports and measures of efficiency do more harm than good? A management faced with recurring situations where intracompany transfers cannot be priced objectively should reconsider the pros and cons of decentralized accounting reports aimed at measuring income and return on investment. In situations of this nature, the use of other measures of performance than those suggested should be investigated.

Assuming the objective is to measure performance, there are several reasons for not basing the transfer price of the selling division on cost. The use of variable costs (or marginal costs) would almost automatically lead to a deficit for the supplying division. The use of full cost, with or without a reasonable profit, would be better than variable costing. The prime difficulty is the determination of the cost of the product. Should actual or standard costs be used? Are inefficiencies to be passed on to the purchasing division? The use of cost as the basis of the transfer price places a large burden on the cost-accounting department. A by-product of a transfer-price system based on cost often is a welter of arguments and hassels on what is cost.

While it is suggested that the selling division use a market price to compute its revenues, the marginal costs of the selling division should be used to determine the cost to the buying division. The use of marginal costs to determine the transfer price to the buying division is a necessary but not a sufficient condition for optimal output decisions.

11.4.2 Decision Making

Four general types of decisions are considered. These are:

1. Make-or-buy.
2. The pricing of an end product.
3. Level of output.
4. Capital-budgeting decisions and decisions to drop products.

All the above decisions should be made on the basis of either marginal or differential cost techniques from the point of view of the corporation as a whole. Hirshleifer has shown systematically that the pricing and output decisions must be solved with the use of the marginal costs of the several divisions, but the individual division's best interests may not be the same as those of the corporation. Neither full costs nor market prices can be used as transfer prices in making these decisions. However, the marginal costs should be compared with the relevant market prices in arriving at a final decision.

The make-or-buy decision requires knowledge of those costs which can be avoided by purchasing the product. This requires a cost breakdown that is not supplied by the market price. The same type of information is required for the decision as to whether or not to drop a product. These are nonmarginal decisions and must be made on the basis of differential-revenue and cost techniques.

The transfer pricing used in capital-budgeting decisions made by a division buying components from another division should be based on the incremental cash inflows and outflows that result from the investment. These flows are tied to variable and semivariable cost, not to the market price of intermediate products purchased from other divisions of the company.

Thus for some decision-making purposes (make-or-buy, capital-budgeting or abandoning a product), the differential costs of the goods transferred from division to division should be known. For decisions such as pricing or output, the marginal costs of the product must be used in order to determine the optimal solutions.

11.4.3 General Financial Accounting

The general financial accounting reports require that inventories be recorded at cost to conform to generally accepted accounting principles. This cost is full cost, including manufacturing overhead but not including any element of unrealized profit (that is, profit not realized by sale to a party outside the corporate organization). This requires that the accounting group in the central office be supplied with unit cost of product by the selling division. The element of divisional profit (or loss) must then be eliminated from the inventory of the purchasing division and the income of the selling division in preparing consolidated financial statements.

11.4.4 Comparing the Methods

No single method of transfer pricing can fill the needs of a decentralized corporation. The uses of the information and the methods that best accomplish the objectives of relevant reporting are summarized in Table 11–1.

Table 11–1   Transfer Pricing and Decision Usage

Use	Method of Pricing
Measuring performance	Market price (negotiated price if market price is unavailable) and marginal cost
Decision making	Marginal cost, variable cost (as a substitute for marginal cost) and differential cost
Generally accepted financial accounting	Full cost of product (excluding intracompany profits)

No pretense of absolute correctness has been made for any of the pricing methods. The admitted inaccuracies must be weighed against the unmeasurable gains resulting from having decentralized operations and decision making. The greater the significance of the intradivisional transfers, the more unreliable are the income measures of the divisions.

11.5   The Economics of Transfer Pricing

The solution to the transfer-pricing problem has sometimes been expressed in naive terms, as if the use of the marginal costs of the selling division (or a competitive price, or a negotiated price) would enable managers to make correct decisions and measure performance. There is no simple solution to the problem of pricing products sold within the company; the solution is complex and requires rigorous analysis. One meaningful analysis presented in the business literature has been made by Hirshleifer, and the analysis which follows is based on his articles in the *Journal of Business*.[7] There are, however, several places where Hirshleifer's articles differ in detail and method from the present approach; thus the reader is encouraged to refer to the original Hirshleifer articles. An alternative approach involves the ideas of mathematical programming. A brief description of this approach is supplied in Appendix 11A.

[7] Hirshleifer, *op. cit.* Also see a later article by Hirshleifer, "Economics of the Divisionalized Firm," *Journal of Business*, April 1957, pp. 96–108.

To simplify the initial explanations of the Hirshleifer approach as much as possible, the following assumptions are made:

1. A manufacturing division makes a product which has no intermediate market; that is, it must be sold to the distribution division.
2. The price of the product sold by the distribution division is set by purely competitive forces, and the company cannot influence the price. The average revenue or price line is horizontal, hence the same line also measures the marginal revenues.

These assumptions are not essential to the basic analysis and are relaxed later.

11.5.1 Optimum Output for the Firm Under Perfect Competition

The first objective is to determine the optimal output for the firm. (Remember that the firm does not have a pricing problem since it faces a price set by purely competitive forces.) Figure 11.1 shows the solution of this problem. A

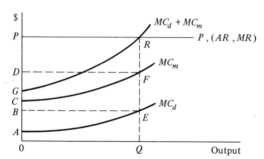

Figure 11.1   Perfect competition for an end product: No intermediate market

marginal-cost curve is drawn for the marginal costs of the distribution division (curve MC_d) and the marginal costs of the manufacturing division (curve MC_m). A curve may be drawn representing the total marginal costs of the firm ($MC_d + MC_m$). The intersection of this total marginal-cost curve with the price line, PP, determines the optimal output of the product. At that point the marginal costs of the product are equal to the marginal revenue of the product since the marginal revenue is equal to the price. The optimal output is OQ.

The firm maximizes its profits if OQ units are produced since production of fewer units means that not enough would be produced to make marginal revenues equal to the marginal costs. Production of more than OQ units means that for each additional unit produced, the costs to the firm are greater than the additional revenues.

The next problem is to determine a reasonable transfer price that will result in the division arriving at the optimal output decision. The manufacturing division should transfer to the distribution division at its marginal cost OD. If the manufacturing division transferred at a higher price, the autonomous distribution division would decrease final sales since the marginal costs of some of the sales would be greater than the division's marginal revenues. A transfer price of OD (the marginal cost of the manufacturing division) will result in an optimal output for the firm. It will be shown, however, that marginal-cost pricing by itself may not be sufficient to ensure that the firm arrives at the optimal output OQ. Other constraints may be necessary.

If the goods are transferred at the marginal cost OD, the profits of the distribution division are equal to the area ABE and the profits of the manufacturing divisions are given by the area CFD, which in sum equals the total profits of the firm, area PGR. The curve of average revenues for the manufacturing division coincides with the marginal-cost curve (since the transfer price is equal to the marginal cost).

11.5.2 The Distribution Division as Monopolistic Buyer

Can the distribution division, by limiting output and acting as a monopolistic buyer, maximize its own profit at the expense of a maximum profit

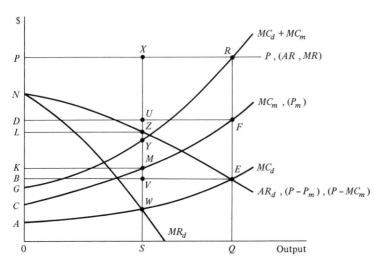

Figure 11.2 Perfect competition for an end product: No intermediate market. Distribution division as a monopolistic buyer

for the firm? Figure 11.2 shows the distribution division acting monopolisticly. Assume that a curve AR_d is drawn, which shows the net average revenue of the distribution division (the difference between the price of the end product, P, and the price P_m which must be paid to the manufacturing division). The curve MC_m and the curve P_m follow exactly the same path since the marginal cost to the manufacturing division represents the minimum price necessary to draw forth an additional unit of product, and P_m is that price.

The curve AR_d passes through point E at an output of OQ units (the optimal output for the firm), since the firm is operating under perfect competition and its average revenue is equal to its marginal revenue. Thus AR_d is equal to $P - P_m$, $AR - P_m$, and $MR - P_m$; and, at an output of OQ, it is equal to the marginal cost of the distribution division.

In addition to the net average-revenue curve, AR_d, the marginal-revenue curve, MR_d, for the distribution division may be drawn. If the distribution division restricts sales to OS and pays the manufacturing division a price equal to the marginal cost OK of the manufacturing division, then the distribution division will be maximizing its own profits since MR_d equals MC_d. The profits of the firm decrease since the output OS is less than the optimal output OQ. The profits of the distribution division are increased at the expense of the manufacturing division and the over-all well-being of the firm. Note that the transfer price OK is the marginal cost of the product, but that in this case the use of marginal cost does not lead to optimal output for the firm.

11.5.3 The Manufacturing Division as Monopolist

It is shown in Figure 11.2 that the profits of the distribution division may be increased if that division acts as a monopolistic buyer. Similarly, the manufacturing division can increase its profits by acting as a monopolistic seller. This is also adverse to the interests of the firm since the firm's total profits will be decreased.

Figure 11.3 shows the results of the manufacturing division acting as a monopolist. Suppose that the manufacturing division correctly assumes that the distribution division requires a net revenue equal to its marginal cost if the division is going to increase its sale of the product. Thus the curve MC_d may be labeled R_d, indicating that this is the minimum net revenue or net price required by the distribution division.

A net average-revenue curve $P - R_d$ or AR_m may be drawn for the manufacturing division, showing the net average revenue to that division. (This is the difference between the price curve of the firm, P, and the average-revenue curve for the distribution division.) A curve may then be drawn representing the marginal revenue to the manufacturing division, MR_m. The manufacturing division will produce OS' units since at that quantity of output the marginal cost $S'M'$ of manufacturing equals the marginal revenue.[8] The manufacturing division will, however, charge a transfer price equal to OL', which is greater than OK', the marginal cost of manufacturing.

---

[8] The primes indicate the point has the same interpretation but a different value. Thus OS and OS' are output levels under different monopolistic behavior; $OS \neq OS'$.

The output OS' that results from this price is less than the optimal output OQ, and the over-all profits of the firm are again less because of the actions of the manufacturing division aimed at increasing its own profits.

Thus the distribution and manufacturing division could enter into a form of competition that might not be desirable in terms of maximizing the profits of the firm as a whole. This analysis argues against allowing the divisions to "battle it out" or negotiate prices. The division with the better poker player may win out to the detriment of the firm as a whole. But even if the manufacturing division charges a price equal to its marginal costs and does not act as a monopolist, this does not ensure an optimal output since the distribution division may be acting as a monopolistic buyer. Both the selling and buying

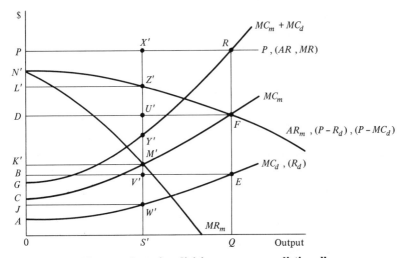

Figure 11.3   The manufacturing division as a monopolistic seller

divisions (the manufacturing and distribution divisions) must be coerced to take the interests of the firm into consideration if the profits of the firm are to be maximized: a way must be found to assure an output of OQ units.

11.5.4 Constant Marginal Costs

Assume now a situation where the marginal costs of both the manufacturing and distribution divisions are constant. This is a reasonable assumption for firms which are not too large and which can expand their facilities without a significant (measurable) change in efficiency. This assumption has the effect of making the MC_m and MC_d lines horizontal. (See Figure 11.4.)

A necessary condition for the firm to produce is

$$MR \geq MC_m + MC_d. \tag{11.1}$$

With perfect competition $MR = P$ and therefore $P \geq MC_m + MC_d$. If the inequality holds, the firm should produce as much as possible.

The distribution division may again act as a monopolist. If so, its average revenue curve is equal to

$$AR_d = P - MC_m = P - P_m$$

where P_m is the price it must pay to the manufacturing division and P is the price of the final product. The average-revenue curve is horizontal and so therefore is the marginal-revenue curve. The optimal solution for the distribution division is still to produce as much as possible so long as strict inequality in equation (11.1) holds.

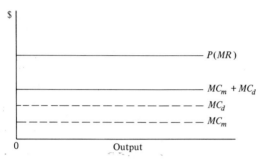

Figure 11.4   Constant marginal costs: Perfect competition

The manufacturing division receives a price equal to its marginal cost of MC_m and incurs marginal costs of MC_m (with constant marginal cost it will have zero profit). The distribution division shows a profit of $(P - P_m - MC_d)$ per unit which is greater than zero if the strict inequality in equation (11.1) holds. Just as the distribution division can act as a monopolistic buyer, so the manufacturing division can act as a monopolistic seller. The results are symmetrical. The distribution division shows no profit and the manufacturing division shows a profit of $(P - P_d - MC_m)$ per unit.

With constant costs for both the manufacturing and distribution divisions, the profits of the firm will be maximized by maximizing output if the strict inequality in equation (11.1) holds. Given strict inequality in equation (11.1) and the fact that both divisions will produce only if their profits are not negative, the transfer price, P_m, must satisfy the relationship

$$P - MC_d \geq P_m \geq MC_m.$$

Optimal output will be reached even if one division acts as a monopolist.

11.5.5   Relaxing the Assumptions of Perfect Competition

Relaxing the assumption of perfect competition, the firm may determine the price at which its product is sold. For example, in order to increase production and sales, the firm may decrease its sale price. Thus, instead of a horizontal line, the average-revenue curve of the firm slopes downward to the right, and the firm has a marginal-revenue curve that is below the average-revenue curve. The optimal output for the firm may be obtained from a graph similar to the one in Figure 11.1, except that the price line (average-revenue curve) is not horizontal, and a marginal curve can be drawn for the end product. The intersection of the total marginal-cost curve and the marginal-revenue curve determines the optimal output. This occurs at U.

Constant Marginal Costs: Imperfect Competition
Consider first the case of constant marginal costs. In this situation the previous conclusions are altered only slightly. (See Figure 11.5.) The optimal

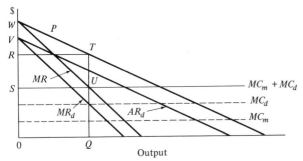

Figure 11.5   Constant marginal costs: Imperfect competition

solution for the firm is an output of OQ units (where the firm's marginal cost equals its marginal revenue) and a price of OR. This output will be attained even though one of the divisions acts as a monopolist. If the distribution division acts as a monopolist $P_m = MC_m$ and the cost per unit to the distribution division is

$$P_m + MC_d = MC_m + MC_d.$$

Hence its output remains unchanged at OQ. Alternatively, the average and marginal revenue curves for the distribution division can be constructed as before. The result is the same: an output of OQ units.

The profits of the distribution division equal the profits of the firm and are represented by area $RSUT$ in Figure 11.5. The manufacturing division shows zero profits. If the manufacturing division acts as a monopolist, its profits will be $RSUT$ and the distribution division will show no profit.

As was true for the case of perfect competition, the optimal activity is achieved with constant costs, despite the efforts of one division to act as a monopolist. If the transfer price to the manufacturing division satisfies the inequality $P - MC_d > P_m > MC_m$, say to assure the manufacturing division a profit, the optimal output will not be reached. With perfect competition and constant marginal costs optimal output could still be reached.

In order for the firm's profits to be maximized, the firm must assure that the distribution division sells OQ. Using a transfer price of $P_m = MC_m$ is sufficient to accomplish this objective in this case.

Increasing Marginal Costs: Imperfect Competition

Consider now the case where marginal costs are increasing for both divisions. If it is desired to find the optimal output for each division with the aim of maximizing its income instead of the income of the firm, then a diagram similar to Figure 11.2 may be used. The average revenue of the distribution division would again be obtained by subtracting the price curve of the manufacturing division (P_m) from the average-revenue curve of the end product. A marginal-revenue curve similar to the MR_d curve is obtained. The distribution division acting as a monopolistic buyer could restrict output to the intersection of this marginal-revenue curve and its marginal-cost curve.

The best transfer price for decision making is the marginal cost to the manufacturing division; but the use of marginal cost does not ensure that the purchasing division will not act as a monopolistic buyer. Centralized action is required to ensure that the optimal output is attained. One means of obtaining the desired output level is for central management to establish the output levels of the divisions. Another means would be for it to establish a price for all purchases by the distribution division from the manufacturing division equivalent to OD in the example graphed in Figure 11.2. Still another means of achieving the maximum output is for the central office to provide a subsidy payment to the division acting as a monopolist. The subsidy payment schedule would shift the marginal-revenue curve of the monopolistic division to coincide with its average-revenue curve determined without the subsidy.

11.5.6 Competitive Intermediate Markets

Up to this point it was assumed that the product could be sold only to the distribution division. Suppose that the intermediate product can also be bought or sold by the manufacturing division in a purely competitive market at a price p, and that the end product is sold in a purely competitive market at a price P. Figure 11.6 shows that the manufacturing division should produce OQ_m units of product (use the second quadrant of Figure 11.6) and that the distribution division should sell OQ_d units. The unit output of the manufacturing division does not have to equal the units sold by the distribution division.

The curves are explained as follows:
P, AR, MR is the price curve of the end product.
p is the market price of the intermediate product.

MC_m is the marginal-cost curve of the manufacturing division.

MC_d is the marginal-cost curve of the distribution division.

DRT or $MC_m + MC_d$ is the sum of the marginal-cost curves of the manufacturing and distribution divisions. The marginal-cost curve DRT is based on the assumption that the product of the manufacturing division must be sold to the distribution division and the distribution division must buy from the manufacturing division.

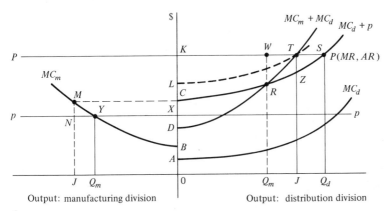

Figure 11.6 Competitive intermediate and final markets

CRS is the sum of MC_d plus p, the marginal cost of the distribution division and the intermediate price of the product. The curve is based on the assumption that all products produced at a marginal cost of less than the competitive price p have a marginal cost to the distribution division equal to the opportunity cost p.

DRS is the sum of $MC_d + MC_m$ up to Q_m and $MC_d + p$ thereafter. It is the marginal cost curve for the firm.

The manufacturing division would produce OQ_m units since if it produced more its marginal cost would then exceed the market price p. The distribution division would not pay in excess of the market price p to the manufacturing division since it could purchase the product in the market for that price. Thus the marginal-cost curve of the distribution division would be the sum of the marginal costs of the distribution division, MC_d, plus p, the effective cost of the intermediate product. The transfer price should be p, the competitive price, which is also the marginal cost of the manufacturing division at an output of OQ_m. The distribution division would buy OQ_m from the manufacturing division, $OQ_d - OQ_m$ from outside, and obtain a profit of $CRSK$. The profits to the manufacturing division are BYX.

The marginal-cost curve of the firm is given by DRS; the sum of the marginal costs of the two divisions up to an output of OQ_m and $p + MC_d$ thereafter. The profits to the firm are therefore $DRSK$. (Note, since $DRSK = CRSK + DRC$, $BYX = DRC$.)

If the additional requirement were made that the distribution division could sell only the product of the manufacturing division, then the competitive price p of the intermediate product would not be relevant to the decision.[9] The relevant costs would be the marginal costs of the manufacturing division and the marginal costs of the distribution division. The solution would be similar to the solution illustrated in Figure 11.1. Referring to Figure 11.6, the output would be OJ and, using the same marginal cost of OX as the transfer price, the manufacturing division would show a profit of $BYX - YNM$.

Restricting the distribution division to selling only the product of the manufacturing division reduces the number of units sold by the distribution division from OQ_d to OJ. The number of units sold by the manufacturing division increases from OQ_m to OJ. There is a loss in profit to the manufacturing division and also a loss in profit is suffered by the distribution division. The total loss of profit to the firm is the area RST. The profits of the firm decline from $DRSK$ to $DRTK$. The transfer price may be the marginal cost to the manufacturing division, but the distribution division is being penalized (as is the firm) by management's restricting the distribution division to selling only products made by the manufacturing division. The loss is partly due to the greater cost of the $OJ - OQ_m$ units and partly to a smaller output. If the transfer price used were to be the new marginal cost for OJ units, OC, the new marginal-cost curve for the distribution division would be LT, output would still be OJ, and company profits $DRTK$. The only result would be a shift of profits to the manufacturing division of $YXCM = CRTL$.

11.5.7 Transfer Pricing and Decision Making

The limitations of transfer pricing for decision making should be carefully noted. The fact that using marginal costs as the basis for the transfer prices may not lead to the optimal output decision at the division level has been discussed. Indeed, there is no one method of transfer pricing that can be used for all varieties of decision making and performance evaluation.

Consider the problem of whether or not to drop a division. Assume that the transfer-pricing system uses marginal costs, that a computation of the income of the division manufacturing component parts indicates that the income computed in accordance with accounting procedures is negative, and that a computation of the contribution of the division to the recovery of fixed costs directly identified with the division indicates that the division is not making any contribution. Should the division be abandoned? Not necessarily. The production of parts may have the effect of increasing the profits of the division that manufactures a component part. Thus, to determine whether the manufacturing division should be dropped it is necessary to look beyond the

[9] This would restrict total output to OJ and the profits of the firm to $DRTK$.

information obtained from using transfer pricing to the effect of the abandonment on the income of the entire firm. The case illustrated in Figure 11.6 would be an example if the area YNM exceeded the area BYX, and the firm sells only products made by the manufacturing division using a transfer price of OX.

The same type of analysis may be used in make-or-buy decisions. The use of marginal costs as the basis of transfer pricing is not relevant for making a decision unless each unit is priced on the basis of its marginal cost. This is difficult at best, but for a theoretically sound decision it should be attempted by the decision maker. Otherwise a differential-cost analysis procedure should be used.

11.5.8 Transfer Price and The Measurement of Performance—A Paradox

Difficulties of applying the transfer prices to decision making have been noted. There is also an interesting paradox that may result from the use of marginal cost for transfer pricing. If the marginal costs of one division are

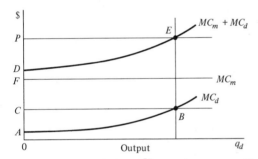

Figure 11.7   Transfer pricing and constant efficiency

constant (its marginal-cost curve is a horizontal line with no increase as production increases), this division shows no profit if the marginal cost is used as the transfer price. (See Figure 11.7 as well as 11.4 and 11.5 and assume that there is no intermediate market for the product.) The profit of the distribution division is ABC, which is equal to the area DEP, the profit of the firm. The manufacturing division makes no profit since it charges a price that is equal to its marginal cost and its marginal-cost curve is horizontal.[10] This emphasizes the importance of using a market price to evaluate the manufacturing division as discussed in section 11.4.1.

A division can determine which type of marginal-cost curve maximizes profits under a given transfer system based on marginal costs. While this may not be consistent with the firm's objective of maximizing company

[10] The same result occurs in the situation where both divisions have constant costs and one acts as a monopolist.

profits, in certain cases inefficiencies that increase marginal costs may actually be desirable from the point of view of, say, the selling division. The use of marginal cost as a transfer price for the product of the manufacturing division provides no incentive for this division to reduce its costs.

11.6 Summary

Attempting to administer the separate components of one industrial firm as if they were separate competing entities frequently results in the necessity for the use of transfer prices for accounting purposes and for decision making. The economic analysis of transfer pricing indicates that the solutions can become extremely complex if the demand and the production of the products are dependent on each other (technological dependence may also be introduced). However, several observations may be made:

1. Marginal cost and the competitive prices of the product being transferred are not necessarily equal. There is an entire schedule of marginal costs, so that this equality, or the appropriateness of the marginal cost, should not be assumed.
2. The use of marginal costs for transfer pricing does not ensure that the company is operating at its optimal output since divisions may act to maximize their own profits to the detriment of the profits of the company (this is also possible if competitive prices are used).
3. The use of marginal-cost transfer pricing may result in weird actions, such as attempting to decrease efficiency or to have an increasing marginal-cost curve in order to increase divisional profits (by increasing marginal costs and thus increasing the price of the product).
4. The transfer-pricing procedure does not generally give good results for nonmarginal decisions such as abandoning a plant and make-or-buy decisions (these decisions require a differential-cost and revenue analysis).

The choice of the transfer-pricing method depends on the information available; for certain decisions transfer prices are not useful at all. The extent to which transfer prices are an artificial compromise should be recognized by the user, so that he may be alert to those cases where they cannot be used for decision-making purposes.[11]

It is likely that in many cases firms have created profit centers which require the use of transfer prices when cost centers would have been a more effective means of controlling costs and measuring performance. The use of a profit

---

[11] Several complications have been omitted from the discussion. Among these are situations of demand dependence for the intermediate and end products, and cost or technological dependence. See Hirshleifer (1957), for discussions of these items.

center requires that revenues be computed, and this in turn requires the use of prices where there may not have been an arms length transaction; in fact, the profit center may not be able to control the number of units sold. Consider a parts division of an automobile company making components of a new model when there is no replacement market. The parts division cannot control the number of units sold and the transfer price cannot help but be somewhat arbitrary. In a situation of this type, it might be more desirable to measure the performance of the parts division by the cost of the product rather than by a fictitious profit figure at least two steps removed from the correctly measured variables (that is, those which are controllable by the parts division).

The first question raised by management must be whether the use of transfer prices is appropriate at all. Only if the answer to this question is yes, should the questions of the method of computing and controlling the transfer price be raised.

APPENDIX 11A

Transfer Prices and Math Programming

Mathematical programming models can be used in transfer pricing problems.[12]

As described in the chapter, setting the transfer price equal to marginal cost is not adequate to assure that the firm's optimal profit will be attained. First there exist the cases where one division acts as a monopolist. Second, one division's activities may affect another's either by using up a scarce resource or by causing an upward shift in another division's cost function by bidding up the price of a scarce resource or causing the division to modify its technology. In either case the division causing the change tends to overproduce since the costs to the other divisions do not enter its analysis. It is also possible for the activities of one division to create external economies, for example, by shifting to the right the demand schedule for the product of another division.

The task of the mathematical model is to induce a division to expand those activities that create external economies and contract those activities that create external diseconomies just enough to produce an optimum of the firm. The means by which this objective is obtained is through the addition to a division's earnings of a per unit subsidy for those activities creating external economies, and a per unit penalty to those activities involving external diseconomies.

[12] See W. J. Baumol, and T. Fabian, "Decomposition, Pricing for Decentralization and External Economies," *Management Science*, September 1964, pp. 1–32. Also see J. E. Hass, "Transfer Pricing in a Decentralized Firm," *Management Science*, February 1968, pp. 310–331, and Whinston, *op. cit.*

In particular where linearity can be assumed, the over-all problem can be decomposed.[13] In essence the divisions submit tentative proposed activity levels to central management based on the constraints attaching to their division and prices supplied by central management. Central management combines these tentative proposals in light of the interdivisional constraints to produce a revised set of scaled down activity levels and associated prices. The process continues in an iterative fashion until an optimum is reached.[14]

The method consists of six steps.

1. The company formulates the model (linear programming in this case) for the entire firm and breaks out the component parts for each division and the central office.
2. Each division submits to the central office an activity plan based upon the unit profit figures assigned to it by the central office.[15]
3. The central office then determines the effects of the divisional solutions on the other divisions and on the company as a whole. This the central office does by solving its own program.
4. The results of the central office solution yield temporary bonus and penalty figures that are used to create new contribution figures for the division's activities.
5. The divisions now resolve their problem using the new activity unit profit figures and resubmit the results.
6. The process is repeated until an optimal plan is determined; that is, until there is no need to modify the per unit profit figures used by the divisions.[16]

The solution technique involves solving the dual. The technique of solution is too complex to illustrate here.[17]

There is, unfortunately, a lack of complete independence in the process. Although the process starts with the actual costs and prices of a division, and one division need know only its own technology, subsequent solutions involve

[13] The decomposition procedure is not restricted to the case where linearity is assumed. But see Hass, *op. cit.* The decomposition procedure is discussed in G. Dantzig, and P. Wolfe, "Decomposition Principle for Linear Programs," *Operations Research*, 1960, pp. 101–111.

[14] The technique is not new having been advanced initially by Pigou. A. C. Pigou, *Wealth and Welfare*, London: Macmillan, 1912, pp. 164–165. Recently it has been expounded by K. J. Arrow, and L. Hurwicz, "Decentralization and Computation in Resource Allocation," *Essays in Economics and Econometrics*, edited by R. Pfouts, Chapel Hill, N.C.: University of North Carolina Press, 1960.

[15] At the first step these are based on market prices and the division's variable costs.

[16] Since only a finite number of plans are possible, the technique assures a solution after a finite number of steps. One application alluded to by Baumol and Fabian, *op. cit.*, p. 1, involves thirty thousand constraints and several million variables.

[17] The reader is referred to Baumol and Fabian, *op. cit.*, for an extensive example.

artificial contribution figures for each activity sent down by the central office. The final solution also involves a direct determination of the activity output levels by the central office despite the previous solutions transmitted by the division. The division managers must be told in the final analysis the resultant activity levels as they emerge from the central office solution. At this point the final decision is made in the central office and is merely communicated to the divisions. In a very real sense this procedure represents only "quasi-decentralization" since the central office makes the final activity-level decisions.

When linearity no longer exists because of the nature of the interdependencies, the functional forms cannot be separated. Two results occur from this situation. First, a gaming problem arises as the interdependent divisions try to anticipate the levels of the variables that are selected by another division but affect their activities. Second, there is an increase in uncertainty resulting from the ambiguity arising because one division's decision variables are dependent in part on the decisions of another division in a way it cannot predict from price data alone.

Several solutions are possible. First, the interrelated divisions could be combined. Second, additional organizational constraints could be introduced into the programming model to mitigate the problem. A third possibility involves building the game problem into the mathematical solution.[18] The final decision in the latter case is essentially like that in which the final activity-level decisions are made by the central office.

QUESTIONS AND PROBLEMS

11–1 Under a marginal-cost transfer-pricing arrangement will a division manager acting to maximize the profits of his division also be maximizing the profits of the corporation?

11–2 What are the advantages and disadvantages of centralization and decentralization of authority?

11–3 What are some of the possible methods of establishing transfer prices? Describe where each might be used to advantage.

11–4 Explain why a distribution (buying) division may act as a monopolistic buyer. Explain the effect on the firm.

11–5 Explain why a manufacturing division (selling division) may act as a monopolistic seller. Discuss the effect on the firm.

11–6 If the transfer price is set equal to the marginal cost of the manufacturing division, will this lead to decisions which will maximize the profits of the firm?

---

[18] See Whinston, *op. cit.*, p. 439.

11–7 Assuming the use of marginal costs as the basis of the prices, are transfer prices useful for such decisions as abandoning a division?

11–8 Assuming a division is performing research for other divisions, at what price should it transfer its completed research (assume the research is one of several products made by the division)?

11–9 If both the distribution and manufacturing divisions act monopolistically, what is the effect on the firm?

11–10 The Regulite Company has two divisions (manufacturing and distribution) acting as profit centers. Since it is a small company it feels that its price is set by its competitors but that it can sell all it can produce at a price of $100 per unit.

The average variable costs for the two divisions are

$$AVC_m = 40 \qquad AVC_d = 10 + 0.005Q.$$

The manufacturing division has $5,000 and the distribution division $1,000 of fixed costs. In addition the corporate headquarters allocates $3,000 of its costs to manufacturing and $2,000 to distribution.

Required:
a. What is the optimum level of production for the firm? What would be the profit of the firm? What is the marginal cost of manufacturing at the optimal output?
b. If you were in charge of the distribution division what price would you offer the manufacturing division? What output would result? What would be the profits of the distribution division?
c. Do the profit figures provide useful performance measures? Explain.

11–11 Suppose that the average variable costs for the two divisions of the Regulite Company in problem 11–10 are

$$AVC_m = 8 + 0.01Q, \qquad AVC_d = 62.$$

There are no fixed costs.

Required:
a. What is the optimum level of production for the firm? What would be the profit of the firm? What is the marginal cost of manufacturing at the optimal output?
b. If you were in charge of the distribution division, what price would you offer the manufacturing division? What output would result?
c. What is the effect in part b on the firm's profits?
d. What profits are shown by the distribution division? Under these assumptions would the profit figures provide good performance measures?

11–12 Suppose that the average variable costs for the two divisions of the Regulite Company in problem 11–10 are

$$AVC_m = 8 + 0.01Q, \qquad AVC_d = 2 + 0.005Q.$$

There are no fixed costs.

Required:

a. What is the optimum level of production for the firm? What would be the profit of the firm? What is the marginal cost of manufacturing at the optimal output?

b. If you were in charge of the distribution division, what price would you offer the manufacturing division? What output would result?

c. What effect is there on company profits. Are the profit figures of the divisions good indicators of performance?

11–13 Suppose that the average variable costs for the two divisions of the Regulite Company in problem 11–10 are

$$AVC_m = 8 + 0.01Q, \qquad AVC_d = 2 + 0.005Q.$$

The price is $100 - .01Q$, and there are no fixed costs.

Required:

a. What is the optimum level of production for the firm? What is the marginal cost of manufacturing? What is the profit of the firm?

b. If you were in charge of the distribution division, what price would you offer the manufacturing division? What output would result?

c. What is the effect on company profits in b? Are the profit figures good indicators of performance?

11–14 (Refer to problem 11–13.) If the manufacturing division were to act as a monopolist, at what price would it sell its product to the distribution division? What output would result? Which division acting monopolistically had the greater impact? Why?

11–15 The Elston Company used the market price of a competitive producer for an identical product as the internal transfer price. The manufacturing division claimed that it should be permitted to charge a higher price. The market price was based on a vendor with a more modern and more efficient plant. The manager of the manufacturing plant was forced to operate with an outdated and inefficient plant. Further, he had no authority to make capital investments or otherwise modernize his plant. He believed he was being penalized for something beyond his control and claimed the practice created bad "managerial psychology."

The vice president for finance ruled that "since the primary objective of the intracompany pricing system was to provide a means of measuring performance against known competitive levels, competitive practice with regard to cost and price must be followed."

Comment on this situation in terms of the use to which the performance measures are being put and the appropriateness of the procedure. Can you think of other reasons besides the efficiency of the plant that might cause other divisions under similar plans to object?

11–16 Using Figures 11.2 and 11.3, determine the profits and the change in profits for the firm and for each division.

11–17 If the firm in Figure 11.6 restricts the distribution division to selling only products made by the manufacturing division, what output will result and what areas represent the profits to each division and to the firm? (Assume marginal cost is used as the transfer price.)

11–18 In the example discussed in the chapter and illustrated in Figures 11.2 and 11.3, under which situation is output most restricted? How can you tell in general which division acting as a monopolist will have the greater effect?

11–19 Assume the top management of the Argon Company requires all divisions to have their activities audited periodically by the Internal Auditing Division. At what price should the audit services be charged to the divisions?

SUPPLEMENTARY READING

BAUMOL, W. J., and T. FABIAN, "Decomposition, Pricing for Decentralization and External Economies," *Management Science*, September 1964, pp. 1–32.

COOK, P. W., "New Technique for Intracompany Pricing," *The Harvard Business Review*, July–August 1957, pp. 74–80.

GOULD, J. R., "Internal Pricing in Firms Where There are Costs of Using an Outside Market," *Journal of Business*, January 1964, pp. 61–67.

HASS, J. E., "Transfer Pricing in a Decentralized Firm," *Management Science*, February 1968, pp. 310–331.

HIRSHLEIFER, J., "Economics of the Divisionalized Firm," *Journal of Business*, April 1957, pp. 96–108.

HIRSHLEIFER, J., "On the Economics of Transfer Pricing," *Journal of Business*, July 1956, pp. 172–184.

National Industrial Conference Board, *Interdivisional Transfer Pricing*, Studies in Business Policy No. 122, 1967.

ONSI, M., "A Transfer Pricing System Based on Opportunity Cost," *The Accounting Review*, July 1970, pp. 535–543.

RONEN, J., and R. COPELAND, "Transfer Pricing for Divisional Autonomy," *Journal of Accounting Research*, Spring 1970, pp. 99–112.

WHINSTON, A., "Price Guides in Decentralized Organizations," in *New Prospectives in Organizational Research*, edited by W. Cooper, H. Leavitt, and M. Shelly, New York: John Wiley, 1962, pp. 405–448.

Chapter 12

Network Methods

Since they appeared in the late 1950s, network methods have achieved considerable application in planning, control, and performance measurement. To apply these methods, subactivities of a major project are specified and arrayed in order of their required completion. This requires the manager to determine those activities that must be completed in series and those that may be worked on in parallel. Probabilistic data concerning both time and cost can be integrated into the analysis for each subactivity. The procedure permits bottlenecks to be identified, the significance of deviations in expected completion times to be evaluated, and it helps in directing resources toward improving project performance. Further, time and cost data provide means of controlling total outlays, evaluating management performance, and predicting both additional costs and delays.

Several network methods are in wide use. This chapter concentrates on presenting the essentials of one of them, the Program Evaluation and Review Technique (PERT).

12.1 The PERT Method

In order for the PERT method to be applicable, several conditions must be satisfied.

1. There must be a well-defined set of activities (or jobs) that, when completed, indicate an end to the project.
2. It must be possible to specify the technological precedence conditions among activities, as well as the activities that can be started and stopped independently of one another.

243

3. Time estimates for each activity are required. These may be in the form of point estimates or probability distributions.

For an example consider the project and the associated network diagram given in Table 12–1.

Table 12–1 Schedule for Project I

Activity Description	Predecessor Activity	Expected Comple- tion Times (weeks)
a	None	8
b	None	7
c	a, b	10
d	None	7
e	c	6
f	d	4
g	f	7

The times will be treated as the means of individual probability distributions, one for each activity.[1] If desired, the entire distribution could be used and simulation methods applied to the solution. This project is diagramed in Figure 12.1.

The circles in Figure 12.1 stand for the jobs or activities indicated by the letter inside; the arrows represent the completion of one task and the beginning of another. The numbers within the circles are the expected completion times. The earliest expected starting time for each activity, given the job-order dependencies, is indicated outside, above, and to the left of each activity. The earliest expected starting time of an activity is defined to be the earliest time an activity can be expected to begin if all previous activities begin at their earliest expected starting times.

The earliest expected finish time for an activity is given by the number outside, below, and to the right of each activity. It is defined as the time an activity is expected to be finished, assuming all predecessor activities begin at their earliest expected starting times and is equal to the earliest expected starting time for the activity plus its expected completion time. Thus, for example, activity c has an expected starting time of eight weeks. Activity c cannot be started until the eighth week since it cannot begin until activities a and b are both completed. Activity b requires an expected time of only seven weeks, but the earliest expected starting time for activity c is eight weeks since activity a has an expected time of eight weeks. The earliest expected

[1] The managerial time estimates are usually considered to follow a beta distribution, and approximate estimates of the expected time are obtained using $E(t) = (t_o + 4t_m + t_p)/6$ where t_o, t_m, and t_p are managerial estimates of the optimistic, most likely, and pessimistic times respectively.

finish time for activity c is the sum of eight weeks plus the expected completion time of ten weeks, a total of $18 = 8 + 10$ weeks.[2] Where several activities feed into one activity—a and b feed into c, for example—the latest of the
completion times of the preceding activities becomes the earliest expected
starting time for the next activity.

An examination of Figure 12.1 indicates that the project's expected completion date is twenty-four weeks. This is true despite the fact that activity g is

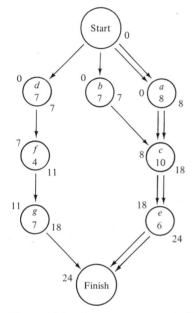

Figure 12.1 A program network diagram: Project I

expected to be completed by the end of the eighteenth week. There are three
distinct paths from the starting activity to the finishing activity in this simple
project. The longest path, start-a-c-e-finish, takes twenty-four weeks and is
defined as the critical path. It is the bottleneck, and if the expected completion
time of the total project is to be decreased, some reduction must be accomplished somewhere in the critical path. The critical path is marked by double
arrows in Figure 12.1.

Suppose for the moment that the project in question did not need to be

---

[2] It is not quite correct to call the figures outside the circles expected times (at least
after the first activities on each path). Where paths are similar in length, ignoring one or
more of them, which is what the method described does, tends to understate the earliest
expected starting times of future activities. Thus, if the probability distributions were
used and if the numbers used are expected times, the earliest expected starting time for
activity c would exceed eight weeks since occasionally activity b would take longer than
activity a.

finished until the thirtieth week. Then with the computations as defined, there would exist an expected available safety factor of six weeks. The project could be delayed for six weeks and still be "expected" to be done on time. The term expected here is a probabilistic concept and implies a substantial probability that the total project time will exceed twenty-four weeks. It also ignores the probability that nonslack paths may delay the project.[3] This time of six weeks is defined as the total slack in the project.

The concept of total slack also applies to each activity. The total slack in an activity is the difference between the earliest expected starting time and the latest time it could be begun without delaying the expected completion date beyond the required date. For all activities on the critical path, the total slack of the activity is the same as that of the project, namely six weeks in this case. For activities not on the critical path the total slack is the difference between the earliest expected starting time and the latest time the activity could begin without delaying the required completion date. Thus the project manager could expect to begin activity f as early as the seventh week. Further, he must begin it by the nineteenth week if the project is to be expected to be completed by the thirtieth week (activity f is expected to take four weeks and activity g seven weeks). Therefore the total slack in activity f is twelve weeks: $19 - 7$.

Another type of slack is the time an activity can be delayed without delaying the expected starting time of another activity. This is referred to as free slack. Some jobs will not have any free slack since free slack requires parallel activities. Indeed, in the present example, only activity b has free slack. The free slack for activity b is one week.[4]

The importance of these slack measures is that they indicate the degree of impact a change in time efficiency has on the over-all expected completion time. Furthermore, they suggest places where resources can be temporarily shifted to improve times on the critical path. The total slack measures show the project manager where he has or does not have elbow room in scheduling activities.

If the probability distributions for the times can be approximated with beta distributions (see footnote 1 for definition of terms), an estimate of the variance for activity i is given by $\sigma_i^2 = 1/36(t_{pi} - t_{oi})^2$. If there is a large number of independent activities on the critical path, the distribution of the total project time for the path can be assumed to be normal and given by the sum of the variances over all activities on the critical path:

$$\sigma^2 = \sum_i \frac{1}{36}(t_{pi} - t_{oi})^2. \tag{12.1}$$

[3] Assuming the probability distribution for the total project completion time is normal, the probability of finishing in twenty-four weeks would be slightly less than 0.5.

[4] This concept is somewhat misleading since a delay of one day in starting activity b may delay the expected starting time for activity c where the term expected is given a probabilistic interpretation.

The variance given by equation (12.1) does not reflect the effect of uncertainty in other paths which may also delay completion and thus has a built-in downward bias. Despite this limitation it can be used to estimate the probability that a project would be finished by a given point in time. For example, if the expected time is 24, σ^2 is 36, and if the project deadline, t, is thirty weeks, then the probability of finishing by the deadline date is given by the standard-normal distribution function

$$N_Z(z) = N_Z\left(\frac{t - t_e}{6}\right) = N_Z\left(\frac{30 - 24}{6}\right) = N_Z(1) = 0.8413.$$

12.2   Resource Allocation in PERT Networks

Suppose now, however, that the required completion time is seventeen weeks; a case of negative total slack. Sometimes nothing can be done about this situation but often the input of more or better resources into the process

Table 12–2   Time Cost Estimates by Activity

Activity	Expected Activity Time	Cost	Cost Increase per Unit of Time Decrease
a	8	$1,000	
	6	1,400	200
	5	1,900	500
b	7	800	
	5	2,000	600
c	10	1,500	
	7	1,800	100
	5	3,000	600
d	7	500	
	6	1,000	500
	3	1,900	300
e	6	1,100	
	5	1,300	200
	4	2,200	900
f	4	800	
	2	1,400	300
g	7	800	
	4	1,400	200
	1	5,000	1,200

permits a shortening of the expected times. For the example of this chapter, assume that the costs associated with different expected activity times are as shown in Table 12–2. Assume further that the cost estimates are independent.

Under these assumptions, shortening one activity for a given cost has no effect on the costs of changing the times on other activities.[5] Finally the assumption is made here that activities must be reduced in accordance with the discrete steps indicated in Table 12–2. (A continuous function could be used if desired.)

The total activity time without any change is expected to be twenty-four weeks, and adding up the costs for each activity yields a total cost of $6,500. This is illustrated in Table 12–3.

Table 12–3   Cost Project 1: 24 Week Completion

Activity	Cost (thousands)
a	$1,000
b	800
c	1,500
d	500
e	1,100
f	800
g	800
Total	$6,500

Since the total expected time is decreased by shortening the critical path, the next step is to search the critical path for the activity with the lowest cost increase per unit of time. The activity with this characteristic is c. Activity c is lowered by three weeks at a cost of $300 or $100 per week. With the incurring of this cost the total cost is now $6,800, the expected time is twenty-one weeks, and the expected duration of the critical path is decreased by three weeks. Since the expected time still exceeds the required time of seventeen weeks, the critical path is searched for the activity with the next lowest cost increase per unit of time decrease. In this project activities a and e are identical. To break the tie one simple rule that might be used is to pick one of the tied activities at random. Suppose activity e is selected. Activity e is shortened by one week for a cost of $200. The total cost is now $7,000, the expected time is twenty weeks, and there is still no change in the critical path.

Continuing the procedure, activity a is now shortened by two weeks at a cost of $400 (the total cost becomes $7,400) and the expected time of the right-hand path is now eighteen weeks. However, the expected time of the project is reduced by only one week, to nineteen weeks, since a new critical path exists; namely, start-b-c-e-finish. Using the new critical path, activities b and c have identical cost increases per time period. Since activity c is relevant to

---

[5] This may not be true in practice as, say, when marginal labor is hired or overtime is required. Where it is not true, allowance must be made for the dependencies, perhaps by using simulation methods.

more paths, it is reduced by two weeks at a cost of $1,200. Total cost is now $8,600, but the expected total time is reduced only to eighteen rather than to seventeen weeks since once again there is a new critical path, namely start-d-f-g-finish. The optimal choice is to decrease activity g by three weeks at a cost of $600. The total cost is now $9,200, the expected time seventeen weeks, and the critical path is start-b-c-e-finish.

It may appear that the problem is finished. This is, however, not quite the case. The path start-d-f-g-finish now requires an expected time of fifteen weeks. Suppose activity g could be increased three weeks at a saving of $600, and instead of following the general procedure described above, suppose activity d were decreased one week at a cost of $500. The expected completion time of seventeen weeks would now also attach to this path and total costs would be reduced by $100 to $9,100. Adjustments of this type should be evaluated before the problem is considered resolved.

The steps used to shorten the total required time are

1. Pick the activity on the critical path with the lowest cost increase per unit of time. If there is a tie, pick one of the tied activities at random. (This is an arbitrary rule.)
2. Decrease the expected activity time by the time saved, compute the expected total time, the total cost, and determine the critical path.
3. Repeat the process until either the expected total time is equal to or less than the required time, there are no more possible time savings, or the total cost exceeds available funds.

Since most project networks are quite complex, it is fortunate that these steps can be programmed for computers.

12.3   Some Problems in Application

The technique described in Sections 12.1 and 12.2 has been extensively employed for analyzing, planning, and scheduling large, complex projects. It is not without its problems, however.[6] Perhaps paramount among these is securing the data necessary to support the analysis. This includes the difficulties attendant in obtaining cost data that can be realistically applied to the scheduling problem. Too often the accounting department data are not relevant to that required by the problem.

A second substantial problem is the difficulty of obtaining useful probabilistic data. The activity-time distributions have traditionally been assumed to be adequately described by beta distributions. In fact, no empirical studies of

[6] See also K. R. MacCrimmon and C. A. Ryavec, "Analytical Study of the PERT Assumptions," *Operations Research*, January 1964, pp. 16–37.

activity-time distributions have been made.[7] The terms optimistic and pessimistic used, in part, to obtain the expected times may be too vague to produce valid estimates of the beta distribution parameters.

The use of probabilistic data in particular has implications for performance evaluation. If both cost and time data are subject to uncertainty, this uncertainty should be recalled when it is time to evaluate the managers who are responsible for a particular activity. Some attempt should be made to consider "normal variability" in his performance on individual tasks and to expect offsetting favorable and unfavorable performance over time and over several tasks. Unfortunately, the observations taken on several tasks may not be independent (for example, if they are worked on concurrently), and time and cost measures on the same activity (and perhaps even on several activities) are usually interrelated. These interdependencies must be considered where they exist. Also, changes in the resources available to the manager, the effects of learning, and favorable or unfavorable conditions (such as weather and strikes) must be considered in estimating the relevant probability distributions and evaluating results.

One possible performance measure that should not be overlooked is the marginal cost added to the project because a manager fails to complete his activity in time or requires the diversion of resources from other activities and hence alters their time or cost performance. Often if one activity is unnecessarily delayed, a new network analysis is required. Computers can and should be programmed to update the network on the basis of actual or estimated data on each activity. As part of this revision, the increase (or decrease) in costs created by an activity, can be computed. These can be used, where estimated in time, to assist in optimal resource allocations. If they are computed after the fact, they can be used in measuring the performance of the manager responsible for the delay by charging them to his budget. It is also important that the effect of delays on the network be promptly relayed to the managers of other activities so they may adjust their plans. The effects of these delays should be considered if the results are used to evaluate performance.

There are several alternate time and cost estimation procedures that could be used. Rough estimates of data could be used until the critical path is located, and effort could then be directed toward better estimate of times for the critical activities. Preconceived biases are common. One way to mitigate the bias problems is to estimate job times in random order. Responders may tend to add times mentally, and this in turn conditions their responses toward reaching a total time within the limit required by the project.

There are problems in establishing the network, including the possibility of omitting activities or misordering activities. Sometimes these problems can

---

[7] An appealing but equally unjustified alternative is the triangular distribution with $E(t) = (a + m + b)/3$ and $\text{var}(t) = [(b - a)^2 + (m - a)(m - b)]/18$ where a and b are the end points and m the most likely (modal) observation.

be reduced by having several groups produce independent networks and comparing the results. Often networks must be modified by the addition of interconnecting paths. Such additions may affect the expected completion time.

One of the more appealing extensions in PERT applications is the incorporation, using simulation, into the analysis of the entire probability distributions for the times and costs of each activity rather than just the mean and variance of those distributions.[8] Furthermore, it is possible to introduce dependencies between the time and cost data as well. Subjective probability distributions are obtained for the relevant variables and the project is simulated using Monte-Carlo techniques. Each simulation run provides project time and cost data for the entire network. An evaluation of the suitability of the implied times and costs associated with the project may be attempted by examining the time and cost distributions. For example, if the time distribution associated with one set of decisions and costs is judged to be unsatisfactory, the simulation could be rerun for a different payment (or payments) to shift an activity's (or several activities') time distribution to the left. Decisions might then be made in terms of the trade-off of money for time saved and the probability of finishing on time. The trade-off may be difficult to evaluate and hence it would be helpful if the benefits from an early finish and penalties for a late finish could be estimated.

Generally there are benefits from finishing a project before the required time. These may include reduced financial charges and increased benefits from early operation. Similarly, there may be penalties including lost contribution margins from a failure to finish by the required completion time. Given a project time distribution resulting from a Monte-Carlo simulation, the expected net effect can be estimated by integrating the product of the function defining the benefits (penalties) with the probability density function for time, $f(t)$, over all values t. This is illustrated in Figure 12.2, when it can be assumed that the benefits from finishing early and the costs from finishing late are linearly related to time.

The integration yields

$$b_u \int_0^{t_b} (t_b - t)f(t)\, dt - b_o \int_{t_b}^{t_c} (t - t_b)f(t)\, dt, \qquad (12.2)$$

where

b_u is the unit dollar benefit from finishing early,
b_o is the unit dollar penalty from finishing late,
t_b is the required time,
t_c is the time such that $f(t) = 0$ for all $t > t_c$.

[8] See, for example, G. L. Thompson, "CPM and DCPM Under Risk," Reprint No. 384, Graduate School of Industrial Administration, Carnegie-Mellon University, 1968. Simulation methods using Monte-Carlo techniques may be excessive. For an alternative see W. H. Parks and K. D. Ramsing, "The Use of the Compound Poisson in PERT," *Management Science*, April 1969, pp. 397–402.

While still in the planning phase, the manager may wish to consider the effect of the reallocation of resources or the use of additional resources to alter the project time distribution. This can be done by altering the activity distributions, presumably at some cost. As the project moves out of the planning and into the execution stage such modifications may become more costly. The results of each reallocation policy could be evaluated by conducting a new simulation, evaluating equation (12.2) and comparing it to the cost of the additional resources committed to the project. This approach explicitly considers the costs involved in a failure to meet the project deadline, the likelihoods of the various completion times and costs, as well as the effects on expected profits of decreasing the completion times of one or more activities.[9]

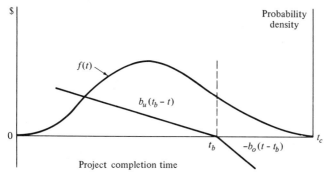

Figure 12.2   Diagram of one simulation

It also implicitly assumes that the policy is found which optimally uses the additional resources. If the assumption is met, additional resources should result in a shift to the left in the resultant project time distribution.

Presumably the relationship between the additional resources committed and the net benefits realized will exhibit marginal decreasing returns. In computing these returns, the net gain obtained in the expectation of the project cost distribution from an early finish should be compared to the cost of obtaining it. The notions of opportunity cost should be used in evaluating the cost of alternative reallocation policies.

Consideration should also be given to the alternative of subcontracting, the use of slack time to shift resources, redesign of the system (for example, to convert series activities into parallel activities), and the use of a different technology.

The PERT technique has already been successfully used in construction, audits, computer installations, institution of control systems, competitive bidding, maintenance programs, new product development, and many other places. With the advent of better techniques for handling some of the prob-

---

[9] The implicit assumption is made here that the net effect can be measured on the basis of the expected monetary values involved.

lems, it should find even more uses as well as being used more effectively in existing applications.

12.4 PERT-Cost and Control

The concept of PERT-Cost provides a useful approach to the control of projects already started.[10] Using this method, figures are kept on actual costs incurred, budgeted costs (adjusted to reflect unforeseen changes, say in prices), and the time activities are completed. This information assists in determining the overexpenditure and time late to date and, thereby, an estimate of the overexpenditure and anticipated time late on the total project. Dividing a project into parts according to both the component activities and the responsible divisions of the firm permits the project manager to pinpoint trouble areas early and perhaps initiate corrective or ameliorating action. It also permits an evaluation of the statement so often made that, "Yes, I'm over the budget, but the work is substantially ahead of schedule." Figures 12.3, 12.4 and 12.5 suggest the essentials of this approach.

Figure 12.3 gives the over-all picture of the project to date. The actual cost has been plotted up to the present time and projected to the expected completion date. The latter date is found by projecting the value-of-the-work-performed line until its height reaches the height of the cost-budget line at the original budgeted completion date. The value of the work performed is the budgeted value of those activities actually completed.

When actual costs exceed the value of the work performed the difference is an overrun. The overrun in the present example is quite large today but is expected to decrease by the time the project is completed. Actual cost less the value of the work performed as a ratio to the value of work performed gives the percentage overrun. This percentage is plotted and extrapolated to the expected completion data in Figure 12.4.

The cost-budget plot indicates just when work should be done as well as its cost. In this case it has taken $b - a$ weeks longer to complete the work done than was budgeted. The amount, $b - a$, then, indicates the time late. Figure 12.3 suggests the project will be even further behind time when it is finished, $b' - a'$. The weeks-late figure is also considered important enough to diagram separately. The fact that the weeks-late figure is predicted to become worse may have some relation to the expected decline in overrun, both in percentage and, somewhat less, in total. It would perhaps be surprising for the weeks-late figure to decline concurrently with a decline in the absolute value of the overrun.

The data on the entire project is perhaps most useful when broken down by tasks, departments, or both. Suppose, for example, the following facts were available on a given activity at the twenty-second week:

[10] See H. W. Paige, "How PERT/Cost Helps the Manager," *The Harvard Business Review*, November–December 1963, pp. 87–95.

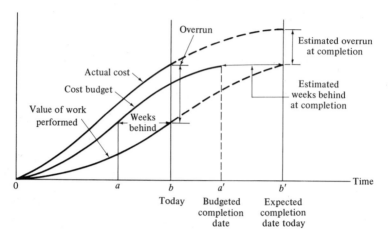

Figure 12.3   Operating schedule of performance

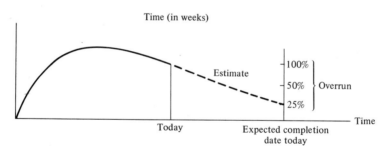

Figure 12.4   Expected overrun

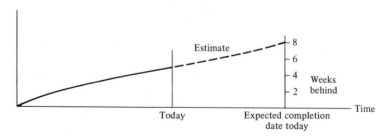

Figure 12.5   Expected time late

Actual cost at week 22	$4.4 thousand
Budgeted value of work performed	$1.8 thousand
Budget time for value of work performed	11 weeks
Cost budget at week 22	$3.8 thousand
Estimated actual cost at completion	$5.4 thousand
Estimated time of completion (total)	36 weeks
Total budgeted value at completion	$4.0 thousand
Budgeted completion time	23 weeks

The above schedule of costs indicates $2.2 thousand of budgeted value, $4 − $1.8, remains to be completed. However, it simultaneously predicts it can accomplish the production task for $1 thousand, $5.4 − $4.4. This optimistic forecast of doing $2.2 thousand of budgeted activity on less than half that in actual expenditures should be questioned. Furthermore, this activity is eleven weeks behind schedule, 22 − 11, while estimating thirteen weeks behind at completion, 36 − 23. This implies a much different level of performance than in the past. While feasible, it too appears questionable in light of an estimate of less costs than budgeted for the remaining work to be completed.

The PERT-Cost technique also provides additional performance measures in terms of overrun and weeks-behind schedule. In particular, it often leads to statements such as the one in the example about future behavior under specified conditions concerning resource availabilities that can be evaluated in terms of later performance.

12.5   Summary

The methods described in this chapter for programming and controlling large projects are appealing for several reasons. They are reasonably easy to understand and can be applied to a wide range of problems. They provide data for immediate and continuing control and re-evaluation, and the graphical techniques provide additional means of communicating and interpreting results as well as of pinpointing critical areas of concern.

New techniques, such as computer simulation, permit larger problems to be treated as well as a more accurate and complete treatment of existing applications. The underlying simplicity and the ability to focus attention on the critical issues involving important projects in a wide range of problem areas makes the technique important to the manager.

The PERT network requirement also requires the manager to think carefully through the logic of the project planning. This exercise can often point up trouble spots early and can suggest the need for redesign when such redesign can be most effectively implemented. Finally, it focuses additional attention on critical-activity time estimates and provides a basis for estimating and scheduling scarce resources.

QUESTIONS AND PROBLEMS

12–1 The chapter indicates that network methods are useful in planning, prediction, control of project cost and time, and performance measurement. Discuss the use of the PERT method in each of these dimensions.

12–2 What problems are created by using the terms optimistic and pessimistic to obtain managerial estimates of the relevant times?

12–3 What problems are created if an activity's completion is delayed?

12–4 Would you suspect that PERT techniques might be useful to builders of motels?

12–5 Can you think of some projects for which PERT would not be a desirable technique?

12–6 A project is diagramed below. The numbers within the circles are the expected completion time in days.

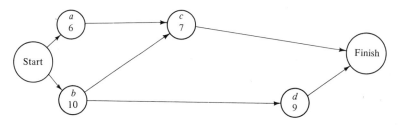

Required:
a. Compute the earliest expected starting time and the earliest expected finishing time for each activity.
b. If the project must be done within twenty-one days, what is the total slack or "safety factor"?
c. What is the critical path?
d. What is the total slack in activity d? In activity c?
e. What is the free slack in activity b? In activity a?

12–7 Assume the following estimates apply to the project described in problem 12–6.

Activity	Optimistic	Pessimistic
a	2	10
b	6	12
c	5	9
d	7	11

Required:
a. Compute an estimate of the variance of the times of each activity.
b. Compute an estimate of the variance of the times of the activities on the critical path assuming that the activities on the path are independent.
c. Assuming the probability distribution of times of the critical path is normally distributed, what is your estimate of the probability of exceeding the twenty-one days that are allowed? Are there reasons to suspect that this estimate is biased? If so, in which direction is the bias?
d. What is the probability that paths a, b, and c will exceed twenty-one days?

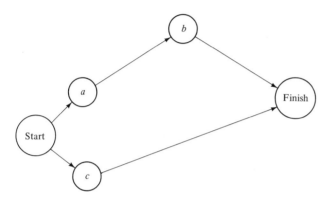

12–8 Consider the following network.
Assume that the probability that path a-b-finish will exceed the allowable time is 0.6 and there is a 0.5 probability of path c-finish exceeding the allowable time. The two paths are independent.

Required: What is the probability that the task will be done on time?

12–9 Assume that the probabilities of completing on time three different (independent) paths are 0.8, 0.9, and 0.6. What is the probability of completing the job on time?

12–10 Assume that the probability of completing three different (independent) paths on time is 0.7 each. What is the probability of completing the job on time?

12–11 Assume that the probability of not completing three different (independent) paths on time is 0.3 for each path. What is the probability of not completing the job on time?

12–12 A firm wants to be 97.5 per cent certain of completing a job within a year. It can organize independent task forces each with profitability 0.6 of success. How many task forces should be organized?

12–13 (This problem is quite a bit longer and more difficult than the others given for this chapter.)

Given the series of tasks and times for the tasks in the following table, answer the questions relating to this specific network.

Suppose you were given the network data in the accompanying table. It is not the normal manner in which you receive data, but can you develop a network diagram from this data similar to those in the chapter? For this purpose the events represent the completion of one or more tasks and the start of new ones. Thus, for example, event 5 occurs when the tasks requiring the expected times of 5.2 and 1.2 hours are completed and the task requiring an expected time of 17.0 hours is begun. Assume work on the project is continuous.

Event (E)	Immediate Predecessor Event(s) (IPE)	Times from IPE to E (Hours)			
		Optimistic Time	Most Likely Time	Pessimistic Time	Expected Time
15	14	2	3	4	3.0
	13	2	5	10	5.3
	12	1	2	4	2.2
	11	3	3	5	3.3
14	10	3	7	16	7.8
	9	4	6	10	6.3
	2	12	15	21	15.5
13	8	12	15	24	16.0
12	7	5	10	16	10.2
11	10	0	0	0	0
	6	2	2	5	2.5
10	5	12	16	26	17.0
9	4	1	1	2	1.2
8	3	3	4	6	4.2
7	3	2	4	5	3.8
6	3	10	14	20	14.3
5	3	3	5	8	5.2
	2	1	1	2	1.2
4	2	2	3	5	3.2
3	1	9	14	22	14.5
2	1	5	8	14	8.5
1 Start	None	0	0	0	0

Required:

a. Set up graphically an appropriate network diagram and indicate the critical path.

b. Explain how the *expected* time values were determined.

c. What are the earliest *expected* arrival times for events 5, 11, and 14?

d. What is the expected completion time for the entire project?

e. What is the most optimistic completion time for the entire project?

f. Suppose the expected time required for the only job necessary to go from event 5 to event 10 were decreased to five hours.

  1. What effect would this have upon the earliest possible expected completion time?

  2. What effect would it have upon the earliest expected time of arrival at event 11?

g. If the expected time to go from event 5 to event 10 were cut by 7.5 hours what would happen to the critical path?

h. How long can the single task between event 3 and event 6 be delayed without delaying the earliest expected time of arrival at event 11?

i. If the entire project must be completed in two days (48 hours) how much total slack exists in the network?

j. Explain how you would find the probability that the entire job will be completed by

  1. The most optimistic completion date?

  2. The expected completion date determined by the critical path?

  3. The target date of two days?

12–14 Consider the following network problem (reflecting perhaps a machine setup) and the associated costs of reducing the most likely time. Assume that

Activity	Immediate Predecessor Event(s)	Optimistic Time (days)	Pessimistic Time (days)	Most Likely Time (days)
A	—	2	5	2
B	—	2	5	4
C	A	3	5	4
D	B	6	12	8
E	C	5	10	7
F	D	3	5	4
G	E	4	10	6
H	A, F	1	2	1
I	G	3	6	5
J	H	4	9	7
K	I, J	2	5	3

Total Cost of Reduction by Days (dollars)

Activity	A	B	C	D	E	F	G	H	I	J	K
1 day	10	14	15	20	20	*	20	20	30	30	30
2 days	30	30	40	40	35	*	35	60	65	65	100

* Cannot be reduced.

the given cost causes the entire distribution to shift to the left by the same amount.[11]

Required:

a. Determine the critical path and the expected completion time.

b. Determine the total slack if the project must be completed in twenty-five days.

c. Estimate the probability that the job will be done in time.

d. What action should the company take to increase the probability of completion to 0.5?

e. If a probability of completion in time of say, 97 per cent were desired, what estimate of the total days to be reduced from the expected time would you make? Would your answer be biased? If so, why?

12–15 Assume that the payoff functions for time early and time late in finishing a particular project are given by $100(24 - t)$ for early finish: $t < 24$, and $200(t - 24)$ for late finish: $t \geq 24$ where t is in days. The early finish function indicates a $100 bonus paid on the contract for each day that the project is finished before the target date twenty-four days away. The penalty function indicates a $200 penalty for each day the project is late. Assume, given present cost and time estimates on the various activities, that the finish date, t, has the following probability distribution

$$f_T(t) = \begin{cases} \dfrac{1}{20}: & 16 \leq t \leq 36 \\ 0: & \text{otherwise.} \end{cases}$$

Required: Compute the expected net bonus to be obtained. Are there any alternatives to accepting this result?

12–16 Suppose that in a given network system the engineering subsystem has the following reported facts for a job that is done uniformly over time in terms of cost incurrence as well as actual activity: cost incurred to date, 6.6 million; cost of work completed (budget), 3.7 million; original budget for engineering, 6.0 million. The engineering department now estimates it will cost a total (including past costs) of $8.1 million to complete its subsystem. The project was expected to take twenty-four weeks. It is now the twenty-second week. Engineering now predicts completion in ten more weeks.

Required:

a. What is the overrun percentage?

b. What is the cost of the work left to be done?

c. How much more does the engineering department propose to spend to complete the task?

d. What is the predicted final overrun?

---

[11] Adapted from Dopuch and Birnberg, *Cost Accounting*, New York, Harcourt, Brace and World, 1969.

e. How far behind in weeks is the process now?

f. If engineering continued at its same rate, how many more weeks would you estimate until completion?

g. Comment on how realistic the engineering departments new predictions are?

SUPPLEMENTARY READING

BERMAN, E. B., "Resource Allocation in a PERT Network Under Continuous Activity Time-Cost Functions," *Management Science*, July 1964, pp. 734–745.

CROWSTON, W., and G. THOMPSON, "Decision CPM: A Method of Simultaneous Planning, Scheduling and Control of Projects," *Operations Research*, May–June 1967, pp. 407–426.

DECOSTER, D. T., "The Budget Director and PERT," *Budgeting*, March 1964, pp. 13–17.

DECOSTER, D. T., "PERT/COST—The Challenge," *Management Services*, May–June 1969, pp. 13–18.

LEVY, F. K., G. L. THOMPSON, and J. D. WIEST, "The ABC's of the Critical Path Method," *The Harvard Business Review*, September–October 1963, pp. 98–108.

MACCRIMMON, K. R., and C. A. RYAVEC, "Analytical Study of the P.E.R.T. Assumptions," *Operations Research*, January 1964, pp. 16–37.

PAIGE, H. W., "How PERT/COST Helps the Manager," *The Harvard Business Review*, November–December 1963, pp. 87–95.

SAITOW, A. R., "CSPC: Reporting Project Progress to the Top," *The Harvard Business Review*, January–February 1969, pp. 88–97.

VAZSONYI, A., "Automated Information Systems in Planning and Control," *Management Science*, February 1965, pp. 2–41.

Chapter 13

An Introduction to Capital Budgeting

Capital budgeting is the process of deciding whether or not to commit resources to projects whose costs and benefits will be spread over several time periods. The problem is to relate the benefits to the costs in some reasonable manner which will be consistent with an objective of maximizing the stockholders' well being.

There are many possible methods of relating a stream of future earnings to the cost of obtaining those earnings. Among these, four methods: cash payback, return on investment, rate of return, and present value, are defined and evaluated in this chapter. The focus of attention is on taking the time value of money into consideration. The concept of risk is discussed in Chapter 16.

13.1 Cash Payback

The cash payback of an investment is the period of time required to recover the initial investment. Thus, if an investment of $10,000 yields $5,000 in net cash proceeds in each of the first two years of use, it would have a cash payback of two years. The available investments may then be accepted or rejected according to the length of their payback periods. An investment with a payback of two years might then be considered desirable while an investment with a payback of three years is rejected. Some firms incorrectly accept or reject investments on the basis of duration of the payback period alone; in fact, for many years payback has been the most common method of capital budgeting in use.

13.2   Return on Investment

The return on investment is equal to the forecasted average income divided by the average investment. This is the same computation that is made in measuring performance, but instead of being computed for one year it is based on the entire life of the investment. Rather than the average investment (i.e., a figure based on the depreciated plant assets), some companies use the initial investment (the undepreciated plant assets). While the choice is not critical in performance evaluation if all comparisons use the same procedure, it may be important to investment decisions.. The average investment is used in this chapter since it is consistent with the performance measure that is normally used to evaluate the investment if it is undertaken.

13.3   Rate of Return or Yield

The rate of return is that rate of discount (interest) that equates the present value of the cash flows to zero. This rate is found by trial and error using different rates of interest. That rate of interest that equates the algebraic sum of the present value of cash outlays and the present value of cash proceeds to zero is the rate of return or the yield of the investment.

It is desirable to understand the implications of the term *rate of return of an investment*. If an investment requires an outlay of $173.55 and yields a net cash flow of $210 at the end of two years, then the rate of interest that equates the present value of $210 and an immediate outlay of $173.55 is the investment rate of return. Equivalently, the following equation can be solved for r:

$$210(1 + r)^{-2} - 173.55 = 0$$

$$(1 + r)^{-2} = 0.8264.$$

Using Table III at the end of this book, r is found to be 0.10. The rate of return is 0.10, since, using this rate, the algebraic sum of the present value of the cash outlays and the present value of the cash proceeds is zero.

Another interpretation of the rate of return is that it is the rate of growth of the investment. Thus the investment may be imagined to grow as follows:

Original investment	$173.55
0.10 return	17.36
Investment plus interest	$190.91
0.10 return	19.09
Final value of investment	$210.00

A third interpretation of rate of return is that it is the highest rate of interest that an investor could pay for borrowed funds to finance the investment being considered and be no worse off than if he did not undertake the investment. This interpretation assumes a conventional investment; that is, an immediate outlay followed by periods of cash flows into the firm. It also assumes that the funds generated by the investment are used to repay the debt plus interest.

If the investment results in several unequal cash proceeds, the analysis is the same, though the computations become more complex. Assume, for example, that an investment required an immediate outlay of $2,810.65 and has an expected life of two years. The forecasted net cash proceeds for the first year are $1,000 and for the second year, $2,000. What is the rate of return and what are the implications of the rate of return? The solution for the rate of return again requires a trial-and-error approach. (If an interest rate results in the present values being positive, a higher rate of discount is used.) After several tries the situation shown in Exhibit 13–1 is obtained. (Note the sum of the present values is zero.)

Exhibit 13–1   Rate of Return Calculations

Year	Proceeds (outlays)	Present Value of a Dollar Discounted at 4%	Present Value of Cash Proceeds
0	($2810.65)	$1.00000	($2,810.65)
1	1000.00	0.961538	961.54
2	2000.00	0.924556	1,849.11
			0

COMPUTATIONS

Original investment	$2,810.65
	× 0.04
Earned first year	$ 112.43
Original investment	+ 2,810.65
Investment available	$ 2,923.08
Cash proceeds withdrawn	− 1,000.00
Investment beginning of second year	$1,923.08
	× 0.04
Earned second year	$ 76.92
Investment beginning of second year	+ 1,923.08
Investment available	$2,000.00
Cash proceeds withdrawn	− 2,000.00
Investment remaining	$ 0.00

At a rate of discount of 4 per cent, the present value of the cash proceeds is equated to the cost of the asset, $2,810.65. Thus the rate of return is 4 per cent. But what does this mean? The asset that cost $2,810.65 earns 4 per cent the first year, and then $1,000 is withdrawn; the remaining investment again earns 4 per cent, and then $2,000 is withdrawn; at this time there will be zero investment left. The asset earned a 4 per cent return during its life.

The rate-of-return capital-budgeting procedure implicitly assumes the above events happen, and in effect assumes the loss in value of the asset for year 1 is $1,000 and for year 2 is $2,000.

Exhibit 13–2 is obtained from the computations illustrating what is meant by rate of return. Note that the total earnings are equal to the difference between the total cash proceeds ($3,000 and the cost of the asset, $2,810.65).

COMPUTATIONS

Exhibit 13–2   Proof of Rate-of-Return Computations

Year	Investment Beginning of Year	Earnings	Return on Investment
1	$2,810.65	$112.43	4%
2	1,923.08	76.92	4%
		$189.35	

The rate of return of an investment is frequently used to determine the desirability of an investment. Either the investments are ranked in order of desirability according to their rates of return (the ranking may be spurious), or all conventional independent investments with a return greater than some selected hurdle rate are accepted and all other investments are rejected.

There is a relation between the rate-of-return and payback approaches. This relationship is illustrated by transforming the mathematical equation for the present value of a level annuity. The present value of an annuity of A dollars for n periods at a rate r per period is

$$P = A\left[\frac{1-(1+r)^{-n}}{r}\right].$$
(13.1)

Dividing by P and multiplying both sides by r, equation (13.1) can be written as

$$r = \frac{A}{P} - \frac{A}{P}\left[\frac{1}{(1+r)^n}\right].$$
(13.2)

The first term on the right-hand side of equation (13.2) is the reciprocal of the payback period since P is the initial investment. The second term is the payback-period reciprocal multiplied by the present-value factor for *n* periods. The larger the effective rate and the life of the investment the closer the right-hand side approximates the reciprocal of the payback period. Note that the payback reciprocal is slightly larger than the rate of return for a project with a finite life. For a project with an unlimited life, the rate of return would be equal to the payback-period reciprocal. In practice, this payback reciprocal is a reasonable estimate of the rate of return when the project life is at least twice as long as the payback period and each year's benefits are the same.

13.4 Present Value

Under the present-value method, cash outlays and cash proceeds are both discounted back to the present period using an appropriate discount rate. If the present value of the cash flows is positive, the investment is considered eligible for further consideration. If the present value of the cash flows is negative, then the investment should not normally be undertaken. (A positive present value does not mean the project will be undertaken, however, since better alternatives may exist, or the risk of the investment may be too great.)

What is the significance of discounting cash flows back to the present? Assume that a firm with a cost of money of 10 per cent is considering an investment which promises to return $11,000 at the end of one year in exchange for an immediate cash outlay of $10,000. The present value of $11,000 discounted back one period at a 10 per cent rate of interest is $10,000. The present value of the outlays is also $10,000; thus, the net present value of the investment is zero. This means that the firm could be just as well off not borrowing from investors and not investing in the project. The cost of borrowing the $10,000 is $1,000, which is equal to the income the investment will earn ($11,000 less $10,000). On the other hand, the firm will be no worse off investing in the project. The investment yields a return equal to the required return and no more. In fact, the rate of return of the investment is 10 per cent, which is equal to the required return.

Now change the illustration by assuming an investment which promises to earn proceeds of $20,000 at the end of period 1 and costs $10,000. The present value of the proceeds is $18,182; the outlay is $10,000. The net present value of the investment is $8,182. This $8,182 is the amount that the firm could afford to pay in excess of the cost of the investment (while paying the cost of borrowing) and still be no worse off than if it had not made the investment. For example, assume it paid $18,182 for the investment and the cost of borrowing is 10 per cent of $18,182, or $1,818. Thus the total outlays would be $20,000 ($18,182 plus $1,818) an amount equal to the expected cash proceeds. The outlay of $18,182 today is equivalent to proceeds of $20,000 a year hence. The computations take into consideration interest of 10 per cent, either by discounting the $20,000 back to the present or by accumulating the $18,182 to the end of the year.

The net present value of the investment is the estimated profit (unrealized, thus not recognized for accounting purposes) at the time of purchase. It is also the amount the firm could pay in excess of the purchase price for the investment, but because of fortuitous circumstances does not have to pay.

13.5 Choosing the Best Method of Decision Making

The example described in Exhibit 13–3 is used to test the four methods that have been proposed. There are three investment proposals and the investment decisions suggested by the different procedures are compared. The relationships to other investments are ignored except as they are incorporated in the discount rate.

Exhibit 13–3   Cash Flows for Investments A, B, and C

Investment Proposed	Initial Outlay (period 0)	Cash Proceeds (period 1)	Cash Proceeds (period 2)
A	$10,000	$10,000	0
B	10,000	1,000	$11,000
C	10,000	5,762	5,762

The cash-payback method would identify investment A as being the most desirable, since it has a payback time of one period. The weakness of this position is indicated by the fact that investment A returns its original investment, but that is all. The cash-payback method fails as an all-purpose device for making investment decisions, since it does not take into consideration the life of the investment after the payback period. Another weakness, not illustrated by the above example, is that the payback method fails to take into consideration the timing of proceeds during the payback period. Thus, while the payback periods of investment B and C are approximately the same, the cash inflows for investment C are more desirable from a timing point of view than those of investment B.

The return on investment for A is zero; thus A is eliminated from consideration if the return-on-investment method is used. The return-on-investment computations for the other two investments are given in Exhibit 13–4.

The return-on-investment computation indicates that investment B is more desirable than investment C. But the return-on-investment procedure also fails to take into consideration the timing of the proceeds. A dollar of proceeds earned in period 2 is given the same weight as a dollar earned in period

1. This failure to take the timing of the proceeds into consideration is one reason the return-on-investment approach should not be used as a general method of making investment decisions.

Exhibit 13–4   Return on Investment Calculations for Investments B and C

Invest- ment	Outlays	Total Proceeds	Net Income	Average Income	Average Investment	Return on Investment
B	$10,000	$12,000	$2,000	$1,000	$5,000	20.0%
C	10,000	11,524	1,524	762	5,000	15.2%

When the rates of return of the two investments B and C are computed, both are found to be 10 per cent. The rate of return of investment A is zero. Before deciding that investments B and C are equally desirable, consider the present value of the two investments, using several interest rates (different assumed costs). At a 10 per cent rate of interest the present values of both investments are zero; thus the investments are equally desirable. This is the same result as was obtained using the rate-of-return procedure. With a discount rate of less than 10 per cent, investment B has a higher present value; but both investments have positive present values. At a rate of interest higher than 10 per cent, investment C has a higher present value than B, but both investments have negative present values. While the rate-of-return and the present-value methods may give different rankings to investments, they lead to the same accept or reject decisions.

If the rate of return of a normal investment is greater than the required return, the investment may be accepted; if the rate of return is less than the required return, then it may be rejected. The same accept or reject decisions are obtained when the required return is used as a rate of discount and the present values of the investments are computed as are obtained by using the rate of return of the investments.

Are the rankings obtained using the present-value or the rate-of-return method the "correct" rankings? Unfortunately, a ranking of investments frequently appears to be correct but is actually only a function of the method used and the assumptions made. Fortunately, for most investment decisions a firm does not have to rank investments, but only has to choose those investments which have a yield greater than the firm's cost of money. If the investments are mutually exclusive, it may be necessary to choose that investment which is the best of a group. This can be done since the failure to undertake a mutually exclusive investment does not invalidate the choice of the discount rate.[1]

---

[1] If an independent investment with a rate of return greater than the required return is rejected, the use of that required return to compute the present values is invalid.

13.5.1 Mutually Exclusive Investments

Mutually exclusive investments are investments which compete with each other; that is, of several investments being considered, only one can be undertaken because of their nature.

A firm may need a tanker to transport oil but may not yet have determined the size or number of tankers which is best. Tankers of all sizes and shapes are in this case mutually exclusive investments. Another illustration of mutually exclusive investments would be brick and wood as materials for building a plant. The initial costs and maintenance costs through the years would be different.

Assume that investments B and C are mutually exclusive investments and that both have 10 per cent rates of return and are otherwise equally desirable. Which is the more desirable, assuming a cost of money of 6 per cent? The present value of the cash flows of the two investments are given in Exhibit 13–5.

Exhibit 13–5   Comparison of Investments B and C

	Investment B				Investment C		
Period	Cash Flows	Present Value Factor	Present Value	Period	Cash Flows	Present Value Factor	Present Value
0	($10,000)	$1.0000	($10,000)	0	($10,000)	$1.000	($10,000)
1	1,000	0.9434	943	1	5,762	0.9434	5,436
2	11,000	0.8900	9,790	2	5,762	0.8900	5,128
			$ 733				$ 564

The present value of the cash flows for investment B is greater than the present value of the cash flows for investment C.

The rate-of-return method may not give correct rankings of mutually exclusive investments, since in a sense the method fails to consider the timing of the cash flows. Mutually exclusive investments with unequal lives provide an example. The rate-of-return method implicitly assumes that the proceeds for the investment with the shorter life can be reinvested at the same rate of interest as the rate of return when two investments are compared. The present-value method, on the other hand, assumes that these proceeds can be invested at the same rate of interest as the cost of money. The later assumption is usually more reasonable. In any case the expected situation should be considered explicitly.[2]

---

[2] Two assumptions that may be important in the present example are those of equal initial outlays and equal lives for investment B and C.

Considering only the incremental cash flows gives the benefit to be gained by the firm from selecting one investment over another. (See Exhibit 13–6.) For another example, assume two investments with the characteristics in Exhibit 13–7.

Exhibit 13–6   Incremental Cash Flows and Their Present Values: Investments B and C

Period	Cash Flows B	Cash Flows C	B – C	Present Value Factor	Present Value B – C
0	($10,000)	($10,000)	0	1.0000	0
1	1,000	5,762	($4,762)	0.9434	– $4,493
2	11,000	5,762	5,238	0.8900	4,662
					$ 169

Exhibit 13–7   Rate of Return for Investments X and Y

Investment	Initial Investment period 0	Cash Proceeds period 1	Rate of Return
X	$10,000	$12,000	20.0%
Y	30,000	35,000	16.7%

The rate-of-return criterion indicates that investment X is superior to investment Y. However, imagine that the difference between the cash flows of investments X and Y are the cash flows of an investment Z. Thus investment Z would have outlays of $20,000 in period 0 and proceeds of $23,000 in period 1, a rate of return of 15 per cent. Assuming a cost of money of 6 per cent, investment Z is desirable. The fact that the cash flows of investment Z are actually the difference between the cash flows of investments X and Y would indicate that investment Y is more desirable than X, since by investing an amount $20,000 greater than investment X, a return of 15 per cent may be earned. The rate-of-return method may be used here to evaluate the incremental benefits, but it is awkward to employ if there are many investment possibilities (an elimination tournament is required). Thus the present-value method is to be preferred.

An additional difficulty with using the rate-of-return method is that some investments may have more than one rate of return. This occurs if, after an outlay, there are periods of positive proceeds followed by periods of negative cash flows (for example, when there are removal costs at the end of the investment's life). This result can also occur with mutually exclusive investments. When an investment has more than one rate of return, it is easier to reach a decision using the present-value method than with the rate-of-return method.

13.5.2 Present-Value and Mutually Exclusive Investments

The present-value method gives the correct decision in judging mutually exclusive investments with unequal lives, but it may be necessary to assume what happens after the asset with the shorter life is discarded. Assume a simple example where there are two mutually exclusive investments C and D with the characteristics given in Exhibit 13–8.

Exhibit 13–8   Cash Flows for Investments C and D

Investment	Initial Investment Period 0	Cash Proceeds Period 1	Period 2	Period 3
C	($10,000)	$12,000		
D	(10,000)	5,000	$5,000	$5,000

Investments C and D may be different types of equipment, with investment C having a life of one year and investment D a life of three years. With a cost of money of 10 per cent, the present values of the cash flows of investments C and D are as given in Exhibit 13–9.

Exhibit 13–9   Present Value of Cash Flows for Investments C and D

Investment	Present Value of Cash Flows
C	$909
D	2,434

Investment D would seem to be the more desirable investment; however, this analysis is incomplete since it fails to take into consideration what will be done at the end of the first year if investment C were selected. The present-value method assumes reinvestment at 10 per cent. But suppose that after one year, equipment of type C (or similar equipment) will again be purchased. Where it is likely that investment C will be repeated at the beginning of periods 2 and 3, the cash flows in Exhibit 13–10 would occur for investment C.

The present value of the cash flows as now presented is $2,488 for investment C; thus C is more desirable than D. Where the mutually exclusive investments have unequal lives, the reinvestment, possibly in similar equipment, must be taken into consideration.

Sometimes it may be difficult to find a common comparison time for two or more mutually exclusive investments. In some situations the lowest common multiple of the lives of the investments results in a length of time longer than the life of the longest lived of the alternatives. For example, consider the relative merits of two types of equipment, one of which has a life of three years and the other of eight years. In a situation of this nature, the equivalent return per year, the returns for perpetuity, or the present value of the investment for twenty-four years could be computed. These three methods of computation all lead to the same decision. Alternately, an attempt to forecast investment alternatives may be feasible.

Exhibit 13–10   Cash Flows for Investment C Modified

	Initial Investment		Cash Flows	
Investment	Period 0	Period 1	Period 2	Period 3
C	($10,000)	($10,000)	($10,000)	
		12,000	12,000	$12,000

Example

Assume that two pieces of equipment have the characteristics given in Exhibit 13–11 and that reinvestment in similar equipment may be assumed. An interest rate of 10 per cent is used.

Exhibit 13–11   Cash Flows for Investments E and F

			Net
	Expected Life	Initial	Cash Proceeds
Investment	(years)	Cost	per Year
E	3	$10,000	5,000
F	8	30,000	6,500

This problem can be solved by taking the lowest common multiple of eight and three, twenty-four years, and computing the expected value assuming reinvestment. An alternative is to compute the present value of each alternative and then find an equivalent yearly annuity.[3] The latter method is illustrated in Exhibit 13–12.

The task is now to find the level annuity, R, which at 10 per cent equals $2,435 for three years and $4,677 for eight years. In symbols: for investment E, $R(2.4869) = \$2,435$ and $R \doteq \$976$ per year; and for investment F, $R(5.3349) = \$4,677$ and $R \doteq \$877$ per year.

---

[3] Since cash inflows are often difficult to associate with a given investment, this approach is often used with cost data to find the equivalent cost per year of doing a given task. The investment with the smaller equivalent cost is preferred.

Exhibit 13–12   Present Value of Cash Flows for Investments E and F

Invest-ment	Expected Life (years)	Initial Cost	Net Cash Proceeds Per Year	Present-Value Factor	Present Value of Proceeds	Net Present Value
E	3	($10,000)	$5,000	2.4869	$12,435	$2,435
F	8	(30,000)	6,500	5.3349	34,677	4,677

To find the value for perpetuity, multiply the equivalent value per year by the present value of a perpetuity. The general formula for the present value of a perpetuity of $1 a period is

$$\text{Present value of a perpetuity} = \frac{1}{r}$$

where r is the appropriate rate of interest.

Since r is equal to 0.10, the factor in this example is 10. The present value of using E forever is 10(976), or $9,760. The present value of using F is $8,770. Since the equivalent yearly annuity of both alternatives is being multiplied by a constant factor of 10, the relative merits of the alternatives are not changed. E remains more desirable than F. Many factors have been omitted, however, such as flexibility and the likelihood of future returns. More important is the assumption that the equipment will be replaced in kind.

13.5.3   Which Method?

The cash-payback method can be rejected because it does not take the entire life of the investment into consideration. The return-on-investment method fails to consider the timing of the proceeds, and thus has severe limitations. The rate-of-return method gives acceptable reject or accept decisions for conventional independent investments except in the special situation where there are several rates of return for an investment. However, the rate-of-return procedure may incorrectly rank mutually exclusive investments for two reasons. In the comparison of two mutually exclusive investments it implicitly assumes reinvestment of proceeds at the same rate of return, and it fails to take into consideration the size of the investment being considered. For these reasons the present-value method should be used as the prime method for making investment decisions.

13.6   Cash Flows for Investment Decisions

One of the important details of capital budgeting that is frequently neglected in discussions of the subject is the computation of the cash flows used in the analysis. The generally used term *cash flows* is not adequately defined. This is a serious omission since the cash flows are the basis of the computations. There are several reasonable definitions for the term *cash flow*. The term is used in this book to describe a procedure that measures the change in cash in each period. Alternately, the capital-budgeting analysis could be based on the change in working capital or the change in funds: The two methods may be equated to each other if receivables and payables of the future are recorded today at their present value. Properly used, there is no material difference between the two procedures.

13.6.1 Cash Flow

The cash-flow procedure assumes that the moment of cash disbursement or cash receipt is the moment at which the change in financial position associated with the investment should be measured. It may be argued that only when the cash is disbursed has the firm suffered any disutility, since only then are real resources, which could be engaged in other earning activities, restricted to this project. For example, the cash may be invested in government securities and interest may thus be earned; but the disbursement of cash either requires that the securities be sold, thus the interest otherwise earned is lost, or that new interest-bearing debt be issued, in which case the costs connected with having debt outstanding are incurred. In like manner, it is argued

Exhibit 13–13   Computation of Forecasted Cash Flow for 1980 for Investment G

Sales (as recorded by accountant) (1)		$100,000
Less: Manufacturing costs of goods sold (2)	$40,000	
Expenses of selling and administration (3)	20,000	60,000
Net revenue after expenses		$40,000
Less: Investment outlays (4)	. . .	
Decrease in revenues from other products (4)	. . .	
Opportunity costs of factors of production (4)	$5,000	
Income tax caused by investment	10,000	$15,000
Less: Changes in working capital and noncash expenses (5)		
Decrease in current liabilities (change the sign for an increase)	$4,000	
Increase in current assets (including noncash expenses)	8,000	12,000
Miscellaneous uses of cash		27,000
After-tax cash flow		$13,000

that until the sales result in cash, which the firm can then put to other uses, there is no real benefit from the transaction. Thus the making of the legal sale and the creation of an account receivable is not important for purposes of analyzing the investment decision; what is important is the receipt or disbursement of cash.

For each period in the life of the investment it is necessary to compute the change in cash resulting from the investment being considered. Exhibit 13–13 indicates how this might be accomplished for one such period.

Explanation of entries:

1. Sales on the accrual basis were $100,000.
2. This is the expense figure taken from the income statement. Usually it is not equal to the out-of-pocket cost of production because of changes in the level of inventories and the inclusion of costs not using cash. These items are picked up as adjustments. (See item 5.)
3. Selling and administration expenses for which a current liability was incurred (or cash disbursed) and which are due to investment G.
4. Investment-type outlays, decreases in revenues from other products (increases due to product complementarily would be positive), opportunity costs (including the use of executive time), associated with this venture are deducted as cash outlays, even though there may not be a cash disbursement since they represent inflows lost elsewhere. The increase in income taxes associated with the investment is calculated after the deduction for any depreciation related to the investment under consideration.
5. The adjustment for the changes in working capital is necessary in order to determine the amount of cash needed to finance these items. The $4,000 is the result of a decrease in current liabilities (using cash). The $8,000 is an increase in current assets (for example, a $33,000 increase in accounts receivable and a $10,000 decrease in inventories) less the amount of fixed costs ($15,000) converted into inventory and cost of goods sold for which no cash disbursement is made, such as depreciation.[4] Note that $33,000 − $10,000 − $15,000 = $8,000.

An increase in current liabilities would be subtracted from the deductions; that is, it would be added to the cash-flow stream. There would be some

---

[4] For example, assume fixed costs in year n of $15,000, for which the cash disbursement was made some years ago, variable costs of $1 per unit, production of 15,000 units, sales of 17,000, and an inventory of 6,000 units at $3 per unit at the start of the year. Under these conditions, assuming all fixed costs are absorbed to product, the cost of sales would be (using FIFO), $3(6,000) + $2(11,000) = $40,000. The inventory *increase* would be $2(4,000) − $3(6,000) = − $10,000. The $40,000 is deducted as cost of sales and the $10,000 is added as the change in inventory. The $15,000 of fixed cost are added as a non-cash expense.

"expenses" that would not actually utilize cash since they would be financed out of current liabilities. Thus the increase in current liabilities is subtracted.

A side computation would be necessary to compute the income taxes of the period associated with this investment. There may be differences between the cash-flow computations and the computations for tax purposes. The person making these computations should be familiar with the tax code or have access to expert tax advice.

13.6.2 Fund Flow versus Cash Flow

The concept of cash flow is relatively simple. The objective in each time period is to compute the change in the cash account caused by investing or not investing in the asset under consideration. This cash-account explanation is easy to understand, and with practice not difficult to apply, though the opportunity-cost concept with the possibility of no explicit cash outlay weakens the cash-account analogy.

The cash-flow procedure seems, however, to ignore the beneficial effects of other changes which may be of significance. For example, assume that in the first operating period it is expected that sales will be $10,000 (all on account) to be collected at the end of period 2, and that the total expenses (including income taxes) are $7,000, all resulting in immediate cash disbursements. There are no other changes expected in the first time period except an increase in depreciation of $1,000 caused by the investment. The total changes are

Increase in accounts receivable	$10,000
Decrease in cash	7,000
Increase in depreciation	1,000
Increase in retained earnings	2,000

The cash-flow procedure would indicate a negative cash flow of $7,000. The computations would be

Sales	$10,000
Less: Out-of-pocket expenses	7,000
Net revenue after expenses	$3,000
Less: Increase in current assets (exclusive of cash)	10,000
After-tax cash flow	($ 7,000)

The negative cash flow of $7,000 correctly measures the change of the cash account. But the measure seems to fail to take into consideration other events that have occurred, such as the increase of $10,000 in accounts receivable and the increase of $2,000 in retained earnings. However, in the next period the $10,000 will be collected, and the cash inflows of that period will be increased by $10,000. But since there is a time delay before collection, the sales of the first period should be recorded at less than $10,000; that is, at the present value of $10,000.

Instead of computing the cash flow, the fund flow could be computed, where fund flow is defined as the change in working capital caused by the investment being considered.

In the present example the fund flow of the first year would be

Sales	$10,000
Less: Out-of-pocket expenses	7,000
Increase in funds	$ 3,000

The fund flow is a positive $3,000, which is the same as the sum of the cash flows of the two periods. The two procedures yield different figures if the time value of money is included in recording the events; that is, if the cash flow of $10,000 in the second time period is discounted back two periods. However, the differences can be reconciled by computing the fund flow on the basis of the present value of the sales of $10,000. This is done in Exhibits 13–14 and 13–15.

For example, at the end of year 1 and assuming a time value of money of 0.1, the present value of the $10,000 to be collected one year hence is $9,091.

Exhibit 13–14   Investment Evaluation: Cash Flow

Period	Cash Flow	Present-Value Factor	Present Value
0	$0	1.0000	$0
1	− 7,000	0.9091	− 6,364
2	10,000	0.8264	8,264
		Net present value	$1,900

Exhibit 13–15   Investment Evaluation: Fund Flow

Period	Fund Flows	Present-Value Factor	Present Value
0	$0	1.0000	$ 0
1	9,091 − 7,000 = 2,091	0.9091	1,900
2	0	0.8264	0
		Net present value	$1,900

The net present value is $1,900 by either technique. Despite the fact that the cash-flow and fund-flow approaches can be reconciled, the former is used almost exclusively for investments since it is easier to apply.

13.6.3 Absolute and Marginal Cash Flows

A complication arises in the computation of cash flows when a new process is being considered to replace the present process. Should the absolute revenues be used (the revenues which would be earned if there were no present process) or the marginal revenues (the incremental revenues which would be earned in excess of what could be earned using the present process)? One possibility is to compute the present value of each alternative method (including abandonment of the project), and choose the method with the highest present value. This bypasses the question of whether the absolute or incremental revenues are appropriate.

Another possible procedure is to determine if the present method would still be undertaken if there were no possibility of improved methods. If the project should be abandoned, then the relative proceeds could not be used. For example, train transportation may be more efficient than truck transportation, but it may be that a truck cannot pay its way; thus a comparison of train with truck is invalid in determining whether a train is economically feasible. If the present method is economically sound, assuming no change in method, then the old method can be compared with the new method and the net savings computed. If the present value of the savings is positive compared with the present value of the outlays, then the new method should be adopted.

13.6.4 Cash Flows and Taxes

The cash flows should be on an after income tax basis. This means that the taxable income of each period must be determined, and that the amount of income tax arising because of the investment should be computed and included as a decrease of the cash proceeds or, possibly, as an increase in liabilities.

Some interesting things occur when both the time value of money and taxes are both included in the analysis. For example, it may be more desirable for a company to allow an account to become a bad debt and claim it as a tax deduction than to try to collect it in the future. Suppose it would cost $2 to collect a $5 account two years hence. With a cost of money of 10 per cent, the present value of the account is ($5 − 2)(0.8264) = $2.48. The present value of the tax deduction, in the presence of taxable income and with a tax rate of 52 per cent, is $0.52 per dollar of deduction or $0.52(5) = $2.60.

An important complication in computing income taxes arising from the opportunity to use accelerated depreciation to compute taxable income allowed under the Internal Revenue Code. With new depreciable property the company will probably choose either the twice-straight-line-declining-balance method, or the sum-of-the-years' digits method. It is difficult to generalize as to which procedure will be better, because the answer is a function of the amount of the salvage, the life of the investment, and the firm's cost of money. Another complication is the fact that the firm has an option to switch from the twice-straight-line to the straight-line method of depreciation at any time. Since the twice-straight-line procedure generally reaches a point where a switch-over is desirable, this privilege should be taken into consideration. The theoretically sound answer to the question of which depreciation method is more desirable to a firm must be solved by computing the present value of the tax deduction that results from following the allowed procedures. The procedure resulting in the highest present value is more desirable.[5]

The amount of depreciation allowable for tax purposes is the relevant figure, not the amount of depreciation to be taken for book purposes. The latter amount does not directly affect the investment decision. However, the cash flows are needed, and since the income tax affects the cash flows and is in turn affected by the amount of depreciation allowable for tax purposes, that amount is of interest.

13.6.5 Some Problems in Cash Flow Analysis

Some of the difficulties in the use of the present value method come from the problem of predicting the relevant cash flows. This problem stems in part from interrelationships which often exist between existing or proposed projects because of the use they make of limited resources. The problem also reflects the uncertainty inherent to both the external factors, such as demand, and internal factors, such as the project-life, that attend any investment. In addition, the classification of costs and knowledge of cost behavior available to the accountant is central to good predictions.

Sophisticated forecasting methods are of help but the essence of the problem remains. The forecasting problem is one reason that the payback method remains in wide use.

A desirable feature of many capital investment projects is the opportunity for the manager to adjust the commitment of resources to a project as information concerning its success is received. This might be thought of as the manager's reaction to the resolution of a project's uncertainty over time. A crude measure of the importance of this uncertainty resolution is the size of the investment and a measure of the rate at which the project's uncertainty is expected to be resolved is supplied by the payback period. This use coupled with the manager's desire for early information confirming the wiseness of

[5] Davidson and Drake found that the sum-of-the-years' digits method maximized the present value of future tax reductions, other things equal, for longer-lived asset lives. S. Davidson and D. F. Drake, "The 'Best' Tax Depreciation Method—1964," *Journal of Business*, July 1964, pp. 258–260.

his decision and the asymmetric payoff function typically applied by organizations in evaluating his success, are strong reasons for the continued use of the payback method in practice. It should be noted, however, that payback should only be used as one of several constraints in accepting a project rather than as the sole criterion.

13.6.6 Cost of Money

Determining the cost of money for a firm is difficult, and this section is no more than a brief survey of the problem. The cost of money is the rate of discount to be applied to future cash flows. This carries with it an implicit assumption that funds may be borrowed or lent at this same rate.

The term *borrowed* implies the obtaining of funds from outside markets. This money may be obtained by the issuance of debt securities or capital stock.

The cost of debt should include not only the explicit interest costs of the debt but also the implicit costs arising from having additional debts outstanding. The implicit costs include the cost of restrictions placed on management and the cost resulting from the increased possibility of bankruptcy, with the result that additional stock equity capital is more expensive. If common stock is used, the cost of new stock equity capital may actually be less than the return demanded by the present stockholders, since the issuance of more common stock may result in decreased costs of raising more debt capital as the capital structure is strengthened.

The cost of money to an average corporation is not a figure that may be determined with certainty. On the other hand, upper and lower limits to this cost can usually be established. For example, the cost of money is greater than the default-free interest rate paid by governmental bodies and less than the return expected by an investor in the common stock of a heavily levered firm in a very risky industry.

It can be argued that the rate of interest used in the compound interest formula to discount for time should not be used to adjust for risk as well as for taking the time value of money into account. If this argument is accepted then the discount rate used for computing the present value of an investment should be closer to the default-free interest rate than to that required by the common stockholders.

While it may properly be argued that the default free rate is appropriate to compute present values, for purposes of this book and considering the desire to find a workable approach to decision making, the use of the firm's borrowing rate to take the time value of money into consideration is reasonable. A more complete prescription is beyond the scope of this book.[6]

---

[6] For a more complete discussion see H. Bierman, Jr., and S. Smidt, *The Capital Budgeting Decision*, New York: Macmillan, 1971, particularly Chapters 8, 9, 17, and 18.

Chapter 16 suggests that if the default-free time value of money is used in the initial evaluation of outcomes from various decisions, another step is necessary to adjust for the riskiness of the situation.

13.6.7 The Present-Value Index

The present-value index is a variant of the present-value approach. Its appeal lies in the fact that seemingly it can be used to rank investments. Unfortunately, the ranking is frequently not useful or correct.

The index is computed by dividing the present value of the cash proceeds exclusive of the initial investment) by the investment.

Example

The X Company has a cost of money of 10 per cent. Assume an investment has the following cash flows:

Period 0	Period 1	Period 2
($1,500)	$1,000	$1,000

The present value of the $1,000-a-period, two-period, cash proceeds is $1,736. The present-value index is 1.16.

$$\text{Present value index} = \frac{1,736}{1,500} = 1.16.$$

One rule to use with an independent investment is: If the index is larger than one, accept the investment. This rule is sound. However, if the index is greater than one, the net present value is also positive, and the computation of the present-value index is unnecessary.

A second rule is: Rank mutually exclusive investments by their indices, and choose the investment with the highest ranking. This rule may lead to correct decisions; but it may just as easily lead to incorrect decisions because of either the scale of the investment or the classification of cash flows.

Example (The Scale Problem).

Assume two mutually exclusive investments with the cash flows given in Exhibit 13–16 and a cost of money of 0.1. Which is the more desirable?

Exhibit 13–16 Cash Flows for Investments J and K and the Present-Value Index

Investment	0	1	2	Present-Value index
J	($1,500)	$1,000	$1,000	1.16
K	(3,100)	2,000	2,000	1.12

The index indicates that J is preferred to K. However, a computation of present values shows that K is better (a net present value of $372 for K compared to $236 for J). The present-value index is a ratio of benefits to outlay and fails to consider the scale of the investment in the same manner that the other ratio measures, such as return on investment and rate of return, fail to do. This point can be seen more clearly by looking at the incremental investment consequent on moving from J to K. Label this investment K − J.

Investment	0	1	2	Present-Value index
K − J	($1,600)	$1,000	$1,000	1.08

The present value of the incremental investment is positive (thus the index is greater than one) and the incremental investment is desirable. The problem of scale can be solved by comparing pairs of investment, but this is unnecessary since the problem is more easily resolved by using present values. Also, the problem of the classification of cash flows still exists.

Example (Classification of Cash Flows)
The second difficulty with the present-value index is that it requires a distinction between deductions from cash proceeds and investment-type outlays. Assume the two mutually exclusive investments given in Exhibit 13–17.

Exhibit 13–17   Cash Flows and Present-Value Index for Investments L and M

Investment	Cash Flows 0	1	2	Present-Value Index
L	($1,500)	$1,000	$1,000	$\frac{1,736}{1,500} = 1.16$
M	(1,500)	(1,000) 2,000	(1,000) 2,000	$\frac{3,472}{3,236} = 1.07$

The present-value index ranks L over M, but inspection of the cash flows of the investments show that the difference is a result of classifying the two $1,000 outlays of M as investments rather than as deductions from cash proceeds. Any procedure depending on arbitrary classifications is resting on an unreliable foundation and for this type of decision, the problem can be avoided.

There is a misconception that the present-value index ranks independent investments. This ranking is not reliable. In addition to the two difficulties described above, if the company does not intend to accept all independent investments with a positive present value (or an index greater than one), then the discount rate is not appropriate and the index ranking is not reliable since the present values used in the index are not computed using the opportunity cost of money. It is not claimed here that the present-value method may be used to rank independent investments. It is claimed only that the present-value method leads to correct decisions involving choices between mutually exclusive investments and gives correct accept or reject decisions when it is applied to independent investments.

13.6.8 Nonconstant Cash Flows

The present value of an investment can be computed by projecting the cash flows of each period. Instead of following this detailed procedure a firm may wish to know the present value of the cash flows with different assumptions of rates of growth or decay applied to the projection of the initial period. The formulas for computing these present values are relatively easy to apply. Formula (13.3) gives the present value of the positive cash flows assuming a continuous rate of growth g. [See Appendix 13A for the derivation of equation (13.3).] To find the net present value of the investment, the initial outlay must be subtracted. All the formulas assume a zero tax rate, or, alternately that the cash flows are on an after tax basis. The assumptions are as follows:

1. Constant rate of growth through time;
2. Cash flows continue forever;
3. In growth situations r exceeds g; otherwise, the present value is infinitely large.

These assumptions give:

$$\text{Present value} = \frac{A}{r - g}, \qquad\qquad (13.3)$$

where A equals the cash flow of the first period, g equals the rate of growth (if flows are declining, the rate of growth is negative), and r equals the rate of discount (continuously compounded).

Example
For increasing cash flows assume that A equals $100, g equals 0.06, and r equals 0.10. (In this situation r is assumed to exceed g):

$$\text{Present value} = \frac{\$100}{0.10 - 0.06} = \frac{100}{0.04} = \$2,500.$$

Example

For decreasing cash flows assume that A equals $100, g equals -0.15, and r equals 0.10:

$$\text{Present value} = \frac{\$100}{0.10 - (-0.15)} = \frac{100}{0.25} = \$400.$$

If g equals 0 (i.e., constant cash flows), then,

$$\text{Present value} = \frac{\$100}{0.10} = \$1,000.$$

A table of values per dollar of initial cash flow can be developed. First, formula (13.3) is revised to read:

$$\text{Present value} = \frac{A}{X} \qquad (13.4)$$

where X is equal to $r - g$ (g is negative if the cash flows are declining). A table of values of $1 divided by X for different values of X can now be developed.

Values of X	Values of $\$1/X$
1.00	1.00
0.50	2.00
0.25	4.00
0.20	5.00
0.10	10.00
0.05	20.00
0.04	25.00
0.03	33.33
0.02	50.00
0.01	100.00

Instead of assuming that the growth in flows continues for an infinite time period, assume that the growth continues only for the life of the investment, say s periods, and there is no salvage value. Formula (13.3) becomes (see Appendix 13A):[7]

$$\text{Present value} = A\left(\frac{e^{(g-r)s} - 1}{g - r}\right) \qquad (13.5)$$

---

[7] The values of e^{-x} may be obtained from Table V.

Example

Assume that A equals \$100, g equals 0.06, r equals 0.10, and s equals 20 years:

$$\text{Present value} = 100\left[\frac{e^{(0.06-0.10)20} - 1}{+0.06 - 0.10}\right]$$

$$= 100\left[\frac{e^{-0.8} - 1}{-0.04}\right]$$

$$= 100\left[\frac{0.449 - 1}{-0.04}\right]$$

$$= 100\left[\frac{-0.551}{-0.04}\right] = \$1,378$$

Previously, when it was assumed that the growth continued for an infinite time period, a present value of \$2,500 was obtained. Thus the assumption of growth for a finite time period, even if it is of a lengthy duration, gives significantly different results from the simpler, but more inexact, assumption of infinite duration. In a situation where there is a decay rate instead of a growth rate, the assumption of an infinite life does little harm since the value of the cash flows is decreasing rapidly. Continued growth and positive salvage values can be added to the analysis.

13.7 The Review Process for Capital-Budgeting Decisions

After the capital-budgeting decision has been made, two control problems remain:

1. Controlling the amount of funds spent purchasing or constructing the investment.
2. Reappraisal of the investment decision once the investment starts operating.

13.7.1 Controlling Investment Expenditures

Capital expenditures are difficult to control since each investment project is usually unique, and neither standards nor past experience can be used in establishing the probable expenditure of funds. When the actual costs differ from the amount originally estimated, the question remains whether the difference is caused by a bad original estimate, by changes in the prices of labor and material, or by inefficiency. The action taken by top management to prevent recurrence of the variance depends on the cause of the variance. Random uncontrollable events can also cause a difference from the estimate, further complicating the analysis. The reasons the actual expenditures exceed the budgeted expenditures are related to all the above items, and it will frequently be impossible to isolate the causes with reasonable accuracy.

For capital investments, actual costs should be compared with budgeted costs. The estimated times related to preparing the investment for operation should also be controlled.

During installation or construction, reports of the percentage completion, the over or under cost expenditure relative to the budgeted costs for the stage of completion, the estimated costs to complete, the time taken relative to the time budgeted for the stage of completion, and the estimated time to complete can enable management to take corrective or cost-saving action (possibly by changing the construction schedule). (The reader is referred to Section 12.4 where such techniques are more fully developed.) Any report should include the probable completion date. A delay in completion of an investment may be costly since interest payments have to be made even if the operations have not yet begun. Thus there are strong incentives to meet the planned date of completion. An expected delay in completion should be explained and differences between actual and budgeted costs may require investigation whether favorable or unfavorable. The ideas developed in Chapters 1 and 2 are relevant.

If the actual costs are overrunning the budgeted costs significantly (say by 20 per cent), it may be necessary for the person in charge of the project to request additional funds. The decision to invest additional funds in the project again is a capital-budgeting decision, and the request should be treated like any other request. The funds already expanded are "sunk" costs, and thus are not relevant to the decision concerning whether or not to invest further funds in the project.

Control of capital expenditures is an extremely inexact procedure since it is often difficult to establish bench marks of performance. However, an estimate of cost is made and defended by the sponsor and the director of a project. This estimate is, at least in part, the basis of the decision to invest; it should be made with care and only after detailed investigation. It is reasonable to use this cost as the bench mark. Large variances should be explained, not shrugged off by saying, "The estimate must have been off." The reason the estimate was off should be reviewed. Furthermore, comparisons of actual and budgeted costs are useful in signaling the necessity for management action.

At a minimum, review of purchase or construction costs gives an incentive for project sponsors to make careful estimates, and for those in charge of construction to have an incentive to control costs and completion times of both the over-all job and the subactivities.

13.7.2 Review of Operating Results

The sponsor of a capital-budget request makes an estimate of revenues and expenses of the future in order to justify the proposed expenditure. If the rate-of-return or the present-value approach is used, a key item forecasted is the net cash proceeds. After the investment has been placed in operation, the actual results should be compared to the estimate information (which formed a basis of the capital-budgeting decision), and the variances should be explained. Similarly a director of the construction or installation of a project should be held accountable for the construction cost and time budget. The selection of items that can be reviewed varies, depending to some extent on the method used to make the capital-budgeting decision.

The budget request usually contains an estimate of the cash-payback period (the length of time required to recover the original investment). A comparison of the actual payback period and the expected payback period is one way of measuring the results of operations and the efficiency of the budget process, but there are several difficulties. The payback period is probably of several years' duration; thus there will be a period with no appraisal of the decision to invest. Also, the appraisal is limited to the payback period; after that period there is no further appraisal. These difficulties might lead instead to a comparison of actual and predicted cash proceeds of each period. The use of cash proceeds eliminates waiting for the cash-payback period to end in order to start the appraisal, and it also corrects the one-shot characteristic of the cash-payback method of review.

The comparison of actual and predicted cash proceeds is a useful method of reappraising capital-budgeting decisions, but it cannot be used in all circumstances. Where the projected cash flow is an incremental value (as when equipment is being replaced), it may not be possible to determine the actual relative cash flow since the costs of using the required equipment after replacement are unknown.

Income (the difference between revenues and expenses) is probably the most widely accepted and used measure of performance, and the return on investment (income divided by investment) is the second. But unless they are carefully used, both these measures are inferior to the use of cash proceeds as a means of reappraising capital-budgeting decisions.

By using cash proceeds the problem of allocating the cost of an investment to specific periods of use is avoided. If income is being used to measure performance, then the depreciation cost of the investment must be computed and used as a revenue deduction since income cannot be computed without taking into consideration the cost of using the investment.

Another popular method of measuring performance is the return on investment. There are two variants of the procedure. Investment can be defined as the gross investment (the accumulated depreciation is not subtracted) or the net investment (the accumulated depreciation is subtracted). There are many difficulties in using this measure, but one of the more important is that with constant (and in some cases decreasing) proceeds, the asset may have an increasing return on investment if the straight-line method of depreciation or any of the decreasing-charge methods of depreciation is used.

It is possible to develop a method of depreciation that allows income and return on investment to be used in appraising capital-budgeting decisions without the distortion introduced by the other depreciation procedures.[8] If such a method of depreciation is not used, the analyst faces the difficult task of disengaging the effect of the depreciation method from the effect of the efficiency or inefficiency of the operations and the capital-budgeting process.

Capital-budgeting expenditures should be controlled during the construction period, and the investment decision must be reappraised once operations have begun. The best means of appraising the decision to invest and the operation of the investment after completion is a comparison of the actual and expected cash proceeds; but this is not always possible. The projected incomes and return on investment may also be used, but if so it is desirable that depreciation charges be handled with care. In many cases reappraisal of the decision is not possible by any of the above methods. For example, an investment that improves the product and prevents lost sales cannot be directly appraised, since the level of sales without the expenditure are unknown.[9]

Finally, capital-budgeting decisions are made under uncertainty. A good decision may turn out to be unsuccessful and still have been the correct decision. For example, most investors would pay $1 for an investment which had a 0.9 probability of an immediate return of $1,000 and a 0.1 probability of $0. However, if the event with a 0.1 probability occurred, the investment appraisal would cause the investment to appear to have been undesirable.

13.8   Summary

This chapter has focused on the making of investment decisions and the control and evaluation of investment expenditures. The most widely used methods, payback and return on investment, are found to be inferior to the discounted cash-flow procedures, rate of return, and present value. For mutually exclusive investments, the present-value method is more easily applied and thus is superior to the rate of return method.

[8] See H. Bierman, Jr., "Depreciable Assets-Timing of Expense Recognition," *Accounting Review*, pp. 613–618, October 1961; and T. R. Dyckman, "Discussion of Accelerated Depreciation and Deferred Taxes: An Empirical Study of Fluctuation Asset Expenditures," *Empirical Research in Accounting, Selected Studies 1967*, pp. 124–138. See also Chapter 17.

[9] The decision to make the improvement should have included estimates of the savings and, thus, implicitly, of the opportunity costs. Evaluations of this and similar projects should at least compare results with those anticipated when the decision was made. See Section 1.1.5 on this issue.

As long as it is assumed that the cash flows are known, the present-value method deals very well with the choice of the acceptable independent investments and the selection of the best of a collection of mutually exclusive investments.

Reappraisal of the capital-budgeting decisions should result in three benefits:

1. The presentation of better information on capital-budget requests,
2. An incentive for the operating departments to meet the income goals which they set on the request form in applying for authority to make a capital expenditure;
3. An incentive for those charged with the installation or construction of the project to optimize with respect to the cost and time budgets given them.

APPENDIX 13A
DERIVATION OF THE PRESENT-VALUE
FORMULAS WHEN THE CASH-FLOWS
CHANGE AT A CONTINUOUS RATE

Derivation of the formula, present value $= A/(r - g)$ for increasing cash flows is as follows. Assume that r is larger than g.

$$\text{Present value} = \int_0^\infty Ae^{gt}e^{-rt}\, dt$$

$$= A \int_0^\infty e^{(g-r)t}\, dt$$

$$-\frac{Ae^{(g-r)t}}{g-r}\bigg|_0^\infty = 0 - \frac{A}{g-r} = \frac{A}{r-g} \qquad (13.3)$$

The derivation of the formula, when growth is assumed to continue for a finite time period and there is zero salvage value, follows.

$$\text{Present value} = \int_0^s Ae^{gt}e^{-rt}\, dt$$

$$= A \int_0^s e^{(g-r)t}\, dt$$

$$= \frac{Ae^{(g-r)t}}{g-r}\bigg|_0^s = A\left(\frac{e^{(g-r)s} - 1}{g-r}\right) \qquad (13.5)$$

QUESTIONS AND PROBLEMS

13–1 Explain how the cash flow of a typical period should be computed. Should interest payments be deducted? Do all the deductions require an explicit cash outlay?

13–2 How would a cash-flow computation differ from a fund-flow computation?

13–3 If the present value of the absolute cash flows of an investment are negative, is it possible for the present value of the relative cash flows of the investment to be positive (i.e., the cash flows resulting from this investment being compared to an alternative)?

13–4 What are some difficulties involved in reviewing capital-budgeting decisions?

13–5 In making investment decisions, what other factors than those discussed in this chapter must be taken into consideration?

13–6 Compute the rate of return of the following investment:

0	− $3,477
1	1,000
2	1,000
10	10,000

13–7 An investment costs $1,000 and promises to return $1,210 two periods from now.
    a. Determine the rate of return of the investment.
    b. Explain in three different ways what is meant by the term *rate of return*. Use this example as the basis of your explanation.

13–8 Compute the net present value of an investment that costs $800 and promises to return $1,000 three periods from now. Assume the time value of money is 0.05 per year. Explain what is meant by the term *net present value of an investment*.

13–9 Compute the rate of return of the following investment:

0	− $2,621
1	1,000
2	1,000
10	10,000

13–10 There are two mutually exclusive investments:

		Cash Flows		
Project	Period 0	Period 1	Period 2	Yield
A	− $10,000	...	$11,664	0.08
B	− 10,000	$5,608	5,608	0.08

You are to advise a client. What information do you need to choose between the two investments? Should he be indifferent?

13–11 Compute the net present value of an investment that costs $800 and promises to return $1,000 three periods from now. Assume the time value of money is 0.10 per year.

13–12 Assume that two pieces of equipment have the following characteristics:

Equipment	Expected Life	Initial Cost	Operating Cost per Year
X	5	$43,295	$4,500
Y	8	60,000	4,000

Required: Assuming a cost of money of 0.05, which piece of equipment is the more desirable if both can do the same job? Ignore taxes and uncertainty.

13–13 The Acutron Company uses a discount rate of 0.05. The following information applies to a projected investment (ignore taxes):

Time 0
Initial outlay of $1,000,000

Time 1	
Net revenue from sales (all cash sales)	$1,080,000
Interest paid	50,000
Net change in bank balance	$1,030,000

Required: Should the investment be accepted?

13–14 A product is currently being manufactured on a machine that results in incremental costs of $7.50 per unit. The rate of production expected in the future is 10,000 units per year, and the sales price per unit is $8.50. It is expected that the old machine can be used without repair for the next ten years.

An equipment manufacturer has agreed to accept the old equipment as a trade-in for a new version. The new machine would cost $200,000 with the trade-in and would result in incremental costs of $5.50 per unit. It has an expected life of ten years, and an expected salvage of $10,000 at that time.

The old equipment could be sold on the open market now for $55,000. It has an expected salvage of $1,000 ten years from now.

Ignore income taxes. The appropriate time-discount rate for this company is 0.05.

Required: What do you recommend the company do?

13–15 Assume the same situation as in problem 13–14 except the resale price now of the old equipment is $100,000.

Required: What do you recommend?

13–16 The Electrolite Company has a cost of money of 0.10. The following two mutually exclusive investments are available (two machines which do the same task). The task will be continued in the foreseeable future.

	X	Y
Initial cost	– $10,000	– $20,000
Other costs per year	– 2,000	– 1,000
Estimated life years	15	20

Required: Which machine should be purchased? Ignore taxes.

13–17 The cost of money of the Blair Company is 0.10. The following mutually exclusive investments are available (ignore taxes):

		Cash Flows		
Project	Period 0	Period 1	Period 2	Yield
W	– $10,000	$6,545	$6,545	0.20
X	– 10,000		14,400	0.20
Y	– 10,000	12,000		0.20
Z	– 30,000	19,400	19,400	0.19

Required: For each of the following pairs of mutually exclusive investments, pick the better of the two.

a. W and X.   d. W and Z.
b. W and Y.   e. Z and Y.
c. Y and X.

13–18 Which of the following three pieces of equipment is the more desirable? Assume that the investments are mutually exclusive.

Type of Equipment	Initial Outlay	Life	Labor Savings per Year	Yield
A	$5,000	1	6,000	0.20
B	16,761	5	5,000	0.15
C	42,883	7	10,000	0.14

The cost of money of the firm is 10 per cent. Assume a tax rate of zero.

13–19 Assume that two pieces of equipment have the following characteristics:

Equipment	Expected Life	Initial Cost	Operating Cost per Year
X	5	$43,295	$4,500
Y	8	60,000	4,000

Required: Assuming a cost of money of 0.08, which equipment is the more desirable? What assumptions are you making? Ignore taxes.

13–20 Assume that two pieces of equipment have the following characteristics:

Equipment	Expected Life	Initial Cost	Operating Cost per Year
X	3	$10,000	$4,500
Y	4	12,000	4,000

Required: Assuming a cost of money of 0.05, which equipment is the more desirable? Ignore taxes.

13–21 Assume the cash flow of the first year is $1,000,000 and that the rate of discount is 0.08. What is the present value of the cash flows assuming that the
  a. Cash flow decreases by 0.02 per year?
  b. Cash flow is constant and continues forever?
  c. Cash flow increases by 0.03 per year forever?
  d. Cash flow increases by 0.09 per year forever?

13–22 Assume that the cost of money is 0.10 and the first period's cash flow is $10,000. Compute the present value of cash flows assuming that
  a. The $10,000 continues for perpetuity.
  b. The $10,000 decays at the rate of 0.15 per year
  c. The $10,000 grows at the rate of 0.08 per year.

13–23 Some persons prefer to compute the present value of the cash flows of an investment, while others prefer to compute the terminal value. Will the choice of the method affect the acceptability of an investment?

13–24 The Happy Valley Mattress Company plans to close down one of its plants. The plant building was originally purchased for $500,000 sixty years ago and has been depreciated on a no-salvage, straight-line basis to a present book value of $200,000. The best offer for the plant building at this time is an offer of $288,000. If the plant is continued in operation for five more years the after tax accounting income will be $63,000 per year. At the end of five years, the plant would be sold for $100,000. If the plant were sold today it would be possible to reduce certain expenditures, for example, general administration, by $20,000 per year for the five years. Under all alternatives the equipment would be retained for standby use. The cost of moving the equipment if sold now or later is $16,000. Assuming a 50 per cent tax rate on all types of income, and considering the time value of money to be 16 per cent, what decision should be made?

13–25 The controller of the Waditap Company has asked a member of his staff to prepare a report on the company's equipment replacement procedure. One of the comments made by the staff member read as follows:

> Present procedure overestimates the profitability of replacement proposals because the investment in inventory, receivables, and working-cash balances is ignored. We have two dollars invested in these assets for every dollar invested in equipment, and, therefore, the average annual investment as computed (with the previously suggested changes) should be tripled in calculating the rate of return on investment.

Evaluate this statement.

13–26 Given a twenty-year project with a payback period of 5.1 years, determine the projects rate of return assuming the cash inflows are uniform over the project's life and the total investment is made immediately.

13–27 Given the limitations of payback, why do you think it is so widely used in practice?

SUPPLEMENTARY READING

BIERMAN, H., and S. SMIDT, *The Capital Budgeting Decision*, New York: Macmillan, 1971.

DEAN, JOEL, *Capital Budgeting*, New York: Columbia University Press, 1951.

HAMMOND, J., "Better Decisions with Preference Theory" *The Harvard Business Review*, November–December 1967, pp. 123–141.

HERTZ, D., "Investment Policies that Pay Off," *The Harvard Business Review*, January–February 1968, pp. 96–108.

HESPOS, R., and P. STRASSMAN, "Stochastic Decision Trees for the Analysis of Investment Decisions," *Management Science*, August 1965, pp. 244–259.

HILLIER, F. S., "The Derivation of Probabilistic Information for the Evaluation of Risky Investments," *Management Science*, April 1963, pp. 443–457.

LUTZ, F., and V. LUTZ, "The Theory of Investment of the Firm," Princeton: Princeton University Press, 1951.

MAGEE, J., "How to Use Decision Trees in Capital Investment," *The Harvard Business Review*, September–October 1964, pp. 79–96.

QUERIN, G. D. *The Capital Expenditure Decision*, Homewood, Ill.: R. D. Irwin, 1967.

ROBICHECK, A. A., and S. C. MYERS, *Optimal Financing Decisions*, Englewood Cliffs, N.J.: Prentice-Hall, 1965.

Chapter 14

The Lease or Buy Decision

An important example of a capital budgeting decision is the lease or buy decision. Should land, a plant, or a piece of equipment be bought or leased?[1]

There is at least one very good reason why leasing might be mutually beneficial to both parties. This is where the lessee (the tenant) has a temporary need (as when a firm rents a building for a temporary excess of inventory) or when a need is recurring but each occurrence is for a short period of time (as when the firm needs only one hour of computer time per day; thus the firm should prefer to share a computer on a lease basis rather than buy one). With most of the other reasons why a firm might want to lease, it is not apparent that both parties benefit. For example, a leasing arrangement may be desirable because of the different expectations of the lessee and the lessor. If the lessor expects a computer to have a life of ten years and the lessee expects a life of five years, it would not be surprising to find that they can arrange a lease contract which both parties consider beneficial, but it may be that only one party actually benefits. The same could be true if both parties estimated different salvage values or if they used a different cost of money.

Artificial institutions and practices also contribute to an incentive to lease. The omission of leases from the balance sheets of corporations which results in an understatement of assets and

[1] For other considerations see Albert H. Cohen, "Long Term Leases," *Michigan Business Studies*, Vol. XI, No. 5, Ann Arbor, 1954; Robert N. Anthony and Samuel Schwartz, "Office Equipment: Buy or Rent?" Management Analysis Center, Inc., Boston, 1957; and "Leasing in Industry," *Study in Business Policy*, No. 127 of the National Industrial Conference Board, 1968; R. F. Vancil, "Lease or Borrow: New Method of Analysis," *The Harvard Business Review*, September–October 1961, pp. 122–136.

liabilities and an overstatement of the return on investment is one such factor even though expert analysts will almost invariably restructure performance measures to include the effects of leases. Leases can be used to make investments seem to be desirable that would otherwise not pass the rate-of-return requirement by the firm (this will be illustrated later).

Some of the advantages to the lessee are disadvantages to the lessor. Thus the payment flexibility (assuming the lease can be cancelled) in the lease is a disadvantage from the point of the lessor. Whether or not the lessee has flexibility depends on the terms of the lease, and flexibility should not just be assumed. The flexibility of a lease is somewhat balanced by the fact that the lessee does not have any residual value in the asset being leased.

A lease contract might also cover maintenance and servicing of the equipment leased. One advantage of such a contract is that it sets a maximum for this cost, thus, in a sense, reducing the risk. However, such a provision also sets a minimum cost since it precludes the possibility of incurring less costs than the amount specified by the contract. Generally a maintenance arrangement could be obtained with or without a lease. This should be considered as a separate issue. Statements that leases are less risky to the lessee than debt to the borrower and hence are less likely to cause bankruptcy than debt should not be automatically accepted; rather, they stand or fall depending on the terms of the lease.

A lease is a form of debt financing and serves a function similar to that of other types of debt. In some situations it may be the only type of financing available, or it may be the cheapest type of financing. In any event, since it is an alternative source of capital, its cost must be compared to the cost of other sources. Unless the lessor can borrow at a lower cost than the lessee there is no inherent reason why the firm acting as lessor should have a lower real cost of money. A contract may occur because of different perceptions of the cost of money. These different perceptions may lead to lease terms that are desirable from the point of view of the lessee while also seeming to be desirable to the lessor.

The analysis begins by assuming that the terms of the lease require that the lease payments be made for the duration of the lease, hence the lease is a form of implicit debt. The procedure does not apply to a lease which can be cancelled readily. Such leases are discussed later in this chapter.

14.1   Borrowing or Leasing

First it is necessary to establish the importance of the question of the rate of interest. The decision frequently depends on the rate of interest that is chosen.

Assume that the choice is between borrowing $50,000 from a bank (making an immediate outlay of $50,000) or paying $18,360 a period for three periods.

Assume the tax rate is zero. With a zero rate of interest the present value or cost of the immediate outlay is $50,000, and the present value or cost of the rental payments is $55,080 ($18,360 times 3, the number of payments). The immediate outlay is a better choice than the three payments of $18,360 a period.

Now increase the rate of interest. The present value of the rental payments becomes smaller as the rate of interest is increased. The cost of the immediate outlay remains the same. At some rate of interest r^*, the present values of the two cost streams are equal, while for larger rates of interest the present value of the rental payments is less than the $50,000 initial outlay. This is shown graphically in Figure 14.1.

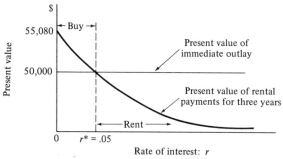

Figure 14.1   Rent versus buy with different interest rates

If the appropriate borrowing rate is less than r^*, the decision should be to buy the equipment since the present value of the immediate outlays resulting from purchase is less than the present value of the rental payments. If the rate of interest (cost of debt) is greater than r^*, the decision should be to rent the equipment. In this example r^* equals 0.05. Assume the rate of interest r (the cost of bank borrowing) is equal to 0.04. The present value of the lease payments is

$$\$18,360 \times 2.77509 = \$50,951$$

and the firm would prefer to buy and borrow compared to renting the equipment. If the cost of debt is greater than 0.05, the decision should be to rent rather than to purchase.

A possible interpretation of the above procedure is that the present outlay or debt equivalent of the three lease payments of $18,360 at 4 per cent is $50,951. Since the present debt equivalent of leasing is more than $50,000, the company should buy and finance the acquisition through borrowing at 4 per cent (the present value of the debt would be $50,000).

The firm has implicitly assumed that the equipment is desirable and should be financed with debt, and the only question is the form of debt, leasing or bank borrowing. The advantage of bank borrowing can be shown clearly if the bank agrees to accept repayment of the $50,000 loan at 0.04 interest in equal annual payments. Each payment to the bank, the first payment due one period from now, would be for $18,017. Given the choice between a series of three debt (bank) payments of $18,017 or three lease payments of $18,360 where the lease is the legal equivalent of debt, the manager should choose the bank payments of $18,017.[2]

14.2 The Investment Decision

The above discussion and Figure 14.1 show that the relative desirability of leasing or borrowing and buying depends on the cost of debt. But the basic investment decision has not yet been considered.[3]

Assume that the investment considered for purchase (and described in Section 14.1) earns proceeds of $21,000 a year for three years, and that the cost of capital is 15 per cent. Table 14–1 presents the decision to purchase the asset using the cost of capital.

Table 14–1   Investment with No Borrowing

Period	Cash Flows	Present Value (15%)
0	($50,000)	($50,000)
1	21,000	18,260
2	21,000	15,880
3	21,000	13,810
		($ 2,050)

The present value of the cash flow is negative, and the investment would be rejected if the cost of capital is used as the discount rate. The cash flows for the leasing alternative are shown in Table 14–2.

Table 14–2 shows leasing has a positive present value and the firm, using conventional procedures, might conclude that leasing is desirable and buying is not desirable. But in the previous section it was concluded that borrowing at 0.04 was superior to leasing. How can it be that the first analysis presents borrowing to be superior to leasing and the second analysis shows leasing to be acceptable but borrowing not to be acceptable?

[2] To avoid implying a bias against leasing, now assume the debt rate is 0.06. Leasing has a present value of $18,360 × 2.6730 or $49,076 and leasing would be more desirable than bank borrowing with a present value of $50,000 and an annual cost of $18,706.

[3] The general method of analysis presented in this chapter was brought to the authors' attention by William D. McEachron.

The paradox arises because of the use of the cost of capital to accomplish the discounting in Table 14–1 (the present value of the cash flows in Table 14–2 is positive as long as the rate of discount used is positive). To reconcile the two presentations, assume the cost of bank borrowing is 0.05 (this is the

Table 14–2   No Investment (Lease)

Period	Investment and Proceeds	Lease Payments	Cash Flow	Present Value (15%)
0	$ 0		$ 0	
1	21,000	($18,360)	2,640	$2,296
2	21,000	(18,360)	2,640	1,996
3	21,000	(18,360)	2,640	1,736
				$6,028

implicit interest being charged on the lease). Assume that a loan of $50,000 can be obtained, the terms being that the loan can be repaid at the rate of $18,360 a year for three years (an interest rate of 5 per cent). The cash flows from the investment and the borrowing to finance the investment are shown in Table 14–3.

Table 14–3   Investment with Borrowing

Period	Investment and Proceeds	Proceeds from Borrowing	Net Cash Flow	Present Value (15%)
0	($50,000)	$ 50,000	$ 0	$ 0
1	21,000	(18,360)	2,640	2,296
2	21,000	(18,360)	2,640	1,996
3	21,000	(18,360)	2,640	1,736
				$6,028

The present value of the cash flows in Table 14–2 is positive, and the indication is that the investment and borrowing should be undertaken. But this is not the conventional analysis, since the positive present value was obtained by incorporating the borrowing of $50,000 and the repaying of the debt into the analysis of cash flows.

Table 14–3 presents the same present value of cash flows as Table 14–2. This arises because of the zero tax rate and the assumption that borrowing an explicit amount of funds carries the same interest rate as the implicit borrowing connected with a lease.

If the lease payments (a form of debt) are included for the lease analysis (Table 14–2) the debt (bank borrowing) should also be included in the analysis as shown in Table 14–3 rather than the analysis in Table 14–1. The buy analysis of Table 14–1 excludes debt, and a comparable analysis should be made for the lease alternative. With a lease the borrowing is implicit in the contract; such implicit borrowing must be eliminated if it is excluded from the buy analysis. This can be done by finding the immediate payment that is equivalent to the lease payments. With an interest rate of 5 per cent, the immediate-payment equivalent to a series of three payments of $18,360 each is $50,000 (the present value of the annuity, with 5 per cent as the rate of discount). Thus, instead of considering three outlays of $18,360, these can be replaced by one outlay of $50,000. The cash flows are given in Table 14–4.

Table 14–4 Lease Payments Converted into an Equivalent Immediate Payment

Period	Cash Flow
0	($50,000)
1	21,000
2	21,000
3	21,000

This series of cash flows is identical to the one presented in Table 14–1, and the same decision should be made in both cases. The cash flows related to the implicit borrowing for the lease situation have been eliminated by computing the immediate-payment equivalent for the lease payments and by considering this payment equivalent to an investment type of outlay. The two investments are now comparable and, in this case, identical.

The choice of the rate of interest to be used to discount the lease payments is often just as cloudy as the computation of the cost of money for the conventional capital-budgeting decision since a lease is a combination of an investment and a borrowing; both these transactions are implicit, and thus not easily separated. In other words, the cost of leasing may not be equal to the cost of borrowing, 0.05. However, defining the cost of leasing as that rate which equates the lease payments to the purchase cost if one exists, 0.05 is obtained.

Any conventional investment with a yield greater than the cost of borrowing can be made to appear acceptable by incorporating into the cash-flow analysis a sufficient amount of debt financing. This is true for leasing or for borrowing from a bank or other sources of debt capital.

Two problems have been highlighted by the lease analysis presented. One is the necessity of making the lease and buy-borrow alternative comparable. The debt cannot be included in the lease analysis and excluded in the buy-borrow alternative. There is the choice of including the debt for both alternatives (Tables 14–2 and 14–3) or excluding it from both alternatives (Table

14–1 and 14–4). But regardless of the treatment of the debt in the investment analysis there still remains the question of the rate of interest to be used in discounting the cash flows. If 15 per cent is used as the discount rate, the investment is not acceptable regardless of how it is financed. (See Table 14–1.)

With no taxes, and if (as was true in this example) the cost of debt and the cost of leasing are equal, and if the cost of debt is used for discounting the investment cash flows for time, including or excluding the debt gives identical present values.[4] Furthermore, both are acceptable at a 0.05 cost of money. This is shown in Table 14–5.

Table 14–5   Comparison of Omitting and Including Financing Costs

	From Table 14–1		From Tables 14–2 and 14–3	
	Investment with No Borrowing		Investment with Debt Flows Included	
Period	Cash Flows	Present Value (0.05)	Cash Flows	Present Value (0.05)
0	($50,000)	($50,000)	0	0
1	21,000	20,000	$2,640	$2,514
2	21,000	19,048	2,640	2,395
3	21,000	18,141	2,640	2,280
		$ 7,189		$7,189

In the illustration being considered the alternatives of purchasing outright and leasing are equivalent. This does not have to be the case; in fact, with the introduction of income taxes and with different estimates of risk and the life of the asset, and different time-value costs for bank borrowing and lease payments, it would rarely be the case that the lease and buy alternatives would give exactly the same present values.

14.2.1 The Income Tax Complication

The income tax complication is relevant to the investment decision. Accelerated depreciation for tax purposes tends to make buying more attractive than leasing since leasing implicitly assumes an increasing-charge depreciation pattern. However, the effect of income taxes must be computed, it cannot be assumed. The present investment provides a useful example because the two alternatives are identical before tax considerations.[5] Suppose

---

[4] The cost of leasing is equal to the cost of debt if the present value of the lease payments, using the cost of debt as the discount rate, is equal to the cost of the asset.

[5] The alternatives are identical since the implicit interest in the lease is equal to the interest payments for the buy-borrow case.

in the present example that the lease payments of $18,360 per period are separated into implicit interest and principal using the cost of leasing of 0.05. The schedule for a loan of $50,000 with a contract interest rate of 5 per cent is shown in Table 14–6. This is also the schedule of debt retirement that could be used for the buy-borrow alternative since the interest costs of leasing and borrowing are equal in this example.

Table 14–6   Separation of Lease into Interest and Principal Payments

1 Period	2 Debt Balance: Beginning of Year	3 Interest (5%) on Debt Balance	4 Rent (Debt Retirement) $18,360 – Interest	5 Depreciation in Buy-Borrow (Straight Line)
1	$50,000	$2,500	$15,860	$16,667
2	34,140	1,707	16,653	16,667
3	17,487	873	17,487	16,667
4	0			

In signing a lease contract services are expected from the asset leased. The periodic payments for these services are "rent" costs plus an amount paid to cover the interest cost on the money tied up in the project. Table 14–6 separates these two costs. The amount paid for rent is as shown in column 4 of Table 14–6. This is the counterpart of depreciation which a firm would incur if it purchased the asset outright. Since in the present example the interest is the same with buy borrow or a lease and the schedule of "rent" is increasing, either a straight-line or decreasing-charge method of depreciation with taxes will make buy borrowing more attractive than leases with a positive cost of money.

Table 14–7   Buy-Borrow: Computation of Income Tax

Period	Gross Proceeds	Depreciation	Interest	Taxable Income	Income Tax (40%)
1	$21,000	$16,667	$2,500	$1,833	$ 733
2	21,000	16,667	1,707	2,626	1,050
3	21,000	16,667	873	3,460	1,384

This analysis does not indicate, however, whether the investment is still acceptable. The income tax for the buy-borrow alternative is calculated in Table 14–7 and the present values of the net cash flows are calculated in Table 14–8.

The present value of the cash flows resulting from the better alternative, the buy-borrow alternative, is $54,341 or $56,433 depending on whether 0.05 or the after tax borrowing rate 0.03 = 0.05 − 0.4(0.05) using a 40 per cent tax rate is used as the discount rate. It is necessary to compare these amounts to the $50,000, the immediate outlay, to reach an accept or reject decision. With both discount rates the decision would be to accept since the present value of the cash flows after taxes is positive with either rate. With a discount rate of 0.15 the decision would be to reject since the present value after taxes is less than $50,000.

Table 14–8 Buy-Borrow: Computation of Present Value of Cash Flows

Period	Gross Proceeds	Income Tax	After-Tax Cash Flow	Present Value (0.05)	Present Value (0.03)
1	$21,000	$ 733	$20,267	$19,302	$19,677
2	21,000	1,050	19,950	18,095	18,805
3	21,000	1,384	19,616	16,944	17,951
				$54,391	$56,433

Leasing gives after tax cash flows of $1,584 per year, ($21,000 − $18,360) (1 − 0.4) = $1,584, and income taxes of $1,056 each year. The total tax payments are about the same but their timing is more favorable under the buy-borrow alternative. The present values of the buy-borrow alternative for the different interest rates are $4,314 with a rate of 0.05 and $4,481 with a rate of 0.03.

With any nonnegative discount rate the present value of leasing is positive.

Without taxes the use of a 0.05 interest cost for both leasing and bank borrowing resulted in the same present value for leasing and buy borrow. With taxes and the remainder of the assumptions unchanged, buy borrow has an advantage compared with leasing if the same borrowing rate is used for both. This arises because the lease arrangement implicitly builds into it an increasing depreciation charge while the tax law allows a constant or a decreasing charge. The present values of the buy-borrow alternative will be higher than the present value of the cash flows associated with leasing, if the costs of leasing and borrowing, without taxes, are equal.[6] The differential will be even larger if the firm buys and uses accelerated depreciation.

Normally there would be differences in the two alternatives before taxes, the leasing cost would not equal the borrowing cost, the salvage value would differ from zero, and so on. In these cases, it is necessary both to establish the present value of both alternatives and to evaluate any nonmonetary factors involved before a choice could reasonably be made.

[6] For the statement to hold for any discount rate, the financing cash flows implicitly included in the lease analysis also have to be included in the buy-borrow alternative (or be excluded from both).

14.2.2 Estimating the Life of the Equipment

In the present example it was assumed that the life of the equipment is known to be three years. Actually, the life of the equipment may not be known with certainty. Any equipment purchased is constantly being challenged by new and more efficient models, and sooner or later it will be replaced by one of these newer models. Thus the life of the equipment being considered is uncertain.

Figure 14.2 shows the different present values of the lease payments and purchase outlays for different assumptions as to the life of the investment (though the lease might be terminated at any time). With a life of zero periods, the lease payments would be zero since no payments would have to be made. The purchase outlay would be $50,000 for all possible lives. If the life of the investment is expected to be zero, or close to zero, it is more desirable to lease.

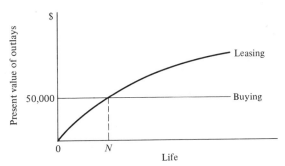

Figure 14.2   Present value of cash outlays with a flexible lease

As the life of the equipment is assumed to increase, the present value of the lease payments increases since they are paid for longer and longer periods of time. Finally a point is reached where the present value of the lease payments is just equal to the cash-purchase outlays, and it is a matter of indifference whether the firm purchases or leases. This occurs at N years in Figure 14.2. If the life is longer than N years, the present value of the lease payments exceeds the cost of purchasing, indicating that it is desirable to buy. This is consistent with the common-sense conclusion that, all things being equal, the longer the economic life of the equipment, the more desirable it is to purchase the equipment.

In the example illustrated in Figure 14.2 it is assumed that the lease is flexible and that it would be void if the equipment is not satisfactory: hence the zero outlay with a zero life. If the lease was not flexible and if there was a firm commitment to make the lease payments even if the equipment turned out to be unusable, then the graph should show the minimum present value of the lease payments associated with each assumed life.

If the equipment has been determined to be desirable, the firm must decide whether to buy or lease. But frequently it will be necessary to include the positive cash flows to determine whether the equipment itself is desirable.

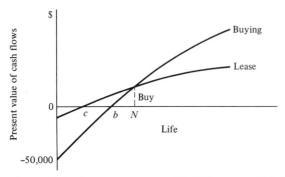

Figure 14.3   Lease versus buy with different possible lives

Figure 14.3 repeats the analysis where the present value of the cash flows is negative up to a life of b years for buying and c years for leasing.

14.2.3 Incorporating Uncertainty

Given the relationships in Figure 14.3, would it be desirable to rent or buy? It would be possible to arrive at a decision if the manager felt that the equipment was likely to last more than N years. A somewhat more exact procedure would be to compute the probabilities of the equipment lasting a different number of years. Each present value could then be weighted by the probability of its lasting that long in order to find a weighted present value.

Example
Assume that analysis indicates uncertain life for a piece of equipment and that management foresees the probabilities of its having different lives as shown in Table 14–9.

Table 14–9   Probability Mass
Function for Equipment Life

Life	Probability
0	0.00
1	0.05
2	0.50
3	0.25
4	0.20
5	0.00
	1.00

The present values of cash flows for buying and leasing for different assumed lives and a new example are given in Table 14–10.

Table 14–10   Present Values of Buy and Lease Alternatives

Assumed Life	Present Value (buy)	Present Value (lease)
1	($30,000)	0
2	0	$10,000
3	30,000	20,000
4	60,000	30,000

If management merely considered the most likely life of two years, the decision would be to lease (a present value of $10,000 versus a present value of zero). However, a more appealing procedure is to multiply the conditional present values for each possible life by the probability of that life occurring.[7] This is done in Tables 14–11 and 14–12.

Table 14–11   Computations: Expected Value of Buying

1 Assumed Life	2 Probability	3 Conditional Present Value (buy)	4 Expected Present Value (column 2 × column 3)
1	0.05	($30,000)	($ 1,500)
2	0.50	0	0
3	0.25	30,000	7,500
4	0.20	60,000	12,000
		Expected value of buying	$18,000

Table 14–12   Computations: Expected Value of Leasing

1 Assumed Life	2 Probability	3 Conditional Present Value (lease)	4 Expected Present Value (column 2 × column 3)
1	0.05	0	0
2	0.50	$10,000	$ 5,000
3	0.25	20,000	5,000
4	0.20	30,000	6,000
		Expected value of leasing	$16,000

[7] The analysis assumes that decisions can be made using expected values or, in other words, a linear utility function for money. Chapter 16 considers the case where the monetary values do not reflect the impact of the events on the decision maker.

The expected value of buying is higher than the expected value of leasing; thus the decision should be to buy. Where there is some probability that the equipment will have a long life, even where the most likely life is short, then it will be necessary to compute the expected value of leasing and purchasing rather than to rely on the decision reached by computing the present values by assuming the most likely life.

If a subjective probability density function over the possible lives is relevant, the better alternative is found in general by multiplying the equation for the payoffs from a given alternative by the equation for the relevant probability density function, integrating and picking the larger expected value. If the payoff equations are linear or nearly so, the choice can be made by selecting the alternative with the largest payoff for the expected life of the equipment.[8]

14.3   Lease or Buy—Land

A corporation which owns land cannot recover the cost of the land through tax deductions unless it sells the land. A corporation which rents land can deduct the rental payments for tax purposes. Assume a cost of money of 5 per cent. If a firm buys land for $2,000,000, it has an immediate outlay of that amount, and there is an implicit capital cost of $100,000 per year before taxes, or $48,000 after taxes. If a firm rents the same land for $100,000 per year, under a 52 per cent tax rate, there is again a net cash outlay of $48,000 (the $100,000 reduces taxes by $52,000). The present value of the outlays of $48,000 per year for perpetuity with an after tax interest rate of 2.4 per cent is $2,000,000. With the facts as given, the cost of renting the land with a lease extending for perpetuity is equal to the cost of the land outright ($2,000,000). This assumes no speculative advantage in owning land.

14.4   Other Considerations

The analysis has been presented as if the only factor which should be considered is the size and timing of the cash flows. Frequently there are nonquantitative factors which might be brought into the analysis. For one

[8] The expected life for the present example (in which the payoffs are a linear function of the life) is 2.60 years. Since this exceeds the intersection value, N equals 1.5 years in this problem, the optimal alternative is to buy. Note that if the expected life were less than point c in Figure 14.2, neither the buy-borrow nor lease alternative would have been attractive.

thing, the owning of equipment does result in risks (and possibly satisfactions) of ownership. The problem of servicing the equipment may exist, though this may frequently be solved by entering into a service contract with the manufacturer or an equipment-servicing agency.

The possibility of more profitable investments is not relevant here. This consideration is incorporated into the analysis by means of the discounting procedures followed in making the decision. If "better" investments are available they should also be accepted.

14.5 Summary

The buy versus lease decision is different from the normal capital-budgeting decision since the economic analysis for the lease alternative incorporates the financing in the cash flows, unless an adjustment is made to eliminate the financing element. This means that the widely accepted practice of evaluating an investment using the cost of capital cannot be used to evaluate the buy alternative if this amount is then to be compared to the present value of the net cash flows of the lease.

Most important, the buy or lease decision raises interesting questions about the choice of a rate of discount and the computation of the cash flows (whether or not financing flows should be included in the analysis).

The procedure recommended in this chapter can be summarized as follows. If present value methods indicate that buying the equipment is appropriate, the question remaining is one of how to finance the purchase: by lease or bank borrowing. This question can be answered by finding the interest rate that equates the lease payments to the purchase price. If this rate is less than the borrowing rate, the firm should lease. If, alternatively, the present value analysis indicates purchase is inappropriate, leasing may still be relevant. This can be determined by first finding the immediate payment equivalent to the future series of lease payments at the borrowing rate and, second, performing a present value analysis on the resultant data using the cost-of-money.

Such features as the possibility of early lease cancellation and the effect of taxes are omitted from this procedure but can be added. Furthermore, if there are other qualitative factors of importance, these must be considered before a final decision is reached.

The chapter also describes a statistical decision theory method for handling the problem of uncertain project life in lease-buy decisions.

It is important for the accountant to be familiar with the necessary inputs to the lease-buy decision such as the relevant cash flows, appropriate tax rates, the effect of depreciation on taxes, and information on expected project lives if he is to provide data relevant to the decision maker.

QUESTIONS AND PROBLEMS

14–1 What are the differences and similarities between a debt contract and a lease contract?

14–2 "Leasing is more desirable than purchasing because of the tax advantage." Discuss.

14–3 Recognizing that part of the lease payment is for interest, and interest is deductible for tax purposes (as is the entire amount of the lease payment): Is it reasonable to exclude the interest in computing the taxable income of the period (that is, not deduct it in computing the income tax for the cash projection)?

14–4 One method of analyzing leases uses both the cost of capital and the cost of debt. Can two rates of discount be used? Does this suggest a general problem?

14–5 "To determine whether a contract is acceptable, discount the cash flows using the cost of capital." Is this reasonable if the contract is a debt contract? A lease contract?

14–6[9] The Elcor Company can contract to make three lease payments of $10,000 each for the use of a piece of equipment. The first payment is to be made immediately and the other payments are to be made in successive years. Assume the cost of debt is 0.05.

Required: Determine the debt equivalent of the lease payments.

14–7 Referring to problem 14–6, if the equipment being leased could be bought for $28,000, should it be purchased or leased? Assume the firm can borrow funds at 0.05 and the equipment is going to be obtained. Assume a zero tax rate for problems 14–7 to 14–11.

14–8 Assume a piece of equipment costs $28,000 and has related cash flows of $10,200 a year for three years. The cash flows are received at the *beginning* of each year. Using a cost capital of 0.10, is the investment desirable?

14–9 Assume $18,000 could be borrowed with the funds being paid back as follows:

Period	
0	
1	10,000
2	10,000

---

[9] Problems 14.6–14.11 are related and should be done consecutively.

Referring to problem 14–8, is the investment now desirable? Assume the initial cash flow could also be used toward the purchase price.

14–10 Referring to problem 14–8, if the company could lease the equipment for $10,000 a year, first payment due immediately, would the equipment be desirable? Assume a cost of debt of 0.05.

14–11 Referring to problem 14–8, if the company could lease the equipment for $9,000 a year with the first payment due immediately, would it be desirable to lease the equipment? Assume other debt costs 5 per cent.

14–12 The Dundee Company is considering leasing a piece of equipment. There are three lease payments of $10,000 due at the end of each of the next three years. The equipment is expected to generate cash flows of $10,500 per year. Assume the cost of debt is 0.05 and the income tax rate is 0.52. The cost of capital is 0.10.

Required:
a. Compute the debt equivalent of the lease payments.
b. Prepare a schedule showing a breakdown of the lease payments into interest and "rent."
c. Compute the income tax of each year and the cash flows after tax of leasing. Include the "rent" but exclude the "interest" component of the lease payment.
d. Compute the present value of the cash flows using 0.10.
e. Should the firm lease the equipment using this calculation?
f. With lease payments of $10,000 per period, what will be the after tax cash flow each year? Is the present value of this flow positive?

14–13 Assume that the equipment described in problem 14–12 can be purchased at a cost of $27,232.

Required: Should the equipment be purchased? Use the sum-of-the-years-digits method of depreciation for tax purposes and a ten per cent discount rate.

14–14 Assume that the life of a piece of equipment is uncertain but that management believes that the probabilities of it having different lives are as follows:

Life	Probability
0	0.00
1	0.20
2	0.30
3	0.40
4	0.10
	1.00

The present values of cash flows for buying and leasing for different assumed lives are as follows:

Assumed Life	Present Value (buying)	Present Value (leasing)
1	$(10,000)	$(2,000)
2	0	4,000
3	11,000	10,000
4	23,000	16,000

Required: Is it more desirable to buy or lease?

SUPPLEMENTARY READING

GANT, D. R., "Illusion in Lease Financing," *The Harvard Business Review*, March–April 1959, pp. 121–142.

GRIESINGER, F. R., "Pros and Cons of Leasing Equipment," *The Harvard Business Review*, March–April 1955, pp. 75–89.

MCEACHRON, W. D., "Leasing a Discounted Cash Flow Approach," *The Controller*, May 1961, pp. 214–219.

VANCIL, R. F., "Lease or Borrow—New Method of Analysis," *The Harvard Business Review*, September–October 1961, pp. 122–136.

VANCIL, R. F., *Leasing of Industrial Equipment*, New York: McGraw-Hill, 1963.

Chapter 15

Applications of Capital-Budgeting Techniques

The present chapter investigates the issues associated with several common capital-budgeting decisions faced by firms. The controller generally plays a substantial role in accumulating the data relevant to such decisions, assisting in the analysis, control, and execution of the projects, and in the evaluation of their success. The four particular decisions selected for examination are illustrative of a wide spectrum of the decisions he may influence. They include:

1. The optimal plant size decision;
2. The make-or-buy decision;
4. Foreign investments and the effect of inflation;
4. Debt refunding.

15.1 Optimal Plant Size

The process of choosing the optimal size of a plant is an interesting theoretical exercise and a question that has important practical significance. Different sized plants have different efficiencies for different levels of operations, require different timing and amounts of cash outflows, and generate different (both as to timing and amount) streams of cash proceeds. The incomes of future periods are affected by the plant-investment decisions made today.

The problem of optimal plant size is an example of a special

313

type of capital-budgeting decision. The investments are mutually exclusive; if one investment plan is accepted, the others are rejected.

In the examples that follow it is assumed that both the relative proportions and the absolute amounts of the factors of production affect the efficiency of the plant. Thus references to changes in size assume that these proportions also change. All theoretically possible plans are being considered.

There are two investment decisions that have to be made. One is whether production is desirable at all. The other is choosing which of several investments can do the best job of production. For example, what size plant should be constructed? If one plant investment is undertaken, all alternative plants will be rejected. Since the alternatives are mutually exclusive, the investment with the highest yield (rate of return) or present-value index (ratio of present value of cash proceeds to investment) may not be the most desirable. The problem can be resolved by using the present-value method.

15.1.1 A Graphic Solution

The accepted theoretical procedure is to plot a series of average total-cost curves for all possible plant sizes and all possible combinations of the factors of production. A smooth curve, called an envelope curve, results, which just touches the cost curve of the most efficient plant for each output.

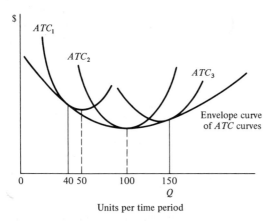

Figure 15.1   Optimum plant size for different outputs

(It does not touch the lowest point or minimum cost point of the curves except for the lowest of all the average total-cost curves.)[1]

In Figure 15.1 there are three plants (or combinations of plants) that give cost curves ATC_1, ATC_2, and ATC_3 for plants 1, 2, and 3, respectively.

[1] See J. S. Bain, *Price Theory*, New York: Henry Holt, 1952, pp. 117–120. Also see E. H. Chamberlin, *The Theory of Monopolistic Competition*, Cambridge, Mass.: Harvard University Press, 1950, pp. 230–259.

Plant 2 is the most efficient plant if output is not a constraint, as evidenced by the fact that it shows the lowest average total cost. But if forty units are to be produced, then plant 1 is the most efficient. At 150 units plant 3 is the most efficient. Note that forty units is not the most efficient point of operations for plant 1. It could actually produce fifty units at a lower average total cost per unit than it could forty units. Nevertheless, plant 1 is the most efficient plant to produce forty units. The plant which could produce forty units at its minimum average total-cost point would not be more desirable, since at forty units its cost would be greater than plant 1's cost.[2]

If it is desired to build a plant to produce 100 units, then plant 2 would be the choice, for at 100 units of production plant 2, which is the most efficient of all the plants, would be operating at maximum efficiency, that is, at the point of minimum average total cost. If the decision were based on a desired production of 150 units, plant 3 would be chosen; but plant 3 would operate at a higher minimum average total cost than plant 2 producing 100 units could do.[3] (Production is for a given time period.)

15.1.2 Quantitative Solutions

Plants of different capacities are mutually exclusive investments. To choose the best of mutually exclusive investments of equal life, the firm can compute the present values of the cash flows of all investment possibilities; the investment with the greatest present value is the best investment. This method does not explicitly use incremental costs, but they are implicit in the solution.

Assume that the forecast for the demand for a product is such that the firm desires to produce seventy units a period as efficiently as possible. The management must choose one of the two following alternatives:

1. A plant that can produce fifty units per period at its most efficient level of output (see ATC_1) in Figure 15.1.
2. A plant that can produce 100 units per period at its most efficient level of output (see ATC_2) in Figure 15.1.

Both plants can produce the expected needs, but the most efficient production capacity of the plant selected may be either less or greater than the 70 unit requirement; thus management must determine the plant size that is optimal, given the objectives of the firm.

Example
The expected (forecasted) cash flows are given in Table 15–1. A two-year life is assumed and taxes are ignored for simplicity.

[2] Depending on the discreteness in plant size, plant 1 may be optimal for fifty units if no plant can be built with a lower average total cost for this level of output.

[3] The concept of optimal plant size is frequently confused with optimal size of the firm. There are similarities, but the discussion here is limited to the narrower interpretation of what is meant by "plant."

Table 15–1   Present Value of Cash Flows for Two Plants

Plant: Described by Most Efficient Output Level	Cash Flows*			Approximate Rate of Return	Present Value (0.10)
	0	1	2		
50	($20,000)	$15,000	$15,000	0.32	$6,033
100	(35,000)	25,000	25,000	0.27	$8,388

  * The net cash flows at a production level of seventy units reflect a higher operating efficiency for the larger plant size and higher initial costs.

At a 0.10 cost of money, the capacity of 100 units per period is the more desirable since it has the higher present value. The lower rate of return is misleading since it ignores the fact that the incremental investment is desirable. The analysis in Table 15–2 indicates that the incremental investment is desirable.

Table 15–2   Incremental Analysis for the Larger Plant

Investment	Cash Flows			Approximate Rate of Return	Present Value (0.10)
	0	1	2		
Incremental Investment	($15,000)	$10,000	$10,000	0.12	$2,355

The analysis in the previous section is correct as far as it goes, but it is incomplete since it considers the costs for only one level of output. Differences in costs may arise due to the operation of the alternative plants at different percentages of their capacity. If probabilities are put on the different output requirements, the expected cost of the different sized plants can be computed.

Example
A Motor Company is considering building an assembly plant. The decision has been narrowed down to two possibilities: a larger plant at a cost of $1 million or a smaller plant for $764,500. The company desires to choose the best plant at a level of operations of 100,000 cars a month. Both plants have an expected life of ten years and are expected not to have any salvage value at the time of their retirement. The cost of money is 10 per cent. Income taxes are ignored for simplicity. The relevant facts are given in Table 15–3.

Table 15–3 assumes that the large plant will have economies of scale; that is, labor efficiencies in terms of the hours of labor necessary to assemble a car. The small plant will have savings on service (for example, heating). The yearly incremental advantage of the larger plant is indicated in Table 15–4. The present value of savings of $50,000 per year is the present value of an annuity of $50,000 for 10 years at 10 per cent: $50,000 × 6.1446 = $307,230.

The incremental present value of the larger plant can be compared to its incremental cost. The present value of the savings ($307,230) resulting from use of the larger plant is $71,730 greater than the $235,500 (that is $1,000,000 − $764,500) of additional outlays required, indicating that the larger plant is more desirable than the smaller plant.[4] However, there are some important

Table 15–3   Yearly Costs for 100,000 Cars per Month

	Large Plant	Small Plant
Initial cost	$1,000,000	$764,500
Direct labor: First shift	500,000	260,000 per year
Second shift		300,000 per year
Overhead	80,000	70,000 per year

elements of the problem which have not yet been considered. What is the possibility of activity being less (or more) than the expected level? How much of the overhead presented in the example is fixed and how much variable? How badly does the company need elbow room for the possibility that the demand will be greater than expected? How important is it to retain flexibility in order to respond to new information?

Table 15–4   Yearly Incremental Advantage per Month of the Larger Plant

	Saving (Dissaving) per Year of Using the Larger Plant
Direct labor: First shift	($240,000)
Second shift	300,000
Overhead	(10,000)
Saving per year of using the larger plant	$ 50,000

Are the costs of possible idle-capacity losses arising from high fixed costs balanced by the ability of the large plant to produce more goods when needed? The small plant is designed to be worked at overtime. If demand increases, the production of the small plant may be increased somewhat by working three shifts as well as on holidays; but the basic fact still remains that the large plant has more reserve capacity. The large plant, however, is more vulnerable to decreases in production since certain costs continue whether the plant produces or not and it costs more.

It is necessary then to consider the desirability of the investment not at

---

[4] The savings could be computed on a monthly basis and discounted (with an appropriate adjustment of the rate), but this refinement would not alter the result.

just one activity level but rather over its entire range of operations. This can be accomplished by weighting the present value of cash flows for different operating rates by the probability of the flows occurring.

Example

Assume that the demand can be approximated by five discrete levels (see Table 15–5). For different levels of operation, the incremental investment of a large plant compared to a small plant is indicated in columns 3 and 4 of Table 15–5. Also shown is the probability of the different levels of demand occurring. By multiplying the probability by the present value, an expected (or weighted) present value is obtained. Since the expected present value of the incremental investment is positive, the larger plant is still desirable.

Table 15–5   Expected Present Value of Incremental Plant Investment: 10-Year Life

Level of Operation Cars per Month	Probability of Demand Level	Present Value of Incremental Investment	Expected Present Value
0	0.10	($235,500)	($23,550)
50,000	0.15	(100,000)	(15,000)
100,000	0.25	71,730	17,933
150,000	0.35	100,000	35,000
300,000	0.15	200,000	30,000
	1.00	Expected present value	$44,383

If the probabilities on the lower two production levels were large enough, either no plant or the smaller plant would have been preferable. (Note that the expected level of activity should not be used for decision purposes in this case because the payoff function given in column 3 is not a linear function of activity.) In some industries firms may use inventories of finished goods as a means of reducing the investment in the plant. By following a policy of building up a finished goods inventory in anticipation of higher demand, firms may employ plants of a smaller capacity than would otherwise be needed.[5] Although omitted for simplicity, tax effects are relevant to the incremental-advantage computation.

15.2   Make or Buy Decisions

The make-or-buy decision may take several forms:

1. To make or buy a product (or a component) the firm is not currently making.

[5] The analysis of this chapter is made in terms of expected monetary values. The next chapter will discuss the case where the monetary values do not adequately reflect the total impact of events on the decision maker.

2. To continue to make or begin purchasing a product the firm is currently making.
3. To make more or less of a product than the firm is currently making.

The three variants of the make-or-buy decision could all be considered capital-budgeting decisions, or they could be considered as incremental-cost-and-revenue decisions with interest a relevant factor. Whether they are treated in one manner or the other depends to some extent on the relative importance of the required investment. Where the investment is large, it is reasonable to consider the make-or-buy decision just as the firm would consider other decisions involving the investment of resources.

15.2.1 Where Significant Resources are Invested

Consider initially a situation where new plant facilities, including a building or equipment, are required in order to make a product. Thus the initial investment is significant. In addition to the investment in plant facilities there is an investment in working capital, for example, cash outlays for rent, financing of material purchases, and so on. First, the series of cash outlays is determined on the assumption that the firm makes the item. This series of cash outlays should be discounted back to the present. The series of cash outlays resulting from making the product would then be compared to another series of cash outlays resulting from purchase. If the present value of this second series of outlays is less than that of the first, the decision (*ceteris paribus*) should be to purchase the product. If the present value of the first series of outlays is less, then the decision should be to invest in the new facilities and make the item.

Costs not requiring cash outlays are included if there is an alternative opportunity connected with using the facilities which give rise to these costs. Thus a piece of equipment may already be owned, but if making the new product results in another product not being made, then there is an opportunity cost connected with making the new product, even though there may not be an out-of-pocket outlay connected with the equipment.[6]

Example
The cost of new equipment needed to produce an item being considered is $25,000. The equipment has an expected life of five years. Other outlays in the beginning of the first period are $1,000. Cash outlays for the next five years are expected to be $2,000 per year if the product is made. If the product is purchased, outlays of $10,000 a year will be required. The cash outlays are assumed to be made at the end of each year. The firm has a cost of money of

---

[6] In determining the savings from making the product, consideration should be given to the decrease in unit cost that results from the learning process. See Chapter 4 on this point.

10 per cent. The cost of purchasing is an annuity of $10,000 for five years. The value of this annuity at 10 per cent is $10,000 (3.7908) = $37,908. The cost of making the product is $25,000 + $1,000 + $2,000 (3.7908) = $26,000 + 7,582 = $33,582. The present value of making the product is less than the present value of purchasing the product; thus the decision should be to make it. A final decision should not be reached without considering the impact of taxes.

This problem is somewhat similar to the problem of buying or leasing discussed in the last chapter, though the debt-like characteristics of a long-term contract are not present. In the buying or leasing decision, the possibility of different service lives was considered. This procedure would also apply to the make-or-buy decision. In the above example, if the part were to be used for only four years, and if the equipment had no other use or salvage value, then the decision would be to buy the part.

15.2.2 No Resources Required

Next assume a situation where there is and will be idle capacity in the plant and in the machinery presently owned (the opportunity cost of these facilities is therefore zero), and that there is no significant investment in working capital required. In this case the firm could compute the incremental costs of producing the product and compare them with the incremental costs connected with purchasing the product. Note that the incremental costs are used. The accounting costs (which may include an allocation of fixed-overhead costs which would be incurred in any event) are not relevant. Since there may be more than one unit produced, the marginal cost of one unit is also not relevant; the incremental costs are relevant.

Example
The Creighton Company is attempting to determine whether to make or buy a component part presently being produced. The cost of purchasing the part would be $10 per unit. There is and will be excess capacity in the plant, and there is and will be free machine time. The cost of the product in the most recent time period was:

Direct labor	$ 3.00
Material	4.50
Fixed overhead (allocated)	2.50
Variable overhead (identified with product)	1.00
	$11.00

Assume that the fixed overhead would be incurred in any event, and thus there are outlays of only $8.50 identified with the manufacture of the product.

The amount would be less if some of the variable overhead were the result of an arbitrary allocation. Since the product could not be purchased for less than $10, it would seem desirable to make the product at an incremental cost of $8.50.

If the assumption of free machine time and idle-plant capacity were removed, then some or all of the fixed costs might be included. In fact it is conceivable that the opportunity costs used for decision making are higher than the accounting costs.

In this example the assumption is made that the product is already being produced. This assumption is not necessary to the analysis, except that it lends an air of reliability to the cost information relative to making the product. Exactly the same analysis is appropriate if the product were not currently in production. The rule to follow is to include only those costs that are incremental to the decision; those costs incurred only if the product is made. Income lost if the product is made is also an incremental cost. Once again consideration should be given to taxes. In considering the decision to buy, for example, the firm should decide what is to be done with the unused equipment. If it can be disposed of, the tax effects of early retirement are relevant.

In the solution just suggested, interest is not considered. Generally speaking, the making of any product requires the commitment of new capital resources; thus interest should be taken into consideration. One method of incorporating interest, is to compute the present values of the cash flows of the several alternatives. A second possibility is to compute the relevant costs per unit and include an interest cost per unit. The complete exclusion of interest in the analysis of inventory decisions or the computation of product costs would result in a bias toward investment in work in process rather than in plant and equipment. This is not desirable. All investments involving resource allocations should be placed on a comparable basis by the recognition of interest costs incurred.

15.2.3 Other Factors

The firm should also take into consideration qualitative factors such as the advantages and disadvantages of having several sources of supply, the quality of the product and the possibility of improvements in the product, the possibility of better uses of managers, and the risks of the industry the firm is entering.[7] The quantitative analysis may not enable the firm to make the final decision independently of other information, but it supplies a very important factor in making the decision, namely, the answer to the question of the direct impact of the make-or-buy decision on the profitability of the enterprise. Furthermore, the decision maker may be able to decide whether

---

[7] Sometimes the qualitative factors can be given quantitative values by asking, for example, how much might be paid to obtain the safety features of a given alternative.

he would be willing to sacrifice the quantitative difference between two alternatives for the qualitative advantages of the previously less attractive choice.

15.3 Inflation and Interest Rates

When inflation is present it must be considered in computing the "real" cost of borrowing (the real interest rate) to the firm. The real rate is lower than the stated or contractual rate (the nominal rate) when there is inflation. The real rate should not be used in discounting cash flows for capital budgeting unless the cash flows are expressed in constant dollars.

Let
A = amount borrowed.
S = amount to be repaid (A plus the amount of interest).
p_0 = price index at beginning of period.
p_1 = price index at end of period.
r = real interest rate.
S^* = amount to be repaid in terms of constant, beginning-of-period, dollars.

$$S^* = S(p_0/p_1). \tag{15.1}$$

Hence, to convert the amount to be paid at the end of the period into beginning-of-the-period purchasing power, S is multiplied by the ratio of the price indices. The formula and examples below assume that money is borrowed for a period of one year. Solving for the real interest rate:

$$A = \frac{S^*}{1 + r}, \qquad A(1 + r) = S^*$$

$$r = \frac{S^*}{A} - 1, \quad \text{and, using (15.1), } r = \frac{Sp_0}{Ap_1} - 1 = \frac{Sp_0 - Ap_1}{Ap_1}. \tag{15.2}$$

Example
A = $1,000
S = $2,000
p_0 = 100
p_1 = 150
The nominal interest rate here is $S/A - 1 = 2 - 1 = 1.00$.

$$S^* = S\left(\frac{p_0}{p_1}\right) = \$2,000\left(\frac{100}{150}\right) = \$1,333,$$

$$r = \frac{S^*}{A} - 1 = \frac{1,333}{1,000} - 1 = 1.333 - 1 = 0.333,$$

or,

$$r = \frac{Sp_0}{Ap_1} - 1 = \left(\frac{2,000}{1,000}\right)\left(\frac{100}{150}\right) - 1 = 1.333 - 1 = 0.333.$$

Although the nominal (stated) interest rate on the loan is one, the effective or "real" rate is 0.333.

Example
    $A = \$1,000$
    $S = \$1,200$
    $p_0 = 100$
    $p_1 = 130$
The nominal interest rate is 0.20.

$$S^* = S\left(\frac{p_0}{p_1}\right) = 1,200\left(\frac{100}{130}\right) = \$923$$

$$r = \frac{S^*}{A} - 1 = \frac{923}{1,000} - 1 = -0.077,$$

(a negative real interest rate).

The real rate is negative in this case indicating the lender will suffer a real loss.

Example
    $A = \$1,000$
    $S = \$1,200$
    $p_0 = 100$
    $p_1 = 110$
The nominal interest rate is again 0.20.

$$S^* = 1,200 \times \frac{100}{110} = \$1,091;$$

$$r = \frac{S^*}{A} - 1 = \frac{1,091}{1,000} - 1 = 0.091.$$

This may be the most typical case. The real rate is positive but substantially less than the nominal rate.

15.3.1 Capital-Budgeting Implications

Assume that the price level is expected to double in the next twelve months. There is an interest rate of 100 per cent demanded by the banks (that is, for every dollar borrowed, two must be paid one year later). The one-year investment described in Table 15–6 is being considered.

Using the indicated interest rate of 100 per cent, the investment (which has a rate of return of 40 per cent) should be rejected. With a real interest rate

Table 15–6 Foreign Investment Cash Flows

Period	Cash Flows
0	$-1,000
1	1,400

of $r = (Sp_0/Ap_1) - 1 = [2,000(100)/1,000(200)] - 1 = 0$ per cent, the investment would seem to be desirable; however, this would be an incorrect use of the real interest rate.

If the funds were borrowed at a cost of 100 per cent, the cash flows would be as given in Table 15–7.

Table 15–7 Cash Flows from Investment and Borrowing

Period	Investment	Borrowings	Difference
0	$-1,000	$1,000	$0
1	1,400	-2,000	-600

The above analysis indicated that this foreign investment is not desirable if the funds are obtained by borrowing at 100 per cent.[8]

The same conclusion could be reached by adjusting the $1,400 to the beginning of the period purchasing power. Thus $1,400 (100/200) = $700, which leads to a reject decision with an immediate outlay of $1,000 since the net present value is negative using the real interest rate of zero.

Still another way to evaluate this investment is to examine the position of the firm at the end of the year. If it does not accept the investment, it will have experienced no change in the real value of its net assets except that due to inflation. If it accepts the investment its net assets will experience the same effect as well as be reduced by $600, the excess of the loan repayment over the net cash inflows generated by the investment.

An investment must earn a return equal to the cost of money with both the interest rate and the cash flows unadjusted for the change in the price level. If the interest rate is adjusted to reflect the effective cost of the money, with

[8] It should not be implied that if the present value of the differences were positive the investment would be acceptable. Canceling debt against the investment can be used to show that the investment is not acceptable (if the difference is negative); it cannot be used to show that it is acceptable. However, it would be eligible for further consideration.

due regard for inflation, and if this is used as the rate of discount, then the cash flows must be adjusted into dollars of the same purchasing power. In the example being explored, the real rate is 0. The cash flows in terms of beginning-of-period dollars are given in Table 15–8.

Table 15–8   Cash Flows from Investment: Present Period Dollars

Period	Cash Flows	Adjustment Factor	Adjusted Cash Flows (beginning-of-period purchasing power)
0	$ – 1,000	—	$ – 1,000
1	1,400	$\dfrac{100}{200}$	700

The present value of the cash flows is again negative (at a zero rate of discount, the present value is a negative $300).

15.3.2 Foreign Investments

Many firms are expanding operations overseas. In most respects these investments are very similar to those made at home. Yet there are important differences that must be considered. These include different social customs and their impact on the market as well as on employee behavior, problems in the stability of foreign governments, restrictions on a firm's actions including the movement of capital in and out of the country, availability of a trained labor market, capable suppliers and production facilities, tax policies, foreign exchange rates, different market distribution systems, and the likelihood of inflation and currency devaluation, to mention but a few.

Continuing the example of the previous section, would the present investment be desirable if the funds were obtained from another country (say the United States), where the cost of money is 0.10? If $1,000 is borrowed, then $1,100 will have to be returned to investors. If the initial conversion rate between dollars and the foreign currency is one to one, assuming a doubling of the foreign price level and no change in the purchasing power of the dollar, so that the exchange rate becomes two for one, then the $1,400 of foreign currency will convert back to $700 U.S. dollars. This is less than the $1,100, that is; $1,000 + 0.1 ($1,000), required to make this a desirable investment. Thus the investment is again deemed undesirable.

But suppose inflation in the host country is only 10 per cent, the nominal cost of borrowing abroad 20 per cent, and the cost of money in the United States 10 per cent.[9] The real rate abroad is 0.091, $[1,200(100)/1,000(110)] - 1$, and the adjusted net cash flow at the end of the first year

[9] Assume, further, no inflation in the United States.

would be 1,400(100/110) $\doteq$ 1,273. Discounting at the real rate 0.091 gives approximately $1,168 or $168 as the net present value, which shows the investment is now desirable if financed abroad. Given an exchange rate of one to one at the start and one-point-one to one at the end of the period, the $1,400 converts to $1,273 U.S. dollars.[10] Since the cost of money in the United States exceeds the real rate abroad, the project should be financed abroad. Restrictions on capital flows, if present, would add to the argument to finance the investment abroad.

If the funds are already in the foreign country and cannot be removed, then it may be necessary to invest them in absolutely undesirable investments in order to minimize the loss. That is, it may be better to undertake an undesirable investment than to have the funds eaten away by inflation at an even more rapid rate.

Example

Consider now another example involving different capital costs in different countries. Suppose the Clark Manufacturing Company is considering building plants in each of four different countries. The cost of money for the company in each country is given in Table 15–9.

Table 15–9   Borrowing Cost by Country

Country	Cost of Money per Year
United States	0.06
Britain	0.08
Japan	0.10
Brazil	0.40

The cost of money for the Clark Company in the United States is 0.06. What rate of discount and what capital-budgeting procedure should the company use in evaluating investments in the four countries? For ease in exposition assume that the investment has a life of one year and that the cash flows given in Table 15–10 are available in each country. Assume further that each foreign investment must be financed in the host country.

Table 15–10   Foreign Investment Cash Flows

Beginning of Year 1	End of Year 1
($100,000)	$120,000

---

[10] Exchange rates may not move in such a way that they precisely reflect relative inflationary conditions. The actual rate (or rate expected) should be used.

The above cash flows are expressed in the currency of each respective country. For an investment in the United States, and assuming a cost of money of 0.06, the present value is: $- \$100,000 + \$120,000/1.06 = \$13,200$.

The positive net present value of $13,200 indicates that the investment is acceptable, or, more exactly, it indicates that the investment is worthy of further consideration. The riskiness of the venture and qualitative factors should be considered before the investment is finally accepted. Following the above method of analysis and using the capital cost of each country in turn, the investments would be undertaken in all countries except Brazil. (The assumption is made that the capital costs represent the return for the time value of money and do not include an adjustment for risk).[11]

Now assume the same facts as above except that 40 per cent of the investment must be financed by funds from the United States. It is now necessary also to consider possible currency depreciation. The procedure is illustrated using the numbers associated with the Japanese investment and assuming that the expected exchange rate between yen and dollars over the year now changes from 1 yen to 1 dollar, to 1.25 yen to 1 dollar perhaps reflecting a relative inflation of 25 per cent in Japan as compared to the United States.

There are two problems. The first is the choice of the rate of discount to use and the second is the necessity to adjust for currency depreciation. A seemingly reasonable discount rate is obtained by taking a weighted average of the two sources of funds (from the United States and Japan).

	Cost	Proportion of Funds	Weighted Cost
U.S. dollars	0.06	0.40	0.024
Japanese yen	0.10	0.60	0.060
			0.084

Discounting the $120,000 by 0.084 gives: $120,000/1.084 = \$110,700$. Since the cost of the investment is $100,000, the investment has a positive net present value and seems to be acceptable. However, the above analysis is not correct for two reasons. The 0.084 does not consider the end of period conversion rate or the opportunities available in Japan. At the end of the first year if the plant is built the investment will yield 120,000 yen. The investment is financed as shown in Table 15–11.

The total yen available after repayment of the Japanese loan is:

$$120,000 - 66,000 = 54,000.$$

---

[11] Portfolio implications of the several investment opportunities are ignored in this analysis.

Table 15–11   Financing of Japanese Investment

	Initial Loan	Interest	Total Repayment Required
Yen	60,000	6,000	66,000
Dollars	$40,000	$2,400	$42,400

The expected value of the 54,000 yen converted to dollars is

$$\frac{54,000}{1.25} = \$43,200.$$

This amount is received at the end of period 1. The firm can compare the $43,200 to the $42,400, the repayment required at home, or it may discount the $43,200 to the present time using the U.S. borrowing rate and compare it to the amount invested, $40,000:

$$\frac{\$43,200}{1.06} = \$40,750.$$

Using either comparison, the investment is marginally acceptable. Here again the next step is to incorporate the riskiness of the investment and, perhaps, other qualitative factors. With a projected exchange rate of 1.4 yen to 1 the investment would be rejected. The computational procedures are:

1. Compute the cash flows in the currency of the land where the investment is being made.
2. Include in the cash flows the funds from foreign sources which can be borrowed to finance the investment, interest on these funds, and the repayment of this debt.
3. Convert the net cash flow that is available for return to the United States for each time period using the expected conversion rate for the time period.
4. Discount these dollars using the borrowing rate in the United States.
5. And, finally, consider the investment further if the net present value is positive.

If, instead of borrowing funds, financing in the foreign country is in the form of stock equity funds, the analysis is comparable but the end-of-the-period debt repayment is omitted. For an example of foreign equity financing, assume that 60 per cent of the capital is to be obtained from foreign stock equity sources and the rest from U.S. borrowing. The analysis is given in Table 15–12.

The 48,000 yen converts to $38,400 (48,000/1.25), which is inadequate to justify the project for further consideration. Thus the same investment that was accepted when financed by debt earning 0.10 is rejected when the investment is financed entirely by stock because of the increased share of returns that go to

Table 15–12   Net Cash Flows from Japanese Investment: Stock Financing

	Beginning of Year	End of Year
Investment flows	$ – 100,000	$120,000
Foreign equity financing	+ 60,000	
	$ – 40,000	$120,000
Returns allocated to foreign equity investors (0.6 × $120,000)		72,000
Net cash flow	$ – 40,000	$48,000

the foreign investors. The cash flow measured in terms of yen leads to an acceptable investment. When the yen is converted to dollars, the investment is not acceptable if it is financed with 60 per cent foreign stock equity funds and 40 per cent United States dollars.

Intuitive evaluations of the cash flows of foreign investments can be unreliable. It is necessary to include systematically the domestic and foreign borrowing rates, the type of foreign capital to be obtained, and the exchange rates at the relevant dates.

15.4   Debt Refunding

A company with debt outstanding should periodically review the possibility of refunding the debt to take advantage of favorable changes in current interest rates. The problem of refunding has sometimes been treated as if it were a problem separate from other decisions being made in the firm, but actually it is a capital-budgeting decision under uncertainty. To simplify the analysis, the question is limited here to whether or not to replace a debt obligation with another debt contract. The possibility of substituting stock equity securities is passed in order to avoid complications; also there exists a respected theory that this substitution under well-defined conditions would not affect the decision.[12]

[12] See F. Modigliani and M. H. Miller, "The Cost of Capital, Corporation Finance and the Theory of Investment," *American Economic Review*, June 1958.

15.4.1 Bond Refunding under Certainty

Assume that the IOU Company has $100,000 of debt outstanding that pays 6 per cent (i.e., $6,000) interest annually. The bond issue cost and bond discount of the old debt are assumed to be zero to simplify the explanation when taxes are considered. The maturity date of the securities is ten years from the present. Assume that a new ten-year security could be issued that would yield 4 per cent per year. The issue costs would be $8,000, and the bond redemption penalty on the old bonds would be $4,000. Ignoring tax considerations, should the old bonds be replaced with new securities?

The solution using the current effective interest rate is as follows:

1. Determine the interest savings per year resulting from the new contract:

Annual interest of old debt	$6,000
Annual interest of new debt	4,000
Savings per year	$2,000

2. Compute the present value of the savings per year, using the current effective yield. Present value of $2,000 per year for ten years using a 4 per cent discount rate: $2,000 (8.111) = $16,222.
3. Compare the present value of the savings with the present value of the outlays:

Present value of savings	$16,222
Present value of outlays	12,000
Present value of net savings	$ 4,222

Since the net savings are positive (the present value of the savings is greater than the present value of the outlays minus the bond issue cost plus the redemption premium), the refunding of the old investment should be undertaken.

A possible criticism of the above solution centers on the choice of the effective rate of interest of the new security as the appropriate rate of discount for determining the present value of the savings per year, instead of using the corporation's cost of capital or some other discount rate.

The refunding of a bond issue requires an investment of resources today just like any other capital-investment decision. If the cost of capital is used to determine the worth of capital investments, should the same criterion be used in determining whether this refunding should be undertaken?[13] The $12,000 of issue costs and redemption penalty necessary to accomplish the refunding is an investment analogous to other investments, but there are

---

[13] It is not clear that the cost of capital should be used to evaluate investments. However, many firms do use their cost of capital and if it is used the problem described will appear.

several differences. The benefits (savings) promised by this investment are more certain than those available from most investments. Furthermore, the refunding operation reduces the real total debt outstanding (the present value of the debt burden is less), thus strengthening the financial position of the common stockholders and perhaps leading to a higher stock price (all other factors remaining unchanged). The use of the effective rate of interest of the new security to find the present debt equivalent of the series of interest savings (the difference between the interest paid with refunding and the interest which would have to be paid if the bonds were not refunded) is consistent with the improved capital structure.

Continuing the above illustration, assume that the cost of capital is 12 per cent and that this rate is used to discount the cash flows connected with the refunding operation. The computations would be as follows:

1. Compute the present value of the savings per year, using the cost of capital as the appropriate rate of discount: $2,000 (5.65) = $11,300; and
2. Compare the present value of the savings with the present value of the outlays.

Present value of savings	$11,300
Present value of outlays	12,000
Present value of dissavings	$ (700)

Since the present value of the outlays is greater than the present value of the savings, it would seem that the refunding should not take place. The previous solution using the effective rate of interest of the debt suggests that the refunding should take place. If the previous solution is accepted, bond refunding will have a priority over conventional alternative investment opportunities.

The use of the current bond yield rate may give a more reasonable solution since the outlay required actually reduces the amount of debt outstanding. In decisions involving the issue or retirement of debt the yield rate of the new debt is appropriate for discounting the cash flows resulting from the debt. Use of the bond yield rate in refunding is predicated on the assumption that refunding is desirable if it returns more than that yield. Ordinarily a firm has other uses for the cash required for the refunding and these other uses would yield more than the bond yield rate, but these investments will have different risk characteristics from the outlays for refunding. They do not result in an improved capital structure. In the above example, the present value of the debt was reduced by $16,222, the present value of the interest savings; the net savings were $4,222. Furthermore, the certainty of the savings is greater than with the average investment.[14]

[14] Theoretically for other investments, it would be appropriate to use the current interest rate and make a separate adjustment for uncertainty. The decision maker could then decide whether the improvement in capital structure was worth the difference between the savings from refunding and the best alternative use of funds.

15.4.2 The Tax Complication

For a more complete solution of the refunding decision the income tax effect must also be included.

Whether or not particular items are deductible for tax purposes in the year of refunding depends on the exact nature of the transactions and on the tax regulations. If the retirement and issue are separate transactions (there is not an exchange), the costs of retiring the old bonds, including the redemption premiums and the book loss resulting from writing off unamortized bond discount and bond issue costs, are all deductible for tax purposes at the time of retirement.[15] However, the costs of issuing the new bonds have to be written off over the life of the new bonds.

Example (*continued*)
Assume a tax rate of 40 per cent. Should the bonds described earlier be refunded? It is necessary to include the tax effects for each year.

1. There will be a saving equal to 40 per cent of the bond redemption costs of the old securities in the year of issue.

   Tax saving in year 1: 0.40($4,000) = $1,600.

2. Taxes for each year will be decreased by 40 per cent of the portion of the bond issue costs (of the new issue) allocated to the period.

   Allocation of bond issue costs to each year $8,000/10 = $800
   Tax savings occurring each year $800(0.40) = $320

3. The interest expense will be reduced by $2,000 and thus taxes will increase by 40 per cent of this reduction.

Interest decrease	$2,000
Loss on tax deduction	800
Net saving on interest expense	$1,200

4. The net savings each year will be:

After tax savings on interest	$1,200
Savings on taxes	320
Net saving per year	$1,520

---

[15] This is typically a reason for attempting to establish them as separate transactions.

Using 4 per cent, the cost of debt and discounting the tax savings of the first year for one year, the present value of the savings will be

Present value of net savings at 4 per cent	$1,520 (8.111) = $12,329
Tax savings first year at 4 per cent	1,600 (0.962) = 1,539
Present value of savings, allowing for taxes	$13,868

The introduction of income taxes makes the refunding somewhat less desirable in this case. The refunding would cost $12,000, and the present value of the savings is $13,868. In the same situation, without income taxes, the present value of the savings is $16,222. But the effect of income taxes on the solution cannot be assumed to always be in the same direction, since it depends on the size of redemption premiums, the bond issue costs of the new issue, and the unamortized bond issue costs and the discount of the old issue which are deductible in the year of refunding rather than later. It can be properly argued that the after tax interest cost of 2.4 per cent $(0.04(1 - 0.4))$ should be used to accomplish the discounting for time. The use of this discount rate gives:

Present value of net savings	$1,520 (8.983) = $13,654
Tax savings first year	1,600 (0.980) = 1,568
Present value of savings, allowing for taxes	$15,222

The solutions suggested here are based on the assumption that the future tax rates will be the same as the present rate of 40 per cent. If a change in rates is expected, this should be incorporated into the solution.

15.4.3 Extension of Maturity of Debt and Changes in Interest Rates

New issues often extend the maturity of the debt, that is, they push the date of repayment further into the future. All other things being equal, this is desirable, since it reduces the payment pressure accompanying a debt of early maturity.

How does a firm place a dollar value on the fact that the maturity date of the debt is now 1980 instead of 1975? One compromise procedure is to incorporate this factor as a qualitative factor to be considered in favor of refunding if refunding is not clearly advantageous following the quantitative analysis. Alternatively, a monetary value could be estimated and incorporated into the analysis.

15.4.4 Bond Discount

What is the relevance of an unaccumulated bond discount to the refunding decision? The book value of the liability is not relevant to the refunding decision, except through its effect on income taxes. This situation is analogous to the analysis of equipment replacement, where the book value of the asset being replaced is not relevant to the decision except as it affects taxes. Since the bond discount is a valuation account to the face value of the debt, it is not relevant to the refunding decision. This is true no matter how the discount has been accumulated through the years. What is relevant is the impact of the promise to pay an amount in n years and the promise to pay interest for n years. The present value of these promises represents the true liability; the liability recorded on the company's books does not. The computations of the preceding sections appraising refunding were made without reference to the accounting records to determine the balance in the discount account. Whether a book gain or loss will be suffered in the year of refunding as a result of the decision is not relevant to making the decision, if the appropriate computations indicate that refunding is desirable.

The presence of bond discount on the books may result in a loss on retirement of the outstanding bonds. This should be taken into consideration in computing the tax savings of the first year. Since it will increase the tax loss, the presence of bond discount, which is deductible for tax purposes, increases the tax saving and makes refunding more desirable.

15.4.5 Bond Refunding Under Uncertainty

The discussion up to this point has assumed that the contractual interest rate of the debt and the present effective interest rate, which is some rate less than the contractual rate, are given. A more complex problem to solve is whether to refund as soon as the rate of interest falls below a refunding break-even rate, or whether it is more desirable to wait for a further drop in the interest rate. Thus the contractual rate may be 4 per cent, and computations may show that the firm would break-even if it refunded when the bond interest rate fell to 3 per cent. The question remains whether it is desirable to refund if the present rate is 2.9 per cent or wait hoping the rate will drop still lower.

Assume a bond is issued at a contractual rate of 0.04 (a \$1,000 bond paying \$40 a year).[16] If the market rate falls to some rate of interest r_b, the firm just breaks even on refunding with another debt issue that yields r_b. Until the interest rate falls to r_b, the firm has a relatively easy refunding decision; refunding is not desirable. The basic formula giving the conditional net savings from refunding in any period i without considering taxes is:

$$S_{r',i} = (r_c - r')DA_{\overline{n-i}|r'} - C_i + L_i. \tag{15.3}$$

---

[16] The future interest rate is treated here as a discrete random variable.

In the above equation the symbols have the following meaning:

$i = 0, 1, \ldots, n.$

r_c = contractual rate of present outstanding securities.

r' = current interest rate.

$A_{\overline{n-i}|r'}$ = present value of annuity of \$1 a period for $n-i$ periods discounted at r' rate of interest.

C_i = refunding cost (call premiums and bond issue costs), this amount may depend on the period in which the refunding occurs.

D = the maturity value of the debt and the basis for computing the interest payments.

L_i = monetary value placed on lengthening of debt accomplished by refunding. This amount may also depend on when the refunding occurs.

When the break-even rate for the present or zero time period $r_{b,0}$ is inserted for r', equation (15.3) becomes

$$(r_c - r_{b,0})DA_{\overline{n}|r_{b,0}} - C_0 + L_0 = 0. \tag{15.4}$$

The break-even rate can be obtained by trial and error. Since $r_{b,0}$ is a function of the remaining life of the old issue, it must be recomputed each time the refunding decision is considered. (It need be computed only once, however, for a particular period's refunding decision.) The refunding cost, C_i, and the monetary value placed on lengthening the debt are likely to be a function of the time when refunding occurs.

If the interest rate falls below the break-even rate, the firm has to decide whether to refund immediately or to wait in hopes of a still lower rate in the present or some future period. Suppose that management has definite opinions about the probability distribution of the rate in the next and each succeeding time period conditional on the present rate, $r' < r_{b,0}$. The probability mass function for the interest rate in each period given the existing rate, r', can be denoted by $f_R(r \mid r', i)$ where $i = 0, 1, \ldots, n$. Given this information the present expected saving conditional on refunding in each future period can be written as[17]

$$\bar{S}_{r,i} = \left\{ \sum_r [(r_c - r)DA_{\overline{n-i}|r} - C_i + L_i]f_R(r \mid r', i) \right\}(1 + r)^{-i} \tag{15.5}$$

For $i = 0$, equation (15.5) gives the saving from immediate refunding where the probability that $r = r'$ is one. The alternative action is to wait, at least until the next period or until there is a change in the interest rate, whichever

[17] If the future rate of interest is treated as a continuous variable, integration with respect to r replaces summation.

occurs first. The action "wait" should be elected if $\bar{S}_{r,i} > \bar{S}_{r',0}$ for any $i > 0$. Thus, if $\bar{S}_{r,0} = \$10,000$; $\bar{S}_{r,1} = \$9,000$; $\bar{S}_{r,2} = \$11,000$, then refunding should be delayed even if all values of $\bar{S}_{r,i}$ for $i > 2$ are less than \$10,000 using the expected values to make the decision. It does not imply, however, that refunding must wait until period 2. Changes in the interest rate in period i could lead to earlier refunding. If interest rates change, the expected savings of future periods should be recomputed.

The next step in the solution would be to test different decision rules for each period. The decision rules are conditional on the state of the period (that is, on the actual interest rate of the period). Thus in period 2, even if $\bar{S}_{r,2}$ were the greatest expected value, a decision to refund would not be made if the actual rate was above the break-even rate. Taken to its logical conclusion this approach would lead to a dynamic programming approach to the bond-refunding problem.[18]

15.5   Summary

This chapter described the application of capital-budgeting techniques to the optimal plant size, the make-or-buy, the evaluation of investments with inflation and foreign investments, and the bond-refunding decisions. The wide range of decisions discussed illustrates the multitude of possibilities that exist for applying capital-budgeting procedures. Any decision where the results (cash outlays or inflows) are spread out through time is susceptible to solution by using these tools.

QUESTIONS AND PROBLEMS

15–1 Distinguish between determining the optimal size plant and the optimal size firm.

15–2 Is it better to build a small plant and work it intensively (with overtime and double time) or to build a large plant and sometimes have idle capacity?

15–3 Is the plant which offers the highest rate of return (yield) the most desirable plant (in a set of mutually exclusive alternatives)?

15–4 Assume a firm has two alternatives:
  a. Plant A promises to earn a net present value of \$10 million with certainty (assume this is a cost-plus government contract). Instead of plant A, a lárger plant, plant B, could be built.

[18] The bond-refunding problem can also be considered as a dynamic programming problem. See H. M. Weingartner, "Optimal Timing of Bond Refunding," *Management Science*, March 1967, pp. 511–524.

b. Plant B may earn a net present value of $50 million (this outcome has a 0.5 probability) or it may return a negative net present value of $20 million (this outcome also has a 0.5 probability).

Which of the two plants is preferable? Assume the firm's yearly earnings have averaged $5 million a year.

15–5 To make a product, inventories must be increased by a total of $5 million for each year. Should this be considered a cash outlay? Should it be considered as part of the investment to make the product?

15–6 Would you expect the relevant costs for decision making (such as the make-or-buy decision) to be higher or lower than the accounting costs computed on an absorption-costing basis?

15–7 In making the bond-refunding decision should the present value of any interest savings be computed using the cost of capital?

15–8 How does the presence of discount on the bonds which are presently outstanding affect the bond-refunding decision?

15–9 If the new debt will extend the maturity of the debt, how does this affect the bond-refunding decision?

15–10 What are the uncertainties connected with the bond-refunding decision?

15–11 If the present value of the savings are larger than the present value of the outlays connected with refunding, should the decision be to refund? Explain.

15–12 The Tin Can Company must choose between two plants. One is large and has sufficient capacity for working efficiently at the higher ranges of possible sales estimates. The other plant is smaller and is more efficient at lower ranges of sales, but is less efficient if sales are high. The net present values of the two plants are shown with different assumed budgeted sales levels. The probability of attaining that level of sales is also shown.

Level of Expected Sales (as a per cent of budgeted sales)	Probability	Present Value	
		Large Plant	Small Plant
150%	0.10	$50,000,000	$40,000,000
100%	0.70	35,000,000	30,000,000
50%	0.20	(10,000,000)	20,000,000

Required: Which of the two plants should the company build based on the information presented?

15–13 The Ashcot Company has $10 million of debt outstanding which pays 0.05 (that is, $500,000) interest annually. The maturity date of the securities is twenty years from the present.

Assume that a new twenty-year security could be issued which would yield 0.04 per year. The issue costs would be $800,000 and the call premium on redemption of the old bonds is $100,000. Assume a zero tax rate for this company. The cost of capital for the firm is 0.10.

Required: Should the present bonds be refunded?

15–14 (See problem 15–13.) If the corporate income tax marginal rate is 0.52, is the refunding desirable? Use 0.04 as the discount rate in making these computations.

15–15 (See problem 15–13.) How would your answer be modified if the maturity date of the new issue were thirty years instead of twenty years?

15–16 The Bond Company has $10 million of debt outstanding which pays 0.06 annually. The maturity date of the securities is twenty years from the present.

Assume that new securities could be issued which would have the same maturity date. The issue costs of the new securities would be $2.7 million; there is no call premium on the present debt. Assume a zero tax rate.

Required: Determine the rate of interest or yield rate of new securities at which the firm would just break-even if they refunded. Determine this rate to the nearest per cent.

15–17 Assume the same facts as in problem 15–16 except that the issue costs of the new securities are $1,246,000 and that the cost of borrowing at present is 0.05. An analysis of interest-rate changes projected for the near future indicates the following probabilities:

Rate of Interest r	Probability of the Actual Rate of Interest Being Equal to r in the Very Near Future
0.06	0.30
0.05	0.40
0.04	0.20
0.03	0.10
0.02	0.00

Required: Should the firm delay refunding in hopes that the rate will drop?

15–18 The Cascade Company has $1 million of debt outstanding which pays 0.05 interest annually. The maturity date of the securities is twenty years from the present.

Assume that a new twenty-year security could be issued which would yield 0.04 per year. The issue costs would be $800,000, and the call premium on redemption of the old bonds is $200,000. The vice-president for finance suggests that the firm wait until the interest rate goes down to 0.03. An analysis of management's opinions indicate the following:

Length of Time Until an Interest Rate of 0.03 is Reached	Probability of Occurrence
Immediately to 0.5 years	0.10
0.5 to 1.5 years	0.10
1.5 to 2.5 years	0.20
2.5 to 3.5 years	0.10
Over 20 years	0.50
	1.00

Assume a zero tax rate for this company.

Required: Prepare an analysis showing whether it is more desirable to refund now or delay. Take the average time to maturity (for example, for 1.5 to 2.5 years take 2 years) except for immediately to 0.5 years where you can assume an immediate change. Assume the issue costs and call premium remain constant for the being years considered. (Note: The problem ignores other possible rates and changes in the probabilities over time.)

15-19 The Alcott Company operates in a foreign country and has found that it can borrow money at an indicated interest rate of 0.20. It is considering borrowing $1.5 million for a period of one year. The current price index is 150 and the price index is expected to increase to 180 at the end of the year.

   a. What is the expected real interest rate of the borrowed money?

   b. If the $1 million can be invested in the foreign country to yield $1.7 million at the end of one year, is the investment acceptable? Assume the company uses a 0.10 cost of capital for investment decisions in the United States.

   c. If the 1.5 million is already on hand in the foreign country and if there are exchange restrictions preventing the withdrawal of the funds, is the investment described in part b acceptable?

15-20 The Cranston Company operates in a foreign country and has found that it can borrow money at an indicated interest rate of 0.30. The current price index is 100 and the price index is expected to increase to 120. What is the real interest rate?

15-21 In recent years in most countries a 0.15 return after taxes would generally be considered an excellent rate of return. If the cash flows projected for an investment in a country with a large amount of inflation promised a return of 0.15, the investment might not be acceptable from an economic point of view. Explain why this difference exists.

SUPPLEMENTARY READING

BIERMAN, H., and S. SMIDT, *The Capital Budgeting Decision*, New York: Macmillan, 1971.

DEAN, JOEL, *Capital Budgeting*, New York: Columbia University Press, 1951.

GUPTA, S., and J. ROSENHEAD, "Robustness in Sequential Investment Decisions," *Management Science*, October 1968, pp. 18–29.

HAMMOND, J., "Better Decisions with Preference Theory," *The Harvard Business Review*, November–December 1967, pp. 123–141.

HERTZ, D., "Investment Policies that Pay Off," *The Harvard Business Review*, January–February 1968, pp. 96–108.

HESPOS, R., and P. STRASSMAN, "Stochastic Decision Trees for the Analysis of Investment Decisions," *Management Science*, August 1965, pp. 244–259.

HILLIER, F. S., "The Derivation of Probabilistic Information for the Evaluation of Risky Investments," *Management Science*, April 1963, pp. 443–457.

LUTZ, F., and V. LUTZ, *The Theory of Investment of the Firm*, Princeton, N.J.: Princeton University Press, 1951.

MAGEE, J., "How to Use Decision Trees in Capital Investment," *The Harvard Business Review*, September–October 1964, pp. 79–96.

QUERIN, G. D., *The Capital Expenditure Decision*, Homewood, Ill.: R. D. Irwin, 1967.

ROBICHECK, A. A., and S. C. MYERS, *Optimal Financing Decisions*, Englewood Cliffs, N.J.: Prentice-Hall, 1965.

Chapter 16

Utility and Capital Budgeting

Solutions to capital-budgeting decisions frequently assume that the cash flows of all periods are known with certainty. If this assumption is not explicitly made, then an implicit assumption of a mean value is made; that is, the expected value, or what might be called, inaccurately, the best guess of the cash flows. The solution generally accepted among academic authors and a growing number of businessmen is that the present-value method gives the most useful information. If the present value of the cash flows is positive, then the investment is acceptable if it is independent of other investments. If a set of investments are mutually exclusive, then the investment with the largest net present value is the most desirable, assuming the investment periods under consideration are comparable.

Many business firms use the cost of capital (a weighted average of the cost of interest bearing debt and the cost of stock) as the discount rate applied to the expected value of the cash flows. This means of solution can be criticized on two counts. First, the use of the cost of capital incorporates an implicit allowance for risk of a very special nature which is compounded through time. But risk does not necessarily increase at a compound rate through time. Second, it is not always appropriate to consider, as this approach implicitly does, only the expected value of the cash flows and to ignore the other possible values. The notion of risk really has two parts. One involves the fact that more than one thing may occur. This is uncertainty. The other is that the impact of the outcomes on the manager or investor may not be adequately represented by the associated monetary values. This chapter presents a method for separating these two factors so that they may be more appropriately handled. In this respect this chapter departs from the discussion in Chapters 13–15 where the terminology "cost of money" was used explicitly to avoid this problem.

16.1   Investment Decisions under Uncertainty

The present-value method gives information that allows management needs to accept or reject independent investments and to choose the best of mutually exclusive investments. Under conditions of certainty and where the amounts involved are not too large, this information is sufficient for management to make its decisions. But under conditions of uncertainty involving large amounts of money the present-value procedure does not yield a sufficient measure of the desirability of an investment. The capital budgeting method should take risk attitudes into consideration.[1] Utility theory combined with probability theory provides a possible approach.

Assume an investor or manager is offered the choice between two alternatives (or gambles), call them A and B.[2]

Alternative A	Alternative B
0.50 probability of $1,000	1.0 probability of $X
0.50 probability of $0	

For the investor or manager to be *indifferent* between the two alternatives A and B, what value of X should be inserted in the description of alternative B? If it is less than $500, he is somewhat averse to gambling in this situation.[3] If X is more than $500, he requires something for forsaking the opportunity of winning $1,000. The expected monetary value of alternative A is $500. If he is indifferent between alternative A and $500 certain, it is said that his utility function is linear in this range of values.

The point of indifference for many investors and managers occurs when X is less than $500.[4] That is, they are willing to accept a certain sum of less than $500 in place of the gamble represented by alternative A. Questions similar

---

[1] Another consideration is the timing of the information.

[2] Any investment under uncertainty may be thought of as a gamble.

[3] Someone adverse to gambles is someone who would equate a gamble to a certain value less than the gamble's monetary expectation.

[4] If a manager makes decisions on expected monetary values, an increase in the amounts involved may tend to elicit the indicated response.

to the above may be used to determine the entire utility function. For example, assume the following relationship:

$$U(\$X) = 0.5U(\$0) + 0.5U(\$1{,}000)$$

where $U(\$X)$ is the utility of X dollars.

Arbitrarily setting the utility of $0 to be 0 and the utility of $1,000 to be 1, and assuming that the value chosen by the manager for X is $300:[5]

$$U(\$300) = 0.5(0) + 0.5(1) = 0.5$$

The utility of $300 is equal to 0.5. Now suppose the manager is given a chance on a gamble involving $1,000 or $300, both with probabilities 0.5.

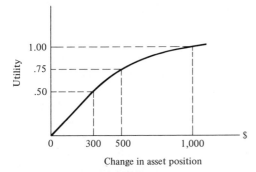

Figure 16.1   A utility function

The monetary expectation of this gamble is $650, but assume the manager is adverse to risk and is willing to accept as little as $500 for certain in place of the gamble. Therefore

$$U(\$500) = 0.5U(\$1{,}000) + 0.5U(\$300) = 0.5(1) + 0.5(0.5) = 0.75.$$

The utility of $500 is 0.75. By asking the manager a variety of similar questions, the entire function can be determined.[6] See Figure 16.1 for an assumed utility function.

The horizontal axis measures the change in the asset position. The vertical axis measures the utility of the change. The utility function shows the utility of different possible changes for an individual. The utility function should be

[5] The first two utility values chosen are arbitrary; that is, the origin and interval scale are not unique. Technically a utility function is unique up to a linear transformation. The choice of a utility of zero for an outcome at least as bad as the worst outcome in the decision situation and unity for an outcome at least as favorable as the best outcome in the decision situation are common but not necessary choices.

[6] The reader is referred to Appendix 16A for an explanation of the procedure's logic.

checked for validity before it is used. This might be done by asking questions concerning gambles implied by the function. Preciseness should not be expected, but perhaps a usable utility function may be obtained. If the utility function is linear, then expected monetary values are a reasonable measure of the desirability of an investment. This is not the case for the present manager: he is adverse to risk. The marginal utility to him for large gains is positive and decreasing.[7]

16.2   Using the Utility Function

Consider again alternative A, described in Section 16.1 as having a 0.5 probability of $0 and a 0.5 probability of $1,000. Assume that the utility of these uncertain payoffs can be read from the utility function of Figure 16.1 (say the utilities are zero and one, respectively). The expected utility is 0.5, 0.5(0) + 0.5 (1.0), in this case. The next step is to determine the certainty equivalent of the gamble. The certainty equivalent is $300 (the utility of $300 is 0.5). The certainty equivalent can be obtained from the graph by entering the vertical axis at 0.5 and finding the value of the asset change on the horizontal axis that has a utility index of 0.5.

The expected monetary value of alternative A is equal to $500, 0.5 ($1,000) + 0.5 (0). Its certainty equivalent is $200 less than the expected monetary value; thus the manager attaches a $200 discount for risk to this alternative.

The discount for risk arises because the monetary values of $1,000 and $0 do not adequately represent the impact of these changes on the manager. If they did there would be no discount. Thus, if the utility function were linear, the expected monetary value of alternative A would have a certainty equivalent of $500. Uncertainty alone then is not sufficient to produce a discount for risk: there must also be an aversion to risk. The information could be presented as follows:

Expected monetary value of alternative	$500
Certainty equivalent	300
Discount for Risk	$200

The general procedure for one gamble may be summarized as follows:

1. Determine the utility of each discrete event (say, possible earnings of $0 and $1,000).
2. Compute the expected utility of the alternative by weighting the utilities of each event by the probability of occurrence.

[7] It is generally assumed that the utility function is bounded from above (i.e., that it approaches a maximum amount).

3. Find the asset change with the same utility as the expected utility. This is the certainty equivalent.
4. Compute the expected monetary value of the investment. Compare the expected monetary value and the certainty equivalent to obtain the discount for risk.

16.3 Complex Alternatives

Instead of one gamble with a 0.5 probability of $1,000 and a 0.5 probability of $0, assume there is an opportunity to enter into two identical gambles (A_1 and A_2) of this nature. Suppose the manager must decide to reject both or engage in both—he cannot accept one gamble and reject the other. Assume the utility function given in Table 16–1 is now relevant.[8]

Table 16–1 Assumed Utility Function

Dollars	Utility Measures for Changes in His Asset Position
$-400	0.00
-200	0.40
0	0.60
75	0.685
200	0.75
300	0.80
500	0.86
600	0.88
800	0.91
1,000	0.95
1,600	0.98
2,000	1.00

Suppose the manager must pay $400 for the opportunity to engage in this double gamble. The double gamble has three possible outcomes. The outcomes together with the expected utilify of the total gamble are given in Table 16–2. The two gambles are independent.

The certainty equivalent for this gamble from Table 16–1 exceeds zero and the gamble would be accepted. This can be determined by comparing the expected utility of the gamble, 0.685 with the utility of $0, which is 0.60. The fact that the certainty equivalent exceeds zero implies that the investor would be willing to pay something to engage in this gamble. If the utility function

[8] A utility function can be developed either for the various asset positions of the decision maker or for changes in the asset position. The latter is done here. It is often assumed that the function so obtained is relevant over a range of initial asset positions for the given decision maker.

were more completely specified, a good approximation of this amount could be determined.

Suppose, however, that the two identical gambles are separable and each requires an investment of $200. An immediate decision is still required for

Table 16–2 Expected Utility Computation: Double Gamble

1 Outcome	2 Probability of Outcome	3 Utility of Outcome	4 Column 2 × Column 3
− $400	0.25	0.00	0.000
600	0.50	0.88	0.440
1,600	0.25	0.98	0.245
		Expected utility	0.685

each investment. Three alternatives exist: namely, accept one gamble, accept both gambles, or reject both gambles. The expected utility of accepting both gambles has just been calculated in Table 16–2 to be 0.685. The utility of rejecting both gambles is 0.60, the utility of $0 net change. The utility from selecting only one of the component gambles is

$$0.5U(-\$200) + 0.5U(+\$800) = 0.5(0.40) + 0.5(0.91) = 0.655$$

which is less than the utility of undertaking both gambles.

The certainty equivalent of this double gamble is $75. The expected utility of accepting double gamble is the greatest of the three choices. The reader may be surprised that the single-gamble alternative yields a lower expected utility given a manager with an aversion to risk. This result is due to the nature of the assumed utility function and the fact that each gamble is relatively desirable.

As a final possibility suppose that the constituent gambles follow one another and that a decision can be made concerning gamble A_2 after the result of gamble A_1 is known. Since a single gamble here has an expected utility of 0.655 which exceeds the utility of doing nothing, 0.60, gamble A_1 should be accepted. Whether gamble A_2 should be accepted depends on the change, if any, in the investor's utility function due to the results of gamble A_1. If the utility function for changes in his asset position is essentially unaffected by the result of the first gamble, the second gamble will also have a utility index of 0.655 and be acceptable.

In none of the above cases is it correct to assume that the expected utility of immediately accepting both gambles A_1 and A_2 is twice 0.655 (the utility of one of the two constituent gambles). This would incorrectly assume that $U(A_1 + A_2) = U(A_1) + U(A_2)$, a condition that holds only for linear utility functions. It is also incorrect to assign the double gamble a certainty equivalent of twice the certainty equivalent of one of the constituent gambles, since this assumes $E[U(A_1 + A_2)] = E[U(A_1)] + E[U(A_2)]$. This relation also holds generally only for linear utility functions.

The components of a gamble cannot usually be separated, evaluated, and then recombined. This has relevance to the investor considering several investment simultaneously and to the manager involved in selecting a set of capital projects at a point in time.

The general procedure is to:

1. List all the possible monetary outcomes.
2. Determine the probability of each outcome.
3. Assign utility measures to each outcome.
4. Compute the expected utility of the gamble.

The sum of money with this expected utility is called the certainty equivalent. Decisions between alternatives can be made using the expected utilities or the certainty equivalents.

Instead of finding the certainty equivalent the manager might be interested in finding the amount he would be willing to pay for the privilege of gambling. There is no reason to assume that this amount is equal to the certainty equivalent. That is, the amount the investor is willing to make as an outlay may be different from the amount he would be willing to accept for certain in lieu of the gamble.

Example
Ask yourself how much you would be willing to pay for one of the gambles described above. Also ask yourself the minimum amount you would be willing to accept for certain rather than gambling (one gamble). Compare your two answers.

16.4 Time Discounting

Most investments differ from the gamble described above, since the benefits do not occur instantaneously but are spread out through time. The situation involving the double gamble could, for example, be thought of as a two-period investment, the outlay occurring in period 0, the first gamble in period 1, and the second gamble in period 2. Instead of dealing with immediate amounts, the investor must concern himself with inflows and outflows that take place over different time periods. In addition, the outcomes connected with the investment will require utility measures.

The theory dealt with so far in this chapter is not easily applied to long-run investments where the cash flows are significantly separated in time, and where the date of resolution of the uncertainty is very important. Where the date when the outcome is known is important, the necessary time adjustments cannot be adequately made by discounting because some evaluations depend upon information obtained near the resolution date. Further, some alternatives permit strategic information to be obtained earlier than do others. While progress is being made on these issues, practically useful and theoretically satisfying methods are not yet available.

16.4.1 Independent Cash Flows

One method that has appeal and that offers a reasonable approximation requires that all cash flows for a given project first be discounted for time. If, for the moment, the yearly cash flows can be considered independent events, a computation of the present values of all possible cash flows together with their probabilities can be made. After converting the present value of the cash flows associated with each possible set of events into utility measures, a decision can be based on the expected utility calculations.

There remains the problem of choice of rate of interest used in the discounting. In computing present values, managers frequently use the cost of capital. The possibility of the cash flow not being realized and the reaction of the investor to this possibility are assumed to be effectively incorporated into the analysis using this rate. The use of the cost of capital (which implicitly incorporates a risk allowance) is assumed to take "normal" risk into consideration. With the proposed procedure the possibility that the cash flow will not occur is taken into account by the probabilities, and the investor's reaction to the monetary amounts involved is taken into account via the utility function. Thus it is now appropriate to use a default-free measure for time discounting, say, the interest rate associated with long-term government securities. This rate combined with an explicit statement of the probabilities, is a more effective way of incorporating uncertainty into the analysis than using different rates of discount for different investments or ignoring uncertainty entirely.[9]

Assume a situation where the investment consists of the cash flows given in Table 16–3 (assume the cash flows of each period are independent).

In Figure 16.2, the investment under consideration is represented by a tree diagram. Using a default-free discount rate of 0.05, the figures after the colons show the present values of the possible results. The probability of each outcome in this case is $(0.5)(0.5) = 0.25$.

---

[9] Some authors prefer to consider risk in terms of the variance (and sometimes higher moments) of the return distribution. This method is perhaps easier from the point of view of calculations but it does not provide a clear indication of just how the risk is being weighted. In part this is because risk has two elements, namely, the uncertainty of the cash flow, a probabilistic problem, and the inability in some cases to measure the impact of events on the decision maker with a single quantitative measure, money.

Now if the monetary values calculated at the end of the tree are valid measures of the impact of the outcomes on the decision maker, the expected value of the investment, $0.25(-\$400) + 0.25(\$507) + 0.25 (\$552) + 0.25$

Table 16–3   Investment Cash Flows

Period	Proceeds
0	($400) outlay
1	0.5 probability of $0 and 0.5 probability of $1,000
2	0.5 probability of $0 and 0.5 probability of $1,000

($1,459) = $539, can be used as the value of this investment in decision making. Since the net expected value is positive the investment is desirable.

If, on the other hand, the amounts are too large to be treated in this manner, or if other considerations are involved, the monetary outcomes must be

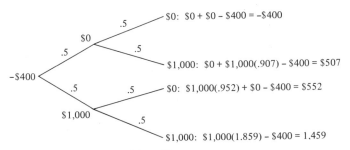

Figure 16.2   Investment tree diagram

converted into utilities. Assume that the utilities of Table 16–1 apply for the present decision maker. Approximation yields the values in Table 16–4.
The expected utility of the investment exceeds the utility of the decision maker's present asset position ($U(\$0) = 0.60$), and therefore the investment is desirable.

Table 16–4   Expected Utility Calculations

1 Net Present Value	2 Utility	3 Probability	4 (Col. 2) × (Col. 3)
– $400	0.00	0.25	0.00
507	0.86	0.25	0.2150
552	0.87	0.25	0.2175
1,459	0.97	0.25	0.2425
		Expected utility =	0.6750

The advantage of this procedure is that it takes into consideration both the probabilities of different events occurring and the reaction of management to the different possible events. Large negative present values would have relatively small (possibly negative) utility measures and thus would be appropriately weighted in computing the expected utility of the investment.

The expected utility of the investment is 0.675. Using Table 16–1, the change-in-asset position which has a utility of 0.675 can be approximated. The value is about $70, that is, $U(\$70)$ is approximately 0.675. This means that the manager should be willing to sell this investment opportunity for $70. Furthermore, using the expected monetary values of the investment and a discount rate of 0.05, the investment has an expected net present value of $539. The discount for risk is therefore $469.

Expected monetary value (present value with 0.05 as rate of discount)	$539
Certainty equivalent of net present value	70
Discount for risk	$469

The $469 is the amount deducted from the present value of the investment because the monetary values of the outcomes are not valid indicators of the impact of the outcomes on the decision maker.

16.4.2 Dependent Cash Flows

In the previous examples it was assumed that the cash flows of the second period were independent of the results of the first period; the results of the second gamble were independent of the results of the first gamble. Now assume the dependency in Table 16–5 exists.

Table 16–5 Investment with Dependent Cash Flows

Period	Proceeds
0	($400) outlay
1	0.5 probability of $0, and 0.5 probability of $1,000
2	Same cash flows as period 1

The relevant tree diagram is given in Figure 16–3:
The expected value of the cash flows is

$$0.5(-\$400) + 0.5(\$1,459) = \$550,$$

which is reasonably close to the previous expectation. From an expected monetary calculation the investment is still desirable. If utilities are computed, the expected utility of this investment, again using Table 16–1, is

$$0.5(0) + 0.5(0.97) = 0.485.$$

Since the utility of the decision maker's present asset position, $0 net change, is 0.6, the investment is not desirable. The change in decision from the previous situation is due to the assumed dependency in the cash flows.

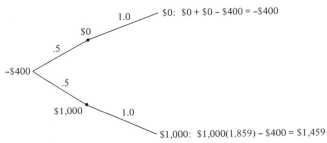

Figure 16.3 **Compound investment diagram**

Dependency of the type illustrated tends to lead to the probability of larger profits and larger losses; the more moderate possibilities are eliminated. This reduces the desirability of the investment if the utility function is one which reflects increasing marginal aversion to losses and decreasing marginal utility to gains as is the case for the function in Table 16–1.

16.4.3 Continuous Probability Distributions

Most of the examples developed in this chapter assume that only two events are possible in each of the operating periods. The possible number of events can be increased to as large a number as desired. In fact the number of events may be infinite; instead of a series of discrete probabilities (a probability mass function), a probability density function may be relevant. With a density function, earnings may take on any value within certain limits.

The procedure using a probability density function is essentially the same as previously illustrated with one modification. Because the utility function is difficult to express mathematically, it may be easier to simulate the expected utility of the earnings of each time period.

Assume, for example, that the net cash flows of a period are normally distributed, with a mean of $10,000 and a standard deviation of $3,000. The simulation procedure is as follows. Take a number, say, *d*, from a table of standard normal deviates (or have an electronic computer generate the number). The number d is the number of standard deviations from the mean. It is necessary to convert the number d to a cash-flow observation.

$$Y = \bar{M} + d\sigma$$

where Y is the cash-flow observation, $\bar{M}$ the mean cash-flow, d the random observation, and σ the standard deviation. Say d is equal to -1.5, the first observation is

$$Y = 10,000 - 1.5(3,000)$$
$$Y = \$5,500.$$

The \$5,500 earnings would then be discounted back to the present. The cash flow for each period would be computed with separate random selections and discounted back to the present and the present value summed for one trial life. This assumes the cash flows of each period are independent.

The utility function for the manager (see Figure 16.1 for example) could be used to determine the utility for the net present value of each draw (this is sometimes referred to as a Monte-Carlo simulation). The process would be repeated for many trials and the utility for each trial (each trial leading to a present value) would be recorded. The sum of these utilities divided by the number of observations gives the average utility of the uncertain earnings. The last step is to convert the average utility to a certainty equivalent in the same manner used to find the certainty equivalent of \$70 for the expected utility of 0.675. Enter the vertical axis at the value of the average utility and read the value on the horizontal axis which has that value of utility. An investment with an expected utility greater than $U(\$0) = 60$ would be an acceptable investment. Furthermore, the expected utilities could be used to make a choice between two investments.

It is not necessary to assume that the earnings are normally distributed. Other continuous probability distributions could be used (though often with more difficulty).

16.4.4 A Mathematical Solution

If the cash flows of each period are considered to be independent of one another, it is possible to obtain mathematically a distribution of the net present value of the investment and to use this as the basis of the expected utility computation.

Assume the appropriate rate of discount is r, the cash flow of period i is Y_i, and the variance of the cash flows of the ith period is σ_i^2. The mean value of the cash flows of the ith period is $\bar{Y}_i$, and the mean value of the distribution of net present values is

$$\text{Mean} = \sum_{i=0}^{n} (1 + r)^{-i} \bar{Y}_i. \tag{16.1}$$

The variance of the net present value distribution (with independent flows) is given by:

$$\sigma^2 = \sum_{t=0}^{n} (1 + r)^{-2t} \sigma_i^2.$$ (16.2)

It should be noted that the discount factor in equation (16.2) is raised to an exponent equal to twice the number of periods. For example, consider the values in Table 16–6.

Table 16–6   Characteristic of an Investment

Period	Mean Value Cash Flow	Standard Deviation of the Cash Flow
0	$ – 1,600	100
1	1,000	200
2	2,000	300

The mean value of the distribution of the present value is equal to the present value of the mean values of each period. This value is computed in Table 16–7 using a 0.05 rate of discount.

Table 16–7   Calculation of Mean Value

Period	Mean Value	Discount Factor	Present Value
0	$ – 1,600	1.0000	$ – 1,600
1	1,000	0.9524	952
2	2,000	0.9070	1,814
		Mean =	$ 1,166

The computation of the variance of the distribution of net present values is similar to the mean calculation except that the discount factor is raised to twice the period rather than the number of the period. The calculations are given in Table 16–8.

Table 16–8   Variance Calculation

Period	Square of Standard Deviation	Discount Factor $(1 + r)^{-2t}$	Product
0	10,000	1.0000	10,000
1	40,000	0.9070	36,280
2	90,000	0.8227	74,043
		Variance =	120,323

The square of the standard deviation (or the variance) is equal to 120,323. The standard deviation is therefore equal to approximately 347. With the standard deviation and the mean value of the probability distribution it is possible to determine the utility of this investment by the simulation method illustrated in Section 16.4.3.

16.5 The Law of Large Numbers and Investments

An approximate statement of the law of large numbers is that if the probability of a success is p on any one trial, and if a large number of trials are performed, the proportion of successes will differ from p by a very small amount. If a fair coin is tossed, the probability of a head is 0.5, but

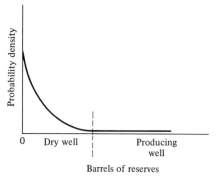

Figure 16.4   Drilling one well

after tossing the coin once there is a 0.5 probability that the proportion of heads observed so far is zero (that the coin came up tails). If the coin is tossed a million times, the proportion of heads will be very close to 0.5. Even though the number of heads will no doubt differ from 500,000, the number of heads divided by the number of tosses will be close to 0.5.

This law of probability can be applied to investment analysis. Consider drilling for oil. If an independent organization raises enough capital to drill one well, the probability of an economic well may be 0.1, and the probability of the equivalent of a dry well may be 0.9. Taking into consideration the entire range of possibilities, the distribution of outcomes may appear as in Figure 16.4.

Figure 16.4 shows a high probability that the one well will be nonproducing. If, instead of an independent driller, one of the major oil companies drills 500 wells during the year, then the probability distribution of the possible events is different. There is a very small probability that all 500 wells will be dry and there is an even smaller probability that all five hundred will be producers. Figure 16.5 shows how the probability distribution of barrels of reserves per well will change; a very important observation is that the variance of the reserves per well decreases as the number of wells drilled increases. The variance of the distribution of the proportion of successful wells drilled also decreases as the number of wells drilled increases.

By drilling a large number of wells an oil company can eliminate the rather large possibility of complete failure that is present with drilling a single well. Furthermore, an expert can predict the proportion of producing wells to be found by drilling 500 wells and come reasonably close to his prediction (the variance in his prediction will be small). The same manager's prediction about the results of drilling any one well could be completely off; that is, the well could be dry, or it could be a producer. Thus, in one sense, the drilling of a large number of wells decreases the risk associated with drilling for oil.

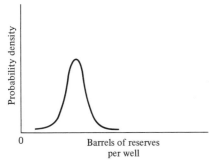

Figure 16.5　Drilling 500 wells

It is possible for an investor's utility function to be such that he would not be willing to finance completely the drilling of one well where only one well was to be drilled, but he would be willing to participate in the drilling of the 500 wells to the extent of buying 1/500 of the ownership. For this reason large oil companies may be considered reasonable investments by individuals who are essentially conservative in their investment policies.

16.6　An Appraisal of the Procedure

The procedure described in this chapter has several weaknesses. First, it assumes the same utility function is relevant for series of investments. This weakness can be corrected conceptually by changing the utility function as investments are accepted. Carrying this out operationally in a meaningful manner is likely to be quite difficult.

The assumption was made in all except one example that the cash flows of each period were independent. This assumption can be changed readily without damaging the basic analysis, though the details of calculation are modified. However, the decision process becomes much more complex if the acceptance of one investment changes the expected cash flows of other investments and if it is recognized that the acceptance of one investment affects the willingness of an investor to accept further investments.

The suggested procedure for solving decision problems involving several time periods offers a method of incorporating attitudes toward outcomes that is more effective than just using the one cash flow figure as is done in the conventional present-value procedure. Making decisions on the basis of monetary expectations is reasonable if the dollar amounts involved are small. The underlying assumption is that the utility function is linear with respect to money when the dollar amounts are small. However, if the amounts are large in relation to the magnitude of operations of the entity making the decision, then expected utility is usually more appropriate for making decisions than expected monetary values. This can also be true if other factors surrounding an investment are important and not measurable in terms of marginal adjustments in the cash flows.

One by-product of the utility approach is that it permits a default-free discount rate to be used in computing the present value. This eliminates the necessity of computing the cost of capital. More important, the risk of an investment is brought directly and systematically into the analysis (though separate from the time discounting).

Despite the fact that the determination of the utility function for the manager(s) of a corporation is not well defined, it is still desirable that some assumption relative to the utility function be made and that decisions be made that are consistent with that function. If this is not done, it is implicitly assumed that the utility function is linear. No organization has a utility function which is linear over all possible outcomes; thus the technique presented in this chapter has relevance to all organizations. The measure used to indicate the desirability (or acceptability) of the investment is incomplete unless it incorporates the impact of the outcomes on the firm.

An individual's aversion to risk seems to be related to amounts that are large in comparison to the size of expenditure he can authorize rather than to the financial position of the firm.[10] This can induce conservative behavior the firm would like to prevent.[11] The accountant should be aware of the behavioral effects of his control techniques on the type of decisions made by the manager. Control techniques should be designed to motivate the behavioral pattern desired by the organization.

It is also useful to bring the uncertainty of the cash flows into the decision by dealing explicitly with the probabilities implicit in the problem. Although

[10] Swalm, R. O., "Utility Theory-Insights into Risk Taking," *The Harvard Business Review*, November–December 1966, pp. 123–135.
[11] One reason for this behavior lies perhaps in corporate control procedures that are unduly hard on failures versus the rewards for success.

difficult, it is necessary to estimate the probabilities of the relevant events. The normal information-processing system of a firm prevents a point estimate of the uncertain cash flow. The extent of the confidence of the person or persons responsible for the estimate is not known by the receiver of the information. The use of such terms to describe uncertainty as *optimistic, reasonable chance*, and *quite likely* are susceptible to various interpretations and hence lead to difficulties in implementation.[12]

The discussion of uncertainty and utility in this chapter has not systematically considered the "portfolio" question, though the assumptions of independence and dependence of the cash flows for the two-time period situation was very close to the portfolio question. Investments may be related to each other so that if one is successful the other is successful (this is described as statistical dependency with positive correlation). The opposite extreme is where the success of one investment is accompanied by failure of the other (the investments are dependent and negatively correlated). The third situation is where the results of the investments are independent of each other (the investments have zero correlation). The risk associated with an investment is a function of how it relates to the other investments of the firm. An apparent risky investment may not be at all risky when it is considered in relationship to other investments of the firm. On the other hand, while a firm might willingly undertake a single investment of a given kind, it might reasonably hesitate to undertake several, all of which are positively correlated with each other. Although this is an extremely important area, a complete analysis is beyond the coverage of this book. In addition to the portfolio investments of the firm, the fact that investors also have portfolios of investments affects the decisions of the corporation.

16.7 Summary

Large size investments cannot be made as if the cash flows are known with certainty when this assumption is not valid. The use of expected monetary value is not likely to be appropriate except for investments involving relatively small commitments of resources.

One solution is to evaluate investments using utility analysis. Even when all the results occur in one time period, the application of utility analysis is difficult because of the necessity of deriving a utility function for the person or persons making the investment. The analysis becomes more complex when the consequences are spread through time. Nevertheless, utility analysis

---

[12] See D. H. Woods, "Improving Estimates that Involve Uncertainty," *The Harvard Business Review*, July–August 1966, pp. 91–98, and J. S. Hammond, "Better Decisions with Preference Theory," *The Harvard Business Review*, November–December 1967, pp. 123–141, for further discussions of these issues.

offers insights into the making of capital-budgeting decisions under conditions of uncertainty and is, therefore, a valuable tool.

A reader may ask why these concepts, which are so useful to making rational capital budgeting decisions, are introduced so late in the book. Several other chapters have already discussed the same general type of decision problem. The explanation is that much information can be obtained from the computations that assume certainty. Also, present corporate practice frequently fails to use to the fullest extent possible even the present-value method. Hence, decision making in the area of internal investments can be improved by the wider use of the present-value method. However, the goal is to incorporate information about uncertainty and utility into the analysis, and so produce a measure which enables decision makers to separate investments into acceptable and unacceptable classifications. The need for incorporating utility considerations into the analysis for major investments leads to some procedure similar to that described in this chapter.

If the formal utility analysis is rejected then it should be apparent to the reader that no one measure of investment desirability is sufficient for investment appraisal. It is necessary to know how the investment may fare under a wide range of circumstances and how the investment's performance is tied to the performance of other investments, already undertaken and currently being considered.

APPENDIX 16A
UTILITY FUNCTIONS AND GAMBLES

In Section 16.1 a portion of a utility function is derived for an investor. The procedure used rests on some psychological assumptions, several of which have been challenged in the literature. One very important assumption is that if two gambles involve the same two prizes, the decision maker prefers the gamble with the larger probability of winning the larger prize.

The technique used to determine a utility function in essence reduces all gambles so that they involve only two reference outcomes or prizes. These outcomes may be given arbitrary utility indices of zero and one. The reference outcomes are selected so that the larger is at least as favorable as any outcome in the gamble being considered and the smaller is at least as unfavorable as any outcome.

In the example described in Section 16.1, the two reference outcomes are $1,000 and $0. These outcomes may be assigned utility indices of one and zero, respectively. Now suppose the decision maker is offered a fifty-fifty gamble on $1,000 or $300 versus a gamble involving $1,000 and $0 with probabilities of 0.7 and 0.3, respectively. The fifty-fifty gamble can be simulated by a box and chip analogue. Suppose there are 100 chips in a box, fifty marked win $1,000 and fifty marked win $300. One chip will be selected and the payment indicated will be made. Now the investor in Section 16.1 indicated that he is indifferent between $300 and a fifty-fifty gamble involving prizes of $1,000 and $0. Thus the fifty chips marked win $300 could be divided in half, with twenty-five marked win $1,000 and twenty-five marked win $0. There would now be 75 chips marked win $1,000 and 25 marked win $0. In this manner the original gamble is converted into a gamble involving only the reference outcomes with a probability of $0.50 + 0.25 = 0.75$ of winning $1,000.[13] Since 0.75 exceeds 0.7 and the outcomes are identical, the initial gamble ($1,000 or $300 each with probability 0.5) must be preferred. The expected utility calculations give the first gamble an expected utility of 0.75:

$$0.5[U(\$1,000)] + 0.5[U(\$300)] = 0.5[1] + 0.5[0.5] = 0.75,$$

and a utility to the second gamble of 0.7 since

$$0.7[U(\$1,000)] + 0.3[U(\$0)] = 0.7[1] + 0.3[0] = 0.70.$$

Thus the expected utility method also leads to a preference for the first gamble.

QUESTIONS AND PROBLEMS

16–1 A company estimates the expected cash flows of year 5 to be $10,000. If this figure is used in the investment analysis, what assumption (or assumptions) is (are) being made?

16–2 What is the maximum amount you would pay for a gamble that involved the following two alternatives?

Alternative 1: 0.5 probability of $1,000
Alternative 2: 0.5 probability of $0.

What does this imply about your utility function?

16–3 For you to be indifferent between the following two gambles, what value of X must be inserted?

Gamble A	Gamble B
0.5 probability of $1,000 0.5 probability of $0.	1.0 probability of $X

[13] The choice of zero and one permits probability numbers to serve as utilities. Recall that 0.75, the chance of winning in the reference gamble, was the utility of the certain monetary amount of $500 found to be equivalent to the same gamble in Section 16.1. Other choices besides zero and one could be used if desired.

What does this imply about your utility function? Compare your answer to the answer you gave to problem 16–2.

16–4 Why might you expect the utility function for earnings (or for money) to have an upper bound? Why might you expect it to have a lower bound?

16–5 Some suggest that risk should be taken into consideration by the use of a risk discount rate which is added to the default-free interest rate. This assumes that risk causes the cash forecast of a period to be worth a given fixed percentage less than an equal amount of cash in the previous period (this is in addition to the interest factor). Is this a good way of incorporating risk into the analysis? Can you think of a situation where the risk of future cash flows is less than the risk associated with cash flows of immediate time periods?

16–6 Would the utility function of a firm change after making an investment? Why?

16–7 When is it reasonable for a firm to base decisions on the expected monetary values and to ignore utility considerations?

16–8 In making a utility function for a corporation, how would you handle the situation where different corporate executives had different utility functions?

16–9 If the analysis did not try to incorporate utility considerations into the investment analysis, would the investment decisions of the firm still be affected by the utility functions of the individual corporate executives? Assume some degree of decentralization.

16–10 If the firm is small enough for the president (and owner) to make all the decisions, is it necessary to make a formal analysis using utility functions? Explain.

16–11 The following utility function of Mr. Jay will be used for problems 16–11 and 16–12.

Change in Net-Asset Position:	
Dollars	Utility Measures
$-3,000	-3,000
-1,000	-1,000
-600	-500
-500	-350
0	0
100	100
500	150
1,000	200
2,000	350
4,000	500
9,000	680
10,000	700

Assume there is a gamble which has 0.5 probability of $10,000 and 0.5 probability of $0.

Required:
a. What is the utility measure of the gamble?
b. What is the amount Mr. Jay would be willing to accept for certain to cause him to be indifferent to the two choices?
c. Would Mr. Jay be willing to pay $1,000 for this gamble?
d. What is the expected monetary value of the gamble?
e. What is the risk discount?
f. Would you describe Mr. Jay as financially conservative?

16–12 Assume there is a gamble which has a 0.5 probability of $4,000 and 0.5 probability of $1,000.

Required:
a. What is the utility measure of the gamble?
b. What is the amount Mr. Jay would be willing to accept for certain to cause him to be indifferent to the two choices?
c. Would Mr. Jay be willing to pay $1,000 for this gamble?
d. What is the expected monetary value of the gamble?
e. What is the risk discount?

16–13 The following problem attempts to illustrate the simulation of the mean utility of a cash flow which has a normal probability density function.

The earnings of a period are normally distributed with a mean of $100,000 and a standard deviation of $20,000. Assume the following values of d were obtained from a table of standard normal deviates.

d
0.40
1.35
−0.83
2.50

The following values were obtained from the utility function:

Dollars	Utility Measures
$ 0	0
83,400	10,000
108,000	15,000
110,000	16,000
127,000	19,000
150,000	20,000

Required:

a. Compute the four earnings observations.
b. Using the utility function, determine the utility observation for each earning observation.
c. Determine the mean utility.
d. Determine the certainty equivalent.

16–14 Assume the following utility function applies to the Arnot Corporation.

Change in Net-Asset Position: Dollars: Present Value	Utility Measures
$ – 20,000	– 400
– 10,000	– 100
0	0
7,200	80
8,600	90
10,000	100
18,600	140
20,000	150
30,000	190
35,800	200
40,000	220
60,000	240

a. Would the corporation accept an investment which requires an outlay of $10,000 and will either be a complete failure or generate cash flows of $30,000 within a week if each possibility has a 0.5 probability?
b. What would be your recommendation if the probabilities were 0.65 of failure and 0.35 of success?

16–15 Assume the same utility function as in problem 16–14.

a. Should the Arnot Corporation undertake the following investment? Assume a 0.05 discount rate is appropriate.

Period	Cash Flow
0	$ – 10,000
1	$ 0 with 0.5 probability
	$ 30,000 with 0.5 probability

b. What would be your recommendation if the probabilities were 0.6 of failure and 0.4 of success?

16–16 Assume the same utility function as in problem 16–14. The Arnot Corporation has been offered an investment which costs $20,000. The investment has 0.5 probability of not generating any cash the first day and 0.5 probability of generating $30,000. It also can generate $0 or $30,000 with the same probabilities the second day (the outcomes are independent of the day). Should the firm accept the investment?

16–17 Assume the same situation as in problem 16–16 except that the transactions take place in successive years instead of days. The discount rate is 0.05. Should the firm accept the investment?

16–18 Assume the same investment as in problem 16–16 except the cash flows of the second will be the same as for the first day (the outcomes are dependent). Should the firm accept the investment?

16–19 Assume the expected cash flows of an investment are as follows:

Period	Mean Value	Standard Deviation
0	– $ 8,000	$500
1	10,000	1,000
2	10,000	2,000

Compute the mean, variance, and standard deviation of the net present value distribution assuming the cash flows of each period are independent. Use a 0.05 rate of discount.

16–20 Determine whether the following investment is acceptable.

Period	Cash Flows
0	($1,000)
1	0.5 probability of $2,100 cash flow
	0.3 probability of $1,050
	0.2 probability of $0

The firm has a cost of money of 0.05. The utility function of the corporation has the following values (interpolate if you need other values).

Dollars: Present Value	Utility
$ – 1,000	– 300
0	0
500	50
1,000	70
1,050	75
1,300	85
1,500	90
2,000	100
2,100	101
3,000	125

SUPPLEMENTARY READING

BIERMAN, H., and S. SMIDT, *The Capital Budgeting Decision*, New York: Macmillan, 1971.

DEAN, JOEL, *Capital Budgeting*, New York: Columbia University Press, 1951.

HAMMOND, J., "Better Decisions with Preference Theory," *The Harvard Business Review*, November–December 1967, pp. 123–141.

HERTZ, D., "Investment Policies that Pay Off," *The Harvard Business Review*, January–February 1968, pp. 96–108.

HESPOS, R., and P. STRASSMAN, "Stochastic Decision Trees for the Analysis of Investment Decisions," *Management Science*, August 1965, pp. 244–259.

HILLIER, F. S., "The Derivation of Probabilistic Information for the Evaluation of Risky Investments," *Management Science*, April 1963, pp. 443–457.

LUTZ, F., and V. LUTZ, "The Theory of Investment of the Firm," Princeton, N.J.: Princeton University Press, 1951.

MAGEE, J., "How to Use Decision Trees in Capital Investment," *The Harvard Business Review*, September–October 1964, pp. 79–96.

QUERIN, G. D., *The Capital Expenditure Decision*, Homewood, Ill.: R. D. Irwin, 1967.

ROBICHECK, A. A., and S. C. MYERS, *Optimal Financing Decisions*, Englewood Cliffs, N.J.: Prentice-Hall, 1965.

Chapter 17

Present-Value Accounting Used in Performance Evaluation

After an investment decision has been made and the investment has been acquired there is the necessity of evaluating the performance of the investment. To reduce possible misunderstanding the term *asset* could be used in place of *investment* since this evaluative process applies to all assets.

Sometimes it is impossible to evaluate an isolated investment (or asset) and it is necessary instead to evaluate the utilization of groups of assets because of their jointness. Thus the recommendations of this chapter are not always applicable with the degree of accuracy indicated. One necessary condition for the application of present methods is that the costs and benefits of the investment are measurable in dollar terms.

17.1 Definition of the Problem

Previous chapters have recommended the use of cash flows in making investment decisions. However, after the asset has been acquired the evaluation is likely to be based on measures of income and return on investment. A component of both measures is depreciation. The primary objective of this chapter is to present a method of depreciation to be used in performance evaluation, that is consistent with the cash-flow procedure used in the investment decision-making process.

365

Define:

$V(t)$ to be the present value of the cash flows of an investment at the end of period t.

$V(0)$ is the present value at the end of period 0 or the beginning of period 1.

$D(t)$ to be the depreciation for the tth period.

$Y(t)$ to be the income for the tth period.

$N(t)$ to be the net revenues for the tth period (revenues less costs other than depreciation).

$r(t)$ to be the return on investment for the tth period computed using the beginning of the period investment.

Then $D(t)$ is equal to

$$D(t) = V(t - 1) - V(t)$$

if there is no additional external investment; $r(t)$ is equal to

$$r(t) = \frac{Y(t)}{V(t - 1)}.$$

and $Y(t)$ is equal to

$$Y(t) = N(t) - D(t).$$

To avoid complications, the following example assumes that the actual decrease in value for each period is the same as the expected decrease.

Example

Assume that an asset costs $17,355 and earns proceeds of $10,000 a year for two years. The cash is received at the end of each period. The time value

Table 17–1   Characteristics of Investment

Period t	Investment, End of Period: $V(t)$	Depreciation $D(t)$	Income $Y(t)$	Return on Investment $r(t)$
0	$17,355	...	...	...
1	9,091	$8,264	$1,736	10%
2	0	9,091	909	10%

of money is 10 per cent. The yield of the investment is 10 per cent (the present value of $10,000 for two years at 10 per cent is $17,355).

The investment has the values, decreases in values, and performance measurements given in Table 17–1 for the two years of its existence.

The values of $Y(t)$ are:

$$Y(t) = N(t) - D(t)$$
$$Y(1) = 10,000 - 8,264 = 1,736$$
$$Y(2) = 10,000 - 9,091 = 909.$$

Using this depreciation procedure, the returns on investment of each period (proceeds less depreciation divided by net investment) are the same percentage and equal to the yield of the investment as anticipated upon purchase.

If the straight-line method of depreciation is used, the results in Table 17–2 are obtained:

Table 17–2   Return on Investment Calculation

Period	Investment, End of Period	Depreciation	Income	Return on Investment
0	17,355.00	...	...	...
1	8,677.50	8,677.50	1,333.50	7.7%
2	0	8,677.50	1,333.50	15.4%

The return on investment increases from an unsatisfactory (in that it is less than cost of money) 7.7 per cent to a pleasing 15.4 per cent for a situation where the cash proceeds that were used to predict the expected yield of 10 per cent actually occur.

There is a deficiency in a system that forecasts one thing and when the forecasted event actually occurs reports something different. The present investment promises a 10 per cent return and constant proceeds, but only if the reporting method suggested in this chapter is used will the reported return be consistent with the rate used in the decision model. Hence, in a situation where the benefits are constant, the depreciation used in evaluating the investment should not be straight-line depreciation if return on investment is to be used in performance evaluation. Furthermore, accelerated depreciation would further distort the measurement problem. In fact, only one depreciation schedule will be consistent, in the present sense, with a given investment. And this schedule may not be related to any of the common depreciation schemes presently used by accountants.

It is now necessary to be more explicit about what is meant by the term *cash proceeds* and to distinguish between the amount that is needed for purposes of computing depreciation and the amount that is used in the basic investment analysis. The objective is to develop a timetable of depreciation that is internally consistent with the decision, and at the same time gives reasonable measures of income and return on investment.

17.2   Time-Adjusted Revenues and Expenses

The use of cash proceeds in computing depreciation is correct only in the unlikely set of circumstances where the time-adjusted measures of revenues and expenses coincide with the cash-flow computations. If the two are different for any period, then it is desirable to explain the difference and, if possible, to reconcile the two sets of numbers.

To avoid confusion with accounting practices that may not be accurate enough for these purposes, it is desirable to use the terms *time-adjusted revenues* and *time-adjusted expenses* to describe items that appropriately take into consideration the time value of money.

The inadequacy of using cash proceeds rather than time-adjusted net revenues can be illustrated by a short example.

Example

An investment costs $8,264, and will repay $10,000 after two years. The time value of money is 10 per cent and $8,264 is the present value of the expected $10,000 receipt two years hence. The use of the cash-proceeds approach results in the schedule given in Table 17–3 and the income statement given in Table 17–4.

Table 17–3   Investment Cash Flows

	Period 0	Period 1	Period 2
Cash flows at end of period	$ – 8,264	$ ...	$10,000
Investment at beginning of period		$8,264	$ 9,091
Appreciation of investment		827	909
Depreciation		...	(10,000)
Investment at end of period		$9,091	$ 0

Table 17–4   Income Statements Using Cash Proceeds

	Period 1	Period 2
Cash flows	$ 0	$10,000
Plus: Appreciation	827	909
	$827	$10,909
Less: Depreciation	...	10,000
Income	$827	$ 909

In both period 1 and period 2 the return on investment is 10 per cent. Now add the information that the cash flow of $10,000 at the end of two periods is the result of a sale on account at the end of period 1. The value of the receivable at the time of the sale is $9,091. Using accrual accounting, this $9,091 is recognized as revenue in period 1, and there is an apparent large profit in period 1 and large loss in period 2, as illustrated in Table 17–5.

Table 17–5   Income Statements Using Cash-Flow Depreciation

	Period 1	Period 2
Sales revenue—accrued	$9,091	
Interest revenue—implicit on receivable	0	$ 909
Total Revenue	$9,091	$ 909
Cash-flow appreciation		
(depreciation)	827	(9,091)
Net income (loss)	$9,918	($8,192)

It is necessary to refine the depreciation procedure. Rather than basing the depreciation on the cash proceeds, the calculation must be based on the time-adjusted net revenues (revenues less the expenses exclusive of depreciation, all adjusted for the timing of the receipts and disbursement of cash). The analyst must be careful to separate the basic investment that gives rise both to cash and to increases in accounts receivable and other secondary investments that may arise. The account receivable in the present example is such a secondary investment.

Table 17–6   Time-Adjusted Investment and Return on Investment

	Period 1	Period 2
Time-adjusted revenues	$9,091	$ 0
(Depreciation) appreciation	(8,264)	909
Income	$ 827	$ 909
Investment beginning of year	$8,264	$9,091
Return on investment	10%	10%

The basic investment has a value of $8,264 at the beginning of period 1, and zero value at the end of that period. The depreciation of the first period is therefore $8,264. The receivable has a value of $9,091 at the end of period 1 and a value of $10,000 at the end of period 2. Based on the difference in the value of the receivable at the beginning and end of the second year, the receivable appreciated $909 during period 2. This information is the basis of the schedule given in Table 17–6.

In this example the depreciation of the investment for a period is based on the decrease in value of the asset during the period; but it is necessary to define how to compute the values at the several moments in time and the decreases in value. The manager making the investment decision is not concerned with how the accountant measures the revenues of each period, and he may erroneously assume that the cash-flow estimates can be used as the basis for computing the value decreases.

This assumption does not affect the investment decision since the present value of the cash proceeds and the present value of the time-adjusted revenues and expenses are identical. It is only when the analysis shifts from the over-all profitability of the investment to a period-by-period profitability analysis that the difference between the cash-flow depreciation and the time-adjusted revenues and expense depreciation makes a difference (and then only if the cash flows are not equal for each period to the time-adjusted net revenues).

The cash-flow depreciation procedure incorrectly combines the analysis of two assets, the original investment and the account receivable acquired as a result of the original investment. Using accrual accounting, cash-flow depreciation does not necessarily match revenues and the expenses of earning those revenues. A significant economic event has occurred when a sale takes place and the business has a legal claim against the customer. The accountant properly recognizes revenue at the moment of sale. Since the revenue is recognized before the cash is received, it is also appropriate to incorporate this consideration into the depreciation calculation. This may be accomplished by defining the depreciation in terms of the decrease in value of the original investment, where the value is measured by discounting the future net time-adjusted revenues.

Table 17–7 Time-Adjusted Revenues and Present Values

	Period 1	Period 2	Total
Time-adjusted revenues	$2,545	$ 400	
Present-value factors	0.9091	0.8264	
Present value at time 0	$2,314	$ 331	$2,645

To illustrate, consider an investment of $2,645 that provides cash flows of $2,000 at the end of period 1 and $1,000 at the end of period 2. The present value of these two cash flows at 0.10 is also $2,645. Add the information that in period 1 the cash sales are $2,000 and the charge sales are $600, and that the charge sales to be collected a year later have a present value of $545 at the end of period 1 (that is, they are discounted at 10 per cent). There are $400 of cash sales at the end of period 2. The time-adjusted revenues and present values are given in Table 17–7.

The present values of the basic investment and the decreases in its values are given in Table 17–8 where the $364 figure for year 1 is the value of the second year's cash sales at the end of the first year. The $2,281 of depreciation for period 1 may also be computed by taking the difference between the present value of the first period's revenues and the appreciation of the second period's revenues in period one. The present value of the first period's revenues consists of $1,818 in cash sales, $2,000 (.9091), plus $496 in credit sales, $600

Table 17–8 Present Value of Basic Investment and Decreases in Value: Time-Adjusted Revenue Method

End of Period	Value of Basic Investment	Decrease in Value (depreciation)	Present Value of Accounts Receivable	Appreciation of Receivable
0	$2,645	...	...	...
1	364	$2,281	$545	...
2	0	364	...	$55

(.8264), a total of $2,314. The initial value of period two's cash sales is $331; that is, $400 (.8264). This initial value appreciates by $33 during the first period, $331 (.10). The difference of $2,281 (which is $2,314 − $33) is the first year's depreciation.

The income statements for the two years are given in Table 17–9 (ignoring rounding errors).

Table 17–9 Time-Adjusted Income Statements for Investment

	Period 1	Period 2	Investment Receivable	Total Period 2
Time-adjusted revenue	$2,545	$400		$400
Depreciation	2,281	364		364
Appreciation			$ 55	55
Income	$ 264	$ 36	$ 55	$ 91
Investment at start of period	$2,644	$364	$545	$909
Return on investment	10%	10%	10%	10%

The results of period 2 are divided into two parts above since there are two assets earning income, the basic investment and the derived accounts receivable.

17.2.1 Reconciliation of the Two Depreciation Methods

It would be disconcerting if two depreciation schedules (and equivalently two different value-decrease schedules) result from the same set of economic data. Continuing the previous example, and using the cash-flow method, the schedule of values and decreases in value given in Table 17–10 is obtained.

Using the time-adjusted revenues there is depreciation of $2,281 for year 1 and $364 for year 2. The differences arise because in using the time-adjusted

Table 17–10   Present Value of Basic Investment and Decreases in Value: Cash-Flow Method

Time	Value	Decrease in Value
0	$2,645	...
1	909	$1,736
2	0	909

revenue method the increase in the accounts receivable is recognized as a depreciation of the primary asset. In like manner, the cash-flow depreciation of period 2 recognizes the decrease in the receivable that has already been recognized under the time-adjusted revenue method in period 1. Table 17–11 attempts to reconcile the two depreciation schedules.

Table 17–11   Reconciliation of Depreciation: Time-Adjusted Revenue Method and Cash-Flow Method

Period	Cash-Flow Depreciation	Conversion of Investment to Receivable	Time-Adjusted Net Revenue Depreciation
1	$1,736	$545	$2,281
2	909	− 545	364

17.2.2   Yields Greater than the Time Value of Money

All the examples to this point assume that the net present value of the investment is zero; that is, the yield of the investment equals the time value of money for this firm. Now assume the yield is greater than the time value of money.

Example
An investment is expected to give an adjusted net income of $10,000 at the end of period 1 and $20,000 at the end of period 2. (It can also be assumed that these are cash flows, with the cash flows and time-adjusted net revenues being equal.) The cost of the investment is $25,619 (the investment has a 10 per cent yield). The firm's time value of money is 5 per cent.

If 5 per cent is used as the discount rate, a value of $27,664 is obtained at time zero and the results of operations given in Table 17–12 are relevant.

Table 17–12   Results of Operations: 5 per cent

Period	Investment, End of Period	Depreciation	Income	Return on Investment
0	$27,664			
1	19,048	$ 8,616	$1,384	5%
2	0	19,048	952	5%

The investment that cost $25,619 had an immediate value increment to $27,664 (an increase of $2,045) and that value then earned 5 per cent over its life.

If the $25,619 had been used as the basis of the accounting and if a 10 per cent time-value factor had been used, the results would appear as in Table 17–13.

Table 17–13   Results of Operations: 10 per cent

Period	Investment, End of Period	Depreciation	Income	Return on Investment
0	$25,619			
1	18,182	$ 7,437	$2,563	10%
2	0	18,182	1,818	10%

A difficulty with using this schedule is that the time value of money has been defined to be 5 per cent and the value of the investment at time zero is $27,664, not $25,619. As a compromise the two procedures might be combined as in Table 17–14.

Table 17–14   Combining the Results

Period	Income Using 5%	Portion of Income Unrealized (at time of acquisition) Profit Realized During Period	Total Realized Income (income using 10%)
1	$1,384	$1,179	$2,563
2	952	866	1,818

The income using 5 per cent might be used for purposes of performance evaluation for the manager operating the investment and the total income using 10 per cent might be reported to stockholders where there is more of a requirement for obtaining objective evidence before reporting income. That is, income should not be reported externally at the time of purchase just because the decision maker is optimistic about the prospects. On the other hand, the schedule based on the 10 per cent return could be used. If the manager makes propitious investments, the measure of his performance should reflect the increase in the return he is able to make. In other words, deviations from expected results or, in this case, from the required minimal return, appear as improved rates of performance.[1]

17.3 Imputed Interest

As a supplement to the return on investment calculation, the effect of the utilization of assets can be incorporated into the measurement of performance by deducting implicit interest from the operating income of the period. Thus, if $40,000,000 of assets are utilized during a period and if the interest cost is 0.05, an implicit interest charge of $2,000,000 can be deducted from the operating income. If the operating income were $3,000,000 it would be $1,000,000 after the deduction of the implicit interest.

Thus management might be told:

1. The return on investment was $3,000,000/$40,000,000 = 0.075.
2. The amount of $1,000,000 was earned over and above the implicit interest cost charged on the assets utilized.

There are two difficulties with the procedure of charging implicit interest. The most important is that it may be that not all the interest cost of a period should be an expense. For example, an asset may be purchased today at a cost of $10,000 with a promised return of $11,025 two years from now. At 5 per cent there is an interest cost of $500 after one year, but this is not an expense but rather an increase in the value of the asset (after one period the cost basis of the asset should be adjusted to $10,500; the cost basis includes the implicit interest cost of $500).

The difficulty can be solved by allocating the interest cost between the assets and expenses of the period. This allocation requires judgment, but there is no escaping the need for the allocation if the firm is going to avoid distortions in incentives.

The second difficulty follows from the first. If the cost basis of the asset is

---

[1] The fact that depreciation taken for taxes has implications for cash flows through its effect on tax obligations adds another dimension to the problem that is not considered here. One appealing means of dealing with this complication is to consider the tax-payment deduction associated with an asset because of depreciation as a separable asset. Alternately, and easier from a practical point of view, this tax effect can be considered in determining the value of the asset and the relevant depreciation schedule for it. See T. R. Dyckman, "Discussion of Accelerated Depreciation and Deferred Taxes: An Empirical Study of Fluctuating Asset Expenditures," *Empirical Research in Accounting: Selected Studies*, Chicago: The Institute of Professional Accounting, Graduate School of Business, University of Chicago, 1967, pp. 124–138.

adjusted from $10,000 to $10,500 and then to $11,025, no operating income is reported when the expected revenues of $11,025 are earned.

There is no income above the implicit interest cost of $1,025 and the $10,000 explicit cost of the asset. However the other side of the implicit interest cost of $1,025 is implicit interest revenue. This revenue should be recognized during some time period if the implicit interest cost is recognized. The income statement should have at least three subtotals:

Revenues	$xxxxx
Less: Expenses	xxxxx
Operating income	$xxxxx
Less: Implicit interest cost	xxxxx
Income after interest cost	$ xxx
Plus: Implicit interest revenue	xx
Change in stockholders' equity	$ xxx

Example

The facts in Table 17–15 relate to a firm with a cost of money of 0.05. The cost of the asset is $18,594.

Table 17–15   Revenues and Expenses by Periods

	Period 1	Period 2
Revenues	$25,000	$25,000
Less: Out-of-pocket expenses	15,000	15,000
	$10,000	$10,000

First the depreciation and operating incomes of the two time periods are computed in Table 17–16 in accordance with the depreciation method developed earlier in this chapter.

Table 17–16   Depreciation and Operating Income

t	$V(t)$	$D(t)$	Operating Income
0	$18,594		
1	9,524	$9,070	$930
2	0	9,524	476

The returns on investment are 0.05 for both years. If the firm computes the implicit interest cost for the two years, its net income is as given in Table 17–17.

Table 17–17   Net Income Calculated

	Period 1	Period 2
Operating income	$930	$476
Less: Implicit interest cost		
0.05 × 18,594	930	
0.05 × 9,524		476
Income	$0	$0

To complete the procedure, the implicit interest revenue of the two time periods should be added. The complete presentation of operating results is given in Table 17–18.

Table 17–18   Operating Results by Periods

	Period 1	Period 2
Revenues	$25,000	$25,000
Less: Out-of-pocket expenses	15,000	15,000
Depreciation	9,070	9,524
	$24,070	$24,524
Operating income	$930	$476
Less: Implicit interest cost	930	476
Income after interest	$ 0	$ 0
Plus: Implicit interest revenue	930	476
Change in stockholders' equity	$ 930	$ 476

Taking the last line and dividing by the investment at the beginning of the period, a return on investment of 0.05 is obtained for both years.

The above procedure is somewhat awkward since interest is already taken into account in the depreciation computation and the deduction of the implicit interest is redundant. There is at least as much information in the $930 operating income figure, the changes in this number, and the return on investment as there is in the $0 income after interest measure.

Now suppose the capital consumption of a period is defined "To be equal to the present value of the expected future benefits of that period."[2] Thus the basic capital consumption for period 1 is $9,524 and for period 2 is $9,070. It is now necessary to compute the interest cost and implicit interest revenue

[2] The concept of capital consumption used here may be reconciled to the depreciation notions discussed earlier in this chapter by suitable adjustments for interest costs and revenues.

as associated with the two investments of $9,524 for the first period and $9,070 for the second period. Table 17–19 identifies the implicit interest costs and revenues of the two time periods.

Table 17–19   Implicit Interest Cost and Revenues by Period

	Investment	Interest in Period 1	Interest in Period 2	Total Implicit Interest Cost
Cost of period 1's revenue	$9,524	$476	...	$ 476
Cost of period 2's revenue	9,070	454	$476	930
Total interest revenue		$930	$476	$1,406

The related income statements are supplied in Table 17–20.

Table 17–20   Income Statements by Periods

	Period 1	Period 2
Revenues	$25,000	$25,000
Less: Out-of-pocket expenses	15,000	15,000
Capital consumption	9,524	9,070
	$24,524	$24,070
Operating Income	$ 476	$ 930
Less: Implicit interest cost	476	930
Income after interest cost	$ 0	$ 0
Plus: Implicit interest revenue	930	476
Net change in stockholders' equity	$ 930	$ 476

The returns on investment for both time periods are again 0.05.

Using different procedures it was possible to obtain constant returns on an investment of 0.05 for the two periods. One strong warning is necessary. A wrong combination of interest calculations and depreciation method will result in meaningless income measures. The interest and the depreciation calculations must be consistent with each other.

17.4   Interest as a Cost of Product

Through the years accountants have argued whether or not interest was a cost of an inventoriable nature similar to material and labor costs. While the question is theoretically interesting and there are arguments both pro and con, it is subordinate to the primary question of how interest should be incorporated into the decision-making process. The following sections review briefly the technique for incorporating interest into the manufacturing accounts.

A method suggested for incorporating interest into the accounts is to compute the interest on the assets utilized and allocate this interest to departments and absorb it into the cost of product. Assuming a value of money of 6 per cent and incremental assets of $100,000, the entries to accomplish the inclusion of interest are as follows:[3]

Implicit Interest Cost		Implicit Interest Revenue	
(1) 6,000	(2) 6,000	(3) 5,000	(1) 6,000

Manufacturing Costs		Income	
(2) 6,000	(4) 5,000	(4) 5,000	(3) 5,000

Explanation of entries
1. Records the interest cost and the interest revenue earned on the funds tied up in incremental assets ($100,000 × 6%). Part of the credit would be to "interest payable" if there is debt outstanding.
2. Records the transfer of the $6,000 implicit interest to the manufacturing account.
3. Transfers $5,000 of the interest revenue to the income account.
4. Transfers $5,000 of the manufacturing costs to the income account (five sixths of the inventory has been used).

The above entries assume that five sixths of the goods worked on during the period were sold and thus five sixths of the interest is expensed during the period. For the portion of the manufactured product still on hand, it would be incorrect to recognize interest revenue since the funds are invested in goods not yet sold. Since five sixths of the goods worked on during the period were sold, and one sixth are still in inventory, it is appropriate to recognize only five sixths of $6,000 or $5,000 as income for the period. Interest cost of $5,000 appears as revenues (the net effect of implicit interest on the income of the period being zero). The $1,000 balance in implicit interest revenue could be formally closed to the manufacturing account (or inventory accounts) or merely subtracted from the inventories. The net effect of recognizing implicit interest on income in the manner indicated is zero.

The question of whether or not interest should be considered a cost of product and treated in a manner comparable to costs of material and labor is

---

[3] Depreciable assets should be excluded from the asset total on which interest is being computed if interest is being taken into account via the depreciation method.

less important than how the interest cost of the resources committed to a project may be incorporated into the decision-making process. It is suggested that computing the present value of cash flows will frequently be a reasonable and adequate method of accomplishing this objective.

If it is desired to present a unit cost of product for decision making and measuring performance, then the cost of product should include interest cost on the incremental assets. For assets already owned the cost measure used should be the interest on the opportunity cost of employing the resources in other projects. Thus interest would be computed on the increase in working capital which is required by the project. But where the machinery and equipment have other uses than the one being considered, the opportunity cost of the equipment should be used as the measure of cost.

17.5   Implicit Interest and Break-Even Analysis[4]

Implicit interest also has an impact on traditional break-even analysis. One of the differences between most economic and accounting approaches to break-even analysis concerns the treatment of the cost of money. The economists include it as a cost while the accountants do not. The latter, however, evaluate (or leave it to management to evaluate) profits in terms of the required return on investment that is implied relative to the cost of money to the firm. Thus both recognize the importance of the cost of money but consider it at different points in the analysis.

The cost of money can be incorporated into conventional break-even analysis (which assumes constant price, linear variable cost, constant inventory levels, etc.) by discounting the relevant cash flows. Figure 17.1 assumes no long-lived assets. The traditional break-even volume, computed using a zero interest rate, is at an activity of x_1. The fixed cost is $0A$ dollars. Introducing a positive rate of interest causes the discounted value of the total revenues to decline for a given activity level. The same is true for total costs. If the fixed costs were all incurred over the same period and under the same timing assumed for the revenue and variable-cost flows, the fixed costs would drop to $0B$ and the break-even activity level would remain unchanged. This is illustrated by the dashed line, with the same slope as the line labeled Total cost: $r > 0$, emanating from point B.

But if the fixed costs are incurred at the start of the period, the break-even point is affected by the discounting.[5] The result is a revised break-even

[4] The development here follows R. Manes, "A New Dimension to Break-Even Analysis," *The Journal of Accounting Research*, Spring 1966, pp. 87–100. The reader is encouraged to read the original article.

[5] The costs of an investment can often be converted into annual costs by leasing. Additional costs are incurred in the process due to the postponement of payment and these costs are among those that traditional break-even analysis ignores if the asset is purchased.

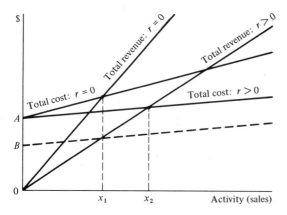

Figure 17.1 The effect of incorporating the cost of money into the break-even analysis: No long-lived assets

point, x_2, which exceeds the break-even point ignoring the cost of money. In the following example there is a long-lived asset servicing several periods.

Example

Assume a situation with the following characteristics:

Variable cost per unit	$0.50
Sales price per unit	$2
Fixed costs of initial investment	
(assume the investment is avoidable)	$100,000
Life of proposed activity	5 years
Annual operating outlays	$20,000
Salvage value of investment after 5 years	$0
Assumed cost of money	0.15

Let D_5 be the present value of a 5-year annuity with a 0.15 cost of money. Then

$$D_5 = \frac{1}{(1 + 0.15)} + \frac{1}{(1 + 0.15)^2} + \frac{1}{(1 + 0.15)^3} + \frac{1}{(1 + 0.15)^4} + \frac{1}{(1 + 0.15)^5}$$

$$= \frac{1 - (1 + 0.15)^{-5}}{0.15} = 3.3522.$$

The break-even level is given by x_b where

$$100,000 = (2 - 0.50)D_5 x_b - 20,000 D_5 = 1.5 x_b(3.3522) - 20,000(3.3522)$$

and

$$x_b = 33,227 \text{ units per year.}$$

If the interest rate were ignored, the break-even level would be

$$\frac{100,000 + 5(20,000)}{5} = 1.50x_b$$

and x_b equals 26,667 units per year.

The effect of adding the cost of money in this case increases the break-even quantity by nearly 25 per cent.[6]

17.6 Summary

The difficulties in performance evaluation include all of the problems of measuring unit costs, income, and assets. Any evaluation of performance must consider the limitations of the measures being used as the basis of the evaluation.

The examples have illustrated the computation of depreciation in situations where the cash flows of a period differ from the time-adjusted net revenues of a period because of the presence of sales made on account. In situations where there are expenses not requiring the immediate disbursement of cash because of the possibility of delaying payment (current liabilities may be increased), an analysis analogous to that associated with the accounts receivable would be appropriate.

The chapter also examines briefly the effect of implicit interest on revenues and product cost. Interest also affects break-even analysis, increasing the break-even level over that obtained in traditional analysis.

QUESTIONS AND PROBLEMS

17–1 An asset costs $18,594 and will earn proceeds of $10,000 a year for two years. The cash is received at the end of each period. The time value of money is 0.05.

Required:

a. Compute the yield of the investment.

b. Compute the depreciations in the value of the asset, the incomes, and the returns on investment for the two years of life.

17–2 An asset costs $27,665 and will earn proceeds of $10,000 in year 1 and $20,000 in year 2. The time value of money is 0.05.

---

[6] The method used here can be extended to include the effect of taxes, depreciation policy, growth or decline in future sales, and the effects of inflation. This would take the analysis further afield than the authors wish to go. The interested reader is referred to Manes, *op. cit.*, *passim*, for a discussion of these points.

Required:

a. Compute the yield of the investment.

b. Compute the depreciations in the value of the asset, the incomes and returns on the investment for the two years of life.

17–3 An asset costs $28,118 and will earn proceeds of $20,000 in year 1 and $10,000 in year 2. The time value of money is 0.05.

Required:

a. Compute the yield of investment.

b. Compute the depreciations in the value of the asset, the incomes and the returns on investment for the two years of life.

17–4 An asset costs $20,000 and earns proceeds of $11,000 in year 1 and $10,500 in year 2. The time value of money is 0.05.

Required:

a. Compute the yield of the investment.

b. Compute the depreciations in the value of the asset, the incomes and returns on investment for the two years of life.

17–5 An asset costs $20,000 and will earn proceeds of $12,000 in year 1 and $11,000 in year 2. The time value of money is 0.10.

Required:

a. Compute the yield of the investment.

b. Compute the depreciations in the value of the asset, the incomes, and the returns on investment for the two years of life.

17–6 An asset costs $18,594 and will earn cash proceeds of $10,500 a year for two years; the first payment is to be received two years from now. The sales of $10,500 will be made at the end of periods 1 and 2 and the collections at the end of periods 2 and 3. The time value of money is 0.05.

Required: Compute the depreciations, the incomes, and returns on investment for the life of the investment.

17–7 An asset costs $27,665 and will earn proceeds of $10,500 in year 2 and $21,000 in year 3. The time value of money is 0.05. The sales will be made at the end of periods 1 and 2 and the collections at the end of periods 2 and 3.

Required: Compute the depreciations, the incomes, and returns on investment.

17–8 An asset costs $17,355 and will earn proceeds of $10,000 a year for two years. The cash is received at the end of each period. The time value of money is 0.05.

Required:

a. Compute the yield of the investment.

b. Compute the depreciations, incomes, and returns on investment.

17–9 An asset costs $25,619 and will earn proceeds of $10,000 in year 1 and $20,000 in year 2. The time value of money is 0.05.

Required:
a. Compute the yield of the investment.
b. Compute the depreciations, income, and returns on investment.

17–10 Assume that the Alstar Company is considering the investment described in 17–9. The company uses a straight-line method of depreciation for financial accounting purposes and management is very sensitive to the effect an investment will have on income and earnings per share.

Required: Should the company undertake the investment assuming the cash flows are known with certainty and 0.05 is an appropriate discount rate?

17–11 Accountants typically ignore implicit interest in break-even analyses. What is the effect of this behavior? Is the effect important?

17–12 A recent proposal in the literature suggests that a firm may want to consider its growth rate of income as reflected in its published accounting statements in its decision making.[7] In particular, the firm may select among investments subject to limitations placed on the minimum percentage growth in earnings to be reported. Is it reasonable for a firm to be concerned about its reported growth in income? What problems do you see in using the suggested procedure? What remedies might you suggest?

17–13 Consider a situation in which a firm has received the first order from a new customer. Assume that:
1. The firm has excess capacity at the present time.
2. The marginal revenues exceed variable costs.
3. There are no externality problems.
4. The problems of cost justification under the Robinson-Patman Act can be ignored, and
5. The new customer is likely to maintain purchases in periods when unexpected declines occur in the orders from other customers.

Present arguments, from a risk standpoint, to accept the order as well as from the traditional marginal viewpoint.

17–14 Is the variance of an investment the best measure of risk of that investment?

17–15 Does a project with uncertain returns necessarily add to the firm's overall risk?

17–16 Can you argue from a risk standpoint that a firm with several divisions might be justified in using different required rates of return with each?

SUPPLEMENTARY READING

BACKER, M., "Additional Considerations in Return on Investment Analysis," *N.A.A. Bulletin*, January 1962, pp. 57–62.

[7] See E. Lerner and A. Rappaport, "Limit DCF in Capital Budgeting," *The Harvard Business Review*, September–October 1968, pp. 133–139.

BIERMAN, H., JR., "A Further Study of Depreciation," *The Accounting Review*, April 1966, pp. 271–274.

COUGHLAN, J., "Contrast Between Financial-Statement and Discounted-Cash Flow Methods of Comparing Projects," *N.A.A. Bulletin*, June 1960, pp. 5–20.

DEARDEN, J., "The Case Against ROI Control," *The Harvard Business Review*, May–June 1969, pp. 124–135.

DEMSKI, J. S., "Predictive Ability of Alternative Performance Measurement Models," *Journal of Accounting Research*, Spring 1969, pp. 96–115.

DEMSKI, J. S., "The Decision Implementation Interface: Effects of Alternative Performance Measurement Models," *The Accounting Review*, January 1970, pp. 76–87.

FURLONG, W., "Risk Income and Alternative Income Concepts," *N.A.A. Management Accounting*, April 1967, pp. 25–29.

MAURIEL, J., and R. ANTHONY, "Misevaluation of Investment Center Performance," *The Harvard Business Review*, March–April 1965, pp. 98–105.

SHWAYDER, K., "A Proposed Modification to Residual Income—Interest Adjusted Income", *The Accounting Review*, April 1970, pp. 299–307.

SOLOMONS, D., *Division Performance: Measurement and Control*, New York: Financial Executives Research Foundation, 1965.

Tables

Table I. Normal Probability Distribution Function (Probabilities That Given Standard Normal Variables Will Not Be Exceeded—Left Tail)*

$$N_z(-z). \text{ Also } N_z(z) = 1 - N_z(-z).$$

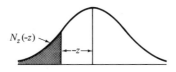

$-z$	0.00	0.01	0.02	0.03	0.04	0.05	0.06	0.07	0.08	0.09
.0	0.50000	0.49601	0.49202	0.48803	0.48405	0.48006	0.47608	0.47210	0.46812	0.46414
.1	0.46017	0.45620	0.45224	0.44828	0.44433	0.44038	0.43644	0.43251	0.42858	0.42465
.2	0.42074	0.41683	0.41294	0.40905	0.40517	0.40129	0.39743	0.39358	0.39874	0.38591
.3	0.38209	0.37828	0.37448	0.37070	0.36693	0.36317	0.35942	0.35569	0.35197	0.34827
.4	0.34458	0.34090	0.33724	0.33360	0.32997	0.32636	0.32276	0.31918	0.31561	0.31207
.5	0.30854	0.30503	0.30153	0.29806	0.29460	0.29116	0.28774	0.28434	0.28096	0.27760
.6	0.27425	0.27093	0.26763	0.26435	0.26109	0.25785	0.25463	0.25143	0.24825	0.24510
.7	0.24196	0.23885	0.23576	0.23270	0.22965	0.22663	0.22363	0.22065	0.21770	0.21476
.8	0.21186	0.20897	0.20611	0.20327	0.20045	0.19766	0.19489	0.19215	0.18943	0.18673
.9	0.18406	0.18141	0.17879	0.17619	0.17361	0.17106	0.16853	0.16602	0.16354	0.16109
1.0	0.15866	0.15625	0.15386	0.15151	0.14917	0.14686	0.14457	0.14231	0.14007	0.13786
1.1	0.13567	0.13350	0.13136	0.12924	0.12714	0.12507	0.12302	0.12100	0.11900	0.11702
1.2	0.11507	0.11314	0.11123	0.10935	0.10749	0.10565	0.10383	0.10204	0.10027	0.09853
1.3	0.09680	0.09510	0.09342	0.09176	0.09012	0.08851	0.08691	0.08534	0.08379	0.08226
1.4	0.08076	0.07927	0.07780	0.07636	0.07493	0.07353	0.07215	0.07078	0.06944	0.06811
1.5	0.06681	0.06552	0.06426	0.06301	0.06178	0.06057	0.05938	0.05821	0.05705	0.05592
1.6	0.05480	0.05370	0.05262	0.05155	0.05050	0.04947	0.04846	0.04746	0.04648	0.04551
1.7	0.04457	0.04363	0.04272	0.04182	0.04093	0.04006	0.03920	0.03836	0.03754	0.03673
1.8	0.03593	0.03515	0.03438	0.03362	0.03288	0.03216	0.03144	0.03074	0.03005	0.02938
1.9	0.02872	0.02807	0.02743	0.02680	0.02619	0.02559	0.02500	0.02442	0.02385	0.02330
2.0	0.02275	0.02216	0.02169	0.02118	0.02068	0.02018	0.01970	0.01923	0.01876	0.01831
2.1	0.01786	0.01743	0.01700	0.01659	0.01618	0.01578	0.01539	0.01500	0.01463	0.01426
2.2	0.01390	0.01355	0.01321	0.01287	0.01255	0.01222	0.01191	0.01160	0.01130	0.01101
2.3	0.01072	0.01044	0.01017	0.00990	0.00964	0.00939	0.00914	0.00889	0.00866	0.00842
2.4	0.00820	0.00798	0.00776	0.00755	0.00734	0.00714	0.00695	0.00676	0.00657	0.00639
2.5	0.00621	0.00604	0.00587	0.00570	0.00554	0.00539	0.00523	0.00508	0.00494	0.00480
2.6	0.00466	0.00453	0.00440	0.00427	0.00415	0.00402	0.00391	0.00379	0.00368	0.00357
2.7	0.00347	0.00336	0.00326	0.00317	0.00307	0.00298	0.00289	0.00280	0.00272	0.00264
2.8	0.00256	0.00248	0.00240	0.00233	0.00226	0.00219	0.00212	0.00205	0.00199	0.00193
2.9	0.00187	0.00181	0.00175	0.00169	0.00164	0.00159	0.00154	0.00149	0.00144	0.00139
3.0	0.00135	0.00131	0.00126	0.00122	0.00118	0.00114	0.00111	0.00107	0.00104	0.00100
3.1	0.00097	0.00094	0.00090	0.00087	0.00084	0.00082	0.00079	0.00076	0.00074	0.00071
3.2	0.00069	0.00066	0.00064	0.00062	0.00060	0.00058	0.00056	0.00054	0.00052	0.00050
3.3	0.00048	0.00047	0.00045	0.00043	0.00042	0.00040	0.00039	0.00038	0.00036	0.00035
3.4	0.00034	0.00032	0.00031	0.00030	0.00029	0.00028	0.00027	0.00026	0.00025	0.00024
3.5	0.00023	0.00022	0.00022	0.00021	0.00020	0.00019	0.00019	0.00018	0.00017	0.00017
3.6	0.00016	0.00015	0.00015	0.00014	0.00014	0.00013	0.00013	0.00012	0.00012	0.00011
3.7	0.00011	0.00010	0.00010	0.00010	0.00009	0.00009	0.00008	0.00008	0.00008	0.00008
3.8	0.00007	0.00007	0.00007	0.00006	0.00006	0.00006	0.00006	0.00005	0.00005	0.00005
3.9	0.00005	0.00005	0.00004	0.00004	0.00004	0.00004	0.00004	0.00004	0.00003	0.00003

* By symmetry this table also gives the area in the right tail for $+ z$.

Table II. Normal Probability Density Function: $n_z(z)$

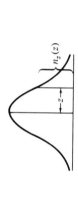

z	0	0.01	0.02	0.03	0.04	0.05	0.06	0.07	0.08	0.09
0.0	0.3989	0.3989	0.3989	0.3988	0.3986	0.3984	0.3982	0.3980	0.3977	0.3973
0.1	0.3970	0.3965	0.3961	0.3956	0.3951	0.3945	0.3939	0.3932	0.3925	0.3918
0.2	0.3910	0.3902	0.3894	0.3885	0.3876	0.3867	0.3857	0.3847	0.3836	0.3825
0.3	0.3814	0.3802	0.3790	0.3778	0.3765	0.3752	0.3739	0.3725	0.3712	0.3697
0.4	0.3683	0.3668	0.3653	0.3637	0.3621	0.3605	0.3589	0.3572	0.3555	0.3538
0.5	0.3521	0.3503	0.3485	0.3467	0.3448	0.3429	0.3410	0.3391	0.3372	0.3352
0.6	0.3332	0.3312	0.3292	0.3271	0.3251	0.3230	0.3209	0.3187	0.3166	0.3144
0.7	0.3123	0.3101	0.3079	0.3056	0.3034	0.3011	0.2989	0.2966	0.2943	0.2920
0.8	0.2897	0.2874	0.2850	0.2827	0.2803	0.2780	0.2756	0.2732	0.2709	0.2685
0.9	0.2661	0.2637	0.2613	0.2589	0.2565	0.2541	0.2516	0.2492	0.2468	0.2444
1.0	0.2420	0.2396	0.2371	0.2347	0.2323	0.2299	0.2275	0.2251	0.2227	0.2203
1.1	0.2179	0.2155	0.2131	0.2107	0.2083	0.2059	0.2036	0.2012	0.1989	0.1965
1.2	0.1942	0.1919	0.1895	0.1872	0.1849	0.1826	0.1804	0.1781	0.1758	0.1736
1.3	0.1714	0.1691	0.1669	0.1647	0.1626	0.1604	0.1582	0.1561	0.1539	0.1518
1.4	0.1497	0.1476	0.1456	0.1435	0.1415	0.1394	0.1374	0.1354	0.1334	0.1315
1.5	0.1295	0.1276	0.1257	0.1238	0.1219	0.1200	0.1182	0.1163	0.1145	0.1127
1.6	0.1109	0.1092	0.1074	0.1057	0.1040	0.1023	0.1006	0.09893	0.09728	0.09566
1.7	0.09405	0.09246	0.09089	0.08933	0.08780	0.08628	0.08478	0.08329	0.08183	0.08038
1.8	0.07895	0.07754	0.07614	0.07477	0.07341	0.07206	0.07074	0.06943	0.06814	0.06687
1.9	0.06562	0.06438	0.06316	0.06195	0.06077	0.05959	0.05844	0.05730	0.05618	0.05508

z	.00	.01	.02	.03	.04	.05	.06	.07	.08	.09
2.0	0.05399	0.05292	0.05186	0.05082	0.04980	0.04879	0.04780	0.04682	0.04586	0.04491
2.1	0.04398	0.04307	0.04217	0.04128	0.04041	0.03955	0.03871	0.03788	0.03706	0.03626
2.2	0.03547	0.03470	0.03394	0.03319	0.03246	0.03174	0.03103	0.03034	0.02965	0.02898
2.3	0.02833	0.02768	0.02705	0.02643	0.02582	0.02522	0.02463	0.02406	0.02349	0.02294
2.4	0.02239	0.02186	0.02134	0.02083	0.02033	0.01984	0.01936	0.01888	0.01842	0.01797
2.5	0.01753	0.01709	0.01667	0.01625	0.01585	0.01545	0.01506	0.01468	0.01431	0.01394
2.6	0.01358	0.01323	0.01289	0.01256	0.01223	0.01191	0.01160	0.01130	0.01100	0.01071
2.7	0.01042	0.01014	$0.0^2 9871$	$0.0^2 9606$	$0.0^2 9347$	$0.0^2 9094$	$0.0^2 8846$	$0.0^2 8605$	$0.0^2 8370$	$0.0^2 8140$
2.8	$0.0^2 7915$	$0.0^2 7697$	$0.0^2 7483$	$0.0^2 7274$	$0.0^2 7071$	$0.0^2 6873$	$0.0^2 6679$	$0.0^2 6491$	$0.0^2 6307$	$0.0^2 6127$
2.9	$0.0^2 5953$	$0.0^2 5782$	$0.0^2 5616$	$0.0^2 5454$	$0.0^2 5296$	$0.0^2 5143$	$0.0^2 4993$	$0.0^2 4847$	$0.0^2 4705$	$0.0^2 4567$
3.0	$0.0^2 4432$	$0.0^2 4301$	$0.0^2 4173$	$0.0^2 4049$	$0.0^2 3928$	$0.0^2 3810$	$0.0^2 3695$	$0.0^2 3584$	$0.0^2 3475$	$0.0^2 3370$
3.1	$0.0^2 3267$	$0.0^2 3167$	$0.0^2 3070$	$0.0^2 2975$	$0.0^2 2884$	$0.0^2 2794$	$0.0^2 2707$	$0.0^2 2623$	$0.0^2 2541$	$0.0^2 2461$
3.2	$0.0^2 2384$	$0.0^2 2309$	$0.0^2 2236$	$0.0^2 2165$	$0.0^2 2096$	$0.0^2 2029$	$0.0^2 1964$	$0.0^2 1901$	$0.0^2 1840$	$0.0^2 1780$
3.3	$0.0^2 1723$	$0.0^2 1667$	$0.0^2 1612$	$0.0^2 1560$	$0.0^2 1508$	$0.0^2 1459$	$0.0^2 1411$	$0.0^2 1364$	$0.0^2 1319$	$0.0^2 1275$
3.4	$0.0^2 1232$	$0.0^2 1191$	$0.0^2 1151$	$0.0^2 1112$	$0.0^2 1075$	$0.0^2 1038$	$0.0^2 1003$	$0.0^3 9689$	$0.0^3 9358$	$0.0^3 9037$
3.5	$0.0^3 8727$	$0.0^3 8426$	$0.0^3 8135$	$0.0^3 7853$	$0.0^3 7581$	$0.0^3 7317$	$0.0^3 7061$	$0.0^3 6814$	$0.0^3 6575$	$0.0^3 6343$
3.6	$0.0^3 6119$	$0.0^3 5902$	$0.0^3 5693$	$0.0^3 5490$	$0.0^3 5294$	$0.0^3 5105$	$0.0^3 4921$	$0.0^3 4744$	$0.0^3 4573$	$0.0^3 4408$
3.7	$0.0^3 4248$	$0.0^3 4093$	$0.0^3 3944$	$0.0^3 3800$	$0.0^3 3661$	$0.0^3 3526$	$0.0^3 3396$	$0.0^3 3271$	$0.0^3 3149$	$0.0^3 3032$
3.8	$0.0^3 2919$	$0.0^3 2810$	$0.0^3 2705$	$0.0^3 2604$	$0.0^3 2506$	$0.0^3 2411$	$0.0^3 2320$	$0.0^3 2232$	$0.0^3 2147$	$0.0^3 2065$
3.9	$0.0^3 1987$	$0.0^3 1910$	$0.0^3 1837$	$0.0^3 1766$	$0.0^3 1698$	$0.0^3 1633$	$0.0^3 1569$	$0.0^3 1508$	$0.0^3 1449$	$0.0^3 1393$
4.0	$0.0^3 1338$	$0.0^3 1286$	$0.0^3 1235$	$0.0^3 1186$	$0.0^3 1140$	$0.0^3 1094$	$0.0^3 1051$	$0.0^3 1009$	$0.0^4 9687$	$0.0^4 9299$
4.1	$0.0^4 8926$	$0.0^4 8567$	$0.0^4 8222$	$0.0^4 7890$	$0.0^4 7570$	$0.0^4 7263$	$0.0^4 6967$	$0.0^4 6683$	$0.0^4 6410$	$0.0^4 6147$
4.2	$0.0^4 5894$	$0.0^4 5652$	$0.0^4 5418$	$0.0^4 5194$	$0.0^4 4979$	$0.0^4 4772$	$0.0^4 4573$	$0.0^4 4382$	$0.0^4 4199$	$0.0^4 4023$
4.3	$0.0^4 3854$	$0.0^4 3691$	$0.0^4 3535$	$0.0^4 3386$	$0.0^4 3242$	$0.0^4 3104$	$0.0^4 2972$	$0.0^4 2845$	$0.0^4 2723$	$0.0^4 2606$
4.4	$0.0^4 2494$	$0.0^4 2387$	$0.0^4 2284$	$0.0^4 2185$	$0.0^4 2090$	$0.0^4 1999$	$0.0^4 1912$	$0.0^4 1829$	$0.0^4 1749$	$0.0^4 1672$
4.5	$0.0^4 1598$	$0.0^4 1528$	$0.0^4 1461$	$0.0^4 1396$	$0.0^4 1334$	$0.0^4 1275$	$0.0^4 1218$	$0.0^4 1164$	$0.0^4 1112$	$0.0^4 1062$
4.6	$0.0^4 1014$	$0.0^5 9684$	$0.0^5 9248$	$0.0^5 8830$	$0.0^5 8430$	$0.0^5 8047$	$0.0^5 7681$	$0.0^5 7331$	$0.0^5 6996$	$0.0^5 6676$
4.7	$0.0^5 6370$	$0.0^5 6077$	$0.0^5 5797$	$0.0^5 5530$	$0.0^5 5274$	$0.0^5 5030$	$0.0^5 4796$	$0.0^5 4573$	$0.0^5 4360$	$0.0^5 4156$
4.8	$0.0^5 3961$	$0.0^5 3775$	$0.0^5 3598$	$0.0^5 3428$	$0.0^5 3267$	$0.0^5 3112$	$0.0^5 2965$	$0.0^5 2824$	$0.0^5 2690$	$0.0^5 2561$
4.9	$0.0^5 2439$	$0.0^5 2322$	$0.0^5 2211$	$0.0^5 2105$	$0.0^5 2003$	$0.0^5 1907$	$0.0^5 1814$	$0.0^5 1727$	$0.0^5 1643$	$0.0^5 1563$

Example: $n_z(3.57) = n_z(-3.57) = 0.0^3 6814 = 0.0006814$.

Reproduced by permission from A. Hald, *Statistical Tables and Formulas*, New York: John Wiley, 1952.

Table III. Present Value of $1.00

$$(1 + r)^{-n}$$

n/r	1.0%	1.1%	1.2%	1.3%	1.4%
1	.990099	.989120	.988142	.987167	.986193
2	.980296	.978358	.976425	.974498	.972577
3	.970590	.967713	.964847	.961992	.959149
4	.960980	.957184	.953406	.949647	.945906
5	.951466	.946769	.942101	.937460	.932847
6	.942045	.936468	.930930	.925429	.919967
7	.932718	.926279	.919891	.913553	.907265
8	.923483	.916201	.908983	.901829	.894739
9	.914340	.906232	.898205	.890256	.882386
10	.905287	.896372	.887554	.878831	.870203
11	.896324	.886620	.877030	.867553	.858188
12	.887449	.876973	.866630	.856420	.846339
13	.878663	.867431	.856354	.845429	.834654
14	.869963	.857993	.846200	.834580	.823130
15	.861349	.848658	.836166	.823869	.811766
16	.852821	.839424	.826251	.813296	.800558
17	.844377	.830291	.816453	.802859	.789505
18	.836017	.821257	.806772	.792556	.778604
19	.827740	.812322	.797205	.782385	.767854
20	.819544	.803483	.787752	.772345	.757253
21	.811430	.794741	.778411	.762433	.746798
22	.803396	.786094	.769181	.752649	.736487
23	.795442	.777541	.760061	.742990	.726318
24	.787566	.769081	.751048	.733455	.716290
25	.779768	.760713	.742142	.724042	.706401
26	.772048	.752437	.733342	.714750	.696648
27	.764404	.744250	.724646	.705578	.687029
28	.756836	.736152	.716054	.696523	.677544
29	.749342	.728143	.707563	.687585	.668189
30	.741923	.720220	.699173	.678761	.658963
35	.705914	.681883	.658692	.636311	.614712
40	.671653	.645586	.620554	.596516	.573432
45	.639055	.611221	.584624	.559210	.534924
50	.608039	.578685	.550775	.524237	.499002

Table III. Present Value of $1.00 (cont'd)

n/r	1.5%	1.6%	1.7%	1.8%	1.9%
1	.985222	.984252	.983284	.982318	.981354
2	.970662	.968752	.966848	.964949	.963056
3	.956317	.953496	.950686	.947887	.945099
4	.942184	.938480	.934795	.931127	.927477
5	.928260	.923701	.919169	.914663	.910184
6	.914542	.909155	.903804	.898490	.893213
7	.901027	.894837	.888696	.882603	.876558
8	.887711	.880745	.873841	.866997	.860214
9	.874592	.866875	.859234	.851667	.844175
10	.861667	.853224	.844871	.836608	.828434
11	.848933	.839787	.830748	.821816	.812988
12	.836387	.826562	.816862	.807285	.797829
13	.824027	.813545	.803207	.793010	.782953
14	.811849	.800734	.789781	.778989	.768354
15	.799852	.788124	.776579	.765215	.754028
16	.788031	.775712	.763598	.751684	.739968
17	.776385	.763496	.750834	.738393	.726171
18	.764912	.751473	.738283	.725337	.712631
19	.753607	.739639	.725942	.712512	.699343
20	.742470	.727991	.713807	.699914	.686304
21	.731498	.716526	.701875	.687538	.673507
22	.720688	.705242	.690143	.675381	.660949
23	.710037	.694136	.678607	.663439	.648625
24	.699544	.683205	.667263	.651708	.636531
25	.689206	.672446	.656109	.640185	.624662
26	.679021	.661856	.645142	.628866	.613015
27	.668986	.651433	.634358	.617746	.601585
28	.659099	.641174	.623754	.606823	.590368
29	.649359	.631077	.613327	.596094	.579360
30	.639762	.621139	.603075	.585554	.568558
35	.593866	.573747	.554328	.535584	.517492
40	.551262	.529970	.509521	.489879	.471013
45	.511715	.489534	.468336	.448074	.428708
50	.475005	.452183	.430479	.409837	.390203

Table III. Present Value of $1.00 (cont'd)

n/r	2.0%	2.1%	2.2%	2.3%	2.4%
1	.980392	.979432	.978474	.977517	.976562
2	.961169	.959287	.957411	.955540	.953674
3	.942322	.939556	.936801	.934056	.931323
4	.923845	.920231	.916635	.913056	.909495
5	.905731	.901304	.896903	.892528	.888178
6	.887971	.882766	.877596	.872461	.867362
7	.870560	.864609	.858704	.852846	.847033
8	.853490	.846826	.840220	.833671	.827181
9	.836755	.829408	.822133	.814928	.807794
10	.820348	.812349	.804435	.796606	.788861
11	.804263	.795640	.787119	.778696	.770372
12	.788493	.779276	.770175	.761189	.752316
13	.773033	.763247	.753596	.744075	.734684
14	.757875	.747549	.737373	.727346	.717465
15	.743015	.732173	.721500	.710993	.700649
16	.728446	.717114	.705969	.695008	.684228
17	.714163	.702364	.690772	.679382	.668191
18	.700159	.687918	.675902	.664108	.652530
19	.686431	.673769	.661352	.649177	.637237
20	.672971	.659911	.647116	.634581	.622302
21	.659776	.646338	.633186	.620314	.607716
22	.646839	.633044	.619556	.606368	.593473
23	.634156	.620023	.606219	.592735	.579563
24	.621721	.607271	.593169	.579408	.565980
25	.609531	.594780	.580400	.566382	.552715
26	.597579	.582547	.567906	.553648	.539761
27	.585862	.570565	.555681	.541200	.527110
28	.574375	.558829	.543720	.529032	.514756
29	.563112	.547335	.532015	.517138	.502691
30	.552071	.536078	.520563	.505511	.490909
35	.500028	.483169	.466894	.451183	.436015
40	.452890	.435482	.418759	.402694	.387259
45	.410197	.392502	.375586	.359415	.343955
50	.371528	.353763	.336864	.320788	.305494

Table III. Present Value of $1.00 (cont'd)

n/r	2.5%	2.6%	2.7%	2.8%	2.9%
1	.975610	.974659	.973710	.972763	.971817
2	.951814	.949960	.948111	.946267	.944429
3	.928599	.925887	.923185	.920493	.917812
4	.905951	.902424	.898914	.895422	.891946
5	.883854	.879555	.875282	.871033	.866808
6	.862297	.857266	.852270	.847308	.842379
7	.841265	.835542	.829864	.824230	.818639
8	.820747	.814369	.808047	.801780	.795567
9	.800728	.793732	.786803	.779941	.773146
10	.781198	.773618	.766118	.758698	.751357
11	.762145	.754013	.745976	.738033	.730182
12	.743556	.734906	.726365	.717931	.709603
13	.725420	.716282	.707268	.698376	.689605
14	.707727	.698131	.688674	.679354	.670170
15	.690466	.680440	.670569	.660851	.651282
16	.673625	.663197	.652939	.642851	.632928
17	.657195	.646390	.635774	.625341	.615090
18	.641166	.630010	.619059	.608309	.597755
19	.625528	.614045	.602784	.591740	.580909
20	.610271	.598484	.586937	.575622	.564537
21	.595386	.583318	.571506	.559944	.548627
22	.580865	.568536	.556481	.544693	.533165
23	.566697	.554129	.541851	.529857	.518139
24	.552875	.540087	.527606	.515425	.503537
25	.539391	.526400	.513735	.501386	.489346
26	.526235	.513061	.500229	.487729	.475554
27	.513400	.500059	.487077	.474445	.462152
28	.500878	.487387	.474272	.461522	.449127
29	.488661	.475036	.461803	.448952	.436470
30	.476743	.462998	.449663	.436723	.424169
35	.421371	.407232	.393581	.380400	.367673
40	.372431	.358183	.344494	.331341	.318702
45	.329174	.315042	.301530	.288609	.276254
50	.290942	.277097	.263923	.251388	.239459

Table III. Present Value of $1.00 (cont'd)

n/r	3.0%	3.1%	3.2%	3.3%	3.4%
1	.970874	.969932	.968992	.968054	.967118
2	.942596	.940768	.938946	.937129	.935317
3	.915142	.912481	.909831	.907192	.904562
4	.888487	.885045	.881620	.878211	.874818
5	.862609	.858434	.854283	.850156	.846052
6	.837484	.832622	.827793	.822997	.818233
7	.813092	.807587	.802125	.796705	.791327
8	.789409	.783305	.777253	.771254	.765307
9	.766417	.759752	.753152	.746616	.740142
10	.744094	.736908	.729799	.722764	.715805
11	.722421	.714751	.707169	.699675	.692268
12	.701380	.693260	.685241	.677323	.669505
13	.680951	.672415	.663994	.655686	.647490
14	.661118	.652197	.643405	.634739	.626199
15	.641862	.632587	.623454	.614462	.605608
16	.623167	.613566	.604122	.594833	.585695
17	.605016	.595117	.585390	.575830	.566436
18	.587395	.577224	.567238	.557435	.547810
19	.570286	.559868	.549649	.539627	.529797
20	.553676	.543034	.532606	.522388	.512377
21	.537549	.526706	.516091	.505700	.495529
22	.521893	.510869	.500088	.489545	.479235
23	.506692	.495508	.484582	.473906	.463476
24	.491934	.480609	.469556	.458767	.448236
25	.477606	.466158	.454996	.444111	.433497
26	.463695	.452142	.440888	.429924	.419243
27	.450189	.438547	.427217	.416190	.405458
28	.437077	.425361	.413970	.402894	.392125
29	.424346	.412571	.401133	.390023	.379231
30	.411987	.400166	.388695	.377564	.366762
35	.355383	.343516	.332055	.320988	.310300
40	.306557	.294885	.283669	.272890	.262530
45	.264439	.253140	.242334	.231999	.222114
50	.228107	.217304	.207021	.197235	.187920

Table III. Present Value of $1.00 (cont'd)

n/r	3.5%	3.6%	3.7%	3.8%	3.9%
1	.966184	.965251	.964320	.963391	.962464
2	.933511	.931709	.929913	.928122	.926337
3	.901943	.899333	.896734	.894145	.891566
4	.871442	.868082	.864739	.861411	.858100
5	.841973	.837917	.833885	.829876	.825890
6	.813501	.808801	.804132	.799495	.794889
7	.785991	.780696	.775441	.770227	.765052
8	.759412	.753567	.747773	.742030	.736335
9	.733731	.727381	.721093	.714865	.708696
10	.708919	.702106	.695364	.688694	.682094
11	.684946	.677708	.670554	.663482	.656491
12	.661783	.654158	.646629	.639193	.631849
13	.639404	.631427	.623557	.615793	.608132
14	.617782	.609486	.601309	.593249	.585305
15	.596891	.588307	.579854	.571531	.563335
16	.576706	.567863	.559165	.550608	.542190
17	.557204	.548131	.539214	.530451	.521838
18	.538361	.529084	.519975	.511031	.502250
19	.520156	.510699	.501422	.492323	.483398
20	.502566	.492952	.483532	.474300	.465253
21	.485571	.475823	.466279	.456936	.447789
22	,469151	.459288	.449643	.440208	.430981
23	.453286	.443328	.433599	.424093	.414803
24	.437957	.427923	.418129	.408567	.399233
25	.423147	.413053	.403210	.393610	.384248
26	.408838	.398700	.388823	.379200	.369825
27	.395012	.384846	.374950	.365318	.355943
28	.381654	.371473	.361572	.351944	.342582
29	.368748	.358564	.348671	.339060	.329723
30	.356278	.346105	.336231	.326648	.317346
35	.299977	.290007	.280378	.271077	.262093
40	.252572	.243002	.233803	.224960	.216460
45	.212659	.203616	.194965	.186689	.178772
50	.179053	.170613	.162578	.154929	.147646

Table III. Present Value of $1.00 (cont'd)

n/r	4.0%	4.1%	4.2%	4.3%	4.4%
1	.961538	.960615	.959693	.958773	.957854
2	.924556	.922781	.921010	.919245	.917485
3	.888996	.886437	.883887	.881347	.878817
4	.854804	.851524	.848260	.845012	.841779
5	.821927	.817987	.814069	.810174	.806302
6	.790315	.785770	.781257	.776773	.772320
7	.759918	.754823	.749766	.744749	.739770
8	.730690	.725094	.719545	.714045	.708592
9	.702587	.696536	.690543	.684607	.678728
10	.675564	.669103	.662709	.656382	.650122
11	.649581	.642750	.635997	.629322	.622722
12	.624597	.617435	.610362	.603376	.596477
13	.600574	.593117	.585760	.578501	.571339
14	.577475	.569757	.562150	.554651	.547259
15	.555265	.547317	.539491	.531784	.524195
16	.533908	.525761	.517746	.509860	.502102
17	.513373	.505054	.496877	.488840	.480941
18	.493628	.485162	.476849	.468687	.460671
19	.474642	.466054	.457629	.449364	.441256
20	.456387	.447698	.439183	.430838	.422659
21	.438834	.430066	.421481	.413076	.404846
22	.421955	.413127	.404492	.396046	.387783
23	.405726	.396856	.388188	.379718	.371440
24	.390121	.381226	.372542	.364063	.355785
25	.375117	.366211	.357526	.349054	.340791
26	.360689	.351788	.343115	.334663	.326428
27	.346817	.337933	.329285	.320866	.312670
28	.333477	.324623	.316012	.307638	.299493
29	.320651	.311838	.303275	.294955	.286870
30	.308319	.299556	.291051	.282794	.274780
35	.253415	.245033	.236935	.229113	.221556
40	.208289	.200434	.192882	.185621	.178641
45	.171198	.163952	.157019	.150386	.144038
50	.140713	.134111	.127824	.121839	.116138

Table III. Present Value of $1.00 (cont'd)

n/r	4.5%	4.6%	4.7%	4.8%	4.9%
1	.956938	.956023	.955110	.954198	.953289
2	.915730	.913980	.912235	.910495	.908760
3	.876297	.873786	.871284	.868793	.866310
4	.838561	.835359	.832172	.829001	.825844
5	.802451	.798623	.794816	.791031	.787268
6	.767896	.763501	.759137	.754801	.750494
7	.734828	.729925	.725059	.720230	.715437
8	.703185	.697825	.692511	.687242	.682018
9	.672904	.667137	.661424	.655765	.650161
10	.643928	.637798	.631732	.625730	.619791
11	.616199	.609750	.603374	.597071	.590840
12	.589664	.582935	.576288	.569724	.563241
13	.564272	.557299	.550419	.543630	.536931
14	.539973	.532790	.525710	.518731	.511851
15	.516720	.509360	.502111	.494972	.487941
16	.494469	.486960	.479571	.472302	.465149
17	.473176	.465545	.458043	.450670	.443421
18	.452800	.445071	.437482	.430028	.422709
19	.433302	.425498	.417843	.410332	.402964
20	.414643	.406786	.399086	.391538	.384141
21	.396787	.388897	.381171	.373605	.366197
22	.379701	.371794	.364060	.356494	.349091
23	.363350	.355444	.347717	.340166	.332785
24	.347703	.339813	.332108	.324586	.317240
25	.332731	.324869	.317200	.309719	.302422
26	.318402	.310582	.302961	.295533	.288295
27	.304691	.296923	.289361	.281998	.274829
28	.291571	.283866	.276371	.269082	.261991
29	.279015	.271382	.263965	.256757	.249753
30	.267000	.259447	.252116	.244997	.238087
35	.214254	.207201	.200385	.193801	.187438
40	.171929	.165475	.159270	.153302	.147564
45	.137964	.132152	.126590	.121267	.116172
50	.110710	.105540	.100616	.095926	.091459

Table III.   Present Value of $1.00 (cont'd)

n/r	5.0%	5.1%	5.2%	5.3%	5.4%
1	.952381	.951475	.950570	.949668	.948767
2	.907029	.905304	.903584	.901869	.900158
3	.863838	.861374	.858920	.856475	.854040
4	.822702	.819576	.816464	.813367	.810285
5	.783526	.779806	.776106	.772428	.768771
6	.746215	.741965	.737744	.733550	.729384
7	.710681	.705961	.701277	.696629	.692015
8	.676839	.671705	.666613	.661566	.656561
9	.644609	.639110	.633663	.628268	.622923
10	.613913	.608097	.602341	.596645	.591009
11	.584679	.578589	.572568	.566615	.560729
12	.556837	.550513	.544266	.538096	.532001
13	.530321	.523799	.517363	.511012	.504745
14	.505068	.498382	.491790	.485292	.478885
15	.481017	.474197	.467481	.460866	.454350
16	.458112	.451187	.444374	.437669	.431072
17	.436297	.429293	.422408	.415640	.408987
18	.415521	.408461	.401529	.394720	.388033
19	.395734	.388641	.381681	.374853	.368153
20	.376889	.369782	.362815	.355986	.349291
21	.358942	.351838	.344881	.338068	.331396
22	.341850	.334765	.327834	.321052	.314417
23	.325571	.318521	.311629	.304893	.298309
24	.310068	.303064	.296225	.289547	.283025
25	.295303	.288358	.281583	.274973	.268525
26	.281241	.274365	.267664	.261133	.254768
27	.267848	.261052	.254434	.247990	.241715
28	.255094	.248384	.241857	.235508	.229331
29	.242946	.236331	.229902	.223654	.217582
30	.231377	.224863	.218538	.212397	.206434
35	.181290	.175350	.169609	.164062	.158701
40	.142046	.136739	.131635	.126726	.122004
45	.111297	.106630	.102163	.097887	.093793
50	.087204	.083150	.079289	.075610	.072106

Table III.   Present Value of $1.00 (cont'd)

n/r	5.5%	5.6%	5.7%	5.8%	5.9%
1	.947867	.946970	.946074	.945180	.944287
2	.898452	.896752	.895056	.893364	.891678
3	.851614	.849197	.846789	.844390	.842000
4	.807217	.804163	.801125	.798100	.795090
5	.765134	.761518	.757923	.754348	.750793
6	.725246	.721135	.717051	.712994	.708964
7	.687437	.682893	.678383	.673908	.669466
8	.651599	.646679	.641801	.636964	.632168
9	.617629	.612385	.607191	.602045	.596948
10	.585431	.579910	.574447	.569041	.563690
11	.554911	.549157	.543469	.537846	.532285
12	.525982	.520035	.514162	.508361	.502630
13	.498561	.492458	.486435	.480492	.474627
14	.472569	.466343	.460204	.454151	.448184
15	.447933	.441612	.435387	.429255	.423215
16	.424581	.418194	.411908	.405723	.399636
17	.402447	.396017	.389695	.383481	.377371
18	.381466	.375016	.368681	.362458	.356347
19	.361579	.355129	.348799	.342588	.336494
20	.342729	.336296	.329990	.323807	.317747
21	.324862	.318462	.312195	.306056	.300044
22	.307926	.301574	.295359	.289278	.283328
23	.291873	.285581	.279431	.273420	.267543
24	.276657	.270437	.264363	.258431	.252637
25	.262234	.256096	.250107	.244263	.238562
26	.248563	.242515	.236619	.230873	.225271
27	.235605	.229654	.223859	.218216	.212720
28	.223322	.217475	.211788	.206253	.200869
29	.211679	.205943	.200367	.194947	.189678
30	.200644	.195021	.189562	.184260	.179111
35	.153520	.148512	.143673	.138996	.134475
40	.117463	.113095	.108893	.104851	.100963
45	.089875	.086124	.082533	.079094	.075802
50	.068767	.065585	.062553	.059665	.056912

Table III. Present Value of $1.00 (cont'd)

n/r	6%	7%	8%	9%	10%	11%
1	0.9434	0.9346	0.9259	0.9174	0.9091	0.9009
2	0.8900	0.8734	0.8573	0.8417	0.8264	0.8116
3	0.8396	0.8163	0.7938	0.7722	0.7513	0.7312
4	0.7921	0.7629	0.7350	0.7084	0.6830	0.6587
5	0.7473	0.7130	0.6806	0.6499	0.6209	0.5935
6	0.7050	0.6663	0.6302	0.5963	0.5645	0.5346
7	0.6651	0.6227	0.5835	0.5470	0.5132	0.4817
8	0.6274	0.5820	0.5403	0.5019	0.4665	0.4339
9	0.5919	0.5439	0.5002	0.4604	0.4241	0.3909
10	0.5584	0.5083	0.4632	0.4224	0.3855	0.3522
11	0.5268	0.4751	0.4289	0.3875	0.3505	0.3173
12	0.4970	0.4440	0.3971	0.3555	0.3186	0.2858
13	0.4688	0.4150	0.3677	0.3262	0.2897	0.2575
14	0.4423	0.3878	0.3405	0.2992	0.2633	0.2320
15	0.4173	0.3624	0.3152	0.2745	0.2394	0.2090
16	0.3936	0.3387	0.2919	0.2519	0.2176	0.1883
17	0.3714	0.3166	0.2703	0.2311	0.1978	0.1696
18	0.3503	0.2959	0.2502	0.2120	0.1799	0.1528
19	0.3305	0.2765	0.2317	0.1945	0.1635	0.1377
20	0.3118	0.2584	0.2145	0.1784	0.1486	0.1240
21	0.2942	0.2415	0.1987	0.1637	0.1351	0.1117
22	0.2775	0.2257	0.1839	0.1502	0.1228	0.1007
23	0.2618	0.2109	0.1703	0.1378	0.1117	0.0907
24	0.2470	0.1971	0.1577	0.1264	0.1015	0.0817
25	0.2330	0.1842	0.1460	0.1160	0.0923	0.0736
26	0.2198	0.1722	0.1352	0.1064	0.0839	0.0663
27	0.2074	0.1609	0.1252	0.0976	0.0763	0.0597
28	0.1956	0.1504	0.1159	0.0895	0.0693	0.0538
29	0.1846	0.1406	0.1073	0.0822	0.0630	0.0485
30	0.1741	0.1314	0.0994	0.0754	0.0573	0.0437
35	0.1301	0.0937	0.0676	0.0490	0.0356	0.0259
40	0.0972	0.0668	0.0460	0.0318	0.0221	0.0154
45	0.0727	0.0476	0.0313	0.0207	0.0137	0.0091
50	0.0543	0.0339	0.0213	0.0134	0.0085	0.0054

Table III. Present Value of $1.00 (cont'd)

n/r	12%	13%	14%	15%	16%	17%
1	0.8929	0.8850	0.8772	0.8696	0.8621	0.8547
2	0.7972	0.7831	0.7695	0.7561	0.7432	0.7305
3	0.7118	0.6931	0.6750	0.6575	0.6407	0.6244
4	0.6355	0.6133	0.5921	0.5718	0.5523	0.5337
5	0.5674	0.5428	0.5194	0.4972	0.4761	0.4561
6	0.5066	0.4803	0.4556	0.4323	0.4104	0.3898
7	0.4523	0.4251	0.3996	0.3759	0.3538	0.3332
8	0.4039	0.3762	0.3506	0.3269	0.3050	0.2848
9	0.3606	0.3329	0.3075	0.2843	0.2630	0.2434
10	0.3220	0.2946	0.2697	0.2472	0.2267	0.2080
11	0.2875	0.2607	0.2366	0.2149	0.1954	0.1778
12	0.2567	0.2307	0.2076	0.1869	0.1685	0.1520
13	0.2292	0.2042	0.1821	0.1625	0.1452	0.1299
14	0.2046	0.1807	0.1597	0.1413	0.1252	0.1110
15	0.1827	0.1599	0.1401	0.1229	0.1079	0.0949
16	0.1631	0.1415	0.1229	0.1069	0.0930	0.0811
17	0.1456	0.1252	0.1078	0.0929	0.0802	0.0693
18	0.1300	0.1108	0.0946	0.0808	0.0691	0.0592
19	0.1161	0.0981	0.0829	0.0703	0.0596	0.0506
20	0.1037	0.0868	0.0728	0.0611	0.0514	0.0433
21	0.0926	0.0768	0.0638	0.0531	0.0443	0.0370
22	0.0826	0.0680	0.0560	0.0462	0.0382	0.0316
23	0.0738	0.0601	0.0491	0.0402	0.0329	0.0270
24	0.0659	0.0532	0.0431	0.0349	0.0284	0.0231
25	0.0588	0.0471	0.0378	0.0304	0.0245	0.0197
26	0.0525	0.0417	0.0331	0.0264	0.0211	0.0169
27	0.0469	0.0369	0.0291	0.0230	0.0182	0.0144
28	0.0419	0.0326	0.0255	0.0200	0.0157	0.0123
29	0.0374	0.0289	0.0224	0.0174	0.0135	0.0105
30	0.0334	0.0256	0.0196	0.0151	0.0116	0.0090
35	0.0189	0.0139	0.0102	0.0075	0.0055	0.0041
40	0.0107	0.0075	0.0053	0.0037	0.0026	0.0019
45	0.0061	0.0041	0.0027	0.0019	0.0013	0.0009
50	0.0035	0.0022	0.0014	0.0009	0.0006	0.0004

Table III.   Present Value of $1.00 (cont'd)

n/r	18%	19%	20%	21%	22%	23%
1	0.8475	0.8403	0.8333	0.8264	0.8197	0.8130
2	0.7182	0.7062	0.6944	0.6830	0.6719	0.6610
3	0.6086	0.5934	0.5787	0.5645	0.5507	0.5374
4	0.5158	0.4987	0.4823	0.4665	0.4514	0.4369
5	0.4371	0.4190	0.4019	0.3855	0.3700	0.3552
6	0.3704	0.3521	0.3349	0.3186	0.3033	0.2888
7	0.3139	0.2959	0.2791	0.2633	0.2486	0.2348
8	0.2660	0.2487	0.2326	0.2176	0.2038	0.1909
9	0.2255	0.2090	0.1938	0.1799	0.1670	0.1552
10	0.1911	0.1756	0.1615	0.1486	0.1369	0.1262
11	0.1619	0.1476	0.1346	0.1228	0.1122	0.1026
12	0.1372	0.1240	0.1122	0.1015	0.0920	0.0834
13	0.1163	0.1042	0.0935	0.0839	0.0754	0.0678
14	0.0985	0.0876	0.0779	0.0693	0.0618	0.0551
15	0.0835	0.0736	0.0649	0.0573	0.0507	0.0448
16	0.0708	0.0618	0.0541	0.0474	0.0415	0.0364
17	0.0600	0.0520	0.0451	0.0391	0.0340	0.0296
18	0.0508	0.0437	0.0376	0.0323	0.0279	0.0241
19	0.0431	0.0367	0.0313	0.0267	0.0229	0.0196
20	0.0365	0.0308	0.0261	0.0221	0.0187	0.0159
21	0.0309	0.0259	0.0217	0.0183	0.0154	0.0129
22	0.0262	0.0218	0.0181	0.0151	0.0126	0.0105
23	0.0222	0.0183	0.0151	0.0125	0.0103	0.0086
24	0.0188	0.0154	0.0126	0.0103	0.0085	0.0070
25	0.0160	0.0129	0.0105	0.0085	0.0069	0.0057
26	0.0135	0.0109	0.0087	0.0070	0.0057	0.0046
27	0.0115	0.0091	0.0073	0.0058	0.0047	0.0037
28	0.0097	0.0077	0.0061	0.0048	0.0038	0.0030
29	0.0082	0.0064	0.0051	0.0040	0.0031	0.0025
30	0.0070	0.0054	0.0042	0.0033	0.0026	0.0020
35	0.0030	0.0023	0.0017	0.0013	0.0009	0.0007
40	0.0013	0.0010	0.0007	0.0005	0.0004	0.0002
45	0.0006	0.0004	0.0003	0.0002	0.0001	0.0001
50	0.0003	0.0002	0.0001	0.0001	0.0000	0.0000

Table III. Present Value of $1.00 (cont'd)

n/r	24%	25%	26%	27%	28%	29%
1	0.8065	0.8000	0.7937	0.7874	0.7813	0.7752
2	0.6504	0.6400	0.6299	0.6200	0.6104	0.6009
3	0.5245	0.5120	0.4999	0.4882	0.4768	0.4658
4	0.4230	0.4096	0.3968	0.3844	0.3725	0.3611
5	0.3411	0.3277	0.3149	0.3027	0.2910	0.2799
6	0.2751	0.2621	0.2499	0.2383	0.2274	0.2170
7	0.2218	0.2097	0.1983	0.1877	0.1776	0.1682
8	0.1789	0.1678	0.1574	0.1478	0.1388	0.1304
9	0.1443	0.1342	0.1249	0.1164	0.1084	0.1011
10	0.1164	0.1074	0.0992	0.0916	0.0847	0.0784
11	0.0938	0.0859	0.0787	0.0721	0.0662	0.0607
12	0.0757	0.0687	0.0625	0.0568	0.0517	0.0471
13	0.0610	0.0550	0.0496	0.0447	0.0404	0.0365
14	0.0492	0.0440	0.0393	0.0352	0.0316	0.0283
15	0.0397	0.0352	0.0312	0.0277	0.0247	0.0219
16	0.0320	0.0281	0.0248	0.0218	0.0193	0.0170
17	0.0258	0.0225	0.0197	0.0172	0.0150	0.0132
18	0.0208	0.0180	0.0156	0.0135	0.0118	0.0102
19	0.0168	0.0144	0.0124	0.0107	0.0092	0.0079
20	0.0135	0.0115	0.0098	0.0084	0.0072	0.0061
21	0.0109	0.0092	0.0078	0.0066	0.0056	0.0048
22	0.0088	0.0074	0.0062	0.0052	0.0044	0.0037
23	0.0071	0.0059	0.0049	0.0041	0.0034	0.0029
24	0.0057	0.0047	0.0039	0.0032	0.0027	0.0022
25	0.0046	0.0038	0.0031	0.0025	0.0021	0.0017
26	0.0037	0.0030	0.0025	0.0020	0.0016	0.0013
27	0.0030	0.0024	0.0019	0.0016	0.0013	0.0010
28	0.0024	0.0019	0.0015	0.0012	0.0010	0.0008
29	0.0020	0.0015	0.0012	0.0010	0.0008	0.0006
30	0.0016	0.0012	0.0010	0.0008	0.0006	0.0005
35	0.0005	0.0004	0.0003	0.0002	0.0002	0.0001
40	0.0002	0.0001	0.0001	0.0001	0.0001	0.0000
45	0.0001	0.0000	0.0000	0.0000	0.0000	
50	0.0000					

Table III. Present Value of $1.00 (cont'd)

n/r	30%	31%	32%	33%	34%	35%
1	0.7692	0.7634	0.7576	0.7519	0.7463	0.7407
2	0.5917	0.5827	0.5739	0.5653	0.5569	0.5487
3	0.4552	0.4448	0.4348	0.4251	0.4156	0.4064
4	0.3501	0.3396	0.3294	0.3196	0.3102	0.3011
5	0.2693	0.2592	0.2495	0.2403	0.2315	0.2230
6	0.2072	0.1979	0.1890	0.1807	0.1727	0.1652
7	0.1594	0.1510	0.1432	0.1358	0.1289	0.1224
8	0.1226	0.1153	0.1085	0.1021	0.0962	0.0906
9	0.0943	0.0880	0.0822	0.0768	0.0718	0.0671
10	0.0725	0.0672	0.0623	0.0577	0.0536	0.0497
11	0.0558	0.0513	0.0472	0.0434	0.0400	0.0368
12	0.0429	0.0392	0.0357	0.0326	0.0298	0.0273
13	0.0330	0.0299	0.0271	0.0245	0.0223	0.0202
14	0.0253	0.0228	0.0205	0.0185	0.0166	0.0150
15	0.0195	0.0174	0.0155	0.0139	0.0124	0.0111
16	0.0150	0.0133	0.0118	0.0104	0.0093	0.0082
17	0.0116	0.0101	0.0089	0.0078	0.0069	0.0061
18	0.0089	0.0077	0.0068	0.0059	0.0052	0.0045
19	0.0068	0.0059	0.0051	0.0044	0.0038	0.0033
20	0.0053	0.0045	0.0039	0.0033	0.0029	0.0025
21	0.0040	0.0034	0.0029	0.0025	0.0021	0.0018
22	0.0031	0.0026	0.0022	0.0019	0.0016	0.0014
23	0.0024	0.0020	0.0017	0.0014	0.0012	0.0010
24	0.0018	0.0015	0.0013	0.0011	0.0009	0.0007
25	0.0014	0.0012	0.0010	0.0008	0.0007	0.0006
26	0.0011	0.0009	0.0007	0.0006	0.0005	0.0004
27	0.0008	0.0007	0.0006	0.0005	0.0004	0.0003
28	0.0006	0.0005	0.0004	0.0003	0.0003	0.0002
29	0.0005	0.0004	0.0003	0.0003	0.0002	0.0002
30	0.0004	0.0003	0.0002	0.0002	0.0002	0.0001
35	0.0001	0.0001	0.0001	0.0000	0.0000	0.0000
40	0.0000	0.0000	0.0000			
45						
50						

Table III.   Present Value of $1.00 (cont'd)

n/r	36%	37%	38%	39%	40%	41%
1	0.7353	0.7299	0.7246	0.7194	0.7143	0.7092
2	0.5407	0.5328	0.5251	0.5176	0.5102	0.5030
3	0.3975	0.3889	0.3805	0.3724	0.3644	0.3567
4	0.2923	0.2839	0.2757	0.2679	0.2603	0.2530
5	0.2149	0.2072	0.1998	0.1927	0.1859	0.1794
6	0.1580	0.1512	0.1448	0.1386	0.1328	0.1273
7	0.1162	0.1104	0.1049	0.0997	0.0949	0.0903
8	0.0854	0.0806	0.0760	0.0718	0.0678	0.0640
9	0.0628	0.0588	0.0551	0.0516	0.0484	0.0454
10	0.0462	0.0429	0.0399	0.0371	0.0346	0.0322
11	0.0340	0.0313	0.0289	0.0267	0.0247	0.0228
12	0.0250	0.0229	0.0210	0.0192	0.0176	0.0162
13	0.0184	0.0167	0.0152	0.0138	0.0126	0.0115
14	0.0135	0.0122	0.0110	0.0099	0.0090	0.0081
15	0.0099	0.0089	0.0080	0.0072	0.0064	0.0058
16	0.0073	0.0065	0.0058	0.0051	0.0046	0.0041
17	0.0054	0.0047	0.0042	0.0037	0.0033	0.0029
18	0.0039	0.0035	0.0030	0.0027	0.0023	0.0021
19	0.0029	0.0025	0.0022	0.0019	0.0017	0.0015
20	0.0021	0.0018	0.0016	0.0014	0.0012	0.0010
21	0.0016	0.0013	0.0012	0.0010	0.0009	0.0007
22	0.0012	0.0010	0.0008	0.0007	0.0006	0.0005
23	0.0008	0.0007	0.0006	0.0005	0.0004	0.0004
24	0.0006	0.0005	0.0004	0.0004	0.0003	0.0003
25	0.0005	0.0004	0.0003	0.0003	0.0002	0.0002
26	0.0003	0.0003	0.0002	0.0002	0.0002	0.0001
27	0.0002	0.0002	0.0002	0.0001	0.0001	0.0001
28	0.0002	0.0001	0.0001	0.0001	0.0001	0.0001
29	0.0001	0.0001	0.0001	0.0001	0.0001	0.0000
30	0.0001	0.0001	0.0001	0.0001	0.0000	
35	0.0000	0.0000	0.0000	0.0000		
40						
45						
50						

Table III.   Present Value of $1.00 (cont'd)

n/r	42%	43%	44%	45%	46%	47%	48%
1	0.7042	0.6993	0.6944	0.6897	0.6849	0.6803	0.6757
2	0.4959	0.4890	0.4823	0.4756	0.4691	0.4628	0.4565
3	0.3492	0.3420	0.3349	0.3280	0.3213	0.3148	0.3085
4	0.2459	0.2391	0.2326	0.2262	0.2201	0.2142	0.2084
5	0.1732	0.1672	0.1615	0.1560	0.1507	0.1457	0.1408
6	0.1220	0.1169	0.1122	0.1076	0.1032	0.0991	0.0952
7	0.0859	0.0818	0.0779	0.0742	0.0707	0.0674	0.0643
8	0.0605	0.0572	0.0541	0.0512	0.0484	0.0459	0.0434
9	0.0426	0.0400	0.0376	0.0353	0.0332	0.0312	0.0294
10	0.0300	0.0280	0.0261	0.0243	0.0227	0.0212	0.0198
11	0.0211	0.0196	0.0181	0.0168	0.0156	0.0144	0.0134
12	0.0149	0.0137	0.0126	0.0116	0.0107	0.0098	0.0091
13	0.0105	0.0096	0.0087	0.0080	0.0073	0.0067	0.0061
14	0.0074	0.0067	0.0061	0.0055	0.0050	0.0045	0.0041
15	0.0052	0.0047	0.0042	0.0038	0.0034	0.0031	0.0028
16	0.0037	0.0033	0.0029	0.0026	0.0023	0.0021	0.0019
17	0.0026	0.0023	0.0020	0.0018	0.0016	0.0014	0.0013
18	0.0018	0.0016	0.0014	0.0012	0.0011	0.0010	0.0009
19	0.0013	0.0011	0.0010	0.0009	0.0008	0.0007	0.0006
20	0.0009	0.0008	0.0007	0.0006	0.0005	0.0005	0.0004
21	0.0006	0.0005	0.0005	0.0004	0.0004	0.0003	0.0003
22	0.0004	0.0004	0.0003	0.0003	0.0002	0.0002	0.0002
23	0.0003	0.0003	0.0002	0.0002	0.0002	0.0001	0.0001
24	0.0002	0.0002	0.0002	0.0001	0.0001	0.0001	0.0001
25	0.0002	0.0001	0.0001	0.0001	0.0001	0.0001	0.0001
26	0.0001	0.0001	0.0001	0.0001	0.0001	0.0000	0.0000
27	0.0001	0.0001	0.0001	0.0000	0.0000		
28	0.0001	0.0000	0.0000				
29	0.0000						
30							
35							
40							
45							
50							

Table IV. Present Value of $1 Received per Period

$$\frac{1 - (1 + r)^{-n}}{r}$$

n/r	1.0%	1.1%	1.2%	1.3%	1.4%
1	.99010	.98912	.98814	.98717	.98619
2	1.97040	1.96748	1.96457	1.96167	1.95877
3	2.94099	2.93519	2.92941	2.92366	2.91792
4	3.90197	3.89237	3.88282	3.87330	3.86383
5	4.85343	4.83914	4.82492	4.81076	4.79667
6	5.79548	5.77561	5.75585	5.73619	5.71664
7	6.72819	6.70189	6.67574	6.64975	6.62391
8	7.65168	7.61809	7.58473	7.55158	7.51864
9	8.56602	8.52432	8.48293	8.44183	8.40103
10	9.47130	9.42070	9.37048	9.32066	9.27123
11	10.36763	10.30732	10.24751	10.18822	10.12942
12	11.25508	11.18429	11.11414	11.04464	10.97576
13	12.13374	12.05172	11.97050	11.89007	11.81041
14	13.00370	12.90971	12.81670	12.72465	12.63354
15	13.86505	13.75837	13.65286	13.54852	13.44531
16	14.71787	14.59780	14.47911	14.36181	14.24587
17	15.56225	15.42809	15.29557	15.16467	15.03537
18	16.39827	16.24934	16.10234	15.95723	15.81398
19	17.22601	17.06167	16.89955	16.73961	16.58183
20	18.04555	17.86515	17.68730	17.51196	17.33908
21	18.85698	18.65989	18.46571	18.27439	18.08588
22	19.66038	19.44598	19.23489	19.02704	18.82237
23	20.45582	20.22353	19.99495	19.77003	19.54869
24	21.24339	20.99261	20.74600	20.50348	20.26498
25	22.02316	21.75332	21.48814	21.22752	20.97138
26	22.79520	22.50576	22.22148	21.94228	21.66803
27	23.55961	23.25001	22.94613	22.64785	22.35505
28	24.31644	23.98616	23.66218	23.34438	23.03260
29	25.06579	24.71430	24.36975	24.03196	23.70079
30	25.80771	25.43452	25.06892	24.71072	24.35975
31	26.54229	26.14691	25.75980	25.38077	25.00962
32	27.26959	26.85154	26.44249	26.04222	25.65051
33	27.98969	27.54851	27.11709	26.69519	26.28255
34	28.70267	28.23789	27.78368	27.33977	26.90587
35	29.40858	28.91977	28.44237	27.97608	27.52058
40	32.83469	32.21950	31.62051	31.03722	30.46915
45	36.09451	35.34358	34.61463	33.90692	33.21972
50	39.19612	38.30136	37.43540	36.59715	35.78557

Table IV.   Present Value of $1 Received per Period (cont'd)

n/r	1.5%	1.6%	1.7%	1.8%	1.9%
1	.98522	.98425	.98328	.98232	.98135
2	1.95588	1.95300	1.95013	1.94727	1.94441
3	2.91220	2.90650	2.90082	2.89515	2.88951
4	3.85438	3.84498	3.83561	3.82628	3.81699
5	4.78264	4.76868	4.75478	4.74094	4.72717
6	5.69719	5.67784	5.65859	5.63943	5.62038
7	6.59821	6.57267	6.54728	6.52204	6.49694
8	7.48593	7.45342	7.42112	7.38904	7.35716
9	8.36052	8.32029	8.28036	8.24070	8.20133
10	9.22218	9.17352	9.12523	9.07731	9.02976
11	10.07112	10.01330	9.95598	9.89913	9.84275
12	10.90751	10.83987	10.77284	10.70641	10.64058
13	11.73153	11.65341	11.57604	11.49942	11.42353
14	12.54338	12.45415	12.36583	12.27841	12.19189
15	13.34323	13.24227	13.14241	13.04363	12.94592
16	14.13126	14.01798	13.90600	13.79531	13.68588
17	14.90765	14.78148	14.65684	14.53370	14.41206
18	15.67256	15.53295	15.39512	15.25904	15.12469
19	16.42617	16.27259	16.12106	15.97155	15.82403
20	17.16864	17.00058	16.83487	16.67147	16.51033
21	17.90014	17.71711	17.53674	17.35900	17.18384
22	18.62082	18.42235	18.22689	18.03439	17.84479
23	19.33086	19.11649	18.90549	18.69782	18.49341
24	20.03041	19.79969	19.57276	19.34953	19.12995
25	20.71961	20.47214	20.22887	19.98972	19.75461
26	21.39863	21.13399	20.87401	20.61858	20.36762
27	22.06762	21.78543	21.50837	21.23633	20.96921
28	22.72672	22.42660	22.13212	21.84315	21.55958
29	23.37608	23.05768	22.74545	22.43925	22.13894
30	24.01584	23.67882	23.34852	23.02480	22.70749
31	24.64615	24.29017	23.94152	23.60000	23.26545
32	25.26714	24.89190	24.52460	24.16503	23.81300
33	25.87895	25.48416	25.09793	24.72007	24.35035
34	26.48173	26.06708	25.66168	25.26529	24.87767
35	27.07559	26.64083	26.21601	25.80088	25.39516
40	29.91585	29.37684	28.85172	28.34005	27.84144
45	32.55234	31.90411	31.27438	30.66254	30.06799
50	34.99969	34.23854	33.50121	32.78684	32.09457

Table IV. Present Value of $1 Received per Period (cont'd)

n/r	2.0%	2.1%	2.2%	2.3%	2.4%
1	.98039	.97943	.97847	.97752	.97656
2	1.94156	1.93872	1.93588	1.93306	1.93024
3	2.88388	2.87828	2.87269	2.86711	2.86156
4	3.80773	3.79851	3.78932	3.78017	3.77105
5	4.71346	4.69981	4.68622	4.67270	4.65923
6	5.60143	5.58258	5.56382	5.54516	5.52659
7	6.47199	6.44719	6.42252	6.39800	6.37363
8	7.32548	7.29401	7.26274	7.23168	7.20081
9	8.16224	8.12342	8.08488	8.04660	8.00860
10	8.98259	8.93577	8.88931	8.84321	8.79746
11	9.78685	9.73141	9.67643	9.62191	9.56783
12	10.57534	10.51068	10.44660	10.38310	10.32015
13	11.34837	11.27393	11.20020	11.12717	11.05483
14	12.10625	12.02148	11.93757	11.85452	11.77230
15	12.84926	12.75365	12.65907	12.56551	12.47295
16	13.57771	13.47077	13.36504	13.26052	13.15718
17	14.29187	14.17313	14.05581	13.93990	13.82537
18	14.99203	14.86105	14.73172	14.60401	14.47790
19	15.67846	15.53482	15.39307	15.25318	15.11513
20	16.35143	16.19473	16.04019	15.88777	15.73744
21	17.01121	16.84107	16.67337	16.50808	16.34515
22	17.65805	17.47411	17.29293	17.11445	16.93863
23	18.29220	18.09413	17.89915	17.70718	17.51819
24	18.91393	18.70140	18.49231	18.28659	18.08417
25	19.52346	19.29618	19.07272	18.85297	18.63688
26	20.12104	19.87873	19.64062	19.40662	19.17664
27	20.70690	20.44930	20.19630	19.94782	19.70375
28	21.28127	21.00813	20.74002	20.47685	20.21851
29	21.84438	21.55546	21.27204	20.99399	20.72120
30	22.39646	22.09154	21.79260	21.49950	21.21211
31	22.93770	22.61659	22.30196	21.99365	21.69151
32	23.46833	23.13084	22.80035	22.47668	22.15968
33	23.98856	23.63452	23.28801	22.94886	22.61688
34	24.49859	24.12783	23.76518	23.41042	23.06336
35	24.99862	24.61100	24.23207	23.86160	23.49937
40	27.35548	26.88180	26.42004	25.96985	25.53087
45	29.49016	28.92849	28.38244	27.85151	27.33520
50	31.42361	30.77317	30.14252	29.53095	28.93777

Table IV. Present Value of $1 Received per Period (cont'd)

n/r	2.5%	2.6%	2.7%	2.8%	2.9%
1	.97561	.97466	.97371	.97276	.97182
2	1.92742	1.92462	1.92182	1.91903	1.91625
3	2.85602	2.85051	2.84501	2.83952	2.83406
4	3.76197	3.75293	3.74392	3.73494	3.72600
5	4.64583	4.63248	4.61920	4.60598	4.59281
6	5.50813	5.48975	5.47147	5.45329	5.43519
7	6.34939	6.32529	6.30134	6.27751	6.25383
8	7.17014	7.13966	7.10938	7.07929	7.04940
9	7.97087	7.93339	7.89619	7.85924	7.82254
10	8.75206	8.70701	8.66230	8.61793	8.57390
11	9.51421	9.46103	9.40828	9.35597	9.30408
12	10.25776	10.19593	10.13464	10.07390	10.01369
13	10.98318	10.91221	10.84191	10.77227	10.70329
14	11.69091	11.61034	11.53059	11.45163	11.37346
15	12.38138	12.29078	12.20116	12.11248	12.02474
16	13.05500	12.95398	12.85409	12.75533	12.65767
17	13.71220	13.60037	13.48987	13.38067	13.27276
18	14.35336	14.23038	14.10893	13.98898	13.87052
19	14.97889	14.84443	14.71171	14.58072	14.45142
20	15.58916	15.44291	15.29865	15.15634	15.01596
21	16.18455	16.02623	15.87015	15.71629	15.56459
22	16.76541	16.59476	16.42663	16.26098	16.09775
23	17.33211	17.14889	16.96849	16.79084	16.61589
24	17.88499	17.68898	17.49609	17.30626	17.11943
25	18.42438	18.21538	18.00983	17.80765	17.60877
26	18.95061	18.72844	18.51005	18.29538	18.08433
27	19.46401	19.22850	18.99713	18.76982	18.54648
28	19.96489	19.71589	19.47140	19.23134	18.99561
29	20.45355	20.19092	19.93321	19.68029	19.43208
30	20.93029	20.65392	20.38287	20.11702	19.85625
31	21.39541	21.10519	20.82071	20.54185	20.26846
32	21.84918	21.54502	21.24704	20.95510	20.66906
33	22.29188	21.97370	21.66216	21.35710	21.05837
34	22.72379	22.39152	22.06637	21.74816	21.43670
35	23.14516	22.79875	22.45995	22.12856	21.80438
40	25.10278	24.68525	24.27798	23.88067	23.49303
45	26.83302	26.34453	25.86927	25.40682	24.95677
50	28.36231	27.80396	27.26210	26.73615	26.22555

Table IV.   Present Value of $1 Received per Period (cont'd)

n/r	3.0%	3.1%	3.2%	3.3%	3.4%
1	.97087	.96993	.96899	.96805	.96712
2	1.91347	1.91070	1.90794	1.90518	1.90244
3	2.82861	2.82318	2.81777	2.81237	2.80700
4	3.71710	3.70823	3.69939	3.69059	3.68182
5	4.57971	4.56666	4.55367	4.54074	4.52787
6	5.41719	5.39928	5.38146	5.36374	5.34610
7	6.23028	6.20687	6.18359	6.16044	6.13743
8	7.01969	6.99017	6.96084	6.93170	6.90274
9	7.78611	7.74993	7.71400	7.67831	7.64288
10	8.53020	8.48683	8.44379	8.40108	8.35868
11	9.25262	9.20159	9.15096	9.10075	9.05095
12	9.95400	9.89485	9.83620	9.77808	9.72045
13	10.63496	10.56726	10.50020	10.43376	10.36794
14	11.29607	11.21946	11.14360	11.06850	10.99414
15	11.93794	11.85204	11.76706	11.68296	11.59975
16	12.56110	12.46561	12.37118	12.27780	12.18545
17	13.16612	13.06073	12.95657	12.85363	12.75188
18	13.75351	13.63795	13.52381	13.41106	13.29969
19	14.32380	14.19782	14.07346	13.95069	13.82949
20	14.87747	14.74085	14.60606	14.47308	14.34187
21	15.41502	15.26756	15.12215	14.97878	14.83740
22	15.93692	15.77843	15.62224	15.46832	15.31663
23	16.44361	16.27393	16.10682	15.94223	15.78011
24	16.93554	16.75454	16.57638	16.40100	16.22834
25	17.41315	17.22070	17.03138	16.84511	16.66184
26	17.87684	17.67284	17.47226	17.27503	17.08108
27	18.32703	18.11139	17.89948	17.69122	17.48654
28	18.76411	18.53675	18.31345	18.09412	17.87867
29	19.18845	18.94932	18.71458	18.48414	18.25790
30	19.60044	19.34949	19.10328	18.86170	18.62466
31	20.00043	19.73762	19.47992	19.22721	18.97936
32	20.38877	20.11409	19.84488	19.58103	19.32240
33	20.76579	20.47923	20.19853	19.92355	19.65416
34	21.13184	20.83339	20.54121	20.25513	19.97501
35	21.48722	21.17691	20.87327	20.57612	20.28531
40	23.11477	22.74563	22.38534	22.03365	21.69030
45	24.51871	24.09227	23.67708	23.27277	22.87900
50	25.72976	25.24827	24.78058	24.32621	23.88471

Table IV. Present Value of $1 Received per Period (cont'd)

n/r	3.5%	3.6%	3.7%	3.8%	3.9%
1	.96618	.96525	.96432	.96339	.96246
2	1.89969	1.89696	1.89423	1.89151	1.88880
3	2.80164	2.79629	2.79097	2.78566	2.78037
4	3.67308	3.66438	3.65571	3.64707	3.63847
5	4.51505	4.50229	4.48959	4.47695	4.46436
6	5.32855	5.31109	5.29372	5.27644	5.25925
7	6.11454	6.09179	6.06916	6.04667	6.02430
8	6.87396	6.84536	6.81694	6.78870	6.76063
9	7.60769	7.57274	7.53803	7.50356	7.46933
10	8.31661	8.27484	8.23340	8.19226	8.15142
11	9.00155	8.95255	8.90395	8.85574	8.80792
12	9.66333	9.60671	9.55058	9.49493	9.43976
13	10.30274	10.23814	10.17413	10.11072	10.04790
14	10.92052	10.84762	10.77544	10.70397	10.63320
15	11.51741	11.43593	11.35530	11.27550	11.19654
16	12.09412	12.00379	11.91446	11.82611	11.73873
17	12.65132	12.55192	12.45368	12.35656	12.26056
18	13.18968	13.08101	12.97365	12.86759	12.76281
19	13.70984	13.59171	13.47507	13.35992	13.24621
20	14.21240	14.08466	13.95861	13.83422	13.71147
21	14.69797	14.56048	14.42488	14.29115	14.15925
22	15.16712	15.01977	14.87453	14.73136	14.59024
23	15.62041	15.46310	15.30813	15.15545	15.00504
24	16.05837	15.89102	15.72625	15.56402	15.40427
25	16.48151	16.30407	16.12946	15.95763	15.78852
26	16.89035	16.70277	16.51829	16.33683	16.15834
27	17.28536	17.08762	16.89324	16.70215	16.51429
28	17.66702	17.45909	17.25481	17.05409	16.85687
29	18.03577	17.81766	17.60348	17.39315	17.18659
30	18.39205	18.16376	17.93971	17.71980	17.50394
31	18.73628	18.49784	18.26395	18.03449	17.80937
32	19.06887	18.82031	18.57661	18.33766	18.10334
33	19.39021	19.13157	18.87812	18.62973	18.38628
34	19.70068	19.43202	19.16887	18.91111	18.65859
35	20.00066	19.72203	19.44925	19.18218	18.92069
40	21.35507	21.02772	20.70803	20.39578	20.09076
45	22.49545	22.12179	21.75771	21.40292	21.05712
50	23.45562	23.03853	22.63302	22.23871	21.85522

Table IV.   Present Value of $1 Received per Period (cont'd)

n/r	4.0%	4.1%	4.2%	4.3%	4.4%
1	.96154	.96061	.95969	.95877	.95785
2	1.88609	1.88340	1.88070	1.87802	1.87534
3	2.77509	2.76983	2.76459	2.75937	2.75416
4	3.62990	3.62136	3.61285	3.60438	3.59594
5	4.45182	4.43934	4.42692	4.41455	4.40224
6	5.24214	5.22511	5.20818	5.19132	5.17456
7	6.00205	5.97994	5.95794	5.93607	5.91433
8	6.73274	6.70503	6.67749	6.65012	6.62292
9	7.43533	7.40157	7.36803	7.33473	7.30165
10	8.11090	8.07067	8.03074	7.99111	7.95177
11	8.76048	8.71342	8.66674	8.62043	8.57449
12	9.38507	9.33085	9.27710	9.22381	9.17097
13	9.98565	9.92397	9.86286	9.80231	9.74231
14	10.56312	10.49373	10.42501	10.35696	10.28957
15	11.11839	11.04105	10.96450	10.88874	10.81376
16	11.65230	11.56681	11.48225	11.39860	11.31586
17	12.16567	12.07186	11.97912	11.88744	11.79680
18	12.65930	12.55702	12.45597	12.35613	12.25747
19	13.13394	13.02308	12.91360	12.80549	12.69873
20	13.59033	13.47077	13.35278	13.23633	13.12139
21	14.02916	13.90084	13.77426	13.64941	13.52623
22	14.45112	14.31397	14.17876	14.04545	13.91402
23	14.85684	14.71082	14.56694	14.42517	14.28546
24	15.24696	15.09205	14.93949	14.78923	14.64124
25	15.62208	15.45826	15.29701	15.13829	14.98203
26	15.98277	15.81005	15.64013	15.47295	15.30846
27	16.32959	16.14798	15.96941	15.79381	15.62113
28	16.66306	16.47260	16.28542	16.10145	15.92062
29	16.98371	16.78444	16.58870	16.39641	16.20749
30	17.29203	17.08400	16.87975	16.67920	16.48227
31	17.58849	17.37176	17.15907	16.95034	16.74547
32	17.87355	17.64818	17.42713	17.21029	16.99758
33	18.14765	17.91372	17.68438	17.45953	17.23906
34	18.41120	18.16880	17.93127	17.69850	17.47036
35	18.66461	18.41383	18.16821	17.92761	17.69192
40	19.79277	19.50162	19.21710	18.93904	18.66726
45	20.72004	20.39141	20.07097	19.75848	19.45368
50	21.48218	21.11925	20.76608	20.42236	20.08777

Table IV. Present Value of $1 Received per Period (cont'd)

n/r	4.5%	4.6%	4.7%	4.8%	4.9%
1	.95694	.95602	.95511	.95420	.95329
2	1.87267	1.87000	1.86734	1.86469	1.86205
3	2.74896	2.74379	2.73863	2.73349	2.72836
4	3.58753	3.57915	3.57080	3.56249	3.55420
5	4.38998	4.37777	4.36562	4.35352	4.34147
6	5.15787	5.14127	5.12475	5.10832	5.09196
7	5.89270	5.87120	5.84981	5.82855	5.80740
8	6.59589	6.56902	6.54232	6.51579	6.48942
9	7.26879	7.23616	7.20375	7.17156	7.13958
10	7.91272	7.87396	7.83548	7.79729	7.75937
11	8.52892	8.48371	8.43885	8.39436	8.35021
12	9.11858	9.06664	9.01514	8.96408	8.91345
13	9.68285	9.62394	9.56556	9.50771	9.45038
14	10.22283	10.15673	10.09127	10.02644	9.96223
15	10.73955	10.66609	10.59338	10.52141	10.45018
16	11.23402	11.15305	11.07295	10.99372	10.91532
17	11.70719	11.61859	11.53100	11.44438	11.35875
18	12.15999	12.06367	11.96848	11.87441	11.78145
19	12.59329	12.48916	12.38632	12.28475	12.18442
20	13.00794	12.89595	12.78541	12.67628	12.56856
21	13.40472	13.28485	13.16658	13.04989	12.93476
22	13.78442	13.65664	13.53064	13.40638	13.28385
23	14.14777	14.01209	13.87835	13.74655	13.61663
24	14.49548	14.35190	14.21046	14.07113	13.93387
25	14.82821	14.67677	14.52766	14.38085	14.23629
26	15.14661	14.98735	14.83062	14.67639	14.52459
27	15.45130	15.28427	15.11998	14.95838	14.79942
28	15.74287	15.56814	15.39636	15.22747	15.06141
29	16.02189	15.83952	15.66032	15.48422	15.31116
30	16.28889	16.09897	15.91244	15.72922	15.54925
31	16.54439	16.34701	16.15323	15.96300	15.77621
32	16.78889	16.58414	16.38322	16.18607	15.99258
33	17.02286	16.81084	16.60289	16.39892	16.19883
34	17.24676	17.02757	16.81269	16.60202	16.39546
35	17.46101	17.23477	17.01308	16.79582	16.58290
40	18.40158	18.14185	17.88788	17.63954	17.39665
45	19.15635	18.86626	18.58319	18.30694	18.03730
50	19.76201	19.44479	19.13584	18.83488	18.54166

Table IV. Present Value of $1 Received per Period (cont'd)

n/r	5.0%	5.1%	5.2%	5.3%	5.4%
1	.95238	.95147	.95057	.94967	.94877
2	1.85941	1.85678	1.85415	1.85154	1.84892
3	2.72325	2.71815	2.71307	2.70801	2.70296
4	3.54595	3.53773	3.52954	3.52138	3.51325
5	4.32948	4.31753	4.30564	4.29381	4.28202
6	5.07569	5.05950	5.04339	5.02736	5.01140
7	5.78637	5.76546	5.74467	5.72399	5.70342
8	6.46321	6.43717	6.41128	6.38555	6.35998
9	7.10782	7.07628	7.04494	7.01382	6.98290
10	7.72173	7.68437	7.64728	7.61046	7.57391
11	8.30641	8.26296	8.21985	8.17708	8.13464
12	8.86325	8.81347	8.76412	8.71517	8.66664
13	9.39357	9.33727	9.28148	9.22619	9.17139
14	9.89864	9.83566	9.77327	9.71148	9.65027
15	10.37966	10.30985	10.24075	10.17234	10.10462
16	10.83777	10.76104	10.68512	10.61001	10.53570
17	11.27407	11.19033	11.10753	11.02565	10.94468
18	11.68959	11.59879	11.50906	11.42037	11.33272
19	12.08532	11.98744	11.89074	11.79523	11.70087
20	12.46221	12.35722	12.25356	12.15121	12.05016
21	12.82115	12.70906	12.59844	12.48928	12.38156
22	13.16300	13.04382	12.92627	12.81033	12.69597
23	13.48857	13.36234	13.23790	13.11523	12.99428
24	13.79864	13.66541	13.53413	13.40477	13.27731
25	14.09394	13.95376	13.81571	13.67975	13.54583
26	14.37519	14.22813	14.08338	13.94088	13.80060
27	14.64303	14.48918	14.33781	14.18887	14.04232
28	14.89813	14.73756	14.57967	14.42438	14.27165
29	15.14107	14.97390	14.80957	14.64803	14.48923
30	15.37245	15.19876	15.02811	14.86043	14.69566
31	15.59281	15.41271	15.23584	15.06214	14.89152
32	15.80268	15.61628	15.43331	15.25369	15.07734
33	16.00255	15.80997	15.62102	15.43560	15.25365
34	16.19290	15.99426	15.79945	15.60836	15.42092
35	16.37419	16.16961	15.96906	15.77242	15.57962
40	17.15909	16.92669	16.69933	16.47687	16.25918
45	17.77407	17.51707	17.26610	17.02101	16.78160
50	18.25593	17.97744	17.70598	17.44131	17.18323

Table IV. Present Value of $1 Received per Period (cont'd)

n/r	5.5%	5.6%	5.7%	5.8%	5.9%
1	.94787	.94697	.94607	.94518	.94429
2	1.84632	1.84372	1.84113	1.83854	1.83597
3	2.69793	2.69292	2.68792	2.68293	2.67797
4	3.50515	3.49708	3.48904	3.48103	3.47305
5	4.27028	4.25860	4.24697	4.23538	4.22385
6	4.99553	4.97973	4.96402	4.94838	4.93281
7	5.68297	5.66263	5.64240	5.62228	5.60228
8	6.33457	6.30931	6.28420	6.25925	6.23445
9	6.95220	6.92169	6.89139	6.86129	6.83139
10	7.53763	7.50160	7.46584	7.43033	7.39508
11	8.09254	8.05076	8.00931	7.96818	7.92737
12	8.61852	8.57079	8.52347	8.47654	8.43000
13	9.11708	9.06325	9.00991	8.95703	8.90463
14	9.58965	9.52960	9.47011	9.41118	9.35281
15	10.03758	9.97121	9.90550	9.84044	9.77602
16	10.46216	10.38940	10.31740	10.24616	10.17566
17	10.86461	10.78542	10.70710	10.62964	10.55303
18	11.24607	11.16043	11.07578	10.99210	10.90938
19	11.60765	11.51556	11.42458	11.33469	11.24587
20	11.95038	11.85186	11.75457	11.65849	11.56362
21	12.27524	12.17032	12.06676	11.96455	11.86366
22	12.58317	12.47189	12.36212	12.25383	12.14699
23	12.87504	12.75748	12.64155	12.52725	12.41453
24	13.15170	13.02791	12.90592	12.78568	12.66717
25	13.41393	13.28401	13.15602	13.02994	12.90573
26	13.66250	13.52652	13.39264	13.26081	13.13100
27	13.89810	13.75618	13.61650	13.47903	13.34372
28	14.12142	13.97365	13.82829	13.68528	13.54459
29	14.33310	14.17959	14.02866	13.88023	13.73427
30	14.53375	14.37462	14.21822	14.06449	13.91338
31	14.72393	14.55930	14.39756	14.23865	14.08251
32	14.90420	14.73418	14.56722	14.40326	14.24222
33	15.07507	14.89979	14.72774	14.55885	14.39303
34	15.23703	15.05662	14.87961	14.70590	14.53544
35	15.39055	15.20513	15.02328	14.84490	14.66992
40	16.04612	15.83759	15.63345	15.43360	15.23792
45	16.54773	16.31922	16.09592	15.87769	15.66437
50	16.93152	16.68598	16.44643	16.21268	15.98455

Table IV.   Present Value of $1 Received per Period (cont'd)

n/r	6%	7%	8%	9%	10%
1	0.9434	0.9346	0.9259	0.9174	0.9091
2	1.8334	1.8080	1.7833	1.7591	1.7355
3	2.6730	2.6243	2.5771	2.5313	2.4869
4	3.4651	3.3872	3.3121	3.2397	3.1699
5	4.2124	4.1002	3.9927	3.8897	3.7908
6	4.9173	4.7665	4.6229	4.4859	4.3553
7	5.5824	5.3893	5.2064	5.0330	4.8684
8	6.2098	5.9713	5.7466	5.5348	5.3349
9	6.8017	6.5152	6.2469	5.9952	5.7590
10	7.3601	7.0236	6.7101	6.4177	6.1446
11	7.8869	7.4987	7.1390	6.8051	6.4951
12	8.3838	7.9427	7.5361	7.1607	6.8137
13	8.8527	8.3577	7.9038	7.4869	7.1034
14	9.2950	8.7455	8.2442	7.7862	7.3667
15	9.7122	9.1079	8.5595	8.0607	7.6061
16	10.1059	9.4466	8.8514	8.3126	7.8237
17	10.4773	9.7632	9.1216	8.5436	8.0216
18	10.8276	10.0591	9.3719	8.7556	8.2014
19	11.1581	10.3356	9.6036	8.9501	8.3649
20	11.4699	10.5940	9.8181	9.1285	8.5136
21	11.7641	10.8355	10.0168	9.2922	8.6487
22	12.0416	11.0612	10.2007	9.4424	8.7715
23	12.3034	11.2722	10.3711	9.5802	8.8832
24	12.5504	11.4693	10.5288	9.7066	8.9847
25	12.7834	11.6536	10.6748	9.8226	9.0770
26	13.0032	11.8258	10.8100	9.9290	9.1609
27	13.2105	11.9867	10.9352	10.0266	9.2372
28	13.4062	12.1371	11.0511	10.1161	9.3066
29	13.5907	12.2777	11.1584	10.1983	9.3696
30	13.7648	12.4090	11.2578	10.2737	9.4269
31	13.9291	12.5318	11.3498	10.3428	9.4790
32	14.0840	12.6466	11.4350	10.4062	9.5264
33	14.2302	12.7538	11.5139	10.4644	9.5694
34	14.3681	12.8540	11.5869	10.5178	9.6086
35	14.4982	12.9477	11.6546	10.5668	9.6442
40	15.0463	13.3317	11.9246	10.7574	9.7791
45	15.4558	13.6055	12.1084	10.8812	9.8628
50	15.7619	13.8007	12.2335	10.9617	9.9148

Table IV. Present Value of $1 Received per Period (cont'd)

n/r	11%	12%	13%	14%	15%
1	0.9009	0.8929	0.8850	0.8772	0.8696
2	1.7125	1.6901	1.6681	1.6467	1.6257
3	2.4437	2.4018	2.3612	2.3216	2.2832
4	3.1024	3.0373	2.9745	2.9137	2.8550
5	3.6959	3.6048	3.5172	3.4331	3.3522
6	4.2305	4.1114	3.9975	3.8887	3.7845
7	4.7122	4.5638	4.4226	4.2883	4.1604
8	5.1461	4.9676	4.7988	4.6389	4.4873
9	5.5370	5.3282	5.1317	4.9464	4.7716
10	5.8892	5.6502	5.4262	5.2161	5.0188
11	6.2065	5.9377	5.6869	5.4527	5.2337
12	6.4924	6.1944	5.9176	5.6603	5.4206
13	6.7499	6.4235	6.1218	5.8424	5.5831
14	6.9819	6.6282	6.3025	6.0021	5.7245
15	7.1909	6.8109	6.4624	6.1422	5.8474
16	7.3792	6.9740	6.6039	6.2651	5.9542
17	7.5488	7.1196	6.7291	6.3729	6.0472
18	7.7016	7.2497	6.8399	6.4674	6.1280
19	7.8393	7.3658	6.9380	6.5504	6.1982
20	7.9633	7.4694	7.0248	6.6231	6.2593
21	8.0751	7.5620	7.1015	6.6870	6.3125
22	8.1757	7.6446	7.1695	6.7429	6.3587
23	8.2664	7.7184	7.2297	6.7921	6.3988
24	8.3481	7.7843	7.2829	6.8351	6.4338
25	8.4217	7.8431	7.3300	6.8729	6.4641
26	8.4881	7.8957	7.3717	6.9061	6.4906
27	8.5478	7.9426	7.4086	6.9352	6.5135
28	8.6016	7.9844	7.4412	6.9607	6.5335
29	8.6501	8.0218	7.4701	6.9830	6.5509
30	8.6938	8.0552	7.4957	7.0027	6.5660
31	8.7331	8.0850	7.5183	7.0199	6.5791
32	8.7686	8.1116	7.5383	7.0350	6.5905
33	8.8005	8.1354	7.5560	7.0482	6.6005
34	8.8293	8.1566	7.5717	7.0599	6.6091
35	8.8552	8.1755	7.5856	7.0700	6.6166
40	8.9511	8.2438	7.6344	7.1050	6.6418
45	9.0079	8.2825	7.6609	7.1232	6.6543
50	9.0417	8.3045	7.6752	7.1327	6.6605

Table IV. Present Value of $1 Received per Period (cont'd)

n/r	16%	17%	18%	19%	20%
1	0.8621	0.8547	0.8475	0.8403	0.8333
2	1.6052	1.5852	1.5656	1.5465	1.5278
3	2.2459	2.2096	2.1743	2.1399	2.1065
4	2.7982	2.7432	2.6901	2.6386	2.5887
5	3.2743	3.1993	3.1272	3.0576	2.9906
6	3.6847	3.5892	3.4976	3.4098	3.3255
7	4.0386	3.9224	3.8115	3.7057	3.6046
8	4.3436	4.2072	4.0776	3.9544	3.8372
9	4.6065	4.4506	4.3030	4.1633	4.0310
10	4.8332	4.6586	4.4941	4.3389	4.1925
11	5.0286	4.8364	4.6560	4.4865	4.3271
12	5.1971	4.9884	4.7932	4.6105	4.4392
13	5.3423	5.1183	4.9095	4.7147	4.5327
14	5.4675	5.2293	5.0081	4.8023	4.6106
15	5.5755	5.3242	5.0916	4.8759	4.6755
16	5.6685	5.4053	5.1624	4.9377	4.7296
17	5.7487	5.4746	5.2223	4.9879	4.7746
18	5.8178	5.5339	5.2732	5.0333	4.8122
19	5.8775	5.5845	5.3162	5.0700	4.8435
20	5.9288	5.6278	5.3527	5.1009	4.8696
21	5.9731	5.6648	5.3837	5.1268	4.8913
22	6.0113	5.6964	5.4099	5.1486	4.9094
23	6.0442	5.7234	5.4321	5.1668	4.9245
24	6.0726	5.7465	5.4509	5.1822	4.9371
25	6.0971	5.7662	5.4669	5.1951	4.9476
26	6.1182	5.7831	5.4804	5.2060	4.9563
27	6.1364	5.7975	5.4919	5.2151	4.9636
28	6.1520	5.8099	5.5016	5.2228	4.9697
29	6.1656	5.8204	5.5098	5.2292	4.9747
30	6.1772	5.8294	5.5168	5.2347	4.9789
31	6.1872	5.8371	5.5227	5.2392	4.9824
32	6.1959	5.8437	5.5277	5.2430	4.9854
33	6.2034	5.8493	5.5320	5.2462	4.9878
34	6.2098	5.8541	5.5356	5.2489	4.9898
35	6.2153	5.8582	5.5386	5.2512	4.9915
40	6.2335	5.8713	5.5482	5.2582	4.9966
45	6.2421	5.8773	5.5523	5.2611	4.9986
50	6.2463	5.8801	5.5541	5.2623	4.9995

Table IV.   Present Value of $1 Received per Period (cont'd)

n/r	21%	22%	23%	24%	25%
1	0.8264	0.8197	0.8130	0.8065	0.8000
2	1.5095	1.4915	1.4740	1.4568	1.4400
3	2.0739	2.0422	2.0114	1.9813	1.9520
4	2.5404	2.4936	2.4483	2.4043	2.3616
5	2.9260	2.8636	2.8035	2.7454	2.6893
6	3.2446	3.1669	3.0923	3.0205	2.9514
7	3.5079	3.4155	3.3270	3.2423	3.1611
8	3.7256	3.6193	3.5179	3.4212	3.3289
9	3.9054	3.7863	3.6731	3.5655	3.4631
10	4.0541	3.9232	3.7993	3.6819	3.5705
11	4.1769	4.0354	3.9018	3.7757	3.6564
12	4.2784	4.1274	3.9852	3.8514	3.7251
13	4.3624	4.2028	4.0530	3.9124	3.7801
14	4.4317	4.2646	4.1082	3.9616	3.8241
15	4.4890	4.3152	4.1530	4.0013	3.8593
16	4.5364	4.3567	4.1894	4.0333	3.8874
17	4.5755	4.3908	4.2190	4.0591	3.9099
18	4.6079	4.4187	4.2431	4.0799	3.9279
19	4.6346	4.4415	4.2627	4.0967	3.9424
20	4.6567	4.4603	4.2786	4.1103	3.9539
21	4.6750	4.4756	4.2916	4.1212	3.9631
22	4.6900	4.4882	4.3021	4.1300	3.9705
23	4.7025	4.4985	4.3106	4.1371	3.9764
24	4.7128	4.5070	4.3176	4.1428	3.9811
25	4.7213	4.5139	4.3232	4.1474	3.9849
26	4.7284	4.5196	4.3278	4.1511	3.9879
27	4.7342	4.5243	4.3316	4.1542	3.9903
28	4.7390	4.5281	4.3346	4.1566	3.9923
29	4.7430	4.5312	4.3371	4.1585	3.9938
30	4.7463	4.5338	4.3391	4.1601	3.9950
31	4.7490	4.5359	4.3407	4.1614	3.9960
32	4.7512	4.5376	4.3421	4.1624	3.9968
33	4.7531	4.5390	4.3431	4.1632	3.9975
34	4.7546	4.5402	4.3440	4.1639	3.9980
35	4.7559	4.5411	4.3447	4.1644	3.9984
40	4.7596	4.5439	4.3467	4.1659	3.9995
45	4.7610	4.5449	4.3474	4.1664	3.9998
50	4.7616	4.5452	4.3477	4.1666	3.9999

Table IV. Present Value of $1 Received per Period (cont'd)

n/r	26%	27%	28%	29%	30%	31%
1	0.7937	0.7874	0.7813	0.7752	0.7692	0.7634
2	1.4235	1.4074	1.3916	1.3761	1.3609	1.3461
3	1.9234	1.8956	1.8684	1.8420	1.8161	1.7909
4	2.3202	2.2800	2.2410	2.2031	2.1662	2.1305
5	2.6351	2.5827	2.5320	2.4830	2.4356	2.3897
6	2.8850	2.8210	2.7594	2.7000	2.6427	2.5875
7	3.0833	3.0087	2.9370	2.8682	2.8021	2.7386
8	3.2407	3.1564	3.0758	2.9986	2.9247	2.8539
9	3.3657	3.2728	3.1842	3.0997	3.0190	2.9419
10	3.4648	3.3644	3.2689	3.1781	3.0915	3.0091
11	3.5435	3.4365	3.3351	3.2388	3.1473	3.0604
12	3.6059	3.4933	3.3868	3.2859	3.1903	3.0995
13	3.6555	3.5381	3.4272	3.3224	3.2233	3.1294
14	3.6949	3.5733	3.4587	3.3507	3.2487	3.1522
15	3.7261	3.6010	3.4834	3.3726	3.2682	3.1696
16	3.7509	3.6228	3.5026	3.3896	3.2832	3.1829
17	3.7705	3.6400	3.5177	3.4028	3.2948	3.1931
18	3.7861	3.6536	3.5294	3.4130	3.3037	3.2008
19	3.7985	3.6642	3.5386	3.4210	3.3105	3.2067
20	3.8083	3.6726	3.5458	3.4271	3.3158	3.2112
21	3.8161	3.6792	3.5514	3.4319	3.3198	3.2147
22	3.8223	3.6844	3.5558	3.4356	3.3230	3.2173
23	3.8273	3.6885	3.5592	3.4384	3.3253	3.2193
24	3.8312	3.6918	3.5619	3.4406	3.3272	3.2209
25	3.8342	3.6943	3.5640	3.4423	3.3286	3.2220
26	3.8367	3.6963	3.5656	3.4437	3.3297	3.2229
27	3.8387	3.6979	3.5669	3.4447	3.3305	3.2236
28	3.8402	3.6991	3.5679	3.4455	3.3312	3.2241
29	3.8414	3.7001	3.5687	3.4461	3.3316	3.2245
30	3.8424	3.7009	3.5693	3.4466	3.3321	3.2248
31	3.8432	3.7015	3.5697	3.4470	3.3324	3.2251
32	3.8438	3.7019	3.5701	3.4473	3.3326	3.2252
33	3.8443	3.7023	3.5704	3.4475	3.3328	3.2254
34	3.8447	3.7026	3.5706	3.4477	3.3329	3.2255
35	3.8450	3.7028	3.5708	3.4478	3.3330	3.2256
40	3.8458	3.7034	3.5712	3.4481	3.3332	3.2257
45	3.8460	3.7036	3.5714	3.4482	3.3333	3.2258
50	3.8461	3.7037	3.5714	3.4483	3.3333	3.2258

Table IV. Present Value of $1 Received per Period (cont'd)

n/r	32%	33%	34%	35%	36%	37%
1	0.7576	0.7519	0.7463	0.7407	0.7353	0.7299
2	1.3315	1.3172	1.3032	1.2894	1.2760	1.2627
3	1.7663	1.7423	1.7188	1.6959	1.6735	1.6516
4	2.0957	2.0618	2.0290	1.9969	1.9658	1.9355
5	2.3452	2.3021	2.2604	2.2200	2.1807	2.1427
6	2.5342	2.4828	2.4331	2.3852	2.3388	2.2939
7	2.6775	2.6187	2.5620	2.5075	2.4550	2.4043
8	2.7860	2.7208	2.6582	2.5982	2.5404	2.4849
9	2.8681	2.7976	2.7300	2.6653	2.6033	2.5437
10	2.9304	2.8553	2.7836	2.7150	2.6495	2.5867
11	2.9776	2.8987	2.8236	2.7519	2.6834	2.6180
12	3.0133	2.9314	2.8534	2.7792	2.7084	2.6409
13	3.0404	2.9559	2.8757	2.7994	2.7268	2.6576
14	3.0609	2.9744	2.8923	2.8144	2.7403	2.6698
15	3.0764	2.9883	2.9047	2.8255	2.7502	2.6787
16	3.0882	2.9987	2.9140	2.8337	2.7575	2.6852
17	3.0971	3.0065	2.9209	2.8398	2.7629	2.6899
18	3.1039	3.0124	2.9260	2.8443	2.7668	2.6934
19	3.1090	3.0169	2.9299	2.8476	2.7697	2.6959
20	3.1129	3.0202	2.9327	2.8501	2.7718	2.6977
21	3.1158	3.0227	2.9349	2.8520	2.7734	2.6991
22	3.1180	3.0246	2.9365	2.8533	2.7746	2.7000
23	3.1197	3.0260	2.9377	2.8543	2.7754	2.7008
24	3.1210	3.0271	2.9386	2.8550	2.7760	2.7013
25	3.1220	3.0279	2.9392	2.8556	2.7765	2.7017
26	3.1227	3.0285	2.9397	2.8560	2.7768	2.7019
27	3.1233	3.0289	2.9401	2.8563	2.7771	2.7022
28	3.1237	3.0293	2.9404	2.8565	2.7773	2.7023
29	3.1240	3.0295	2.9406	2.8567	2.7774	2.7024
30	3.1242	3.0297	2.9407	2.8568	2.7775	2.7025
31	3.1244	3.0299	2.9408	2.8569	2.7776	2.7025
32	3.1246	3.0300	2.9409	2.8569	2.7776	2.7026
33	3.1247	3.0301	2.9410	2.8570	2.7777	2.7026
34	3.1248	3.0301	2.9410	2.8570	2.7777	2.7026
35	3.1248	3.0302	2.9411	2.8571	2.7777	2.7027
40	3.1250	3.0303	2.9412	2.8571	2.7778	2.7027
45	3.1250	3.0303	2.9412	2.8571	2.7778	2.7027
50	3.1250	3.0303	2.9412	2.8571	2.7778	2.7027

Table IV. Present Value of $1 Received per Period (cont'd)

n/r	38%	39%	40%	41%	42%	43%
1	0.7246	0.7194	0.7143	0.7092	0.7042	0.6993
2	1.2497	1.2370	1.2245	1.2122	1.2002	1.1883
3	1.6302	1.6093	1.5889	1.5689	1.5494	1.5303
4	1.9060	1.8772	1.8492	1.8219	1.7954	1.7694
5	2.1058	2.0699	2.0352	2.0014	1.9686	1.9367
6	2.2506	2.2086	2.1680	2.1286	2.0905	2.0536
7	2.3555	2.3083	2.2628	2.2189	2.1764	2.1354
8	2.4315	2.3801	2.3306	2.2829	2.2369	2.1926
9	2.4866	2.4317	2.3790	2.3283	2.2795	2.2326
10	2.5265	2.4689	2.4136	2.3605	2.3095	2.2605
11	2.5555	2.4956	2.4383	2.3833	2.3307	2.2801
12	2.5764	2.5148	2.4559	2.3995	2.3455	2.2938
13	2.5916	2.5286	2.4685	2.4110	2.3560	2.3033
14	2.6026	2.5386	2.4775	2.4192	2.3634	2.3100
15	2.6106	2.5457	2.4839	2.4249	2.3686	2.3147
16	2.6164	2.5509	2.4885	2.4290	2.3722	2.3180
17	2.6206	2.5546	2.4918	2.4319	2.3748	2.3203
18	2.6236	2.5573	2.4941	2.4340	2.3766	2.3219
19	2.6258	2.5592	2.4958	2.4355	2.3779	2.3230
20	2.6274	2.5606	2.4970	2.4365	2.3788	2.3238
21	2.6285	2.5616	2.4979	2.4372	2.3794	2.3243
22	2.6294	2.5623	2.4985	2.4378	2.3799	2.3247
23	2.6300	2.5628	2.4989	2.4381	2.3802	2.3250
24	2.6304	2.5632	2.4992	2.4384	2.3804	2.3251
25	2.6307	2.5634	2.4994	2.4386	2.3806	2.3253
26	2.6310	2.5636	2.4996	2.4387	2.3807	2.3254
27	2.6311	2.5637	2.4997	2.4388	2.3808	2.3254
28	2.6313	2.5638	2.4998	2.4389	2.3808	2.3255
29	2.6313	2.5639	2.4999	2.4389	2.3809	2.3255
30	2.6314	2.5640	2.4999	2.4389	2.3809	2.3255
31	2.6315	2.5640	2.4999	2.4390	2.3809	2.3255
32	2.6315	2.5640	2.4999	2.4390	2.3809	2.3256
33	2.6315	2.5641	2.5000	2.4390	2.3809	2.3256
34	2.6315	2.5641	2.5000	2.4390	2.3809	2.3256
35	2.6215	2.5641	2.5000	2.4390	2.3809	2.3256
40	2.6316	2.5641	2.5000	2.4390	2.3810	2.3256
45	2.6316	2.5641	2.5000	2.4390	2.3810	2.3256
50	2.6316	2.5641	2.5000	2.4390	2.3810	2.3256

Table IV.   Present Value of $1 Received per Period (cont'd)

n/r	44%	45%	46%	47%	48%	49%
1	0.6944	0.6897	0.6849	0.6803	0.6757	0.6711
2	1.1767	1.1653	1.1541	1.1430	1.1322	1.1216
3	1.5116	1.4933	1.4754	1.4579	1.4407	1.4239
4	1.7442	1.7195	1.6955	1.6720	1.6491	1.6268
5	1.9057	1.8755	1.8462	1.8177	1.7899	1.7629
6	2.0178	1.9831	1.9495	1.9168	1.8851	1.8543
7	2.0957	2.0573	2.0202	1.9842	1.9494	1.9156
8	2.1498	2.1085	2.0686	2.0301	1.9928	1.9568
9	2.1874	2.1438	2.1018	2.0613	2.0222	1.9844
10	2.2134	2.1681	2.1245	2.0825	2.0420	2.0030
11	2.2316	2.1849	2.1401	2.0969	2.0554	2.0154
12	2.2441	2.1965	2.1507	2.1068	2.0645	2.0238
13	2.2529	2.2045	2.1580	2.1134	2.0706	2.0294
14	2.2589	2.2100	2.1630	2.1180	2.0747	2.0331
15	2.2632	2.2138	2.1665	2.1211	2.0775	2.0357
16	2.2661	2.2164	2.1688	2.1232	2.0794	2.0374
17	2.2681	2.2182	2.1704	2.1246	2.0807	2.0385
18	2.2695	2.2195	2.1715	2.1256	2.0815	2.0393
19	2.2705	2.2203	2.1723	2.1263	2.0821	2.0398
20	2.2712	2.2209	2.1728	2.1267	2.0825	2.0401
21	2.2717	2.2213	2.1731	2.1270	2.0828	2.0403
22	2.2720	2.2216	2.1734	2.1272	2.0830	2.0405
23	2.2722	2.2218	2.1736	2.1274	2.0831	2.0406
24	2.2724	2.2219	2.1737	2.1275	2.0832	2.0407
25	2.2725	2.2220	2.1737	2.1275	2.0832	2.0407
26	2.2726	2.2221	2.1738	2.1276	2.0833	2.0408
27	2.2726	2.2221	2.1738	2.1276	2.0833	2.0408
28	2.2726	2.2222	2.1739	2.1276	2.0833	2.0408
29	2.2727	2.2222	2.1739	2.1276	2.0833	2.0408
30	2.2727	2.2222	2.1739	2.1276	2.0833	2.0408
31	2.2727	2.2222	2.1739	2.1276	2.0833	2.0408
32	2.2727	2.2222	2.1739	2.1277	2.0833	2.0408
33	2.2727	2.2222	2.1739	2.1277	2.0833	2.0408
34	2.2727	2.2222	2.1739	2.1277	2.0833	2.0408
35	2.2727	2.2222	2.1739	2.1277	2.0833	2.0408
40	2.2727	2.2222	2.1739	2.1277	2.0833	2.0408
45	2.2727	2.2222	2.1739	2.1277	2.0833	2.0408
50	2.2727	2.2222	2.1739	2.1277	2.0833	2.0408

Table V. Values of e^{-x}

x	0	.01	.02	.03	.04
0	1.000000	.990050	.980199	.970446	.960789
.10	.904837	.895834	.886920	.878095	.869358
.20	.818731	.810584	.802519	.794534	.786628
.30	.740818	.733447	.726149	.718924	.711770
.40	.670320	.663650	.657047	.650509	.644036
.50	.606531	.600496	.594521	.588605	.582748
.60	.548812	.543351	.537944	.532592	.527292
.70	.496585	.491644	.486752	.481909	.477114
.80	.449329	.444858	.440432	.436049	.431711
.90	.406570	.402524	.398519	.394554	.390628
1.00	.367879	.364219	.360595	.357007	.353455
1.10	.332871	.329559	.326280	.323033	.319819
1.20	.301194	.298197	.295230	.292293	.289384
1.30	.272532	.269820	.267135	.264477	.261846
1.40	.246597	.244143	.241714	.239309	.236928
1.50	.223130	.220910	.218712	.216536	.214381
1.60	.201897	.199888	.197899	.195930	.193980
1.70	.182684	.180866	.179066	.177284	.175520
1.80	.165299	.163654	.162026	.160414	.158817
1.90	.149569	.148080	.146607	.145148	.143704
2.00	.135335	.133989	.132655	.131336	.130029
2.10	.122456	.121238	.120032	.118837	.117655
2.20	.110803	.109701	.108609	.107528	.106459
2.30	.100259	.099261	.098274	.097296	.096328
2.40	.090718	.089815	.088922	.088037	.087161
2.50	.082085	.081268	.080460	.079659	.078866
2.60	.074274	.073535	.072803	.072078	.071361
2.70	.067206	.066537	.065875	.065219	.064570
2.80	.060810	.060205	.059606	.059013	.058426
2.90	.055023	.054476	.053934	.053397	.052866
3.00	.049787	.049292	.048801	.048316	.047835
3.10	.045049	.044601	.044157	.043718	.043283
3.20	.040762	.040357	.039955	.039557	.039164
3.30	.036883	.036516	.036153	.035793	.035437
3.40	.033373	.033041	.032712	.032387	.032065
3.50	.030197	.029897	.029599	.029305	.029013
3.60	.027324	.027052	.026783	.026516	.026252
3.70	.024724	.024478	.024234	.023993	.023754
3.80	.022371	.022148	.021928	.021710	.021494
3.90	.020242	.020041	.019841	.019644	.019448
4.00	.018316	.018133	.017953	.017774	.017597
4.10	.016573	.016408	.016245	.016083	.015923
4.20	.014996	.014846	.014699	.014552	.014408
4.30	.013569	.013434	.013300	.013168	.013037
4.40	.012277	.012155	.012034	.011914	.011796
4.50	.011109	.010998	.010889	.010781	.010673
4.60	.010052	.009952	.009853	.009755	.009658
4.70	.009095	.009005	.008915	.008826	.008739
4.80	.008230	.008148	.008067	.007987	.007907
4.90	.007447	.007372	.007299	.007227	.007155

426

Table V.   Values of e^{-x} (cont'd)

x	.05	.06	.07	.08	.09
0	.951229	.941765	.932394	.923116	.913931
.10	.860708	.852144	.843665	.835270	.826959
.20	.778801	.771052	.763379	.755784	.748264
.30	.704688	.697676	.690734	.683861	.677057
.40	.637628	.631284	.625002	.618783	.612626
.50	.576950	.571209	.565525	.559898	.554327
.60	.522046	.516851	.511709	.506617	.501576
.70	.472367	.467666	.463013	.458406	.453845
.80	.427415	.423162	.418952	.414783	.410656
.90	.386741	.382893	.379083	.375311	.371577
1.00	.349938	.346456	.343009	.339596	.336216
1.10	.316637	.313486	.310367	.307279	.304221
1.20	.286505	.283654	.280832	.278037	.275271
1.30	.259240	.256661	.254107	.251579	.249075
1.40	.234570	.232236	.229925	.227638	.225373
1.50	.212248	.210136	.208045	.205975	.203926
1.60	.192050	.190139	.188247	.186374	.184520
1.70	.173774	.172045	.170333	.168638	.166960
1.80	.157237	.155673	.154124	.152590	.151072
1.90	.142274	.140858	.139457	.138069	.136695
2.00	.128735	.127454	.126186	.124930	.123687
2.10	.116484	.115325	.114178	.113042	.111917
2.20	.105399	.104350	.103312	.102284	.101266
2.30	.095369	.094420	.093481	.092551	.091630
2.40	.086294	.085435	.084585	.083743	.082910
2.50	.078082	.077305	.076536	.075774	.075020
2.60	.070651	.069948	.069252	.068563	.067881
2.70	.063928	.063292	.062662	.062039	.061421
2.80	.057844	.057269	.056699	.056135	.055576
2.90	.052340	.051819	.051303	.050793	.050287
3.00	.047359	.046888	.046421	.045959	.045502
3.10	.042852	.042426	.042004	.041586	.041172
3.20	.038774	.038388	.038006	.037628	.037254
3.30	.035084	.034735	.034390	.034047	.033709
3.40	.031746	.031430	.031117	.030807	.030501
3.50	.028725	.028439	.028156	.027876	.027598
3.60	.025991	.025733	.025476	.025223	.024972
3.70	.023518	.023284	.023052	.022823	.022596
3.80	.021280	.021068	.020858	.020651	.020445
3.90	.019255	.019063	.018873	.018686	.018500
4.00	.017422	.017249	.017077	.016907	.016739
4.10	.015764	.015608	.015452	.015299	.015146
4.20	.014264	.014122	.013982	.013843	.013705
4.30	.012907	.012778	.012651	.012525	.012401
4.40	.011679	.011562	.011447	.011333	.011221
4.50	.010567	.010462	.010358	.010255	.010153
4.60	.009562	.009466	.009372	.009279	.009187
4.70	.008652	.008566	.008480	.008396	.008312
4.80	.007828	.007750	.007673	.007597	.007521
4.90	.007083	.007013	.006943	.006874	.006806

Author Index

429

Subject Index